*In a church graveyard in Garmisch, Germany, a headstone
stands against the backdrop of the Alps. Mounted to the stone is
a photo etched on a porcelain circle, an image of a farm boy
hugging a cow. He was killed while serving in World War II.
This book is dedicated to him and all the young men who
answered their countries' calls but never wanted war.*

05. 12. 13.

A HIGHER CALL

Adam Makos is a journalist, historian and editor of the military magazine *Valor*. Makos has interviewed countless veterans from the Second World War, Korea, Vietnam and present-day wars. In 2008 Makos travelled to Iraq to accompany the 101st Airborne and Army Special Forces on their hunt for Al Qaeda terrorists.

Larry Alexander is the author of the *New York Times* bestselling biography *Biggest Brother: The Life of Major Dick Winters, the Man Who Led the Band of Brothers*. He is also is the author of *Shadows in the Jungle: The Alamo Scouts Behind Japanese Lines in World War II* and *In The Footsteps of the Band of Brothers: A Return to Easy Company's Battlefields With Sgt. Forrest Guth*.

THE INCREDIBLE TRUE STORY OF HEROISM AND CHIVALRY
DURING THE SECOND WORLD WAR

A HIGHER CALL

ADAM MAKOS
with LARRY ALEXANDER

ATLANTIC BOOKS
London

First published in the United States in 2012 by Berkley, an imprint of Penguin Group (USA) Inc.

First published in hardback in Great Britain in 2013 by Atlantic Books, an imprint of Atlantic Books Ltd.

Copyright © Adam Makos, 2012

10 9 8 7 6 5 4 3 2 1

A CIP catalogue record for this book is available from the British Library.

Hardback ISBN: 9781782392538
Trade paperback ISBN: 9781782392545
E-book ISBN: 9781782392552

Printed and bound by CPI Group (UK) Ltd, Croydon, CR0 4YY

Atlantic Books
An Imprint of Atlantic Books Ltd
Ormond House
26–27 Boswell Street
London
WC1N 3JZ

www.atlantic-books.co.uk

CONTENTS

INTRODUCTION

ON DECEMBER 20, 1943, in the midst of World War II, an era of pain, death, and sadness, an act of peace and nobility unfolded in the skies over Northern Germany. An American bomber crew was limping home in their badly damaged B-17 after bombing Germany. A German fighter pilot in his Bf-109 fighter encountered them. They were enemies, sworn to shoot one another from the sky. Yet what transpired between the fighter pilot and the bomber crewmen that day, and how the story played out decades later, defies imagination. It had never happened before and it has not happened since. What occurred, in most general terms, may well be one of the most remarkable stories in the history of warfare.

As remarkable as it is, it's a story I never wanted to tell.

———————

GROWING UP, I had loved my grandfathers' stories from World War II. One had been a crewman on B-17s and the other a Marine. They made model airplanes with my younger brother and me, which we invariably destroyed. They took us to air shows. They planted a seed of interest in that black-and-white era of theirs. I was transfixed. I read every book about WWII that I could get my hands on. I knew that the "Greatest Generation" were the good guys, knights dispatching evil on a worldwide crusade. Their enemies were the black knights, the Germans and the Japanese. They were universally evil and beyond re-demption. For being a complex war, it seemed very simple.

On a rainy day my life changed a little. I was fifteen and living in rural Pennsylvania. My siblings, best friend, and I were bored, so we decided to become journalists. That day we started a newsletter on my parents' computer, writing about our favorite thing—World War II aviation. We printed our publication on an inkjet printer. It was three pages long and had a circulation of a dozen readers.

A year later, my life changed a lot. It was the summer after my freshman year in high school when my neighbor, classmates, and teacher were killed. A great tragedy struck our small town of Mon-toursville called "TWA Flight 800." Sixteen of my schoolmates and my favorite teacher were traveling to France aboard a 747 jetliner. They were all members of the school French Club. Their plane exploded, midair, off the coast of Long Island.

I had planned to be with them. I had initially signed up for the trip but faced a tough choice. My Mom had sold enough Pampered Chef products in her part-time job to earn a vacation for our family to Disney World. The only catch was that the Disney trip was the same week as the school trip to France. I chose Disney with my family. I was in Disney when the *USA Today* newspaper appeared on the floor out-side our hotel room to announce the crash, 230 deaths, and the first reference to a shattered small Pennsylvania town. When I returned home, my parents' answering machine was full of condolences. In their haste to identify who had gone with the French Club, someone had posted the roster of the students who had initially signed up for the trip to France, and my name was there.

The funerals were tragic. When school resumed, my neighbor Monica was missing from the bus stop. Jessica always boarded the bus before us, but she was gone. My best friend among any and all girls, Claire, no longer sat next to me in class. And Mrs. Dickey no longer led the lessons. She was a great lady, a lot like Paula Dean, the jovial Southern TV chef. When we picked our adopted French names that we would be called during class hours, I had picked "Fabio." It wasn't even French. But it was funny and Mrs. Dickey let me keep it. That's the kind of lady she was.

Flight 800 taught me that life is precious because it is fragile. I can't say I woke up one day and started living passionately and working faster to make some impact on the world. It never happens in an instant. But looking back, I see that it happened gradually. By the end of high school, my siblings, friend, and I had turned our hand-stapled newsletter into a neatly bound magazine with a circulation of seven thousand copies. While our friends were at football games and parties, we were out interviewing WWII veterans.

We continued the magazine in college and missed all the Greek parties and whatever else kids do in college, because we were meeting veterans on the weekends, at air shows, museums, and reunions. We interviewed fighter pilots, bomber gunners, transport crewmen, and anyone who flew. On our magazine's cover we wrote our mission: "Preserving the sacrifices of America's veterans."

People began noticing our little magazine. Tom Brokaw, who penned *The Greatest Generation*, wrote us a letter to say we were doing good work. Tom Hanks met us at the ground breaking of the WWII Memorial in Washington and encouraged us to keep it up. Harrison Ford met us at the AirVenture air show in Oshkosh, Wisconsin. He read our magazine on the spot and gave us a thumbs-up. So did James Cameron, the director of *Titanic*, when we met him in New York City.

After college, we worked for our magazine full-time. We worked faster and harder because we knew the WWII veterans were fading away. As the magazine's editor, I enforced our three journalistic rules: get the facts right, tell stories that show our military in a good light, and ignore the enemy—we do not honor them. As for that last rule, we never had to worry about ignoring Japanese veterans—there were none in America that we knew of. But the German veterans were different. We crossed paths with them, several times.

At the air show in Geneseo, New York, an old WWII German fighter pilot named Oscar Boesch flew his sailplane for the crowd. He did beautiful gliding routines at age seventy-seven. But did I ever go to talk with him when he stood by his plane alone? No way. In Doylestown, Pennsylvania, I met an old German jet pilot, Dr. Kurt Fox, at a museum unveiling of a restored German jet. Did I care what he had seen or done? Not a chance.

I read about Germans like them in my books, saw them in movies, and that was enough. I agreed with Indiana Jones when he said, "Nazis. I hate these guys." To me, the Germans were all Nazis. They were jackboot zombies who gathered in flocks to salute Hitler at Nuremberg. They ran concentration camps. They worshipped Hitler. Worse, they tried to kill my friends, the eighty-year-old WWII veterans who had become my heroes.

But something began to puzzle me. I noticed that the aging American WWII pilots talked about their counterparts—the old German WWII pilots—with a strange kind of respect. They spoke of the German pilots' bravery, decency, and this code of honor that they supposedly shared. Some American veterans even went back to Germany, to the places where they'd been shot down, to meet their old foes and shake hands.

Are you kidding? I thought. *They were trying to kill you! They killed your friends. You're supposed to never forget.* But the veterans who flew against the Germans thought differently. For once, I thought the Greatest Generation was crazy.

———

I HAD NOT been out of college a year when I called an old American bomber pilot named Charlie Brown. I had heard of him and had sent him a magazine and letter to ask if I could interview him. Legend had it that Charlie's bomber got shot to pieces and there was a twist, although I couldn't quite catch the full story at first. Supposedly he had some unusual connection with a German pilot named Franz Stigler, whom he called his "older brother."

Charlie agreed to an interview then he threw me for a loop. "Do you really want the whole story about what happened to me and my crew?" Charlie asked.

"You bet," I said.

"Then I don't think you should start by talking with me," Charlie said.

"Really?" I asked.

"If you really want to learn the whole story, learn about Franz Stigler first," Charlie said. "He's still alive. Find out how he was raised and how he became the man he was when we met over Europe. Better yet, go visit him. He and his wife are living up in Vancouver, Canada. When you have his story, come visit me and I'll tell you mine."

I was about to make excuses and tell Charlie I had little interest in a German fighter pilot's perspective, when he said something that shut me up.

"In this story," Charlie said, "I'm just a character—*Franz Stigler is the real hero.*"

WHEN I BOOKED my ticket to Vancouver in February 2004, I had to explain to my young magazine partners why I was spending $600 of our limited funds to fly across the continent to break my own rule. I was going to interview, in my words, "a Nazi pilot." I was twenty-three years old. I flew to Vancouver and took a cab into the Canadian countryside. It was raining and dark. The next morning I left my hotel to meet Franz Stigler.

I never envisioned that Charlie Brown had pushed me into one of the greatest untold stories in military history.

I ended up spending a week with Franz. He was kind and decent.

I admitted to him that I thought he was a "Nazi" before I met him. He told me what a Nazi really was. A Nazi was someone who chose to be a Nazi. A Nazi was an abbreviation for a National Socialist. The National Socialists were a political party. As with political parties in America, you had a choice to join or not. Franz never joined them. Franz's parents voted against the Nazis before the Nazis outlawed all other political parties. And here I'd thought it was in every German's blood. I never called Franz a "Nazi" again.

———

AFTER MY WEEK with Franz, I flew to Miami and spent a week with Charlie. We had a blast and drank Scotch each night after my interviews. We published the story of Charlie and Franz in our magazine. Our readers loved it. So, in the next issue, we published a sequel to our first story. But this was not enough. Our readers wanted more. So I asked Charlie and Franz if they would let me write their story as a book, the tale of two enemies. They agreed.

Little did we know that the process of writing this book would span eight years.

What you'll read in the following pages is built around four years of interviews with Charlie and Franz and four years of research, on and off. I say "on and off" because I was still busy with Valor Studios, the military publishing company that our once-tiny newsletter had become. I interviewed Franz and Charlie at their homes, at air shows, over the phone, and by mail.

Charlie and Franz were always gracious and patient. If I had been them, I would have kicked me out and said "That's enough." But Charlie and Franz kept talking, remembering things that made them laugh and cry. I must stress that I simply compiled this story. They lived it. Through the stories they told me, they relived a painful time in their lives—World War II—because they knew that *you* would someday read this book, even if they were not around to read the final copy themselves. This book is their gift to us.

In addition to the foundation of interviews from Charlie and Franz, dozens of other WWII veterans shared their time to talk to me and my staff—from "Doc," the navigator on Charlie's bomber, to a former fourteen-year-old German flak gunner named Otto. Three times my research took me to Europe, where much of this story is set. I toured bomber bases in England with eighty-year-old B-17 pilots and scaled Mount Erice in Sicily, searching for a cave that had once been a headquarters. I followed historians around fighter airfields and into musty bunkers in Germany and Austria. The archivists at the German Bundesarchivs, the National Archives of England, and the U.S. Air Force Historical Research Agency assisted me in finding rare documents.

I've drawn from my magazine adventures, too. The Air Force let me fly in a fighter jet with an instructor pilot to learn fighter tactics. I flew a restored B-17 bomber to feel how it responded to a turn and rode in a B-24 bomber, too. In September 2008, I flew into Baghdad, Iraq, in the cockpit of a C-17 transport. From there I traveled to Camp Anaconda to feel the desert's heat and get a glimpse of a soldier's life by accompanying them on patrols. I figured it was impossible to write about warfare without having ever heard gunfire.

What follows is the book that the old me, with my old prejudices, would have never written. When I first phoned the World War II bomber pilot named Charlie Brown, all I wanted was thirty minutes of his time. But what I found was a beautiful story worth every minute of eight years. The story has plenty of questions about the prudence of war and the person we call the enemy. But mostly it begs a question of goodness.

Can good men be found on both sides of a bad war?

Adam Makos
Denver, Colorado
September 2012

1

A STRANGER IN MY OWN LAND

MARCH 1946, STRAUBING, GERMANY

Franz Stigler buried his hands in the pockets of his long, tattered wool coat as he shuffled along the streets of the small, bombed-out city. The frigid air crystallized his breath in the early morning sunlight. He walked with small, fast steps and hugged himself to keep warm against the wind.

Franz was thirty years old but looked older. His strong jaw was gaunt from weight loss, and his sharp, hawk-like nose seemed even pointier in the icy air. His dark eyes bore hints of exhaustion but still glimmered with optimism. A year after the war had ended, the economy across Germany remained broken. Franz was desperate for work. In a land destroyed and in need of rebuilding, brick making had become Straubing's primary industry. Today he had heard the brick mill was hiring day laborers.

Franz scurried through the town's massive square, Ludwig's Place, his black leather boots clopping along the frozen cobblestones. The square faced east and welcomed the morning sun. In its center sat City

Hall, an ornate green building with a tall white clock tower. The hall's tall windows and carved cherub figurines shimmered. City Hall had been one of the few buildings spared. Around Franz, clumps of other buildings sprawled in the shadows, vacant and roofless, their window frames charred from bombs and fires.

Straubing had once been a fairy-tale city in Bavaria, the Catholic region of Southern Germany where people loved their beer and any excuse for a festival. The city had been filled with a rainbow of houses with red roofs, office buildings with green Byzantine domes, and churches with white Gothic towers. Then on April 18, 1945, the American heavy bombers had come, the planes the Germans called the "Four Motors." In bombing the city's train yards the bombers had destroyed a third of the city itself. Two weeks later, Germany would surrender, but not before the city lost the colors from its rooftops.

The clock chimed, its echo bouncing throughout the square— 8 A.M. A line of German civilians extended across the square from the City Hall, where the American GIs handed out food stamps. Most of the people waited for their stamps in silence. Some argued. Ten years earlier, Hitler had promised to care for the German people, to give them food, shelter, and safety. He gave them ruin. Now the Western Allies—the Americans, British, and French—cared for the German people instead. The Allies called their effort "the reconstruction of Germany." The reconstruction was mostly a humanitarian undertaking but also a strategic one. The Western Allies needed Germany to be the front for the Cold War against the Soviet Union. So the Americans, who occupied Southern Germany and Bavaria, decided to fix what was broken—in Germany's interest, as well as their own.

Rather than traverse around the line of somber people, Franz wiggled through them. Some yelled at him, thinking he was trying to cut in front. Franz kept waddling through the masses. He noticed that the people's eyes were drawn to his boots.

Franz's jacket had moth holes—it had been his father's. His green Bavarian britches had patches on the knees. But his boots were unusual. They covered his calves, and yellow mutton wool peaked over the tops. A silver zipper ran up the inside of each boot, and a black cross strap with a buckle spanned the front of the ankle.

His boots were the mark of a pilot. A year earlier, Franz had worn them proudly in the thin air six miles above earth. There he flew a Messerschmitt 109 fighter with a massive Daimler-Benz engine. When other men walked in the war, he flew at four hundred miles per hour. Franz had led three squadrons of pilots—about forty men—against formations of a thousand American bombers that stretched a hundred miles. In three years, Franz had entered combat 487 times and had been wounded twice, burned once, and somehow always came home. But now he had traded his black leather flying suit, his silk scarf, and his gray officer's crush cap for the dirty, baggy clothes of a laborer. His pilot's boots he kept—they were the only footwear he owned.

As he hurried along the street, Franz saw men and women crowded around the town message board to read its notes held by thumbtacks against the wind. There was no mail service and there were no phone lines anymore, so people turned to the board for word of lost family members. Some seven million people were now homeless in Germany. Franz saw a cluster of women standing behind the lift gate of an American Army truck. From inside the covered truck bed, gum-chewing GIs dropped duffels of laundry to the women while practicing sweet-talking in German. The women giggled and departed, each carrying two bags. They were headed for the old park north of the city where a branch of the Danube River curved along the town. There, the women would kneel on the banks and scrub the GIs' laundry in the icy water. It was cold work but the Americans paid well.

The city's main street ran north to the river. Franz turned, started down it, and encountered a new rush of humanity. He stopped in his tracks and gulped. He was too late. Every building on this block had a long line of men standing in front. They were all looking for work. Some men blew into their hands. Others twisted back and forth at the waist to stay warm. Most were veterans and wore the same gray tunics and long coats they had worn in the war. The thread outlines from patches they had torn away were still visible. Like Franz, they were competing for the scraps of a desolate economy.

The brickyard was farther down the street, and Franz hoped its line was shorter. He kept walking and passed people working in a bombed-out building, its wall open to the street. Under a canvas tarp, men in winter clothes huddled at their desks while repairing small motors. A woman missing an arm walked among them, delivering their work orders.

A honking horn warned Franz to jump to the curb as an American jeep, the Constabulary patrol, raced past—its GI riders wearing clean, white helmets. The Americans provided law and order while a small force of unarmed German police assisted with "local" matters. Some of the German veterans still looked away whenever the jeeps raced by.

Ahead, sitting on the bench where the buses used to stop, Franz saw the footless veteran. Every day the same man sat there in his tattered Army uniform. He looked forty years old but could have been twenty. His hair was long, his stubble gray, and his eyes blinked nervously as if he had seen a thousand hells. He was a vision of a bad past that everyone wanted to forget.

The footless veteran wobbled his mess kit in the air, looking for a handout. Franz fished in his pocket and dropped a food stamp into the man's empty dish. Franz did this every time he saw the veteran, and he wondered if that was why the man always sat on the same bench. The veteran never said thanks or even smiled. He just gazed at Franz forlornly. For a moment, Franz was glad he had flown above the ground war. Six years of hand-to-hand fighting and months in Allied P.O.W. camps had left scores of veterans in the same predicament as the panhandler, listless and broken. But they were the lucky ones. The men captured by the Soviets were still missing.

Franz felt his lunch in his pocket—two slices of oat bread. He was not too proud to take handouts from the victors. Handouts meant eight hundred calories of food a day and survival. When Franz was a pilot, he had been well fed, a tradition begun in the First World War, when pilots were aristocrats who had to live well if they were to die painfully. In WWII, good food was considered a job perk, since no amount of money could convince a man to do what pilots did. During the war Franz had dined on champagne, cognac, crusty bread, sausages, cold milk, fresh cheese, fresh game, and all the chocolate and cigarettes he could handle. After the war, Franz had forgotten the feeling of being full.

A long line of workmen had already gathered at the brickyard. Franz groaned. The line wound down the length of the sidewalk from the destroyed building that had become the mill. These days, bricks didn't have far to travel to be useful—only a block or two away—so the mill had sprung up in the middle of the city.

The men in the brickyard line were a rough mix of laborers. Baking bricks and distributing them was hard work. As Franz approached, they eyed his boots with silent judgment. Franz pretended not to notice. All he wanted was to work and blend in. He had been born an hour away, in tiny Amberg, Germany, where his girlfriend was now living with his mother. Franz had tried to fit in there after the war, but the people knew he had been a fighter pilot and blamed him for the country's destruction. "You fighter pilots failed!" they had yelled at him. "You did not keep the bombs from falling!" So Franz decided to start over in Straubing, where he was a stranger. It was no use. The people of Straubing were as disenchanted with fighter pilots as everybody else in Germany. Once, fighter pilots had been the nation's heroes. Now the hostile eyes of the men around Franz confirmed a new reality. Fighter pilots had become the nation's villains. Franz turned from the glares of the men.

Two American GIs strolled down the street with German girls on their arms. In daylight, they could do this safely. At night they were liable to be attacked. The girls were cold and starving like everyone else, but they faced a choice: date a German man and go hungry, or date an American who could give them coffee, butter, cigarettes, and chocolate. Next to the boyish conquerors from the richest nation in the world, Franz and the German men in their work lines looked emasculated. "He fell for the fatherland, she for cigarettes," the bitter German men would quip.

Finally the line moved forward, and Franz stood in front of a wooden folding table inside the brick mill. Behind the table sat the manager, a bald man with spectacles. Behind him, Franz saw workers packing red clay into molds and wheeling wheelbarrows of bricks. Franz handed his papers to the manager then looked at his boots, hoping the man had not yet noticed them. Franz's papers listed: "1st Lieutenant, Pilot, Air Force." Upon the war's end, Franz had surrendered to the Americans, who were hunting for him because he was one of Germany's top pilots who had flown the country's latest aircraft. The Americans had wanted his knowledge. Franz had cooperated, and his captors had given him release papers that said that he was free to travel and to work. They had him released because his record was clean—he had never been a member of the National Socialist Party (the Nazis).

"So you were a pilot and an officer?" the manager asked.

"Yes, sir," Franz said and looked at the floor.

"Bombers?" the manager asked.

"Fighters," Franz said. He knew the man was baiting him, but Franz was not about to lie. The other workers in line began to whisper.

"So a fighter pilot wants to get his hands dirty now?" the manager said. "He wants to clean up the mess he caused?"

"Sir, I just want to work," Franz said.

Gesturing to the ruined city around him, the manager recited the line Franz had heard countless times before. "You didn't keep the bombs from falling!"

Biting his lip, Franz told the manager, "I just want to work."

"Look elsewhere!" the manager said.

"I need this job," Franz said. He leaned close to the manager. "I've got people to care for. I'll work hard—harder than anyone else."

The other men in line grumbled and crowded closer. "Move along," yelled a voice from behind. Someone pushed Franz. "Stop holding up the line," yelled someone else. They were angry for losing the war. They were angry at Hitler for misleading them. They were angry because another country now occupied theirs. But none of the men who surrounded Franz would admit this. They needed a scapegoat, and a fighter pilot stood right in front of them.

"Get out!" the manager hissed at Franz. "You Nazis have caused enough trouble."

Nazi—the word made Franz's eyes narrow with anger. "Nazi" was the new curse word the Germans had learned from the Americans. Franz was no Nazi. The Nazis were known to Franz as "The Party," the National Socialists, power-hungry politicians and bureaucrats who had taken over Germany behind the fists of violent, disenchanted masses. They shouldn't have ever been in charge. They'd only come to power after the elections of 1933, when twelve parties campaigned for seats in Germany's parliament. Each party won a portion of the vote—there was no majority winner. In the end, the National Socialists won the most votes—44 percent of Germany had voted in their favor. This 44 percent gave the Nazis, and their leader, Adolf Hitler, enough seats in parliament to eventually seize dictatorial powers. Soon after, Hitler and his Nazis outlawed all future elections and all other political parties except for theirs, which became known as "The Party." Hitler and The Party took over Germany after 56 percent of the country had voted against them.

Franz felt the blood beginning to boil behind his ears. He had been just seventeen, too young to vote in the 1933 election although his parents had voted against The Party. When Franz had come of age, he had never joined The Party. The Party had ruined his life. "I'm not a Nazi!" Franz told the manager. "All I want is to work."

"Be a man and move along," yelled someone from the line of men. Others jostled Franz. He felt the wind of angry breath on his neck.

"Get off my back!" Franz shouted to them, twisting his shoulders. Nothing bothered Franz more than someone standing too close behind him. It was his fighter pilot's survival instinct to fear anyone or anything that approached from his back, his "six o'clock." Franz knew if he turned around to face the angry men it would only start a fight, so he avoided eye contact with any in the crowd.

The manager picked up a phone mounted on the wall. Its line ran out the shattered window and into the street. He made a call, then told the other workers, "The police are coming."

"Please don't," Franz said. "I've got a family to care for."

The manager just sat back, his arms folded. Franz removed his cap, revealing a dent in his forehead where an American .50-caliber bullet had hit him in October 1944 after piercing his fighter's armored windshield. Franz pointed to the dent and said, "Don't rile me!"

The manager laughed. Franz fished inside his pocket and slapped a piece of paper on the table. It was a medical form from his former flight doctor, who had written that Franz's head injury and its resulting brain trauma "could trigger adverse behavior." In reality, Franz had not suffered brain damage, just a dented skull. The doctor had given him the slip as a sort of "get out of jail free" card for anything Franz said or did wrong.

The manager took the note, read it, and crumpled it up.

"An excuse for cowardice!" he told Franz.

"You have no idea what we did!" Franz said, clenching his fists. He had watched his fellow fighter pilots fight bravely until they died, one by one, while The Party's leadership called them "cowards," deflecting the blame for the destruction of Germany's cities onto them. In reality, Franz and his fellow fighter pilots never stood a chance against the Allies' industrial might and endless warplanes. Of the twenty-eight thousand German fighter pilots to see combat in WWII, only twelve hundred survived the war.

Franz leaned close to the man and whispered in his ear.* Leaning back in his seat, the manager said, "Go ahead, try it."

In one motion, Franz grabbed the manager by his collar, pulled him across the desk, and punched him between the eyes.

The manager stumbled backward into a cabinet. Other laborers seized Franz and slammed him to the floor. One kicked Franz in the ribs. Another punched him in a kidney. Together they ground his face into the dust-covered floor.

"You have no idea!" Franz shouted, his cheek pinned to the tiles.

———————

THREE GERMAN POLICE officers arrived and blew their whistles to part the mob. The laborers lifted their knees from Franz's back. The police hauled Franz up to his feet. The officers were strong and well fed by their American overseers. Franz wanted to run but could not escape.

With tears in his eyes, the manager told the police that Franz had demanded work ahead of the others and refused to leave. The angry mob confirmed the manager's story.

Franz denied the accusations, but he knew a losing battle when he saw one. He was going to jail. But he needed to get his papers back. Franz told the officer in charge that the manager held them.

The officer motioned for the other police to take Franz away.

"Wait! He still has my medical form!" Franz objected. The manager handed over the note. The officer uncrumpled the waiver and read it to the other policemen: ". . . head wound, sustained in aerial combat." The officer pocketed both of Franz's papers and announced, "You're still coming with us!"

Franz knew there was no point in resisting. The officers dragged him past the line of workers and into the street. A rush of fearful

---

* Franz would remember what he told the manager: "See, I have a hole here, and if you don't keep quiet I can't control what I'm going to do."

thoughts raced through Franz's mind: *How will I ever find work with an arrest record? What will I tell my girlfriend and mother? How will I provide for them?*

Exhausted from struggling against the mob, hurting from the beating, and overwhelmed with grief, Franz fell limp as the police hauled him away. The toes of his heavy black flying boots dragged against the rough, upturned stones where bombs had fallen.

2

FOLLOW THE EAGLES

THE SMALL BOY sprinted through the open pasture, his feet in tiny brown shoes. He chased the soaring wooden glider as its pilot took off into the sky. The boy wore thick knit Bavarian kneesocks, green knickers, and a white shirt with short sleeves. He ran with arms outstretched. "Go! Go! Go!" he shouted as he waved the machine and its pilot onward. The glider resembled the skeleton of a dinosaur with a web of wires running within it. It flew one hundred feet above the pasture, and the sound of flapping fabric trailed in its wake. The boy followed the glider to the pasture's edge and stopped when he could go no farther. He watched the contraption shrink into the distance over the rolling hills of Bavaria.

The glider soared with a whoosh over a farmer herding cows. An older boy flew the craft and sat in a wicker seat positioned over a ski that ran the glider's length. There was no windshield or instrument panel and only straps across the young pilot's shoulders secured him to the spartan craft. Minutes later, the pilot steered the machine in for a landing. He aimed for a worn white strip of grass in a green field where many landings had happened before. There, on a hill next to the landing strip, sat a short, wide shed where the youngsters and their adult advisors of the glider club were finishing a picnic. The small boy stood waiting at the shed. He held a short-brimmed tweed hat in his hands. The pilot coasted from one hundred feet to fifty feet to twenty-five feet and made a gentle three-bump landing. The pilot put his legs down to keep the glider from tipping over as the small boy ran up to the machine and darted under its wing. The boy was twelve-year-old Franz Stigler. The pilot was Franz's sixteen-year-old brother, August.

Franz stood alongside the cockpit as August removed his white safety straps. August swung his legs to earth and carefully lowered the glider to rest on its wingtip. Franz handed the hat to August, who removed his goggles and flopped the hat onto his head like an ace after a dawn patrol. August was dressed like Franz, in kneesocks, knickers, and a white shirt with a tiny collar.

The brothers were true Bavarians; both had dark brown eyes, brown hair, and oval faces. August's face was longer and calmer than Franz's. August was straightlaced, a deep thinker, and often wore spectacles. Franz had youthful, chubby cheeks, and he was quiet, although quick to smile. August had been named "Gustel Stigler," but he preferred "August." Franz had been named "Ludwig Franz Stigler," but went by "Franz," which irked the boys' strong, proper, deeply Catholic mother. Their father was easygoing and allowed the boys to call themselves whatever they wanted.

Franz praised August's flight, rehashing what he had seen as if August had not been there. August told Franz he was glad he had paid attention because it would be Franz's turn next. The other eight boys of the glider club converged around the brothers and helped carry the glider up the nearby hill to the flat launch point on top. August was the oldest of the boys and their leader.* Some of the boys were as young as nine and were not yet allowed to fly. But on this day, Franz—age twelve—was scheduled to become their youngest pilot.

Two adults in the glider club followed the boys up the hill. The men hauled a heavy, black rubber rope used to launch the glider. One of the adults was Franz's father, also named Franz. He was a thin man with a tiny mustache and circular spectacles that looped over big ears. He hugged August then helped Franz strap into the glider's thin, basket-like seat. The other adult was Father Josef, a Catholic priest and the boys' teacher, who handled fifth through eighth grades at their Catholic boarding school. Father Josef was in his fifties and had gray hair around the sides of his head. His face was strong, and his eyes were blue and friendly. When Father Josef was gliding, he traded his black robe and flat-brimmed hat for a white shirt and mountaineering pants. A large wooden cross dangled from his neck. Father Josef walked around the glider, checking its surfaces. Both men had flown for the German Air Force in WWI. Franz's father had been a reconnaissance pilot. Father Josef had been a fighter pilot.

Both adults had a habit of downplaying their service in the war. From the bird's-eye perspective of pilots, they had seen the stacks of muddy corpses between the battle lines. When Germany lost the first war, the two men lost their jobs. In the Treaty of Versailles, the victorious French, British, and Americans stipulated that the German Air Force was to dissolve and the Army and Navy were to disarm. Germany also needed to hand over its overseas colonies, allow foreign troops to occupy its western borderlands, and pay 132 billion Deutsche Marks in damages (about $400 billion today). As they paid the price for the war they'd lost, Germany fell into a deep economic depression long before the great global financial collapse of 1929.

---

* "He was the best glider pilot we had," Franz would remember. "We were brothers and best friends."

Franz's father and Father Josef had started the glider club to teach boys to enjoy the only good thing the war had taught them—how to fly. When the men had started the club, neither had enough money to buy a glider for the boys. Franz's father managed horses at a nearby estate. Father Josef had left the military for the priesthood. They told the boys that if they wanted to learn to fly, they would have to build a glider themselves. After school each day for months, August, Franz, and the other boys collected scrap metal and sold it to buy the blueprints for a Stamer Lippisch "Pupil" training glider. Father Josef wrangled a woodshed for them, high on a hill west of Amberg, the ancient, ornate Bavarian town they all called home. There in the shed, on weekends and holidays, the boys began building the glider. Stacks of wood and fabric came first. Blueprints in hand, it took a year for them to build the glider. Safety inspections followed. Administrators from the Department of Transport would not let the boys ride without first checking out the craft. The verdict came back. The boys had done well and were cleared for takeoff.

High on top of the hill, Franz tugged the canvas straps that held his shoulders to the glider's seat. Two other boys held each wingtip to keep the glider from tilting over. Franz's father attached the rubber rope to a hook in the glider's nose, next to where the landing ski curved upward. Father Josef and the other boys took hold of both ends of the rope, three per side. August knelt next to Franz. With a hand on his shoulder, he offered Franz some parting wisdom, "Stay below thirty feet and don't try to turn. Just get the feel of flying, then land." Franz nodded, too scared to speak. August took his place on the rope line. Franz's father reminded him, "Land before you reach the end of the field." Franz nodded again.

Franz's father sat on the ground and held the glider's tail. He was the biggest man and acted as the anchor. He shouted for Father Josef and the others to pull the rope taut. They began to walk down the hill, spreading the rope into a V with the glider at the center, the slack tightening, the rope quivering.

Franz lifted his feet from the ground and extended his tiny legs to the rudder stick. He gripped the wooden control stick that jutted up from a box on the ski between his thighs. The control stick was attached to wires that extended to the wings and tail to make the glider maneuver.

Father Josef and the boys gripped the rope with all their might, pulling out all slack. The cord trembled with energy. "Okay, Franz," Father Josef shouted up to him. "We launch on three!" Franz gave a wave. His heart pounded. Father Josef led the count, "One! Two! Three!" Everyone on the rope sprinted down the hill. The rope stretched with elastic energy, and Franz's father released the tail.

Franz rocketed forward—then instantly straight up. Something was seriously wrong. Instead of a gradual, level takeoff, the glider blasted upward like a missile, carrying its sixty-pound passenger toward the sun.

"Push!" Franz's father screamed. "Push forward!"

Franz jammed the control stick forward. The glider leveled off, nosed downward, then plunged. Frozen with fear, Franz flew straight toward the ground. *Crack!* The glider's nose plowed into the dirt. The machine tipped over, its wings thudding into the grass above Franz's head.

Franz's father, brother, and Father Josef sprinted to the glider. The other boys stood in shock. They were certain that Franz was dead. All they could see was the tops of the wings and the tail jutting into the air.

The two men lifted the machine by the wing and Franz flopped backward, still tied to his seat. He was mumbling and groggy. August unstrapped him and pulled Franz's limp body out of the glider. Slowly, Franz opened his eyes. He was stunned but unhurt. Franz's father clutched his son, hugging and crying at the same time.

"It's my fault, not yours," Franz's father said.

Turning to Father Josef, Franz's father said, "The glider was designed for a heavier passenger—we forgot to compensate." Father Josef nodded in agreement. After a few minutes, Franz walked wobbly from the wreck with August holding him up. He had made his first flight and first crash all at once. "I thought you did pretty well," August told Franz with a grin. "At least you stayed under thirty feet and didn't try to turn!"

THE GLIDER COULD be rebuilt, so the boys worked on it, just as they had built it. Every weekend they would drag the glider's wing from the barn and replace its broken spars over sawhorses in the grass. Franz's task was to re-glue the wing ribs, while the older boys did more precise jobs, like cutting new ribs and fitting them. Franz brushed the glue over the wood's seams heavily, thinking that he would not miss a spot if he coated everything. Franz's father dropped in now and then to inspect their progress. When he came to Franz's work, he looked long and hard at the globs of glue piling up along each seam. Franz stood a few paces back, proudly.

"It's a little sloppy, don't you think?" Franz's father observed.

"I didn't miss a spot," Franz promised.

"There's glue in places that didn't need it," Franz's father elaborated.

"It doesn't bother me," Franz said, "the fabric will cover it."

Franz's father gave him a lesson. "Always do the right thing, even if no one sees it."

Franz admitted it was sloppy, but he promised, "No one will know it's there."

"Fix it," his father advised, "because you'll know it's there."

That day and in the many that followed, when the other boys took breaks from their work to kick the soccer ball, Franz kept working. He wore his fingers bloody by shaving the excess glue with sandpaper. He smoothed the seams of each of the twenty-odd ribs, perfectly. When the boys rewrapped the wings with fabric then coated the fabric with lacquer that would forever seal the glider's skeleton, no one noticed Franz's meticulous work—except for his father and him.

Several months later, Franz shot into the skies with a sandbag tied to his waist. This time he soared, one hundred feet above Bavaria. August ran below, waving Franz onward. Franz saw his craft's wings flex and bend with the turbulence. He could see the curving Danube River to the east. Turning to the south, he could see the foothills of the Alps. Turning west, he saw a swath of forest looming ahead, so he turned hard to avoid it. The air did not rise over a forest or river, every glider pilot knew—you steered for fields and hills where the updrafts lifted your wings. Franz felt the rising air currents and saw birds above him, spiraling upward. August had told him, "The eagles know where the good air is—follow them."

3

A FEATHER IN THE WIND

FRANZ WAITED ON the stone bench. It was just after the midday meal, and the tall walls of his Catholic boarding school loomed around him. Leafy trees above the walls cast thicker shadows. Monks in their brown robes darted along the corridors. Franz wore his school uniform, but his gray pants were grass-stained and his white shirt sullied and rumpled. Franz was now seventeen. The baby fat had melted from his cheeks, revealing a lean, strong jaw. One ear looked inflamed and red.

Franz's mother, Anna, had enrolled him at the school. With August at a university studying to become a teacher, the boys' mother had decided that Franz would follow the path of the cloth. She longed to have a priest or monk in the family, and Franz had no problem with the plan. He loved his mother and cherished his faith. He planned to begin his priesthood studies when he graduated. There was one thing standing in the way of the plan. He had a girlfriend—and she was a secret. Until now.

Wearing his black robe, Father Josef approached the bench where

Franz sat. On the priest's face was a look of uncommon sternness. Graduation was still six months away, yet Franz knew he was in danger of being expelled. Father Josef taught the younger boys at grade school, and although Franz was no longer his student, he had come to Franz's defense once before, when Franz was caught sneaking out on a windless day to fly his glider. But this day was different. Franz had snuck out during lunch and crept down to the brewery at the end of the street. He would have slipped back unnoticed, but the brewmaster had caught Franz in the bushes with his daughter. The brewmaster was a beefy sort and dragged Franz back to school before lunch hour ended—by his ear.

Father Josef knew Franz was a good student and a dutiful son to his parents and God. On Sundays, Franz sang in the boys' choir at St. Peter's Cathedral in Regensburg, forty miles from his home. During the school's daily services he wore the robes of an altar boy.

"It's time to behave like a man," Father Josef told Franz. "A future priest cannot be sneaking out like this."

"You're right, Father," Franz said, hanging his head in shame.

"A man thinks and acts for himself," Father Josef said. "Because he knows he only must answer to God."

Franz nodded.

"Are you certain you want to become a priest?" Father Josef asked.

"I think so, Father."

"I'm not sure you do," Father Josef said. "Your mother wants you to be a priest. What is it that *you* want to do with your life, Franz?"

"I'd love to fly every day," Franz said quickly.

"Then go do it," Father Josef said. "Your mother will get over it."

NEARLY FIVE YEARS LATER, 1937

The muffled roar of three BMW radial engines announced the arrival of the Ju-52 airliner at Munich Airport's posh Lufthansa terminal.

One by one, the plane's passengers entered the terminal, the women in their furs and flapper-era floppy-brimmed hats, and the men in their crisp fedoras and three-piece suits. At their heels trailed luggage bearers in white coats with bags in their gloved hands. The scents of cigar smoke, hair pomade, and French perfume drifted through the bustling breeze of the hustle while upbeat piano music from a nearby lounge jingled over the pace of the traffic. Such was life in Germany in the post-depression 1930s. In this time of renewed optimism and expansive power, the airplane, like the autobahn, was a symbol of national pride and promise.

Lufthansa stewardesses, immaculately coiffed in navy skirts, blouses with flowery collars, and chic headwear, crossed paths in the flux, some leaving the terminal, others heading for their gates. Pilots from every European nationality darted to and fro. Among them was Lufthansa pilot Franz Stigler, now twenty-two years old. Clad in his navy suit with its yellow cuff bands, a crimson tie, and shimmering gold wings on his chest, Franz was a poster pilot for the airlines. He had come a long way since his life-altering talk with Father Josef.

After high school graduation, Franz had studied aeronautical engineering at the university in Würzburg, two hours northwest of his home in Amberg. He liked his studies, but once again he had found himself in trouble. After class one day, a friend pulled Franz aside and invited him to attend the meeting of a secret student club. Franz went along and discovered an underground dueling club where the boys fought with sharpened swords. The boys covered their faces and necks and wore long sleeves and gloves, but still, the swords were real. The rules were simple: they could swipe at one another but never stab. Franz joined because he liked the idea of pretending to be a knight. He picked up a few cuts on the top of his head, but none on his face.

What Franz did not know was that the Catholic Church had an edict outlawing dueling. When the club was discovered, he was caught. Church officials excommunicated him. He wasn't bothered by the edict—it was just part of church policy, he reasoned. His faith remained intact. But Franz felt ashamed for his mother when he heard that every Sunday for six weeks his name had been read aloud during Mass at the cathedral in Regensburg, among the list of the excommunicated.

The embarrassment over, Franz began to tighten his focus solely on his goal to fly. During the weekends, he began flight training at the local airport. It was called "Airline Pilot School," and its instructors taught Franz to fly motor-driven planes at no cost. The government paid for the training because they wanted pilots. Faced with the choice of sitting in a classroom to learn about flying or actually doing it, Franz dropped out of the university and completed his flight training. When Europe's largest airline, Lufthansa, offered Franz a job, he jumped at the chance.

For four years and two thousand hours Franz flew for the airline. His job wasn't typical. Instead of flying commercial airliners, he flew navigators as an international route check pilot. His role was to establish the quickest and safest flying routes between Berlin and London, and over the Alps to Rome and Barcelona. During these long hauls, Franz filled his logbook with passport stamps and flight times. In a glamorous age of air travel, when zeppelins, trimotors, and seaplanes roamed the skies, Franz had never been happier.

But on this day, as Franz walked through the airport, past its art deco lounges, a German Air Force officer waved and approached him. The officer was dressed similarly in a blue-gray blazer with a black tie, except he wore a brown belt and flared riding pants tucked into tall black boots. Two years prior there had not even been a German Air Force. In fact, there had not been one for seventeen years. Then one day in 1935, Hitler defied the Versailles Treaty with the sweep of a pen and reinstituted the German Air Force, the "Luftwaffe."

The officer gave Franz a tall sealed envelope. "Your orders," the officer said, his face grim. "Your country needs your service."

Franz had suspected this day would come.* This was why the government had trained him for free. After the Versailles Treaty had outlawed their Air Force, the German government had secretly trained scores of new pilots like him and funded the national airline—Lufthansa—so that the nation would have seasoned pilots to one day rebuild the Air Force. The routes and times that Franz had been devising for Lufthansa no doubt had also found their way into the hands of the Air Force.

The officer informed Franz that he was to serve as an instructor pilot. He would teach new pilots how to fly long distances using instruments. Franz would remain a civilian, the officer assured him. He would fly his Ju-52 airliner under the banner of the airlines, although his missions would serve the Air Force. The officer promised Franz that they had the airline's blessing.

"Where will I be flying?" Franz asked.

"You like the routes to Spain?"

"I know them."

Franz knew why the Air Force would have an interest in Spain. A year before, the Spanish Civil War had broken out, between the socialist-leaning Republicans and the fascist-leaning Nationalists. Germany was unofficially sending "volunteers" to fight for the fascist side.

"You think it's smart to train pilots by flying them into a war zone?" Franz asked.

"There also may be *supplies* in the belly of your plane," the officer said.

The officer looked to Franz for his response. Franz nodded and accepted the assignment, knowing he had never had a choice in the first place.

---

* "You didn't decide when you became Air Force," Franz would remember. "They decided for you."

A YEAR LATER, SUMMER 1938, EASTERN GERMANY

One thousand feet above the trees, the silver biplane flew in the evening light over the nature preserve within the suburbs of the city of Dresden. The pilots flew from two open cockpits, one in front of the other. The instructor sat in front, the trainee behind him. The plane was a perfect marriage of beauty and ugly functionality. Its radial engine was open to the wind and its spokes stuck out at all angles of the clock. Its landing gear was obtrusively fixed downward. The plane's flanks were long and silver and wore the large black cross of the German Air Force. Painted on its elegantly curved tail was the smaller, crooked cross of The Party, the swastika. The plane was a Heinkel 72 "Cadet," designed for the Air Force as a pilot trainer.

Franz flew the plane from the instructor's front seat. In the cockpit behind him sat a student pilot. After Franz's successful missions to Spain, the Air Force had wanted him to keep training its pilots, and so he remained an instructor. Franz sought to return to the airlines but no longer had a choice—the airlines had given him to the Air Force. In his new role, the Air Force made Franz a head instructor at their pilot school for officers in Dresden. Franz's students were called "cadets," but they were the cream of the crop—some were already officers, and those who were not would become officers upon graduation.

On this evening Franz was supposed to be off duty, but he had volunteered to take a struggling pilot up for some extra practice. The boy was one of the worst flyers of the twenty in his class. Beneath his gray canvas flight helmet, the boy had a strong jaw but fleshy childlike features. His dark blue eyes darted with nervousness. The boy's name was Gerhard Barkhorn, but outside of class, everyone called him Gerd. He was from East Prussia and well mannered. A quiet nineteen-year-old, Barkhorn had told Franz he wanted to fly fighters someday. Franz thought it unlikely but gave him extra practice to help him toward his goal.

Franz taught the B or second level of instructing. In A-level training, pilots like Barkhorn had learned the basics of flying and had soloed after forty "hops." Franz's job now, over the course of five months, was to teach cadets the finer points of flying—skills such as distance flying, navigation, how to handle emergencies, and advanced aerobatics. B school was serious—if a cadet washed out, there was no second chance—he would end up in the infantry. Germany was not yet at war, but everyone sensed the nation was building for one.

As they flew, Franz wondered how Barkhorn had ever soloed successfully. He was jittery and panicky. *This kid is a horrible pilot*, Franz thought. *He should be washed out.* Franz had already pinpointed Barkhorn's problem. The young cadet was thinking himself into a knot. He had to detach his mind and fly by instinct.

The He-72 did not have a radio, so Franz turned and faced Barkhorn.

"Relax!" Franz shouted over the wind. "Feel the plane in your seat, in the stick, in your stomach. Let go of your worry!"

Barkhorn nodded, but Franz noticed his maneuvers remained rigid. Franz signaled to Barkhorn with hand motions to tell him he was taking back the controls. Barkhorn leaned his head against his seat back, defeated. Franz put the biplane into a hard turn and flew north, toward the airfield. But he did not land. Instead, Franz kept flying until they passed over several small lakes nestled among a patch of forest. In the middle of the trees along a lake lay a series of wooden buildings. Franz banked and flew over the buildings. As he dipped the plane's wing for a better view, Barkhorn grinned. People ran out of the buildings, waving. They were all naked! Barkhorn knew he was looking down on the nudist camp that instructors sometimes flew students over as a reward. Franz reached into his cockpit and held up a roll of toilet paper he had placed there. Before the flight, Barkhorn had seen a roll of toilet paper on the floor of his cockpit, too, but thought it was there should they land on some practice field and need to answer nature's call.

Franz banked the plane around for another pass over the nudists. He threw his roll of toilet paper over the cockpit ledge as he flew across the camp. The nudists were accustomed to this and encouraged their children to run to catch the streaming white paper.

Barkhorn and Franz laughed. Circling around, Franz lined up for another pass on the colony. Franz made a throwing motion. Taking the cue, Barkhorn tossed his toilet paper over the side and watched the roll spiral to the children as they ran in circles. Turning back for base, Franz wagged the plane's wings to the nudists. He gave Barkhorn the signal to take over. Barkhorn was so busy laughing he flew smoothly, like a natural pilot.

———————

FRANZ ENJOYED BEING a flight instructor. Every morning when he walked into his classroom, he oversaw four instructors, each of whom looked after four students. The Air Force let him remain a civilian. They paid him his airline salary, which was the equivalent to a major's wages and gave him a major's authority. Franz's final report determined if a cadet earned his wings, and the higher Franz ranked a cadet, the more choice a young pilot would have in picking his next assignment to further training in either single- or multi-engine aircraft. All the cadets vied for single-engine training because that meant fighters, whereas multi-engine aircraft could be bombers, transports, or reconnaissance planes. Franz ultimately gave Barkhorn good scores, and the young pilot qualified for single-engine school.

———————

THE ONLY THING Franz lacked in his new role was rank and the respect that came with it, because he was a civilian. Although most of his pupils were cadets who would be officers one day, some of Franz's students were officers who had been in the military for years and now had decided to become pilots. They presented Franz's biggest challenge. One day, Franz gave a class in navigation. All the while, a captain sat in the back of the room and read a newspaper, ignoring Franz.

Franz had had enough. "Captain," he said, "would you come to the front and read the newspaper out loud so we'll all know what's going on?"

The captain folded his newspaper and walked up to Franz in front of the others. "You have no right to give me orders," the officer said. "You're just a civilian."

Franz felt the back of his neck grow hot. He closed the class, dismissed the pupils, and went straight to the general who ran the school. The general was a hefty fellow and liked Franz because Franz flew him to Munich every Friday so the general could see his doctor. Franz explained the problem with the disrespectful captain.

"Get your logbook," the general told Franz.

"Now write 'Private' next to your name."

Franz did so and looked at the general, confused.

"I'll handle your enlistment papers personally," the general said. "You're now officially a member of the Air Force."

Franz opened his mouth but was at a loss for words.

"As for the unruly captain," the general said, "now you can send him packing."

Franz did and expelled the captain from the school.

The next day the captain tracked down Franz to protest his expulsion—he fumed that a private had cast him out and would keep him from ever becoming a pilot. Franz now wore the blue uniform of a Luftwaffe enlisted man, with a tent cap atop his head, red collar tabs on his tunic, a silver belt buckle, and black boots.

"If you, as a captain, do not know how to behave," Franz said, "how could we have made you into a good pilot?" The captain cursed Franz as he hauled his bags away from the school.

Franz found that his new rank solved some problems, but being a private only got him so far. A few weeks later, while flying home from the doctor in Munich, the general asked Franz how he liked being a private. Franz said it helped, but so many of his students were majors and captains that they still looked down on him. The general was in a good mood, so in the air, he promoted Franz to corporal.

——————

IN EARLY 1939, the cadet who would become Franz's most cherished student waited for him as Franz climbed from his plane after a lesson. Franz was shocked to see his older brother, August, standing before him on the tarmac. Franz knew August had enlisted in the Air Force against their mother's wishes, but the odds that he would be sent to train under Franz seemed incredible.

Franz had not seen August since his brother had left for boot camp. August was on the path to become an officer.* He had already soloed with ease and passed stage A. He would now spend eight months under Franz's tutelage to earn his wings.

Franz knew why August had joined; all young men were being drafted into the military, and August knew that by enlisting first he could pick the branch of service he wanted. August had a lot to lose. He was engaged to the niece of a cardinal, a match their mother had made. August had his education, his job as a high school teacher, his family, his church, and his freedom. "Why risk everything?" Franz had asked him. August had said he was certain a war was coming and he would be drafted. If he had to fight, he preferred to fly.

To be impartial, Franz could have assigned August to another instructor. But Franz did not care what the other cadets whispered. He was burdened by the thought that his brother's survival in combat one day could hinge on his training. So Franz picked August as one of his personal students. For months Franz taught August aerobatics, high-altitude flying, and emergency procedures.

————————

* August had qualified for officer status, unlike Franz, who had not finished his university degree and would have to climb the ranks. The German Air Force was not as rank conscious as other air forces, so even low-ranking airmen and corporals could be fighter pilots.

As their training period wound down, August told Franz that he planned to apply for a twin-engine assignment to fly aircraft that allowed a pilot to "enjoy the ride" instead of the diving and twisting dogfights of fighter pilots. Franz knew that August lacked the killer instinct a fighter pilot needed, but this was a good quality in Franz's eyes. With only weeks remaining that they could be together, Franz gave August extra lessons after class to hone skills a bomber pilot would need—skills such as distance flying, night flying, and flying blind (by instruments only). Franz trained August harder than any other instructor would have. He demanded perfection.

August earned a weeklong vacation prior to his final exams. He decided to go home to spend time with his fiancée. It was a Friday, and that morning Franz had sent him on a long-distance training hop where August had followed his map from airfield to airfield. At each point he was to land and get his logbook stamped by the duty officer in the tower as proof. When August reported back to Franz that evening along with the other students, Franz found that only one pilot was missing a stamp—his brother. August explained that he could not find the duty officer and left without the stamp. Franz knew his brother had been in a hurry. August admitted this was true.

"Hurrying in an airplane can get you killed," Franz told him.

In front of the other cadets, Franz tore up August's holiday papers and canceled his leave. August was shocked and angry. Franz told his brother to go prepare an airplane for more training. August obeyed and left Franz's office, sulking.

The brothers took to the skies, Franz in front, August behind, to practice August's least favorite mission—flying blind. Soon after takeoff, Franz ordered August "under the hood." August pulled a handle and a black cloth covered his canopy, locking him into a cockpit lit only by instruments. Franz flew the plane for a while to disorient August. Then he shouted orders between cockpits and told August which course to steer and for how long. Franz knew that August had no idea where he was going.

An hour and a half later, Franz told August he was taking control of the plane. August asked to remove the hood, which was customary, but Franz denied the request. Franz landed the craft, taxied to a stop, and only then told August he could remove the hood. August started to give Franz a piece of his mind for keeping him in the dark for so long, but he stopped mid-sentence.

Waiting for him by a hangar on the tarmac was his fiancée. August immediately recognized the airport—Regensburg—they weren't back at Dresden—they were home. August's fiancée giggled at the shock on his face. She knew what Franz had done.* August embraced his fiancée and tried to rustle Franz's hair as Franz squirmed away. They were like boys again.

During their weeklong holiday the brothers stayed at their boyhood home on a quiet street in Amberg. While looking for August one afternoon, Franz wandered into his brother's bedroom. There on August's desk, Franz found a stack of letters. Franz picked one up and read it. His hands began to tremble. The letter was a copy of "With Burning Concern," the Vatican's secretly composed message to all of Germany's Catholics. On Palm Sunday, 1937, the letter had been read by every priest, bishop, and cardinal across Germany to their congregations and three hundred thousand copies had been disseminated. Drafted by Munich's Cardinal von Faulhaber and Pope Pius XI, it told German Catholics in carefully veiled terms that National Socialism was an evil religion based on racism that stood contrary to the church's teachings and every man's right to equality. It made reference to "an insane and arrogant prophet" without naming Hitler. When Hitler found out about the letter, he and The Party roared in backlash, outlawing the letter and seizing monks, priests, and any press shops that had printed it.

Franz's mind raced as he set down the letter. Franz wanted to burn

---

* "I had called his girlfriend, his fiancée, and told her, 'We're coming home,'" Franz would remember.

it and the others. He wanted to run. Instead, he waited on the front steps for August to return home. Franz suspected the letters really belonged to August's fiancée, the cardinal's niece. The Catholic clergy of Germany were known enemies of The Party, thanks to their sermons that reviled Hitler, his Gestapo secret police, and the early crimes of the Third Reich. Franz was certain that his brother's fiancée, via her uncle, was dragging his brother into something dangerous: opposition.

When August returned, Franz confronted him, asking him what he was doing with such dangerous literature. August brushed Franz off and said he had found the letters and kept them as a curiosity. Franz reminded August that the letters were dangerous.

"Do you want to wind up in Dachau?" Franz asked him. August scowled. They both knew of Dachau and the concentration camps that existed to "concentrate" in one place any Germans who had angered The Party.

The camps were common knowledge in most German households. The Party wanted the camps to be known, as a deterrent, and had publicized Dachau as their "model camp." The Party had built Dachau in 1933. Any German, regardless of religion or background, could be labeled a "political enemy" and imprisoned there. A year after seizing power, in 1934, The Party had passed a law that made a person's private or public criticism of The Party a crime worthy of a camp sentence.

The Party went to great lengths to show their fellow Germans, and the world, that Dachau was a "civilized" camp. The Party's private security force, the SS, ran the camps and even invited Red Cross representatives and American prison wardens to tour Dachau. The international visitors walked away impressed with what they saw: well-fed prisoners who whistled as they marched to work details, tidy barracks, flower beds, and even a store where the prisoners could purchase tinned food. When the prisoners were released, the SS gave them back their possessions. This was the image of a concentration camp that The Party had fed Franz, August, their fellow Germans, and the world, during the 1930s. The camps were so well publicized that German mothers used to tell their children that if they were bad, they would be taken away to Dachau.*

Seeing Franz's turmoil, August promised to dispose of the letters. Franz did not fault August for opposing Hitler. Franz knew their parents opposed Hitler, too. They always said that Hitler was not their leader. In 1933 they had voted for the BVP (the Bavarian People's Party), the Catholic party that had won a million votes but still fell far short of the National Socialists' 44 percent. As a teenager, Franz had paid little attention to the 1933 election. He was apathetic about politics and not initially alarmed by the National Socialists' victory.† But now, as a twenty-four-year-old man in spring 1939, Franz had come to think of The Party differently than he had as a boy in 1933. He had come to realize that The Party had turned Germany itself into a concentration camp. There were no elections. No freedom of press. No freedom of speech. No freedom to travel. No freedom to choose to serve in the military. No freedom to change things. In the days when possessing an outlawed letter could earn someone a sentence in a camp, the best Franz knew was to stay out of the line of fire, so neither he nor his brother would end up in Dachau.

———

THAT SUMMER, FRANZ pinned the wings on August's uniform when he graduated from flight school. August received his wings in time to

———

* The German civilians weren't the only ones misled about the camps. In a 1937 speech to the German Army, SS leader Heinrich Himmler told them how the prisoners were treated, "The training of men is carried out in these camps in an orderly way. They live in clean huts. Only Germans are capable of such an accomplishment. No other nation would be as humane. Clothes are changed frequently. The men are trained to wash twice a day and to use a toothbrush—something which the majority have never known before."[1] A later chapter will discuss when and how Franz would learn the truth about what was really happening in the camps.

† Franz would remember, "Being Catholic and a well educated family, we just did not buy into the propaganda. My family was anti-Nazi from the early days. I must admit that I was also very indifferent, and thought it was all bullshit to be honest."[2]

wear them when he married his fiancée shortly thereafter. During the wedding ceremony, Franz could not bring himself to look upon his new sister-in-law with much affection. He was still worried. After the wedding, August went to twin-engine school, the path of a bomber pilot, and Franz returned to instructing.

———

THAT AUTUMN 1939, Franz's cadets approached him in the mess hall one morning waving newspapers in their hands. The big, gothic headlines declared: WAR WITH POLAND! The young cadets were smiling and shouting. They wanted Franz's opinion—would their training be hurried so they could get into the war? Franz did not share their glee. War was the last thing he wanted. But in the minds of the flight school cadets, the world's affairs were simple. According to the German papers, the Poles had threatened German farmers on the shared border. Polish troops had attacked a German radio station on the border in order to transmit slander against the Germans, and Hitler had no choice but to declare war. The cadets thought Hitler was right, just like they had reasoned that Germany's other neighbors, Czechoslovakia and Austria, had wanted to become part of the new German empire. The annexation of those countries, that year and the year prior, had been bloodless.

In reality, the Austrians and Czechs had no choice. Germany had been militarily rebuilt and seemed unstoppable. And the "Polish troops" who had raided the German radio station were actually German commandos wearing Polish uniforms. Hitler had ordered this. He wanted a war of expansion, and he lied to his own people to get it. What neither Franz nor any of the cadets could fathom was that Hitler had knowingly picked a fight with much of the rest of Europe, dragging Germany into a repeat of their fathers' war. Britain and France had pledged that if Poland was ever attacked their empires would fight on the Polish side. Hitler attacked Poland anyway. His gamble would eventually cost the lives of more than 4 million German soldiers and more than a million civilians. World War II had officially begun.

ONE YEAR LATER, MID-OCTOBER 1940

Franz worked alone at his desk in an empty classroom. His instructors were out, each training students for war. German troops now occupied all of Europe from Poland to France and had beaten the English back to their island. The "Battle of Britain," as the British called it, was over. The battle had taken place late that summer when the Germans had tried to destroy the British Royal Air Force (RAF) in the sky and to bomb their airfields on the ground. But before the German Air Force could succeed, a grievous mistake shook their focus. During a night raid, a German bomber mistakenly missed its target, an oil depot east of London, and bombed several homes on London's East End neighborhood. Hitler had given orders that British cities were not to be bombed, a far cry from the indiscriminate warfare he ordered against Poland's civilians. But, a few days later, another German bomber hit British homes again. In response, the British sent bombers to attack Berlin, a raid that also missed its military targets and bombed the city's civilians. In a speech Hitler warned the British to stop their attacks on German cities, but it was too late—both sides had stepped over the line. Cities and civilians soon became fair game.

From then on, both sides bombed each other's cities at night and called one another "terror bombers." Franz knew August was on the front lines, flying a Ju-88 bomber, a fast, twin-engine plane with a four man crew. August and his crew had been assigned to bomber group KGr-806 and were based in Caen, France, from where they bombed England at night. At first their targets were airfields and docks. Then they were ordered to bomb cities. Franz knew August would not have liked this, but would have had no choice.

Franz looked up in surprise when he heard the door to his

classroom open slowly. The cadets usually kicked it open in glee after a mission. Franz saw Father Josef standing in the doorway. The priest was dressed in civilian attire but still wore his large wooden cross. Franz moved toward him, his heart racing. Then he stopped. Father Josef was not smiling.

"Sit down, Franz," he said.

Franz stayed standing, his feet frozen. Father Josef was his father's best friend. Franz assumed something must have happened to his father.

The priest's eyes welled with tears.

Franz's legs became wobbly, as if his body knew the answer even before his mind made the suggestion. Father Josef rushed to him and guided him into a seat among the many empty desks.

"August is with God," he said.

———

FRANZ WOULD NOT allow Father Josef to provide him with any details until the following day, when he was able to control his emotions. Father Josef told Franz that August had crashed on takeoff for a night mission to London several days prior on October 10. August and his entire crew had been killed. The reason for the crash was unknown. It had happened at night and all witnesses saw was a flash.

There would be no funeral. August was already buried in Caen, France. Father Josef gave Franz a letter written by August's commanding officer that said that August had died "a hero." Franz tossed the letter aside.

Franz blamed himself for August's crash. He had trained him. *What could I have missed?*

He blamed the people who had built August's plane. *Had they made a mistake?*

He blamed the war. He had believed what Hitler said, that Germany had attacked Poland in self-defense. Franz blamed the British.

In his mind, they had turned a war between two countries into a world war. August had been flying at night, from grass airfields, in dangerous conditions *because of them*. Franz's grief chilled into hate.

Before he could leave to go home and console his parents, Franz reported to the general. The general offered Franz his plane, but Franz refused so that he could ride back with Father Josef. Franz thanked the general for being good to him but said he was resigning. The general appeared shocked. Franz was his best instructor. The general reminded Franz that he could take as much time away as he needed. When he came back, he would always have an instructor job—far from the war.

"Promise me you'll think about it," the general told Franz as he walked out the door.

But the more Franz thought about it, the more he knew exactly what he wanted.

4

FIRE FREE

EIGHTEEN MONTHS LATER, APRIL 7, 1942, THE LIBYAN COASTLINE

Low AND FAST, the twelve tan Messerschmitt Bf-109 fighters blasted over the white beaches of Libya. Climbing over the sea cliffs, the fighters soared above the ruins and Hellenic columns of the ancient Greek city of Appolonia. One 109, far back in formation, flew at an odd angle, banking, one wingtip pointed to earth.

"Stigler, straighten up!" barked the flight leader, Lieutenant Werner Schroer, across the radio. Franz righted his 109, the hottest German fighter of the day. The machine's body was sleek except for an air filter that jutted from the side of the nose.

Franz had not been so happy in ages. He watched over his shoulder as the ruins faded behind his tail. During his Lufthansa days, he had loved to explore the old world's ancient cities.

"Buy a postcard," Schroer radioed Franz. The pilots were all rookies except for Schroer, who had flown in the desert already for a year. Schroer had four "kills," or enemy aircraft destroyed, to his name.

Franz was now a sergeant and a full-fledged fighter pilot, having graduated from boot camp and fighter school with a promotion. With more than four thousand hours of flight time under his belt, he could have flown transports or air sea rescue planes, or he could have stayed an instructor forever. But he had chosen fighters and asked to be transferred to a war theater. It was no secret why. He wanted revenge.

A few days earlier, he had taken possession of his warhorse from the factory in Munich where it had been built. He found it there, waiting on a ramp, already painted in its desert camouflage color scheme, with its white spinner, tan body, and belly the color of a blue robin's egg. The 109 was a new F-model, nicknamed the "Friedrich," the fastest 109 to date. The fighter wore no identification numbers on its flanks—Franz was told they would be assigned when he reached his squadron. On its fuselage and wings it bore the large black cross with white outline, the mark of the German Air Force.

Schroer had met Franz and the other rookies after they had flown to Sicily, the island at the toe of the Italian boot. From Sicily he had led them across the Mediterranean to Africa. From Tunisia, Schroer swung east, and the pilots flew along the coast.

Having passed Appolonia, Franz saw the "Green Mountains," the Al Jabal al Akhdar range, appear below him. The mountains were a lush anomaly in craggy northern Libya. The flight motored over the ancient Islamic city of Derna, where the sun lit the forty-two minarets of the city's mosque. Turning south, Schroer steered the flight into the dry desert, with its rocks, scrub brush, and gullies.

When Franz first saw the desert, he thought of the Christian knights on their crusades for the Holy Land. At fighter school the old instructors, themselves WWI aces, had told Franz and the other rookies that the black cross on their planes' wings and fuselage was an homage to the German Teutonic Knights, whose white shields bore a black cross. "You are their descendants," they told the students. The old WWI pilots were themselves called "the old knights" and they talked of their code. It was unwritten and unspoken. It could only be witnessed and embodied. It was a battle code of honor and chivalry.

When Franz arrived in the desert, he thought their stories were just the whimsical ideals of old veterans. But there, above the sands, he would learn otherwise.

═══════

AHEAD, ON THE white horizon, Franz saw the tan tent peaks of Martuba Airfield, his new home. Entering the traffic pattern to land, Franz was aghast—Martuba looked like a sprawling, isolated campsite. It had countless center-pitched tents in clusters, like villages, no hangars, and just a small whitewashed control tower. A handful of mud-brick blast pens housed fighters along the flight line, but most of the planes sat naked on the sand, baking in the sun.

Following Schroer down, Franz landed on Martuba's sun-bleached runway, with its scars visible from bombings. Taxiing, Franz found his canopy surrounded by blowing sand kicked up from his plane's Daimler-Benz motor. He stopped when a shirtless ground crewman approached through the swirling whiteout. The crewman climbed up onto his right wing and sat on the wingtip. The crewman motioned and pointed for Franz to pull ahead. With hand signals, he guided Franz to park alongside the other new arrivals. Franz shut down his engine, unbuckled his seat belt, and hauled himself from the cockpit. He slid off the wing, his hands stinging from its hot metal. A darkly tanned crewman took Franz's parachute. Franz stretched to work out the kinks. He removed his leather jacket and felt the blazing African sun. Around him, other fighters on the flight line had victory marks on their rudders, white, vertical bars, one for each aerial kill. Franz studied the hash marks. It took five to make an ace. Some of the planes around him had four times that.

Schroer approached Franz. His face was V-shaped and serious, but his eyes were friendly and shy. When he removed his cap to wipe his brow, he revealed that he was balding and looked old for being a young man. He seemed unbothered by the sun, while Franz squinted. Schroer could see Franz's wheels turning and told him it had once taken the "magic 20" victories to earn the Knight's Cross, but now the bench-mark was higher, at least thirty victories, thanks to the fighter pilots on the Eastern Front whose high scoring against easy opponents was spoiling everyone else's dreams. Franz knew the Knight's Cross was Germany's preeminent award for valor, a medal worn around the neck, inspired by the ancient Teutonic Knights.

Schroer told Franz it was time to check into the war. He walked to the control tower, where a few Volkswagen *kuebelwagens*—the Ger-man equivalent of jeeps—were parked. Franz grabbed his duffel from the storage compartment in his plane's fuselage and followed. The tower, Franz would learn, was only for administration. The real ground-to-air coordination happened in an underground bunker next door. Hidden by dirt and marked only by the hum of a generator, Franz saw aircrew and orderlies emerge from the bunker and shield their eyes against the sunlight. This was the headquarters of Fighter Wing 27 (*Jagdgeschwader* 27 or "JG-27"), the legendary "Desert Wing" romanticized in the newsreels. JG-27 had just 120 pilots at full strength. They were the primary fighter force in Africa and served a strategic mission. The Germans wanted to take the Suez Canal in Egypt away from the British. Whoever controlled the canal controlled one of only two waterways into the Mediterranean. The fighting in North Africa had already been raging for a year. It was a pushing con-test. The Germans would push the British one or two hundred miles back toward the canal, into sandy Egypt, then the British would push the Germans back the same distance into craggy Libya. The mission facing JG-27 was daunting. They were to keep the skies clear over the German Army known as the Afrika Korps. Opposing JG-27 was the Desert Air Force, a mixed unit of English squadrons and those from all nations of the British crown. The Desert Air Force outnumbered the pilots of JG-27 five to one.

Franz entered the tower. The narrow room was fitted with wooden benches. High ceilings were held in place by thick beams. Hanging on the wall was a panel of yellow metal cut from a downed British fighter.

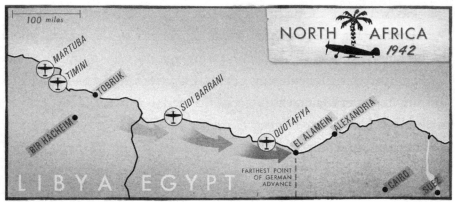

BRYAN MAKOS

Painted on the metal was the plane's nose art—a blue shield with a curved scimitar. Franz joined the other rookies in a line, at attention, when three officers entered and stood before them to announce the new pilots' assignments. The officers wore loose tan shirts and baggy green pants. Under their arms they tucked their white crush caps, like those worn by U-boat captains. One officer, a captain, had groomed his black beard into a sharp goatee. He was Captain Ernst Maak. Franz had never seen facial hair on an officer in Germany. He saw only sternness in Maak's face. The captain barked some names from his list, and the pilots called stepped forward. Maak told the pilots that they now belonged to Squadron 2. The room turned silent.

Maak singled out one of his new pilots, an airman named Helmut Beckmann, and began to address him in a loud, sarcastic voice. "Did you manage to deliver your plane undamaged?"

"Yes sir," Beckmann said.

"Did you land on your wheels or crash on your belly?"

"We did not encounter the enemy," Beckmann said wisely. Franz found himself hoping Maak did not call on him.

"Are you politically inclined?"

"I was in the air force HJ [Hitler Youth], sir!" Beckmann said.

"I'm not interested in that," Maak said. "I'm asking if you are a member of The Party?"

"No, sir!"

"Another big plus for you!" Maak smiled. "Keep it up and you'll do just fine."[1]

"Stigler?" a first lieutenant said calmly, looking around. Shorter and slighter than Maak, the officer seemed serenely confident. He had thick black hair, slicked back, and a square, boyish face. His narrow eyes beamed a sensitive, concerned look. The Knight's Cross dangled from his neck, over the open collar of his crumpled tan shirt. Franz took one look at the thick, black cross as it hung from a red-and-white ribbon and decided that he, too, would one day wear the Cross. Franz clicked his heels and began to salute but stopped when the lieutenant thrust forward an outstretched hand and said, "Welcome to Squadron 4. Follow me."

Franz grinned. He shouldered his bag, relieved that he was not stuck with Maak. Leaning against the door frame, Schroer wished Franz luck.

Outside the shed, the officer flopped his faded white cap on his head. He introduced himself as Lieutenant Gustav Roedel. Franz would learn that Roedel was from Merseburg in Eastern Germany, near Poland. They were the same age. Franz joined Roedel in his *kuebelwagen* for a tour of the base. An enlisted man drove while Roedel explained to Franz that three months earlier the airfield had been owned by the British, before the "Desert Fox" took it back for the Germans. Franz knew the "Desert Fox" was General Erwin Rommel, the commander of the Afrika Korps.

"Can I ask a strange question, Lieutenant?" Franz said.

Roedel nodded.

"What was Maak getting at by asking that pilot if he was a Party member?"

"Never heard someone in uniform speak so brazenly, huh?" Roedel said.

Franz nodded. Roedel explained the rumors that had floated since the Battle of Britain that The Party was going to send "political officers" to infiltrate Air Force squadrons to look for dissention. "Maak hates the thought of that, as we all do," Roedel said. "Let me ask you this—are you a Party member, Stigler?"

"No," Franz said. "I don't need a politician to make me go to war."

Roedel smiled and nodded.

Roedel, Maak, and the others knew that any fighter pilot who was a Party member was a rarity and, most likely, a fanatic. To be a Nazi in the German Air Force, one needed to have joined The Party before enlisting or being drafted, usually at a very young age. Once a man joined the Air Force, the German Defense Law of 1938 forbid him from Party membership.* German civilians could join The Party at any time, as could the SS and the Gestapo. But in the German Air Force, a Nazi fighter pilot was a rarity. It was Roedel's philosophy, like Maak's, to spot such pilots right away, and to keep an eye on them.

When Roedel's driver passed a group of 109s whose cowlings sported leopard heads and the faces of spooked natives surrounded by the outline of Africa, Roedel indicated to Franz that the planes belonged to Squadron 3, home to Germany's most famous pilot of the time—Lieutenant Hans-Joachim Marseille, the twenty-two-year-old ace known as the "virtuoso of all fighter pilots." He had already destroyed more than fifty enemy planes.

"You've heard stories of him?" Roedel said.

Franz nodded. He had read everything he could about "The Star of Africa," as the newspapers called Marseille.

Roedel told Franz the whispers of Marseille's free-spirited rebelliousness were true. Once, as a joke, Marseille ran over Schroer's tent with his *kuebelwagen*. Another time, when passed up for a promotion, he strafed the tent area of his squadron leader. And he had crashed more than one plane into the desert by flying on the edge.

---

* This was due to a German tradition called *Überparteilichkeit*, or "impartiality," the separation of military from politics.

"But despite all the trouble he creates for his commanders," Roedel said, "he is simply too good to ground."

The driver slowed the vehicle to a stop in front of a 109 marked like those around it, with a red and white crest on its cowling. Roedel told Franz that these were the planes of their unit, II Group. The crest on each plane was the logo of the city of Berlin, the unit's home city. The crest was white with a red outline and in the center was a painted black bear, standing, with its tongue lapping. Roedel explained that there were three squadrons in II Group. There was his squadron— Squadron 4—as well as Squadron 5 and Squadron 6. Behind the planes, Franz saw their squadron's headquarters—a wooden shack, several large tents, and a flagpole where a flag hung limply.

Roedel opened a small door and exited the car, indicating for Franz to remain seated. He told the driver to help Franz get situated in his new home. Roedel walked to his 109, a fighter with a yellow number 4 painted on its flanks. Franz noticed that Roedel's fighter wore no victory marks on its tail. With Roedel strapping in and out of earshot, Franz asked the driver, incredulous, how Roedel could wear the Knight's Cross but not be an ace. The driver grinned at the chance to put another rookie in his place. He told Franz that Roedel had thirty-seven victories, some gained in Spain during their civil war, some in Poland, some in Greece, some over the Soviet Union, and the rest in the desert, including one the day before.

"He's one of our best," the driver said. "He just chooses not to flaunt it."

The driver clunked the *kuebelwagen* into gear and pulled away. In the backseat, Franz suddenly felt very stupid.

TWO DAYS LATER, APRIL 9, 1942

The sand-caked tent rustled under a blast of frigid night air. Inside the tent, Franz lay on his cot, awakened by the flapping canvas. He fished for his cigarette lighter, flicked it to life, and read his wristwatch by the dull glow of the flame. It was 4 A.M. He huddled back under his blanket, shivering.

The desert was bitterly cold until the sun arose. Franz remembered that he was due on the flight line at 6 A.M. for his first mission, having flown an orientation flight at the same time the day before. The aces of JG-27 liked to break in the rookies quickly, and Franz preferred this to sitting around.

Quickly he rose and donned his tan desert regulation shirt and black leather flying jacket. Showers were only permitted every few days, as water was precious, so Franz knew not to bother. He stepped into heavy, pale blue flying trousers with on each thigh a large map pocket that extended below his kneecap. He shook out his thick, black leather flying boots to check for scorpions, but only sand poured out. He zipped up his boots and grabbed his rosary from a wooden crate that served as his nightstand. His mother had given Franz the rosary after his confirmation. A silver crucifix dangled from the necklace of small, rectangular black beads. Franz slid his rosary into his jacket's pocket, over his heart, and slipped out of his tent.

In the predawn darkness he wandered through the spartan tent city that was JG-27's desert home. All the tents looked alike. Locating the mess tent at last, Franz ducked inside the flaps and felt the immediate warmth of oil stoves and lively conversation as a handful of pilots ate oatmeal and drank hot coffee. Roedel sipped his coffee in the tent corner while reviewing a battle map. Each squadron sat together like a team. At full strength, a squadron mustered sixteen pilots and planes, but quantities of each were always short due to losses. The pilots' morale remained high, however—they thought they could still win the war.

After slopping his plate full of oatmeal and toast on the chow line, Franz sat down, his mess tin before him. After one bite he was taken aback. His oatmeal tasted like dirt. His coffee tasted like sulfur. The cooks had used the usual brown water to make both.

JG-27 had many Bavarians and Austrians among its pilots, so, like citizens of the same state, Franz found he could make small talk with them. Many of them had been in Africa for a year already. One of the veterans told Franz the standing joke.

"A captured Tommy pilot asked his German captor, 'What do you want with Africa, anyway?' The German replied, 'The same thing you do!' Upon further thought, both men shrugged, not knowing what that was."

The veterans roared in laughter. Franz faked a laugh. He did not understand where they were coming from, at least not yet.

Franz had barely begun to eat when Roedel stood and announced a phrase Franz would learn to dread: "Fire Free." It meant the men could smoke now and that the mealtime was over. Everybody left the mess hall at once. Franz was the last to pick up his dishes. He went to the buffet, where a cook was cleaning up. "Listen," he said. "Save something for me. Otherwise I'll starve to death here!"

Roedel waited outside for Franz. "What are you doing suited up? You don't fly until afternoon."

Franz groaned. Nervousness had made him forget that the night before Roedel had pulled him from a dawn flight and assigned him to a 2 P.M. mission. Afternoon missions were quieter and safer because it was the hottest part of the day, when few wanted to fly.

Franz paced around the base for several hours. By mid-morning it was already a hundred degrees, but he couldn't handle the thought of going back to his tent and simply sitting around. He kept pacing, pausing only to put a T-shirt over his face to ward off swarms of black flies. After lunch he reported to Roedel at the squadron shack and found him suited up to fly. Roedel said he would personally be taking Franz on his first mission, a "free hunt," where the two of them would fly into enemy territory and look for trouble. Together they walked toward the flight line. In the west, the Green Mountains looked yellow under the blazing sun. Upon reaching his fighter, Franz saw that a white number 12 had been painted on its flank. Suddenly "his girl" had a name—*White 12*.

Roedel sat on the tire of Franz's plane, just in front of the wing, and told Franz to take a seat. Roedel looked at Franz as a father might look at a son. "Every single time you go up, you'll be outnumbered," he said.

Franz nodded, wishing Roedel was exaggerating but knowing better.

"Those odds may make a man want to fight dirty to survive," Roedel said, squeezing the bunched-up leather gloves in his hands. "But let what I'm about to say to you act as a warning. Honor is everything here."

Franz shrugged, unsure where Roedel was going with the talk. "What will you do, Stigler, for instance, if you find your enemy floating in a parachute?"

"I guess I've never thought that far ahead yet," Franz said.

"If I ever see or hear of you shooting at a man in a parachute," Roedel said, "I will shoot you down myself."

The words stung.*

"You follow the rules of war for *you*, not for your enemy," Roedel said. "*You fight by rules to keep your humanity.*" Roedel slapped a glove against his palm. "Stick close and we'll come home together." He hopped from the tire. The lesson was over.

A ground crewman helped Franz strap into his parachute that sat on his seat in the cockpit. Shutting the square, glass canopy hood, Franz felt a new sense of dread, as if he had shut his own coffin. Franz pushed the throttle forward and fired a thumbs-up to two ground crewmen, who spun the engine crank. The engine sputtered. The plane belched a snort of white smoke. The propeller began spinning.

---

* There was logic behind Roedel's warning. When a pilot spared a defenseless enemy in a parachute, as was the unspoken practice in the Battle of Britain, if the enemy pilot returned to combat he would be more apt to repeat the gesture. It was for this same reason that the British tried to treat captured German airmen well, housing them in P.O.W. castles and manors. The Germans would write home and tell of their good treatment and hopefully the treatment of British P.O.W.s would improve in turn.

HEIGHT MEANT EVERYTHING to a fighter pilot in the desert. There were few clouds to block the sun, so anytime his opponent looked up, he was blinded. Franz wore sunglasses but still held a hand over his eyes, against his flight helmet, as he flew off Roedel's left wing.

Roedel's plane bumped in turbulence. The Berlin Bear on its nose seeming to dance. Franz looked out over the desert beneath his wings. The ground alternated in shades of brown and tan that indicated gullies and rocky promontories. To the north lay the scrubby green coastal hills and beyond that the pale blue Mediterranean Sea.

The Desert Air Force's American-built Curtiss P-40 fighters usually motored along at eighteen thousand feet, so Roedel led Franz higher, to twenty-five thousand feet, meandering between favorite hunting spots. Franz followed Roedel. Both pilots scanned the brown earth for the enemy aircraft's reddish-tan wings. They flew over the main battlefront, marked only by smoke wisps from exploding artillery shells. The line ran southward from the ocean into the desert.

As they motored east, Roedel's voice crackled over the radio. He pointed out the British port of Tobruk to the north. Franz saw the flat, white city nestled around the ocean in the hazy distance. Tobruk was the strategic prize of North Africa, a door from which supplies and fuel could flow from the sea to the front lines.

"Indians, twelve o'clock low," Roedel said, the code words for having spotted the enemy. Franz saw four Curtiss fighters below, gently weaving left and right in lazy S patterns as they flew on a reconnaissance mission toward the German lines. Desert Air Force planes were most likely flown by English or South African pilots, but the force also contained Australians, Canadians, New Zealanders, Scots, Irishmen, Free Poles, Free French, and even American volunteers. From far above, Franz could see the P-40s' sharp red spinners and painted shark teeth with beady eyes, a frightening war paint the American "Flying Tigers" in China had borrowed from the Desert Air Force. Franz saw the red, yellow, and blue concentric circles on their wings that brazenly marked them as his foe.

Roedel radioed Franz and told him he was attacking and to "stay close." He peeled off and dove toward the enemy. Franz followed, his heart racing. His task was "dive, hit, climb, repeat." This was the fighting style of the 109, a plane that could not turn with its enemies in spiral dogfights, but could outrun and outclimb most of them.

Seven thousand feet below, the P-40 pilots spotted the diving 109s. Franz saw the pack of P-40s break formation and peel wildly upward, aiming their shark mouths directly at him and Roedel. One thousand feet passed by in a split second. The needle in Franz's altimeter whipped counterclockwise, 22,000 feet, 20,000, 18,000.

Roedel's plane obscured half of Franz's windshield as he flew just ahead of him. The P-40s seemed to swell as they climbed on their collision course. Franz had been told that going nose-to-nose with a P-40 was a fatal mistake because each carried six, heavy .50-caliber machine guns, more potent firepower than the 109's two machine guns and single heavy cannon that fired from its nose. But Roedel seemed to know otherwise.

Roedel fired first. Flames spit from the nose of his fighter. His cannon's roar startled Franz. The P-40s' wings twinkled in reply. Franz knew that a combined twenty-four guns were now firing at him. He squeezed off a terrified, blind burst. In training, he had shot at fabric targets towed by biplanes but never while diving toward the earth with the target racing up at him. Roedel's shell casings whipped by his windshield like a rain of brass nails. A P-40 burst into flames. Flaming tracers from the P-40s whipped around Franz's canopy. He swore they were about to collide.

Franz could take it no more. He panicked. Hauling back on the stick, he pulled his fighter into a screaming climb, up and away from the onrushing enemy.

Aiming his plane's nose toward the blue, he ran for the heavens.

Franz tucked his neck into his shoulders, bracing for the thud of lead on his armored headrest, but no bullets followed. "Horrido!" Roedel shouted over the radio. Franz knew this battle cry meant he had shot down an enemy plane and wanted Franz to visually verify its destruction. But Franz was too far away and unable to see a thing.

Franz felt sick. His shoulder straps, the 109's cramped cockpit, his heavy leather jacket, and the sun's blazing rays all seemed to squeeze him. Lifting his neck from his shoulders to look backward, he saw a sight that allowed him to breathe again. The P-40s had not followed him. Instead, they orbited in a defensive circle a mile beneath him, covering one another's tails, expecting a dogfight that was not to be.

As Franz leveled off, a new wave of sickness struck his stomach. He realized he had abandoned his wingman. Worse, his wingman was his leader. Even worse, now he was alone and disoriented, easy prey should the enemy come across him. The fight had ended in mere minutes, as they did in the desert. Franz turned *White 12* in the direction of Martuba. Relying on the ocean as his northern compass point and the sun as his southern point, Franz reasoned that his base lay somewhere in the middle of the horizon.

The sun cooked him through the cockpit glass. He strained his eyes and felt his head grow heavy from shame. Franz shifted his weight over his parachute. He felt something wet in his seat. His first thought was that his plane had been hit and he was feeling its engine coolant. Then he touched a warm, dark patch in his crotch. He had lost control of his bladder. Franz flew until he saw the Green Mountains. Somewhere below, he knew, was home. Navigating in a land without forests or railroads or streets was a challenge Franz had never anticipated when he was teaching cadets to fly.

"There you are," Roedel's voice squawked across the radio. Franz scanned the skies and grimaced when he looked over his shoulder toward the sun. That's where Roedel came from—by habit. A pilot could live longer by always approaching from the sun.

Roedel pulled up on Franz's left wing, the wingman's spot. Roedel could tell that Franz was scared by the way he flew, his plane bobbing and jittering.

"You lead," Roedel told Franz and gave him a heading.

Franz preferred to follow but obeyed orders and flew onward until glints of light blinked below from the arid earth. Squinting, Franz saw small planes lined up along a desert airfield. They were home. Franz landed first and Roedel second.

Franz shut his own engine down and remained in his cockpit, the canopy flipped open. Closing his eyes, he leaned his head against the sweat-covered leather seatback. Lifting himself from his plane, Franz saw ground crewmen approaching so he hurried away, scurrying for his tent, hoping to dodge any embarrassment at the sight of his wet pants.

"Stigler!" Roedel shouted from behind. Franz stopped and approached Roedel, head hung, bracing for a verbal lashing. But instead, Franz was met by a grin.

"Today was a success," Roedel said. "You survived. You brought yourself home. And if you think about it—you'll never be that scared again for the rest of your life."

"I'll confirm your victory, sir," Franz said, "but first I need to change my pants."*

Roedel laughed and slapped Franz on the shoulder "You aren't the first one that's happened to!"

Franz opened the flap to his tent. A blast of heat hit his face. He flopped onto his cot, closed his eyes, and fell into an instant sleep. In the evening he went to the mess tent. He passed through the line and saw that dinner was the same as lunch—a tin of Italian beef his comrades called "Mussolini's Ass." Back home Franz had been picky and would tell his mother, "I'll pass on anything that flies or swims." Little did he know how he would come to regret those words.

---

* "Many times pilots came home, myself included, and we had to change our pants," Franz would remember, "and not just when we were new to combat."

Franz sheepishly sat apart from Roedel and the others. Before every bite, he tried to swat the flies from his food. Sneaking a glimpse at the other pilots, he saw that they ate without brushing away the flies, swallowing a few with each gulp of the tough, sticky meat.

Franz was only a few clean bites into his meal when Roedel stood and announced, "Fire Free!"

Franz looked at Roedel, aghast, his fork frozen in midair.

Roedel saw Franz's wide eyes and full plate, then shouted a line he would use at every meal after that, needed or not: "Fire free—except for Stigler!"

The other pilots laughed. A few whacked Franz on the back with friendly slaps as they departed. With relief, Franz finished his dinner in solitude but knowing he was no longer alone.

The P-40 that Roedel had downed was the only German victory in Africa that day, but the rudder of Roedel's 109 remained unmarked.

5

THE DESERT
AMUSEMENT PARK

NINE DAYS LATER, APRIL 18, 1942

THE SUN BLAZED through the canvas of Franz's tent. His watch read just after 4 P.M. Franz lay on his cot trying to read the only book he had brought to the desert besides his Bible. It was about the lives of the Catholic saints, the heroes of the church. Sweat fell from his forehead and onto the pages. Franz mopped his brow frequently. The flies bothered him more than the heat. They buzzed around his head no matter how hard he swatted them. The more he read, the more Franz was bothered by the hypocrisy of the war he had joined, of people who believed in the same God fighting one another.

A persistent sound outside his tent distracted Franz. I Group's squadrons 1, 2, and 3 were throwing a party in their tent cities to celebrate the one-year anniversary of their time in the desert. Franz had no intention of going to the party, although I Group had invited all the other squadrons and anyone who served at Martuba.

A tap on the fabric of Franz's tent interrupted his self-pity. Franz looked up as Lieutenant Ferdinand Voegl thrust his face inside, his dark, narrow eyes scanning the room and his thin lips curled in a mischievous smile.

They called Voegl "the Birdman" because *vogel* means "bird" in German. Shrewd yet likeable, Voegl was an Austrian and one of Squadron 4's top flight leaders. Voegl was also the squadron's black sheep because he had black hair, black eyes, and a tendency to be dark-minded and quirky.

Franz had yet to fly with Voegl, but he snapped upward on his cot as the officer entered. After seven months in the desert Voegl had scored two kills, on top of his four victories from the Battle of Britain. Like Franz, Voegl wore a light tan shirt and shorts, but instead of boots, Voegl wore sandals with socks.

"The squadron's going to the party," Voegl said. "You're coming with us."

"Would that be right, sir?" Franz asked. "I haven't been here long."

"You've flown in combat, yes?"

"Yes, sir—once."

"Then get up," Voegl said. "You're one of us."

Franz obeyed and followed Voegl outside. The two quickly caught up to the rest of Squadron 4 as the pilots walked toward the sounds of revelry. Roedel was already there, somewhere in the thick of the fun. A circle of tents and booths had been erected in the center of the squadron villages. A sign greeted them: WELCOME TO NEUMANN'S DESERT AMUSEMENT PARK. Franz had heard of Captain "Edu" Neumann—I Group's colorful and beloved leader, more a father figure than commander. This party was his idea.

If Franz had not known that he was sober, he would have sworn that he was drunk. Barrel-chested tankers and tired infantrymen representing the Afrika Korps had turned out, as well as mechanics in their greasy coveralls and even Stuka dive bomber pilots.

The festival's soundtrack boomed from a band of tankers loaned by the Afrika Korps. Franz tapped his hand on his thigh to the lively tuba and accordion beat and wished he had brought his own accordion from home (his mother had made him take lessons). A clanking, creaking old convertible rolled past, honking its horn. The car teemed with pilots, who waved from the backseat, mimicking royalty. They wore pots on their heads, furs, fezzes, grass skirts, and goggles—their best imitation of lunatics. The vehicle had been hauled from a junk pile and brought to life again. Officers and enlisted men alike waited in long lines to ride in it.

Neumann had instructed his men to let off steam, to be eccentric, and to forget where they were for one night. They took his words to heart. Neumann's group had been the first to arrive in Africa. They had Marseille and more aces than any other group due to timing and Neumann's leadership. He was an ace with thirteen victories, but he led better from the ground, coaching, analyzing tactics, and planning missions. He knew when to push his men to bring out their best and when they needed a break.

As Franz and the others strolled through the grounds, they saw pilots riding a flimsy merry-go-round brought in from a coastal city. Others waited before food stands that served tin cups of red wine and sausages flown in from Germany. Men bowled, knocking pins into the sand at homemade bowling lanes. The crack of rifles rang from men shooting at targets against a sand dune backdrop. Squadrons battled each other in a tug-of-war for a bottle of French cognac, and on a sand hill mechanics competed for the title of "strongest man" in a King of the Mountain–styled game called "Knock Lukas Down."

On the fringe of the party, Franz saw Neumann's famous headquarters, a circus wagon. The wagon rode atop four massive wheels. Neumann had first located the wagon while flying in the Battle of France, where the wagon had been abandoned by its traveling circus. Somehow Neumann managed to have it shipped to Africa. The wagon had large windows with brightly colored shutters, and the words NEUMMAN'S COLORFUL CABARET were painted on its sides in tall letters. Franz had never been inside, although he had heard stories that Neumann had a painting of naked native girls, and above each girl he had scrawled a pilot's name upon the man's entry to his unit. With each victory, Neumann would have his orderly paint a grass palm frond on the grass skirt of the pilot's "girl."

A horn's bellow brought the games to a halt. Neumann appeared and stood on a stage of crates. Dressed in his desert fatigues, the captain wore his black hair cropped short. He had calm blue eyes. His chin was small, and when he smiled, he scrunched his face in a happy, unassuming grin.

"Nowhere has it been demonstrated more plainly that no one person can survive without the other as it has here in the desert," Neumann called out. "Nowhere is the *esprit de corps* more important than here!"

The crowd bellowed a shout of agreement.

"Today is therefore declared a day of merriment," Neumann shouted. "Today you can—and should—all paint the town red!"[1]

Applause echoed between the bluffs.

Neumann's men loved him. He was to JG-27 who Rommel was to the Afrika Korps. Everyone called Neumann "Edu," a short clipping of his name, "Eduard," although few knew his story. As a boy Neumann had been orphaned and raised by his grandmother. His lonely upbringing imparted him with a sensitive demeanor, perhaps the very reason he was able to control Marseille and mold him into JG-27's finest fighting weapon.

As the sun set, the men congregated on a hill to watch a variety show. At the back of the audience, Lieutenant Schroer served as the show's emcee and narrated a play-by-play over a loudspeaker from a booth made of crates. A sign painted over his head identified his station—radio martuba. Behind Schroer, technicians adjusted glowing radio dials to transmit his radio show to nearby units.

On the stage made of sand, pilots tried their hand at comedy, and soldiers tried theirs at vaudeville. Between acts Schroer spouted dirty jokes. Neumann introduced Captain Maak, who presented "Maak's World Show"—a series of skits acted out by airmen dressed like belly dancers. The audience roared with laughter. At the climax of the show, Neumann took the stage wearing a genie costume and performed a slapstick magic show set to Schroer's music.

A screeching sound from the speakers suddenly drowned out the sound of laughter. Schroer's music turned to static and he pulled the headphones from his ears. The British must have heard their show, he announced to the crowd. They were jamming his transmissions. The mood grew somber. The men remembered what the games, costumes, food, and drink had tried to make them forget—that they were still at war.

THREE WEEKS LATER, EARLY MAY 1942

In the darkness, Franz stumbled over tent ropes and pegs as he ventured down a small hill into the wadi where Squadron 3 had pitched their tents. He spotted a tent, larger than the others, that served as the pilots' bar and casino. Schroer had told Franz to drop by the bar that night and he would introduce him to Marseille. If the introduction went well, Franz planned to ask Marseille for an autograph.

The Squadron 3 bar itself was a tribute to Marseille, bearing a sign just above the doorway that read: THE STAR OF LIBYA. The sign had been put there during the filming of a newsreel about Marseille, and no one wanted to take it down.

As Franz entered the tent, the rhythm of rumba music blasted from a phonograph, even though such "Americano" music had been banned in Germany. Oriental rugs lined the floor. On the walls hung pictures of actresses and models who had written to Marseille. Franz had heard rumors that Marseille had slept with all of them.

Schroer was there already, watching two men play chess. He spotted Franz and signaled him over. One of the chess players was Marseille, the thin, dashing, bohemian Berliner. He looked the way his

French ancestry suggested he would, with an angular face, arching eyebrows, a sharp nose, and thin lips. He was young, just twenty-two, and wore his long hair swept back over his ears. Had it not been slicked back, it would never pass regulations. He wore the Knight's Cross around his neck.

The other player was a young African man with short fuzzy hair who wore the same tan shirt and shorts as Marseille, but without shoulder boards of rank. He was the former Corporal Mathew Letuku, known to the squadron as "Matthias." Franz had heard of him. Matthias had fought for the South African Army before the Germans had captured him the prior summer. Somehow Matthias had wound up reemployed by Squadron 3 as a driver and bartender for squadron parties, a far better fate for him than languishing in a P.O.W. camp. During duty hours, Matthias doubled as a sort of "batman" (or butler) for Marseille, doing odd jobs such as cooking and laundry. In off hours, Matthias and Marseille socialized and played chess. Matthias helped Marseille improve his English, and Marseille taught German to Matthias. In the process, they had become best friends. In Germany, this would have violated laws meant to keep races apart. But in the desert, Marseille and the pilots of JG-27 accepted Matthias as more than a prisoner—he was their friend.

"Franz, pull up a chair," Schroer said. Marseille and Matthias pushed their game aside. Schroer introduced Franz to Marseille, who sat in a wooden armchair made from shipping crates, a gift from the supply men. Marseille and Schroer had been roommates in flight school and wingmen over the Channel. Marseille had a bottle of French cognac on a nearby table and called for an orderly to bring a snifter glass for Franz. Matthias excused himself to let the pilots talk.

Franz was surprised that Marseille was quietly charismatic and gracious, far from his boisterous reputation.

"Franz is new to the unit," Schroer said.

"Have you scored a victory yet?" Marseille asked.

"Not yet," Franz said, embarrassed. Everyone knew it was JG-27's policy to try to get a new pilot his first victory within ten missions. But for Franz, ten had come and gone.

"There's no reason to apologize for never having killed a man," Marseille said. He poured Franz a tall glass of cognac. "As soldiers, we must kill or be killed, but once a person enjoys killing, he is lost. After my first victory I felt terrible."* An empty cognac bottle later, Marseille and Schroer shared their secrets of combat and survival with Franz, who leaned in close, his eyes lazy from too many drinks.

"Shoot from as close as possible, seventy-five yards or less," they told him.

"Drink lots of milk, it's good for your eyes."

"Stare at the sun a few minutes per day, to build your tolerance."

"Strengthen your legs and abdominal muscles so you can take more Gs."

Franz nodded, forming a foggy mental checklist.

Franz wanted to ask Marseille if all the stories he had heard were true, if Marseille had a flat where he entertained an Italian general's wife, if he had slept with a field marshal's daughter, and if he dated an American lady who worked as a newspaper reporter. But, although those tales of philandering interested Franz, one question burned hotter in his mind. "Is it true you flew over a British airfield and dropped notes to them?" Franz asked.

Marseille knew what Franz was getting at, but he just shrugged with a guilty, thin grin.

Franz had read and heard the story but never had it corroborated. The legend went that Marseille had shot down a British pilot named Byers, who had been badly burned when captured. Marseille

---

* Marseille wrote a letter to his mother the night of his first victory that read, "I keep thinking how the mother of this young man must feel when she gets the news of her son's death. And I am to blame for this death. I am sad, instead of being happy about the first victory."[2]

personally took Byers to the field hospital, where hospital staff told Marseille the prisoner's name and unit. That evening, Marseille flew through British flak to drop a note over Byers's airfield, addressed to his comrades. The note said that Byers was badly wounded but was being cared for. Two weeks later, when Byers died of his wounds, Marseille felt so badly that he flew back through the flak to the British field and dropped another note notifying Byers's friends and sending deepest regrets. It was a gallant act that earned the respect of many in the Air Force except for one: the second most powerful man in The Party, who doubled as the Air Force's leader—*Reichsmarschall* Hermann Goering. Goering had once been an ace in the Red Baron's squadron in WWI but had since become known throughout the Air Force with disdain. Someone had nicknamed Goering "the Fat One," due to his heft, and it had stuck. Goering put out an edict that no pilot should ever again attempt a stunt like the one Marseille had.

"Is the story true?" Franz said to Marseille.

Schroer nodded slightly, for only Franz to see.

"We only need to answer to God and our comrades," Marseille said. To Franz, this sounded like something Father Josef had told him years prior. Curious, Franz asked if Marseille was a man of faith. Marseille revealed that he was a Catholic, too.

As their conversation grew in depth, Franz realized that he was drunk, more drunk than he had ever been. He was not accustomed to liquor, having been raised on Bavarian beer, and had never tried cognac before that night. Franz stood, wobbly, to excuse himself. He thanked Marseille and Schroer for their hospitality and tried to salute but swiped his hand at the wrong angle. Marseille saluted back just as sloppily, with a grin. Marseille's salute was known for always being that bad, sober or drunk. Stumbling into the darkness as the breeze kicked up the sand, Franz realized he had forgotten to ask for an autograph.

SEVERAL NIGHTS LATER

Voegl grew tired of hearing Franz talk in the squadron bar about his meeting with Marseille.

"I want to show you something," Voegl told Franz and pulled him outside. Franz did not feel like a walk in the blowing sand, but he followed his superior. Strolling by the silent rows of parked planes, they stopped at Marseille's *Yellow 14*. Nearby, crewmen worked on another plane's engine by floodlights covered with heavy tarps. Voegl pointed to the rudder of Marseille's plane. "I have twelve kills. But this kid has sixty-eight," he told Franz. "Do you really believe that's possible?"

Franz counted the hash marks silently. Franz had once seen Marseille fighting, alone in the distance while the rest of Marseille's squadron watched his aerial ballet. Franz believed. He also knew of Voegl's intense ambition. Despite being physically weak and the son of a postal worker, Voegl had somehow married the daughter of the German state secretary in Berlin. To Franz, Voegl always seemed to be trying to get somewhere. Rather than cross him, Franz said nothing.

"I'm not trying to slander Marseille," Voegl said. "What I'm saying is that in combat there's seldom time to watch an enemy crash, so there's room for doubt. Marseille gives himself the benefit of that doubt."

Slapping Marseille's rudder, Voegl sulked away into the darkness, back toward the squadron bar.

THREE WEEKS LATER, MAY 31, 1942

Franz settled his 109 down onto the hard desert floor and landed through the dust clouds stirred by Voegl's fighter ahead of him. The rising sun revealed their new home, a destitute, unfinished airstrip called Tmimi that lay some twenty miles east of Martuba, close to the front lines. Rommel had summoned II Group to Tmimi. He was planning a big push but first needed the Air Force's slow, antiquated Stuka dive bombers to soften up the enemy lines. To keep the Stukas from being blown out of the sky, he had called on JG-27. Franz and his comrades had lamented leaving Martuba's primitive comforts, but orders were orders, especially when issued by II Group's new commander—Roedel. Recently promoted, Roedel now led the group's three squadrons—4, 5, and 6. In leaving Squadron 4, Roedel had given Voegl command due to Voegl's seniority, although Roedel still had doubts about him.

Grinning, Franz slid from the wing of his fighter. Voegl ran up and slapped his back. Voegl called the crew chiefs around and announced that Franz had scored his first victory. They had just flown a Stuka escort to a place called Fort Acroma, seventeen miles behind enemy lines. There, with seven 109s they had battled it out against sixteen fighters of the Desert Air Force over a raging sandstorm. Just as Marseille and Schroer had advised him, Franz had waited until a P-40 was close—so close its tail was as tall as a sail in his gun sight when he blasted it from the sky. Franz and Voegl hurried to II Group's headquarters to check in and debrief. They encountered Roedel as he ducked out of the tent's canvas door.

Roedel asked how the mission went. "I got my first kill, sir," Franz said. Roedel's smile slowly disappeared. Franz wondered if he had said something wrong.

"I got two," Voegl added. Roedel seemed unimpressed. He asked if there were any losses.

"Three," Voegl replied. "Fluder, Krenzke, and Gromotka." The missing pilots were from Squadron 6. Fluder had been the squadron leader and Roedel's friend. Franz told Roedel he had witnessed both Fluder's and Krenzke's 109s exploding and was certain that both had been killed.

"Then why are you both smiling?" Roedel asked, his eyes emotional.

"Because of his first kill," Voegl said.

Roedel dropped his arms to his sides.

"You score *victories*, not kills," Roedel told Voegl, frustrated. "Haven't you learned anything?" Turning to Franz, Roedel added, "You shoot at a *machine* not a man."

Voegl muttered something and looked toward the horizon.

Roedel looked like he was going to say something more, but he shook his head and walked away.

Voegl muttered that Roedel had it out for him. He stomped away. Franz knew Voegl was trying to save face. But Franz also knew that Roedel had reason to dislike Voegl. The previous day Voegl had landed and claimed to have shot down three fighters within fourteen minutes, his eighth, ninth, and tenth victories, all in one flight. Voegl's wingman and sidekick, a pilot named Sergeant Karl-Heinz Bendert, had confirmed Voegl's story as a witness. But others in Squadron 4 doubted Voegl's claims. "Marseille could knock down three planes that quickly, but not Voegl," they whispered. Roedel had no proof to overturn Voegl's claims, so he forwarded the victories to Berlin.

Franz sulked back to his tent, alone. He had achieved a fighter pilot's milestone and tasted revenge. Instead of feeling accomplishment, he suddenly felt very hollow.

6

THE STARS OF AFRICA

MOONBEAMS ILLUMINATED a circle of tents on the north edge of the Sidi Barrani Air Base. Franz, Roedel, and a handful of pilots sat within the tents' circle, on thick stones around a campfire. They bantered while Franz ate tinned sardines. He had learned to tolerate anything edible. To the south of their campsite lay JG-27's temporary airstrip, Sidi Barrani, its hard-packed runway glowing white in the moonlight. To the north, the sea sparkled near the coast then faded to blackness in the distance. Behind the tents sat a small, crumbling desert fort.

Normally campfires were forbidden, but Roedel had approved the fire. He reasoned that if a British spotter plane saw the light, they would assume it was just a Bedouin campfire. There was nobody else for miles around anymore. Sidi Barrani lay within Egypt, just forty miles across the border from Libya. Just a few days earlier, the airfield had belonged to the British, evidenced by the empty cigarette packs they had left behind when they retreated. Rommel's push had broken through their lines. He had sacked Tobruk, the British battle capital in the western desert, and had driven the British out of Libya and back into Egypt. Now he was ninety miles to the east, chasing the British deeper and deeper into Egypt while aiming for the Suez Canal.

That month, JG-27 had followed Rommel like a nomadic herd, flying from a new airfield nearly every week. The men flew with renewed vigor, believing the end of the desert war was just beyond the horizon. They also operated under a new, inspirational commander, "Edu" Neumann, who had been promoted to lead JG-27, all nine squadrons. At night, the men slept under the stars. By day, the sight of the unit's fighters lined up on sandy runways reminded Franz of a holiday at the seashore. Between missions, mechanics propped small white umbrellas over the fighters' cockpits to keep the seats cool for the pilots. The pilots found time to sunbathe, and the ground crewmen worked on engines from the backs of trucks. Whenever Franz and the others saw the mechanics hurriedly collapsing the umbrellas, they knew it was time to go back to work.

During one such mission, Franz lost his first airplane of the war. While attacking a desert fort, Franz's plane had been hit from ground fire. He had belly-landed within friendly lines and returned to his unit on a camel after a Bedouin tribesman rescued him. Franz's squadron mates had laughed when they saw him ambling the day after, still bowlegged from the bumpy camel ride.

That night around the campfire, the sound of patrolling Ju-88 night fighters overhead promised Franz and his comrades that the skies were friendly. The sound reminded Franz of his brother, who had flown Ju-88s. Tears filled his eyes, but he brushed them away. A radio glowed on a crate behind the group. Cords led from the radio to a generator that hummed in the distant motor pool. The radio spouted music and military news. Other pilots wandered through. Among them were two of Roedel's squadron commanders, Voegl and Lieutenant Rudi Sinner, who took seats around the fire. Sinner was short and unassuming with a long nose that stood sharply from his calm eyes. He was an Austrian, like Voegl, and had begun his career in the Austrian

Army, tending horses that pulled cannons. Since those days he referred to himself as "just an ordinary soldier," even though he was a seven-victory ace. Roedel had seen promise in Sinner and had appointed him to lead Squadron 6, replacing the commander who had been killed on the day when Franz scored his first victory.

With the radio chattering, a fire going, and tents to shield them from the desert wind, the men enjoyed a luxury they had lacked in weeks prior. They joked that for once they had it better than their British enemies, who they knew received regular rest and weekend leaves to metropolitan cities. They had heard captured British pilots tell them, "Should you chaps ever make it to Alexandria, the Cecil Hotel is your place, and if you find yourselves in Cairo, you must look up the Heliopolis Sports Club."

"They're gentlemen," Sinner said. "You can't ask for a better enemy." The others agreed. Sinner related a story that Lieutenant Willi Kothmann, a JG-27 ace, had told him. "Kothmann warned me that you have to be careful with a captured Tommy pilot," Sinner said, "because he is always planning his escape back to his Pomeranian dog and gambling debts. He will not be comfortable as a prisoner until he has seen to both."

Everyone laughed. Because the German pilots spoke English more readily than any other language, interactions between the two enemies were common. Once when someone asked Marseille why he showed such interest in captured enemy pilots, he said, "I just like to talk to them."[1]

"Where is Kothmann now?" Franz asked.

"He was killed last April," Sinner said sadly.

Voegl scowled. He did not share the others' sporting respect for their enemies. He envied his enemies. They had more pilots and better planes now that their advanced Spitfire fighters were arriving. They did shorter tours and then rotated to England or Australia for quieter duty. Franz could tell that the hardened veterans around him could all use a break. Their clothes were sloppy, their faces gaunt, and their eyes weary. Roedel told the others he was due for leave in a month but was not looking forward to it. Everyone looked at him like he was crazy.

At 9:50 P.M., someone tuned in Radio Belgrade, a station that beamed from the powerful German transmitter in Yugoslavia. Every night at the same time, the station played a recording of Lale Andersen, a German girl in her thirties, singing the song "Lili Marlene." A German soldier named Hans Liep had originally written the song's lyrics as a poem during WWI. Thanks to Andersen's rendition, the song had become the German soldiers' anthem. Like many other homesick warriors, the pilots of JG-27 tuned in nightly. So did their opponents. In Egypt, the British pilots were listening to the same radio show, in silence, in their mess tents. At 9:55 P.M., on cue, Andersen's hypnotically sensual and delicate voice floated from the radio's speaker. She sounded gorgeous. Franz leaned closer, his ear glued to the radio.

Andersen sang of a soldier who often met his girl under the lamp-post outside of his camp, before he was called away to war.

> *Time would come for roll call,*
> *Time for us to part,*
> *Darling I'd caress you*
> *And press you to my heart,*
> *And there 'neath that far-off lantern light,*
> *I'd hold you tight,*
> *We'd kiss good night,*
> *My Lili of the Lamplight,*
> *My own Lili Marlene.*

As the song continued, Franz wondered to himself if Andersen were singing to the men on the steppes of Russia or on the fields of Crete or on the bluffs of France. "Was anyone thinking of us in the desert?" he wondered.

Resting in our billets
Just behind the lines,
Even tho' we're parted,
Your lips are close to mine.
You wait where the lantern softly gleams,
Your sweet face seems
To haunt my dreams,
My Lili of the Lamplight,
My own Lili Marlene.

Beneath the stars, far from home, Franz, like his comrades and enemies across the desert, had tears in his eyes by the time the song trailed to silence.[*]

ONE MONTH LATER, JULY 26, 1942, QUOTAIFIYA, EGYPT

Franz brought his 109 to a halt on the taxiway that paralleled the runway. Ahead, Roedel powered up his plane in morning's yellow light. A vortex of sand blew from beneath the machine's belly. Roedel's fighter's bare rudder flapped left and right, his preflight check. His rudder should have borne forty-five victory marks but still remained unmarked. Their mission that day was the same as many days prior: Stuka escort over the front lines that lay just a ten-minute flight away.

A month earlier JG-27 had come to Quotaifiya, a scorching, flat airfield halfway along the Egyptian coast. British bombers had hit the base only two days earlier. Craters now gave the field character, at least. Before it had been a blank swath of white sand. Even with the ocean nearby, to the north, the heat hovered like a mirage.

---

[*] Franz would remember, "Half of us were crying . . . I can't describe it. We felt left out of everything."

Rommel had ordered JG-27 to this awful place. He had pushed the British back but not far enough to win the war in North Africa. When his advance had petered out, the Germans found themselves staring at the British from across trenches that ran from a coastal train station called El Alamein, deep into the desert. Rommel's great progress would be his undoing. He had stretched his forces far from their ports and supply lines while pushing the British closer to theirs. As British ships steamed into their port at Alexandria, carrying fresh pilots and planes to regenerate the Desert Air Force, the Germans flogged the same pilots and planes harder, sending them on Stuka escorts, often three times a day. The tiresome missions wore JG-27's pilots to the bone. The turning point in the desert air war had arrived.

In the weeks prior, Franz and Roedel had flown together almost daily. On one mission Roedel had downed three Spitfires and Franz had bagged one, his third victory. Franz's fourth and fifth victories followed soon after, and he became classified as an ace. But Franz kept his rudder bare in an effort to emulate Roedel, who had grown larger than life to him.

Roedel gave a fist-forward gesture to show Franz and the others in his flight that he was taking off, a silent signal in case the British were eavesdropping on the radio channel. He began his takeoff roll, his plane's prop blast showering white sand onto Franz's windscreen. Roedel's fighter raced down the runway and shrunk in the distance. But either Roedel in his fatigue or the crewmen who had swept the runways after the bombing raid had failed to notice a piece of debris that lay in the path of Roedel's fighter.

Roedel was at full takeoff speed when he hit the jagged debris. His plane veered off the runway and cartwheeled through the sand.

Franz radioed the control bunker to send firefighters quickly. He and the others cut their engines and sprinted toward Roedel. They never expected to see Roedel emerge from the plane, but he did and ran toward them, shouting, waving his arm, and pointing east.

When the men met Roedel, his glare stopped them in their tracks. He clutched his ribs with one arm. His head was bleeding. "The Stukas!" he shouted at Franz and the others. "You don't stop for one man!" Franz's smile faded. The flight of Stukas was heading unescorted toward the British lines. It was too late to catch up.

When medics arrived, they calmed Roedel down, insisting he lie on a stretcher in the shade of their ambulance. Franz stood by as the medics loaded Roedel into the truck.

"Damn it, now I have to go home," Roedel said with resignation before the medics slammed shut the doors. Franz knew Roedel did not want to go because he did not trust any other officer with the lives of his men.

Before Roedel departed, he appointed a temporary successor from his three squadron leaders based on the only standard he knew they would agree on. He picked the top ace, the man with the most victories. Voegl, with twenty victories, got the nod. Roedel's gesture of impartiality would soon prove one of his biggest mistakes.

———

As THE BLISTERING hot month of August arrived, life at Quotaifiya reached a low point. The men lived like animals. They no longer slept in tents or under the stars. To avoid British strafing, Franz and the others slept in "graves," six- by six-foot holes hacked into the earth, with a sheet of canvas overhead. Here each man kept his cot, blanket, and belongings. The days of showering in freshwater were over. Everyone stank. When the men snuck away once a week to bathe in the ocean, they came back with their skin crusty with salt.

Franz existed with the salt and sand caking his face, lining his hair, and sticking to the dried sweat on his back. The heat at Quotaifiya was often 125 degrees Fahrenheit or hotter. Franz and his comrades developed chapped lips and sores that would not heal, sores the flies loved. Worse was whenever a flight taxied past and blew grains of sand into the men's bloodshot eyes and open cuts. On some days, sandstorms rolled in that settled over the airfield, choking Franz and his comrades with a white hazy cloud.

At night, Franz and the others drank to forget the day. They then stumbled carefully through the "graveyards," careful not to step on the poisonous asps and cobras that came out in darkness. After checking his grave for snakes, Franz said his prayers with his knees in the sand. Then he slid under his blankets and pulled them over his head so spiders would not crawl across his face.

At Quotaifiya, Franz began dreaming of his mother's cooking, of eating his favorite dish, leberkase, a pan-fried Bavarian meatloaf made from finely chopped corned beef, pork, bacon, and onions. He imagined bowls of fresh vegetables, a taste he had long forgotten. Red cabbage, spinach, potato salad, and potato pancakes appeared in his dreams. Then he would awake with his stomach cold and twisted, regretting that he had ever said, "I'll pass on anything that flies or swims."

Within JG-27 it was common knowledge that a man could only endure six months of desert torture before his health fell to pieces. Life at Quotaifiya accelerated that breaking point. Even the Desert Fox, Rommel, had to return to Germany after the desert knocked him out with a sinus infection. Franz knew Voegl and others had somehow withstood eight months of the desert's torture, some 240 days' worth. But he would soon discover that even the bravest of men could crack.

———————

THERE WERE FEW options to escape the desert's misery, among them death, wounds, insanity, and the passing of time. But one man had revealed the only other avenue of escape: victories. Marseille's high scoring saw him flying home to Germany every two months to receive new decorations added to his Knight's Cross—first miniature oak leaves and then miniature swords, each signifying higher degrees of the Cross. Franz, Voegl, and their comrades all watched Marseille leave and wanted to go with him. At a time when desert life was grinding JG-27 to a halt, the competition for victories intensified.

Due to wear and tear from the countless Stuka escorts, the squadrons that once had sixteen fighters each now had, on average, just four planes operational. There were no longer enough planes to go around. When a perfectly good 109 arrived from Germany, the mechanics converged on it like cannibals and stripped its parts to keep several other planes flying. A new question arose in each squadron: "Who gets to fly?"

As the leader of both II Group and Squadron 4, Voegl made that call. Because Roedel had crashed his fighter before Voegl could inherit it, Voegl had taken one of Squadron 4's planes for himself. That left three planes for him to pass around among the squadron's sixteen pilots. He assigned another to his wingman and longtime sidekick, Sergeant Karl-Heinz Bendert. Bendert was a veteran, too, and was known as the squadron's most ambitious pilot. He had a baby face with tiny, pouty lips and was quick to snicker. Voegl gave Franz a plane because he considered him a friend. As if to spite the others, Voegl gave the squadron's fourth and last plane to a replacement pilot, the squadron's new arrival, Sergeant Erwin Swallisch. Swallisch was an "old hare," seasoned in age and experience, with eighteen victories to his name, most from the Eastern Front. Voegl took Bendert as his wingman and assigned Franz to Swallisch but warned Franz, "Swallisch is an expert but watch out, he is ill in the head." Voegl said this because Swallisch had rotated home for instructor duty as a reward but instead requested duty where the fighting was roughest—the desert. Without any say in the matter, Franz had become a member of Voegl's inner circle, a group his peers would call the "Voegl Flight."

Franz met Swallisch when the "ill" pilot introduced himself at Franz's grave. Swallisch had a strong face, a bulbous nose, thick cheeks, and a toothy smile. In talking, Franz discovered that Swallisch was "straight," or "honest and professional." Swallisch, too, had flown in the Spanish Civil War, but as a fighter pilot, and had scored three victories. The two bonded over memories of wine, tapas, and senoritas.

SEVERAL DAYS LATER, AUGUST 4, 1942

At night, Swallisch entered Franz's grave, obviously disturbed. In a hushed tone, Swallisch said he had to tell Franz something, in secret. Franz had not flown that day, due to maintenance on his fighter, but Swallisch told him what he had missed.

Swallisch had flown twice that day, first at dawn when Bendert had summoned him to escort a reconnaissance plane with him. To-gether, they had attacked a dozen P-40s and Swallisch had knocked one from the sky. But on the way home, Bendert said he got one, too, and told Swallisch to confirm his victory, one Swallisch never saw happen. That afternoon Swallisch flew with Bendert again. This time, Swallisch shot down a Spitfire, and again Bendert claimed he had downed a Spitfire, too, one that Swallisch had not witnessed.

Swallisch was disturbed and asked Franz if "loose scoring" was the way of the desert. Franz said it happened. He had been there when everyone questioned Voegl's three claims in one mission, the victories that only Bendert would confirm. Franz and Swallisch agreed they had no choice but to give Bendert the benefit of the doubt.

In the week that followed, the Voegl Flight flew and fought the group's only battles because Voegl ensured that they had the best mis-sions and the planes to fly them. A pattern developed. Whenever the men landed and claimed victories, Bendert always claimed something, and if others claimed a victory, Bendert claimed the same or more. Then came August 10, the day that broke the camel's back. That morning Franz and Swallisch scrambled to intercept British fighters that had been sighted over El Alamein. There, among the thick clouds that bordered the sea, Franz and Swallisch attacked a pack of P-40s and Hurricanes. On their first dive, each claimed a P-40. On the second dive, Franz claimed a Hurricane. But as Franz pulled up to climb and repeat, he saw a terrifying sight behind his tail. Instead of the P-40s breaking into a defensive circle like they always had, they were chasing him! With Swallisch flying ahead of him and unaware of the danger, Franz radioed him with alarm and told him to run—they were being chased. Swallisch radioed back, "Nonsense."

Franz saw the thick clouds along the sea and ran for them. But instead of fleeing with Franz, Swallisch doubled back and flew toward him, flying over Franz's head. Seeing this Franz thought, *Voegl was right—he is ill in the head!*

Franz steered for the safety of the clouds, but kept checking his tail. There, he saw an incredible sight—in a tan streak he watched Swallisch fly head-on into the formation of P-40s, his guns firing. The P-40s peeled in all directions. Swallisch plowed through the melee and somehow emerged on the other side. Franz saw black smoke and knew that someone had been hit. He cursed Swallisch for not escaping with him.

Franz blew out a heavy sigh as the cloud's floating tentacles wrapped around his canopy, enshrouding him in mist, turning the daylight into dimness. Banking westward, he wove through the heavenly white river, following his compass until he popped into the blue, alone, above his desert home. After landing, Franz found Swallisch circling his parked fighter, checking it for damage. Relieved, Franz shouted, "You never go tooth to tooth with a Curtiss!"

"In the east we don't run from Ivan," Swallisch chuckled, "Why start now?"

Franz realized the "ill" pilot's antics were actually his odd brand of bravery. Franz reached out his hand and Swallisch shook it, flashing a big, toothy grin.

Around noon that same day, Voegl and Bendert returned from their flight and found Franz and Swallisch in the mess tent. Franz told Voegl that he and Swallisch had each bagged two planes. Voegl and

Bendert said that they, too, had each knocked down two planes.* Franz and Swallisch gritted their teeth. When Voegl and Bendert had departed, Swallisch and Franz agreed that their group leader and his wingman were up to no good.

In the evening of August 14, Voegl delivered a message from JG-27's commander, Neumann, to Franz and Swallisch. Neumann had ordered the Voegl Flight to assemble on the flight line the next morning. Franz immediately thought that someone was in trouble. When Franz and Swallisch plodded to the flight line the next day, as ordered, Swallisch was sullen. He was certain that Voegl and Bendert were going to drag him and Franz down with them.

But when they reached the flight line, they found Neumann and his staff waiting with photographers. Neumann congratulated the men and said he wanted to celebrate their recent successes. In the weeks prior, the Voegl Flight had kept Neumann's orderly busily painting palm fronds on their girls. In fifteen days they had scored a squadron's worth of victories. Franz had chalked up nine victories, upping his total to fourteen. Swallisch had added fifteen victories, doubling his score to thirty. Voegl posted six victories and now had twenty-six overall. Bendert added sixteen, bringing his total to thirty-four, elevating him among the ranks of Marseille and Roedel as one of JG-27's top ten scorers. With Marseille on leave, the Voegl Flight had become the new "Stars of Africa."

Voegl arrived wearing a white officer's hat like Roedel's and black sun goggles atop its brim. Despite the heat, Bendert wore a fancy green jacket. Franz and Swallisch just wore their everyday attire. The photographers steered the group to Swallisch's plane because Swallisch had unique victory marks—his rudder bore thirty hash marks and the black silhouettes of two ships that he had sunk on the Eastern Front.

---

* Desert Air Force squadron diaries would later reveal that Voegl and Bendert had shot down none of the fighters that they claimed that day. South African Air Force Squadron 2 would report: "Dogfight with two 109's—no results," and Royal Air Force Squadron 80 would report: "On two occasions 2 Me 109Fs were seen, these made dive attacks but they were ineffective."

Voegl joked to Franz that no one would want to be seen by his naked rudder and ordered Franz to paint it up. Franz nodded with reluctance while wondering what Roedel would think.

The photographers arranged the men in a lineup along the plane's rear fuselage. But Swallisch let his arms hang, looking dejected. "Laugh!" a photographer urged. "Tell a joke!" the other said. Franz said something to Swallisch to make him laugh as the shutter snapped.

When Neumann shook each pilot's hand, Franz and Swallisch knew this was their chance to reveal their suspicions of Voegl and Bendert. But they said nothing. They knew it was too late and they were already guilty by association. As other pilots walked past the photo shoot, their glares did all the talking.

That night, while Neumann's orderly painted palm fronds, in the squadron bars around the airfield, the unit's pilots debated the Voegl Flight's meteoric rise. Among the squadrons of I Group, Marseille's group, some pilots gave the "Voegl Flight" a mocking new name: "the Expert Flight." They, too, knew that victories were the key to the Knight's Cross, fan mail, and a ticket home. At the time, Germany had no bigger heroes than her fighter pilots, and even the heroes had a hierarchy according to their scores. The I Group pilots saw the Voegl Flight's soaring claims as Voegl's underhanded attempt for his group to compete against theirs. Had Marseille been there, he might have told his comrades otherwise, for he was the master at scoring multiple victories, day after day. But he was on leave in Germany. In his absence, a few I Group pilots decided: "the Expert Flight" was cheating and had to be stopped.

ONE DAY LATER, AUGUST 16, 1942, OVER EL ALAMEIN

When the Voegl Flight plunged into combat in the early morning of August 16, they did so to answer another flight's cries for help. Two planes from I Group had radioed in distress. The leader of Squadron 2, Lieutenant Hans-Arnold Stahlschmitt, a twenty-one-year-old ace with forty-five victories, and his wingman were badly outnumbered in a dogfight against as many as thirty-eight enemy fighters.

Although Stahlschmitt was a rival, the Voegl Flight scrambled to his aid with a fifth plane in their formation instead of the usual four. That day, Voegl had invited along a rookie, Corporal Ferdinand Just, who had recently arrived with a plane of his own. Voegl was good to the new guys because they were black sheep like him.

After fifteen minutes of fighting, the Voegl Flight and its rookie turned for home, victorious. They had saved Stahlschmitt and his wingman while claiming a combined eleven victories. Even the rookie, Just, had scored his first victory. But it was not what they would claim that would seal the Voegl Flight's fate. It was what they did next.

At three thousand feet over friendly lines, Voegl radioed Just and asked for his ammo status. Just replied that he was "about full." Voegl decided to give the rookie some target practice by playing a game called "Shoot the Shadow." Franz appreciated Voegl's concern for the new guy, but he knew the skies were unsafe and asked Voegl if this was wise. Voegl dismissed Franz and told him, "Stigler, you can play the shadow."

Franz hated being ordered to play a game when he should be watching for enemy fighters. Swallisch promised he would keep an eye out. Franz flew ahead and positioned his plane so its shadow "flew" in front of him on the sands. Voegl ordered Just to get on his wing as he dropped down to one thousand feet.

"See the shadow?" Voegl asked Just. "Kill it."

But the young pilot did not understand.

"Strafe the shadow on the sand," Voegl clarified.

Franz flew straight and level to keep his shadow flat. He heard Just's gunfire crackle beneath him then saw geysers of sand rip through his shadow before Just's 109 peeled off to re-form with Voegl.

Franz flew onward, sweating out the silly game. Voegl ordered

Franz to make things challenging. Franz rolled his eyes. He began snaking right and left using just his rudder, so his shadow stayed flat as it made lazy S patterns. Voegl ordered Bendert and Swallisch to attack the shadow as examples to Just. Both veterans wove along with Franz, mirroring his moves. When they passed beneath Franz, they cut loose with what ammo they had remaining. Each veteran's bullets perfectly tracked the shadow, tossing sand and obliterating rocks. The Voegl Flight was having so much fun in their mock dogfight that they failed to see two black specks paralleling them in the distance by the ocean.

The Voegl Flight landed, claimed their victories, and headed to the squadron tent to celebrate their most momentous day yet. But their rival, Stahlschmitt, had already landed. He and his wingman had marched straight for Neumann's headquarters, now an aboveground bunker after his circus wagon had been destroyed.

The next day a rumor ran rampant throughout the pilot camps. The Voegl Flight was going to be stripped of their victories. Franz and Swallisch could not believe it. They asked around and learned that Stahlschmitt had reported seeing the Voegl Flight in mock dogfights, "emptying their guns into the sand." Stahlschmitt believed that this was the secret behind the Voegl Flight's victories—they would pretend to fight and come home with their ammo exhausted to lie about what they had done.

A day later, Voegl spotted his squadron leaders entering Neumann's headquarters. When Voegl asked why he had not been invited, Neumann's orderly told him, "It's a private matter."

Swallisch took the news hard and grew melancholy. "It's an omen," he told Franz. A fighter pilot since 1936, his victories were his résumé and his life. He was a professional flyer. The hashmarks were all he had to show for his six years of dueling with death. Now he had heard that the pilots of the Voegl Flight would be stripped of all of their victories. It was no longer their two weeks of combat being questioned, but each man's honor.

A DAY LATER, AUGUST 19, 1942

At dawn, Neumann's orderly delivered messages to Franz, Swallisch, Voegl, and Bendert summoning them to report to Neumann's head-quarters that afternoon. Swallisch ran to Franz's dugout, distraught. He was certain that Voegl and Bendert had destroyed them.

"We're to be court-martialed!" he said. Franz's stomach sank.

Voegl and Bendert were dressed in flight gear when they found Franz and Swallisch moping. Voegl said they were answering a scram-ble mission and wanted Franz and Swallisch to come. Bendert was glib as usual. Franz admitted he was not in the mood to fly and Swallisch agreed. Voegl knew what was eating them and reassured Franz and Swallisch that Neumann would see that Stahlschmitt was wrong when they presented their side of the story. Voegl and Bendert departed to fly.

Franz did not fear a court-martial. He feared a court-martial going wrong, and them taking the blame for any loose claims since JG-27 had arrived in the desert. After the midday meal, Franz felt over-whelmed by worry. He lay on his cot in his grave and stared through cracks of light in the canvas ceiling. Around 1:00 P.M. he heard noise above and saw Swallisch peel back the canvas. Swallisch said he was taking a plane up for a maintenance test flight before the meeting with Neumann. Franz thought nothing of it. Many times he had gone flying to clear his head. Before leaving, Swallisch told Franz that re-gardless of the meeting's result he would always think of him as "the best of comrades." Franz knew Swallisch was scared because he had no clout with JG-27 and no relationship with the powers that would be judging him. Franz promised Swallisch that he would en-sure their names were cleared. Swallisch smiled and departed, the can-vas flap swinging behind him. Franz fell asleep. An hour later he opened his eyes with distress when the realization hit him: *Why would a thirty-three-victory ace undertake a maintenance flight? That's a rook-ie's job!*

Franz's heart screamed with alarm. But he was an hour too late.

Swallisch never came back from his maintenance flight. Neumann canceled the meeting. The next day, on the shores north of Quotaifiya, German sentries found Swallisch's body, carried to land by the tide. Some said his plane had malfunctioned. But Franz knew otherwise. Swallisch had wanted to disappear—that's why he had flown out over the sea. There he had committed suicide, diving into the water rather than live to see his victories and honor wrongly stripped from him. On the day Swallisch died, Voegl and Bendert landed from their scramble. Voegl claimed one victory and Bendert another two.

ELEVEN DAYS LATER, AUGUST 30, 1942

A month after his crash, Roedel returned to the unit. Franz found him moving his belongings into his hole in the earth. Roedel had resumed control of II Group, sending Voegl back to Squadron 4. Roedel told Franz he had spent only a week at home in Merseburg and the rest of the time traveling there and back.

"I prefer it here," Roedel admitted, a comment that Franz found odd. Franz tried to explain what had happened with the Voegl Flight, but Roedel cut him off. He had already talked with Neumann, who told him the matter was closed. All the victories in question had been confirmed and sent to Berlin. Franz looked at Roedel with disbelief. Roedel explained that Neumann decided not to pass judgment because he had not been there, flying with them in life-and-death combat. Neumann had decided to give his men the benefit of the doubt.

Franz told Roedel that there had been a breach of honor. Roedel asked Franz if it was worth reopening a closed case. Roedel explained that during the month in question, Bendert had scored his thirtieth victory—"magic 30"—and had been nominated for the Knight's Cross. But Franz told Roedel he had promised Swallisch he would see their names cleared, and there would always be doubt unless the truth was told. Roedel agreed to look into the matter but knew it would get ugly. "You could have saved us a lot of trouble if you had just taken a stand," he told Franz, who nodded in silent agreement.

"I'm afraid you won't be here to see the results," Roedel said. Franz did not understand. "You're going home," Roedel said. "It didn't do me any good, but you might enjoy it."

For a moment, Franz reacted like Roedel had, after his crash. There was something about the simplicity of the desert life, even its hardships, that made him not want to leave.

———————

DURING THE FIRST week of September 1942, Franz found himself sitting on a lonely bench at the far end of the airfield, where Ju-52 transports delivered the unit's supplies. Franz had his orders: hitch a ride on a transport to Libya, then fly to Sicily, then Italy. From there he would take a train to Germany.

Every so often an old sergeant emerged to tell Franz that a Ju-52 was due any minute. The wind sock hung limp. There were no eager rookies checking in for a great adventure, just mechanics linking ammunition belts while orderlies inventoried supplies.

Franz had said good-bye to Roedel, his comrades, and even Marseille, who had just returned from leave. Franz had found Marseille lounging around, strangely reluctant to return to the cockpit. Marseille no longer displayed photos of actresses and models in his dugout and had replaced them with just one framed picture of his girlfriend, Hanneliese, a school teacher. "We just got engaged," Marseille told him. "On my next leave, hopefully at Christmastime, we'll be married. If not, I'm waiting until next Christmas—it's the best time for a wedding." When Franz suggested that Marseille would never be as much fun, the Star of Africa proved otherwise and recited the latest dirty jokes he had learned. Marseille recommended restaurants Franz could visit in Berlin. "Tell them you're my friend," he told Franz, "and they'll throw you out before they'll seat you!"

From his airline days, Franz knew the sound of a Ju-52 by heart. In the distance, the plane landed through a wave of heat. High above, its 109 escorts circled the transport, their duty not completed until the plane had unloaded, reloaded, and was flying back the way it had come.

The Ju-52 taxied to a stop but kept its engines running as crewmen erected a ramp up to the plane's side fuselage. They wheeled barrels from the plane's belly. Franz shouldered his bag as a *kuebelwagen* screeched to a stop behind him. Roedel climbed out.

"I always see my pilots off," Roedel reminded Franz. "I'm just glad we're not talking through a slab of wood."

Franz tucked his hat into his sweaty armpit. Dropping his sea bag, he went to salute Roedel who instead stuck out his hand, just like when they had first met. They shook hands, both serious. They knew there was no guarantee that Franz's plane would make it across the Mediterranean and Roedel had just checked himself back into hell.

The Ju-52's load master grabbed Franz's shoulder and pointed toward the waiting plane. The plane's pilots stared through their windows at Franz, annoyed, eager to get as far from the front as possible. Franz entered the plane and sat uncomfortably in the back, not used to riding. The plane carried him away. The next day he would leave the Dark Continent on a Ju-52 loaded with wounded, groaning Afrika Korps soldiers. As the plane passed over the African coast, this time Franz did not look out the window.

7

THE HOMECOMING

A WEEK LATER, EARLY SEPTEMBER 1942, NEAR AMBERG

FRANZ APPROACHED THE door to the pub. He smoothed his grayish-blue blazer and pulled its yellow collar tabs. His crush cap sat straight on his head, so he cocked it at a jaunty angle like the other veterans did. A tan cloth band encircled the left cuff of his blazer and read AFRIKA, a badge that only men who had fought there could wear. He cinched his black tie. The tie was not just for special occasions. The Air Force fashioned itself as Germany's most gentlemanly military branch. Everywhere but in the desert, German pilots wore ties, even when flying.

Inside the pub, Franz strolled up to the brewmaster's daughter, the girl of his teenage dreams, whose blond hair and busty influence had helped steer him away from the priesthood. Franz beamed a wide smile and removed his hat, revealing his hair neatly slicked back, with the sides and back cropped short. The girl emerged from behind the bar, looked him over, and stopped an awkward foot away from him. Franz gazed at her. She slapped him hard on the cheek. Smarting, Franz looked at her wide-eyed.

"Aren't you ashamed to be here?" the girl snapped.

"What's wrong?" Franz asked, his eyes wide with surprise.

"Get out! Get out! Get out!" she screamed.

Franz hesitated and asked again what he had done wrong. The girl threatened to call her father. Franz ran for the door.

That night, Franz sat with his mother as she sipped a beer. Every night, without fail, she always drank a beer. Franz confessed his woes with the brewmaster's daughter. His mother shrugged with a guilty grin. Franz realized she was somehow behind the slap he had received. He asked his mother what she had done. His mother admitted that when Franz had departed for Africa, he had left so many girlfriends behind that each wrote to her, seeking for news of him. She did not reply. So the girls wrote again and again. Then they started coming to her door to ask about Franz. Annoyed, Franz's mother wrote a letter to each girl that said: "Franz is married! Leave him alone!" Franz broke out laughing at his stern old mother. He knew she probably still prayed he would come to his senses and become a priest.

Franz's holiday was supposed to last eight weeks, but he found himself wanting to return to the desert sooner. When he biked around Amberg, his friends' parents told him where their boys had been deployed. Every morning when he rustled open his newspaper, the headlines revealed bad news from the African front. JG-27 lost forty-victory ace Sergeant Gunther Steinhausen, and a day later, fifty-nine-victory ace Stahlschmitt, both killed.

Three weeks later, the headlines screamed in big black letters that Squadron 3's hero of the desert, Marseille, was dead. Franz read the story in shock. It said that Marseille had died bailing out of his fighter after a combat mission. But Franz knew there had to be more to the story that no one was saying. The Desert Air Force could never kill Marseille.

As his leave wound down in October, Franz's orders changed; he was told not to return to his unit because JG-27 was withdrawing from the desert. Africa had become a lost cause for the Germans. The British had launched an attack from El Alamein, a push that Rommel was unable to stop. In early November, as the Germans retreated, a new foe landed behind them in Casablanca: the Americans. When the first American flyer was captured, Neumann invited the pilot to join him for breakfast. Neumann was amazed that the American, a major, wore only a one-piece, olive-green flight suit. Neumann looked upon the enemy flyer with great worry as the American happily ate his breakfast. He knew that behind that one man stood the might of the American industrial empire. Neumann lost his appetite.

Around the table with his father and Father Josef, Franz came to the same conclusion—and worse. They agreed that the war had already been decided, ever since June 1941, when Hitler attacked the Soviet Union and opened a two-front war. Hitler had told his people that Stalin was about to attack them, but the truth did not matter. The older men had already lost a war in 1918 and knew how a nation's doom played out. They knew at that moment, in November 1942, that Germany was going to lose the Second World War.

"What do I do now?" Franz asked his elders.

"You're a German fighter pilot," Franz's father said. "That's all there is to it."

Father Josef nodded, having been a fighter pilot himself. Although he never spoke of his war stories, he told Franz something he would never forget.

"Don't worry," he said. "We fight our best when we're losing."

8

WELCOME TO OLYMPUS

SIX MONTHS LATER, APRIL 13, 1943, NORTHWEST SICILY

HIDDEN IN THE shade of an olive tree, the white nose cone of the gray Bf-109 began to spin, its black blades catching the midday sunlight that snuck through the branches. The engine whined, coughed, and belched white smoke before settling into a powerful rhythm. Franz sat in the cockpit, a pipe clenched in his teeth. He wore just his tent cap, no flight helmet, no ear protection, and worked the throttle of the new 109.

Mechanics in oil-stained T-shirts and baggy khakis watched from the side of the spinning prop. Sicily was as hot as the desert, but unlike Africa, Sicily had trees, flowers, and streams around which high scrub bushes grew. At Trapani Airfield, the Squadron 6 mechanics preferred to work in the shade at the south corner of the base, far from the "big target" hangars on the north end. The lead mechanic leaned into the cockpit and studied the gauges.

"She's still running hot," Franz insisted to the mechanic who leaned in to hear Franz's words. *Yellow 2* was a new Gustav, or G-4, model, fresh from the factory. With its new camouflage scheme, the fighter looked like a sleek gray shark as it vibrated in the olive grove. The plane's flanks and wings were pale gray, its belly had hints of blue, and a wavy, dark gray swath ran along the fighter's spine. A yellow 2 stood starkly from its camouflage.

Franz shut down the plane and hopped out. The mechanic insisted that Franz must be imagining problems. Franz reminded the mechanic that a G model had killed Marseille.

Franz had learned the story of Marseille's death when he reunited with the unit. When JG-27 had been issued the new G models, Marseille had refused to fly his and had barred his pilots from doing so because the plane's new, more powerful Daimler-Benz engine was prone to failure. After General Albert Kesselring heard that Marseille was casting doubt on the G, he ordered Marseille to fly the new plane anyway.

That's how Marseille died. He had been flying home from a mission when a gear in his G model's engine shattered and broke the oil line. Smoke billowed into his cockpit, blinding and disorienting him. Marseille failed to notice that his plane had slipped into a dive. When he jumped, instead of falling beneath the plane, the airflow sucked his body into the plane's rudder. The same rudder that had borne his 158 victory marks had smashed Marseille's chest, rendering him unconscious and unable to deploy his chute. Marseille's friends had watched helplessly as he fell to earth. His comrades later returned to the airfield in a *kuebelwagen* with Marseille's body resting across their laps. In a palm grove, they displayed his casket in the bed of a truck. After burying Marseille, they gathered in a tent and listened to his favorite song, "Rumba Azul," on his gramophone. A month later, they had to be removed from combat due to shattered morale.

The mechanic promised Franz he would take a look. His men reached for their tools, propped up the engine cowlings with rods, and began ratcheting off the engine cover.

Franz departed, darting across the runway with his life preserver in one hand and his flight helmet in the other. Small, silver flare car-

BRYAN MAKOS

tridges lined the tops of his boots like bullets. The flares were a necessity now that he regularly flew over water.

Across the runway to the north lay the small village of Milo, with its flat, white roofs. Beyond it stood the massive dusty-looking Mount Erice, which looked like it belonged in the American badlands. Roedel kept his headquarters there, in a cave just below the summit. Atop Erice, an ancient, abandoned Norman castle clung to the mountain's eastern lip. Called "Venus Castle," the towers and walls had been built over an ancient temple to the Roman Goddess, Venus. Franz often envisioned ghostly knights staring down on the airfield from the ramparts. A month earlier, the group had deployed to Trapani Airfield from Germany. Roedel had promoted Franz to staff sergeant and placed him in Squadron 6 under Rudi Sinner, thinking the humble pilot a better influence than Voegl, whom Roedel had dispatched to lead a detachment in Africa.

Franz ambled along the flight line where the new 109s of Squadron 6 sat in gray brick blast pens held together by white mortar. Squadron 6 was nicknamed "the Bears," because they had made the Berlin Bear their mascot and painted it on their patches. Franz saw his comrades lounging in the grottos behind their planes. The pilots sprawled in white lawn chairs and sipped herbal tea and iced limoncello. Franz felt the cool breeze of the ocean and thought how Sicily seemed a far better place than Africa.

Franz stopped in his tracks. The wind carried a rumble that Franz had come to dread in the days before. It was the deep hum of a swarm of metal wasps high above. *Thump! Thump! Thump!* Three bursts of anti-aircraft fire exploded on the edge of the airfield, the signal for "Air Raid!"

Pilots ran from the grottos for their 109s. Franz sprinted toward his plane. His heavy, fur-lined flying boots pounded the dry earth, and Franz wished he wore slim cavalry boots like the pilots had in the Battle of Britain days.

The droning grew louder. Franz glanced up between strides and saw twenty or thirty little white crosses at fifteen thousand feet on the southern horizon, flying toward him. His fears were confirmed—they were the Four Motors—the planes the Americans called the "B-17 Flying Fortress."

Still running, Franz neared the mechanics' grotto. He saw the lead mechanic emerge, waving his arms. "She's not ready!" the mechanic shouted. Franz cursed his new 109. Wheeling, Franz decided that if his own plane was down, then he could borrow someone else's. At the first blast pen, he found a 109 fueled and ready, its cockpit open. A crewman waited with the starter handle, ready to crank the plane to life, while another waited on the wing root to help a pilot strap in. Franz grabbed the handhold behind the cockpit to haul himself up, but another hand pulled him back down. A voice shouted at his back, "She's mine, Franz!" Franz turned to see Lieutenant Willi Kientsch pull himself up and onto the wing. Willi looked more like a pale Italian teenager than a fighter pilot. His black eyebrows drooped like arches over his lazy eyes. Short, slight, and scrappy, Willi was just twenty-two years old but already had seventeen victories, the same as Franz. Franz cursed and ran to find another plane. Although Franz and Willi were tied for victories, they were not rivals. Willi was Franz's best friend in the squadron, and Franz knew he had the right to claim his plane. At the next 109, Franz got as far as the wingtip when another pilot shouted, "Don't even think about it!" as he tossed his helmet up to the crewman and climbed aboard.

A red flare arced through the sky across the airfield, the signal for everyone to hide in a bomb shelter. From a slit trench behind the blast pens, a mechanic shouted for Franz to take cover. Franz could see the trench was full already with mechanics who watched the sky.

Franz kept running. The next 109 that Franz reached had taxied out before he could commandeer it. Farther down the line, another 109 taxied away. Beyond that, one pilot cut his motor, hopped from his plane, and ran, his self-preservation instincts kicking in. Another pilot saw this and followed, then another.

Franz looked up—the B-17s were now large white crosses in a line. He counted twenty-six bombers. Slowly they turned to make a run over the airfield. They were almost overhead. Franz swore he could see little black holes in their bellies, their bomb bays open. Willi and his wing-man took off down the runway past Franz, adding insult to injury.

It was too late to get to a plane. Franz knew he needed to get as far from the airfield as possible. He spotted a distant patch of trees where he had seen men digging a shelter the day before, and he ran in its direction. He spotted the slit trench and slid in, knocking away a round wooden pole that spanned its length. When his boots squished into the earth, Franz knew why the trench was unoccupied—it was not a shelter. It was a latrine. The pole had been there for the men to steady their rears upon. Luckily, the latrine was new and only looked to have been used a few times. Repulsed, Franz tried to climb from the latrine, but the sound of bombs whining from above chased him back in. He scurried to the end of the trench and peered over the edge.

The earth shook as the first plane dropped its bombs on the runway. A second barrage followed. A third. A fourth. Franz buried his face into the island's sandy dirt and clutched the rosary in his shirt pocket. Explosion after explosion detonated, each a brilliant five-hundred-pound flash. Fighters along the flight line evaporated in bursts of flame that erupted from the revetments. The earth upheaved, spitting dirt. Steel fragments flew in all directions, chopping trees in ragged halves.

Franz clutched his ears, but this only made the concussions hurt worse. He grabbed his throat as each blast sucked the air out of his lungs. He closed his eyes from the painful flashes of light. He wanted to vomit as his equilibrium spun. The bombs cracked, time and again, each a supersonic wave that pounded Franz like a lightning storm slapping the earth.

Then, just as suddenly, the earth stopped shaking. Silence arrived. The B-17s had dumped their payloads and droned away. The attack was part of the Allies' new offensive, Operation Flax. The Americans and British knew that Hitler had refused to evacuate the Afrika Korps from the desert and that the only thing keeping Rommel from collapse was his supply line from Sicily. Operation Flax was the Allied plan to slice that umbilical cord of bullets, fuel, and food.

Franz's ears rang. As he pulled himself from the trench, he lost his balance and fell facedown. Through his orbiting vision, he saw fires on the flight line. In the blast pens, cracked wings and upturned tails protruded where 109s had once perched. Squinting through the spins, Franz peered toward the mechanics' grotto. There through the smoke Franz saw *Yellow 2*. His Gustav still sat, proudly intact and on its gear, while others all around the field burned. Franz slapped the earth with joy.

THAT SAME EVENING

Franz and Willi drove the Squadron 6 *kuebelwagen* up the winding road that climbed the side of Mount Erice. The road was rough and full of hairpins. Franz kept the car in low gear, its tires kicking up yellow dust. Below the summit, the mountain became smooth. Franz pulled into a small roundabout where other *kuebelwagens* sat at the mouth of a cave, with camouflaged netting draped over them. Rock piles spewed from the cave, a sign of "home improvements" to the unit's mountainside headquarters. Franz and Willi walked to the cliff to soak in the majestic view. On many nights the pilots congregated there to smoke. They felt more at home above the earth than on its face.

At their feet lay Milo. Farther south sat the airfield, with its runway shaped like a bone and a circular turnabout at each end, where planes could warm their engines before takeoff. Above them loomed the stark walls of Venus Castle. To the east lay clusters of Mediterranean farms and olive groves that vented from the day's heat. Beyond the farms lay brownish-gold fields of durum wheat, still golden in the fading sunlight. To the west lay the ancient coastal city of Trapani. It was built around a half-moon bay, and the city came alive at sunset as Mediterranean villages did when their oil lamps were lit. Willi always acted unimpressed by the scenery and instead bragged about the skiing near his hometown, Kisslegg, where he had been a master skier before the war. When he wasn't bragging about the mountains, Willi boasted about his small town's domed church. It was built along a lake where people would stroll after Mass. Franz sensed the innocence of Willi's hometown pride as he looked at the young pilot, whose white officer's crush cap always looked like he had borrowed it from his father.

"Welcome to Olympus," Roedel shouted as he sauntered from the cave that doubled as his headquarters. Franz had known he would be there. The airfield below was Roedel's kingdom and the mountain and its castle, his estate. His squadrons—4, 5, and 6—were now the "Knights of Sicily." Outfitted with new planes and refilled with new pilots, the squadrons' new mission was to defend the island and the supply convoys to Africa. With only forty-two planes, II Group was shouldering a mission meant for all of JG-27. Due to the broadening war front, the wing had splintered and would never operate as one again. Instead, Neumann, who operated from an airfield in the center of Sicily, was dispatching some of his squadrons to France and others to Greece. For support, Roedel had the Italians, whose pilots were brave but known for their outstanding aerobatic flying rather than their fighting prowess. He also had the three ghost squadrons of Fighter Wing 53 (JG-53), whose battered planes sat derelict at the northern end of the airfield, their pilots at home, resting from African duty.

Relaxing around the *kuebelwagen*, Franz, Willi, and Roedel lit up and swapped stories. Franz pulled out his pipe and bag of tobacco, a new habit. He tamped the tobacco into the pipe with the brass of a spent machine gun shell. Roedel and Willi lit cigarettes. They talked about the raid that day and lamented the loss of eight fighters, bombed on the ground. Willi had caught up to the Four Motors north of the island and knocked one down, a significant accomplishment. A bomber victory carried bonus points that brought a pilot much closer to "magic 30" and the Knight's Cross. A fighter victory was worth one point, but a bomber victory was worth three points because a bomber was a more challenging adversary.

Invariably, their conversation steered back to the old days in Africa. Willi had barely known Franz there, but he knew of the "Voegl Flight." Roedel explained that he, himself, had been dragged into the controversy. Just days after his return, Roedel had scored his fifty-third victory, when someone started a rumor that he, too, had inflated his victories.

Secretly, Roedel had taken action. When Voegl and Bendert claimed new victories, he sent out the unit's camera-equipped 109 and Fiesler Storch reconnaissance planes to the spots where they said their vanquished foes had crashed. When the searches found nothing, Roedel confronted Voegl and Bendert. He knew they had entered combat; there were witnesses to that much. But both claimed victories that could not be verified.*

---

* Roedel would remember, "I do not think that it was a matter of intentionally lying about their victories, but it was proven to have been gross negligence in claiming victories simply because a pilot shoots at an aircraft, maybe getting hits, but not confirming the crash or the pilot getting out. The situation stained all involved in the Group and that flight, and even Stigler and I were questioned. Bad business really." [1]

Roedel could have hung Voegl and Bendert out to dry. But he knew that exposing them could have turned JG-27 into the laughing stock of the Air Force. So Roedel dealt with them privately. He kept them on the flight roster and gave them a second chance to repair the damage they had done. He allowed Voegl to retain his leadership of Squadron 4, and he did not interfere with Bendert's Knight's Cross nomination. But as punishment, Roedel kept both men in the desert as long as he could. After Roedel confronted them, Voegl scored only once more and Bendert stopped scoring altogether. But Voegl and Bendert became team players once again, flying mission after mission without victory claims. They fought harder than before, as if driven to make amends for what they had done to Swallisch. By the time JG-27 left the desert, their month of bad judgment had been forgotten.

Without fail, Franz's evening talks with Roedel took on a negative tone. It seemed that the longer Roedel looked at the horizon, the more haunted he became by the vision of the horrors still happening in Africa.

"We're next," he said between drags on his cigarette. "It's impossible to succeed here." Franz drew deeply from his pipe, its embers glowing. They all had heard the rumor that the enemy now had five thousand planes in Africa. In silence, the men looked past the beautiful Sicilian sunset and to the southern horizon, where darkness overtook the skies.

THREE DAYS LATER, APRIL 16, 1943

Spiraling upward in their 109s through scattered clouds above the airfield, Franz and Willi saw smoke rising on the other side of Olympus. The gray plumes bellowed from the port of Palermo on the island's north coast. The Four Motors had bombed the docks and power station there, sinking two ships. Franz, Willi, and twenty-one of their comrades had scrambled too late. The skies were otherwise empty. It was 4:30 P.M., and the Four Motors had just spoiled the dinner dates Franz had lined up for him and Willi in Trapani.

From Olympus, the controllers radioed the flight to alert them that P-38 fighters had been sighted above the Gulf of Palermo. Franz had never seen a P-38, but he had heard the name the boys in Africa gave the new American fighter—"the Fork-Tailed Devil." The P-38 was rumored to spit a hose of fire from five machine guns and a cannon, all packed in its nose. Supposedly it could snap from level flight into a loop in a blink.

From his fighter, *Yellow 3*, Willi radioed Franz and said he had a hunch where the bombers were. Two days before, after the B-17s had obliterated the airfield, Willi had caught them north of Sicily, turning west to reverse course and skirt the island on their way home to North Africa. Willi wagered that now the Four Motors would be flying the same route. He told Franz they could intercept the bombers west of the island if they hurried.

Franz liked the idea of pursuing "the herd," as the bombers were called, instead of "the Fork-Tailed Devils." The call was Willi's—he was leading the flights because their squadron commander, Sinner, had been banged up several weeks earlier after a crash landing on the airfield. Despite the fact that Willi was younger than him, Franz respected Willi's rank and courage.

Willi steered the flights west and poured on the coals. Their G models seemed to surge with joy at the chance to run open-throttle. As the flights motored across the island and over the sea, the clouds revealed their speed. The G's new motor had 120 more horsepower than the F, its propeller blades were broader, and it was faster, capable of four hundred miles per hour at altitude. The G was still poor for dogfighting. Its faster speed made its turning radius even wider. And the G was a killer on takeoff. If a pilot applied too much power too quickly it would torque roll, flipping onto its back and into the runway.

"There's the herd!" someone shouted across the radio. Willi was right. Ahead, Franz saw them: the Four Motors. Like a black cloud they flew at twenty-four thousand feet over a tiny fishermen's island called Marettimo. They were B-17s of the 97th Bomb Group. Willi led the squadron in a gentle turn behind the bombers until they were flying in the same direction at the same altitude. The pack of 109s spread out into a trail formation, each flight of four following the one ahead of it, as they gained ground on the heavies.

Franz squinted through the illuminated ring of his gun sight. The Four Motors were several miles ahead, flying toward the late-afternoon sun. He could make out their mustard-brown bodies and white bellies. They flew in a box formation, an arrangement of twenty-one planes that stacked diagonally like steps toward the heavens. This allowed the bombers' gunners to lend fire support to one another.

Franz's heart pounded. He found his plane rising and dipping with the shaking of his hand, and he noted the irony that he was flying like a rookie again. Through his bulletproof windshield, a welcomed improvement of the G model, Franz watched Willi lead the 109s ahead of him into their attack run. Franz's flight was next in line.

Although the bombers were lighter and faster without their bombs, the fighters slowly crept up on them from behind using their one-hundred-plus-mile-per-hour speed advantage. As Willi's flight approached the bombers at six hundred yards' distance, gunners on all twenty-one bombers opened fire. A stream of tracers converged around and in front of the tiny fighters. Willi's flight panicked and returned fire too soon, leaving a dirty gun smoke trail in their wake. They broke away and dove for safety, all too eager to let Franz's flight try.

Suddenly there were no 109s in front of Franz, just smoke-stained air between him and the bombers. He had no experience in attacking bombers and was unsure of the right way to go about it. Franz radioed his flight, instructing them to fall behind him. They would simply attack one after the other. He was too scared to think of any last advice or words of bravado. "Let's go," he simply said. One of his pilots confirmed his transmission. The other two said nothing, too scared to speak.

Starting at one thousand yards from the bombers, Franz turned onto his gun run. He was alarmed to discover that attacking from tail was agonizingly slow. He knew to fire at a hundred yards then break away. But flying the first nine hundred yards to reach that point would take eighteen long seconds.

Franz aimed for the lowest bombers so he and his flight could make the quickest getaway possible. He passed nine hundred yards in two seconds. Then eight hundred. Then seven hundred. At six hundred yards he could see that the bombers' flanks displayed white American stars surrounded by yellow circles. The bomber crews could see him, too, and their tail and ball turret gunners opened fire, eighty-four guns, tracking him in the lead like a spotlight on a stage actor.

Each gun spit seven sharp .50-caliber bullets per second. At five hundred yards, with tracer bullets zipping past his canopy, Franz realized the awful truth of the tail attack. *You cannot do this and not be hit.*

At four hundred yards he saw the massive wingspan of a B-17 fill the ring of his gun sight. He squeezed a burst of his cannon for one second before he lost his nerve, snap-rolled his fighter inverted, and broke away. The pilots behind him did the same, some firing, but others too scared to squeeze a trigger.

When Franz pulled out of the dive, he looked up through the canopy roof and saw the bombers' white bellies high above him, motoring upward and away, unscathed. Franz wondered how he had missed the bombers—the enemy's wings had filled the ring of his gun sight. But, like Willi before him, Franz had failed to recognize a new variable. The massive, 104-foot wingspan of a B-17 was far different than the 40-foot wings of a fighter—it filled the gun sight faster although it was farther away. That day all of the 109 pilots' shots fell short. They had yet to learn that a bomber's wingspan needed to extend *beyond* the ring of the gun sight before it was time to shoot.

For the young American bomber crews, it had been a resounding although exaggerated victory. They would report being attacked by

"40 enemy planes" without loss and would later write simply: "Enemy aircraft fired at bombers from distance."

———————

WILLI PULLED UP on Franz's wing as their flights re-formed behind them. Willi jokingly asked if Franz wanted to try again. "I'd rather be a coward for seven seconds than a long time dead," Franz said. So Willi radioed the others: "Mission complete, return to base." The attack had carried them southwest of Marettimo Island, so Willi steered northeast toward the island.

Not a minute had gone by before someone radioed, "Fighters! Eleven o'clock low!" Franz leaned forward against his straps and peered ahead of his left wing. He saw green silhouettes just two thousand feet below him. At sixteen thousand feet they motored in the opposite direction, toward Africa. Franz's eyes went wide. Each fighter had two engines, one attached to each large wing. The engines' booms extended back like fork blades connecting to a small tail. They were P-38s, ten of them, the Fork-Tailed Devils of the 82nd Fighter Group. The Americans called their planes "Lightnings."

Eager to redeem himself from his botched run on the bombers, Willi radioed Franz to say he was attacking. Willi knew no bounds when it came to pushing his luck, so Franz agreed to cover him. Willi dismissed his flight, as did Franz. It was like the desert again, two experts against many.

Franz followed Willi into a dive toward the P-38s. Both knew they had to hit them from astern or from behind, anywhere but from the front. Head-on, the Lightnings had them outgunned.* The P-38 pilots spotted the 109s too late.

———————

* Franz would remember, "One cardinal rule we never forgot was: avoid fighting a P-38 head-on. That was suicide. Their armament was so heavy and their firepower so murderous that no one ever tried that type of attack more than once."[2]

With height, speed, and surprise on their side, Franz and Willi swept across the P-38 formation from above, their guns blazing. Willi riddled a P-38 from wingtip to wingtip. Franz's bullets stitched the right engine of another. Round and round they danced with the P-38s. Willi's bullets hit another P-38 that spun from the sky. But the P-38s seemed reluctant to duel. After each joust they steered back onto their original southward course. All at once, they leveled their wings toward Africa and ran from the fight.

Convinced he and Franz had routed the P-38s, Willi began to chase them. But Franz warned Willi that the P-38s would only lead him out to sea, where he would run out of fuel. Willi reluctantly abandoned his pursuit.

Franz tipped his wing and looked down on the P-38 he had wounded. It was circling downward, its engine coughing black smoke. Suddenly the hood of its canopy tumbled away in the slipstream. The pilot stood in the cockpit then dove toward the rear of the wing. The draft sucked his body under the forked tail. He free-fell from twelve thousand feet, passing through the clouds. "Pull it!" Franz shouted at the American, urging him to open his chute. When the pilot's parachute finally popped full of air, Franz felt relief. The pilot drifted lazily downward while his P-38 splashed into the sea. Franz flew lower and saw the P-38 pilot climb into a tiny yellow raft against the whitecaps.

Franz radioed Olympus to tell them to relay the American's position to the Italians. He guessed they were seventy kilometers west of Marettimo and asked if the island could send a boat to pick up the man. For a second, Franz considered hovering over the man in the raft like an aerial beacon to steer a boat to the spot, but he shook the thought from his mind. It would put him at risk. If a prowling flight of enemy fighters found him, Franz knew he, too, could be shot into the sea. Franz and Willi departed the scene, leaving the pilot in his raft to fate. As they flew away, Franz wished the man a strong westerly wind.

The American who looked up from the raft was Second Lieutenant Conrad Bentzlin, a young man from a large Swedish-American family in Saint Paul, Minnesota. He was quiet and hardworking, having taught himself English in high school. He had paid his way through the University of Minnesota by working for the government's Civilian Conservation Corps program, cutting firebreaks in the forests of northern Minnesota. Among his buddies of the 82nd Fighter Group, Bentzlin was known as "the smartest guy in the unit."

Far from shore Bentzlin floated alone. A day later, another flight of P-38s flew over him and, through a hole in the clouds, saw him waving his arms from a raft. But he was in the middle of the sea and they could do nothing. Bentzlin would never be seen again.*

When Franz and Willi landed at Trapani, they hurried to fill out their victory claims in the operations shack. Willi claimed two P-38s and Franz one. Willi was cheerful because they had chased away an entire flight of Fork-Tailed Devils, but Franz felt a sense of regret. He had seen his enemy in the raft. He mentally put himself in that man's shoes, floating alone as the sea grew choppy and storm clouds rolled in, without water or food. "That's war," Franz told himself as he lit a cigarette, another new habit. With each drag of smoke, he put the American pilot farther out of his mind. He scrawled his signature on the paperwork so he and Willi could go celebrate in Trapani, where black-haired "bella donnas" and bottles of sweet Marsala wine were calling.

---

* Conrad Bentzlin had a younger brother, Carl, who would become a navigator on a B-24 that would be shot down over Vienna. Like Conrad, he became "missing in action" and never would return. When Conrad was shot down, his sister, Betty, was sixteen. For years after the war, Betty always looked for him in crowds.

9

THE UNSEEN HAND

TWO WEEKS LATER, LATE APRIL 1943, TRAPANI, SICILY

FRANZ AND WILLI waited nervously in the courtyard of the villa on a hillside overlooking Trapani Bay. The high noon sun cast sharp shadows on the dried fountain that languished in the courtyard's center between a cluster of palm trees. Willi flicked his cigarette nervously. All Roedel had told them was that General Adolf Galland had ordered that they report to the villa, the general's new headquarters. Franz and Willi knew Galland's face from postcards, the news clips before cinema films, and from the boxes of cigars he endorsed. He was a national hero, a ninety-four-victory ace and Germany's youngest general at age thirty-one. All of Germany's fighter pilots fell under his command.

Franz and Willi had pressed their tropical dress uniforms—tan blazers with white caps—and had assumed Galland either intended to decorate them with some awards or wanted their report on the disastrous supply convoys to Africa. In the week prior, Franz and Willi had flown to Africa daily, escorting transports with supplies for the doomed Afrika Korps. They had seen the Allies' aerial blockade and had watched as the seas grew covered with the burning wreckage of German transports and floating men. Allied fighters were shooting down thirty Ju-52s per week, and the Germans had begun naming days after big losses, such as "the Palm Sunday Massacre" followed by "the Holy Thursday Massacre."*

Roedel opened the tall wooden doors of the villa and ushered Franz and Willi inside. Roedel nervously raised his eyebrows to Franz, as if to say, "Be prepared." Franz had not seen Roedel since the shakeup when Galland had named him the new leader of JG-27. Neumann was gone. No one knew if he had been promoted or replaced, but he had had to leave his beloved JG-27 to work on Galland's staff in Germany. Roedel chose Schroer to take his spot and lead II Group.

Passing through a vast room beneath a high ceiling with wooden beams, they found Galland outside on a patio, relaxing after his lunch at a small, circular table. The sea lay behind him. Galland's thin smile beamed from beneath his black mustache. His slicked black hair and black eyebrows gave him a dark, menacing quality. A bad crash had made his face more rugged. The crash had flattened his nose and sunken his eyebrows over his eyes. Still, Galland remained a dashing lady's man and unrepentant bachelor. He wore a tan, short-sleeved shirt that made his black Knight's Cross dangle boldly.

Across from Galland sat his deputy, Colonel Gunther Luetzow, also a legendary pilot at only thirty-one years old. Luetzow was known as "the Man of Ice" because he showed little emotion, on the ground or in the air, where he had scored 104 victories and earned the Knight's Cross. Slender in build, his face was scrunched by a thick nose and his small eyes always looked serious, either deep in thought or piercing with worry. Only a few people had ever seen him smile. Luetzow had

* One of the transports that managed to escape Tunisia carried a pilot Franz knew well: his old squadron leader, Voegl. But Voegl did not leave Africa on his feet. On April 19, in Tunisia, his fighter had collided with another on takeoff. Badly burned, Voegl was sent home. He would recover slowly and later lead a pilot training school for the remainder of the war.

another side that few witnessed, in which he was a family man who cherished his wife, small son, and daughter.

Franz and Willi saluted the seated general and colonel and remained at attention as Roedel took a seat at Galland's table.* Roedel and Galland were old friends, going back to the Battle of France, where Roedel had been Galland's wingman on the day when Galland scored his first victory.

Galland lit up a thick cigar, a trademark affectation he had discovered while flying in the Spanish Civil War. Galland loved cigars so much he had an electric cigar lighter installed in his 109. Galland's 109 was legendary for other reasons. Franz had never seen the plane, but Galland was said to have customized it with extra machine guns and had his personal nose art, a custom-designed cartoon of Mickey Mouse, painted alongside the cockpit.

Turning to Franz and Willi, Galland told them in his soft, proper, voice that he had come to Sicily to manage the African debacle and more—to investigate a threat far greater to Germany—the Four Motors. Galland confirmed what all the pilots knew, that American heavy bombers were pounding Germany from one direction—England. But if they attacked from the Mediterranean, too, such a two-pronged attack would be impossible to defend against.

"They have to be stopped, here," Galland said.

Galland turned to Franz and Willi.

"You are the pilots who shot down the P-38s on April 16—yes?"

"Yes, General," they replied.

"Then why did you run from the bombers to go and battle against fighters?" Galland asked.

Franz and Willi were lost for words. Galland reiterated the record for them. The heavies had bombed Trapani on April 11, 12, and 13, yet only one Four Motor was knocked down. On April 16, the heavies re-

---

* The stiff armed "Nazi salute" would not be mandated until summer 1944. Instead, the Air Force men saluted like any other nation's pilots but with a heel click.

turned, and twenty-three pilots flew against them and scored nothing but P-38s. Galland told them that Goering received every mission report by teletype and had seen their claims himself. "The *Reichsmarshall* always asks for the victory figures first and losses second," Galland said.

"This says what he thinks of his pilots." Galland's voice carried a tone of disdain. Galland and Goering had been at odds since the Battle of Britain, when Goering first accused the fighter pilots of cowardice. Goering had once asked Galland what he needed to improve his pilots' fighting spirit, and Galland had replied, "An outfit of Spitfires for my squadron." It was a verbal insult that Goering never forgot.

Luetzow's face grew cold at the mention of Goering's name. Luetzow had, in fact, given Goering his Air Force–wide nickname, "the Fat One." Luetzow hated Goering because he was an ignoble man who now sat at the head of the once noble Air Force.* Goering had led the fifty thousand brownshirts—The Party's thugs—who had "monitored" the polling booths during the 1933 elections, intimidating voters and suppressing opposition.

Roedel interrupted Galland to remind him that II Group was still fresh to the theater and that Lieutenant Kientsch had the unit's first success against a B-17. Prodded by Roedel, Willi told the story of downing the B-17. He shocked everyone by confessing that the B-17 he had destroyed had actually been a straggler. Hit by flak, it fell from formation and he finished it. Franz suddenly wished Willi could filter his thoughts with as much talent as he flew with.

Galland assured Roedel that he was not questioning his leadership. Rather, he simply needed answers from his pilots. Galland got to the point and asked Franz and Willi again, "Why did you let the bombers escape?"

"Because we fired from too far away because of their defensive fire," Willi admitted.

---

* Galland would remember, "It was as if he [Luetzow] never exhibited any emotion except anger, and ironically, this was usually directed at Goering, and never the enemy."[1]

"Ah," Galland said. "Goering calls that 'cowardice,' but I personally believe it is a matter of tactics."

His ire raised at the hint of cowardice, Franz interrupted the general and said, "Sir, it's the tail approach that's the problem—it's all we're taught and it's stupid."

The three Knight's Cross holders at the table turned toward Franz. Willi looked straight ahead like a ghost. Galland leaned across the table, his cross dangling like a threat. The rumor was that Galland's cross was so heavy due to its twenty-four embedded diamonds that he needed to wear a woman's garter under his collar to support it. Galland let a smile curl and said, "It's about time someone agrees with me! But tell me, why do you hold this opinion of yours?"

"The tail approach will only get us killed," Franz said. "It is too slow. We need to attack from the front, with speed."

Galland banged his fist on the table. "I told my group commanders the same thing—'Lead your men from head-on, in close formation!' But they said the new approach would be too fast."

"A good pilot will find a way," Franz said.

Galland's eyes lit up and he agreed. He was a brave pilot and valued that characteristic in others.

Galland gave his cigar another light and seemed to mellow. Seeing the general satisfied, Roedel motioned for Franz and Willi to leave. They saluted Galland. Before departing, Franz wheeled and asked Galland a question that had been burning in his mind since the Spanish Civil War.

"Sir, is it true that in Spain you flew in your bathing suit?"

Galland laughed and nodded. Franz explained that he had heard the rumor when he was flying transports into Spain. "We delivered your bullets," Franz said.

Galland smiled. "Pull up a chair," he ordered, motioning for Franz and Willi to sit.

"Seems we've got an old comrade here," he said to Luetzow with a grin.

ALTHOUGH GALLAND HAD summoned Franz and Willi to call them on the carpet, by the end of their visit he had offered Franz a cigar and told Franz to call him "Dolfo," as his friends did. Franz discovered that he and Galland had a common bond, albeit tragic. Both had lost a brother in the war. Galland told a story of how he and his two younger brothers, Paul and Wutz, loved playing with electric trains as boys. Both of his younger brothers became fighter pilots and were stationed together in France when Galland commanded Fighter Wing 26 (JG-26). Galland cleared an outbuilding of his château headquarters, bought a set of electric trains, and called his brothers together. Like small boys, they set up the trains and played long into the night. Galland's brother Paul had been shot down and killed the autumn prior to his meeting with Franz. Wutz still flew FW-190 fighters, and Galland worried about his safety. Luetzow mentioned he had a brother in the Navy and said that he "had no idea where he went wrong." When Galland laughed, Franz realized Luetzow had been telling a joke, although his face remained stone cold.

He had not always been a stone-faced "Man of Ice." Luetzow had once been a scholar, a track star, and a pilot whom his comrades affectionately called "Franzl" because he was "popular with all ranks because of his easy charm and warm personality."[2] In Spain, he had been the first pilot ever to score a victory in the 109, then a new machine. But when he came home he saw the values of The Party and how the 44 percent had taken over Germany. Luetzow wrote in his diary, "The omnipresent, primitive anti-Semitism in the Reich pisses me off."[3] Luetzow became conflicted. He had been raised in a Prussian military family. His father was an admiral and had taught him that a professional soldier should separate himself from politics. So Luetzow continued to fly and fight until June 1942, when a dark event on the Eastern Front led to the end of his combat career.

Only Galland knew of the dark event that haunted Luetzow. Luetzow had been the commander of Fighter Wing 3 (JG-3) on an airfield outside of Kharkov in the Ukraine, when SS soldiers came to commandeer his services. They wanted Luetzow to lend them any non-flyers he could spare to help them round up people they called "undesirables." Luetzow knew the reputation of the SS and knew that whatever they were planning, it could not be good. When Luetzow refused to help them, the SS threatened to go around him. Luetzow called his entire wing to the tarmac in dress uniform—the pilots, the orderlies, and even the mechanics. Luetzow told them what the SS had asked of him and said he would remove his Knight's Cross and resign from the Air Force if any of his men complied with the SS's request.[4]

When The Party learned of Luetzow's speech, rumors circulated that he would be court-martialed and perhaps even shot. Galland heard this and was worried for his friend. He removed Luetzow from command of the wing, probably saving his life. The general put Luetzow on his staff and under his protection. Galland agreed with what Luetzow had done and would thereafter call him "a man above all others."

A WEEK LATER, MAY 8, 1943

In rickety lawn chairs, Franz, Roedel, and Schroer lounged in the mid-morning sun in front of the airfield's Operations Office. Spent cigarettes piled up in ashtrays beside them, the product of waiting to greet Fighter Wing 77 (JG-77), which was due to land at any minute. The Ops Office sat at the airfield's north end and looked like a roadside fruit stand, a strange contrast to the bombed-out hangars nearby. From the office's open door, Franz heard the excited voices of the JG-77 pilots across the radio. They had sighted Sicily, were entering the traffic pattern to land, and sounded like men who had just been given a second lease on life. They had just escaped Africa.

Roedel and Schroer were obligated to greet JG-77, but Franz was not. He had just landed from a flight and had stuck around, eager to see the reinforcements arrive. II Group desperately needed them. Nearby, in JG-53's tarmac space, mechanics were still mending the unit's battered fighters, using manpower to hoist off wings and lower propellers to earth. On paper, JG-53 had transferred three squadrons to Trapani, but their lineup was so depleted they resembled just one squadron. Each plane in JG-53 wore the same crest on its nose, a white diamond with a black spade set within it. For that reason they were known as the "Ace of Spades Wing."

Roedel recounted the little-known story of JG-53. During the battle for Britain in spring 1940, Goering had discovered that the wife of JG-53's commander was Jewish. So Goering made the commander and his staff strip the spade crests from their planes. In its place, Goering made them paint a red stripe, a mark of shame. To get back at Goering, the commander and his staff painted over the swastikas on their tails and flew that way all summer. Finally Goering could stand it no longer. He sacked the commander and replaced him. But he allowed the commander's men to repaint the spades on their planes. Only then did they agree to put Goering's swastika back on their tails.

Franz smiled at Roedel's disdain for Goering, even though he knew Roedel was taking a risk in even telling such a story. The Party had ears everywhere. An orderly stuck his head from the door and reported that JG-77 had entered the circuit to land.

———

FRANZ KNEW FOR certain the battle for Africa had been lost when he saw the battered 109s of JG-77 touch down. They taxied to the open pens where he and the others sat. The planes' tan bodies and blue bellies were riddled with bullet holes and covered with oil, sand, and gunpowder residue. Roedel spotted the plane of JG-77's commander, Major Johannes "Macky" Steinhoff—the plane had forward-facing arrows on its flank instead of numbers. Alarmed, Roedel ran to the plane, with Franz and Schroer following.

JG-77's commander slid from the plane's wing. Steinhoff was tall and lanky and had a lean, tired, face. Above his high cheeks his light blue eyes hung sadly and his nose curved gently downward, compounding his look of worry. Those who knew Steinhoff looked up to him as a father figure, although he was only thirty-two.

Steinhoff embraced Roedel, his old friend from flying school, then hurried nearby to one of his unit's fighters that had rolled to a halt. Bypassing the plane's pilot, Steinhoff darted behind the wing and fiddled with the wireless radio hatch in the fuselage, where the black cross had been painted and the first aid kit was housed. He opened the hatch and leaned into the fighter's storage compartment. Steinhoff reached, struggled, then pulled a man out of the plane—*by his feet.*

The man hugged Steinhoff then fell to the ground and kissed the dirt. As the propellers of the other planes wound down to stillness, Steinhoff rushed to another fighter and popped the hatch, freeing a man inside while the plane's pilot buried his face against his gun sight, exhausted.

Steinhoff's pilots had left their tools, bullets, and spare parts in Africa, but they had not abandoned their mechanics. Instead, the pilots had helped the mechanics crawl into the dark, claustrophobic confines of the fighters' bellies. There they rode out a forty-five-minute flight from hell. No room to wiggle. No parachutes. No hope of escape.

Franz, Schroer, and the men of JG-27 quickly realized what was happening. They rushed to help Steinhoff get the weary JG-77 pilots and mechanics to shade. Mechanics hugged one another and slapped one another on the back. A few cried tears of joy. A few vomited in the bushes. Some were bloody and bandaged. From one fighter they pulled two mechanics. On the wing of another they helped the pilot stand, his nerves frayed. Ambulances raced to the scene.

"So much for reinforcements," Franz said to Schroer as they steadied a mechanic, his arms over their shoulders.

JG-77 had flown from the Cape Bon Peninsula, where the Germans and Italians were making their last stand in Africa. They had raced low over the waves to Sicily. A few 109s had been shot down during the crossing, each crash costing two lives, as the pilots bravely stayed with their planes rather than jump and leave their mechanics. Only 40 of JG-77's 120 planes made it out of Africa.*

Having cared for his men, Steinhoff trudged over to Roedel to formally report his unit's arrival. From Roedel's side, Franz saw that Steinhoff wore a haggard grin and looked like he was about to collapse. He knew Steinhoff's name. The man was a national hero with 134 victories, almost all won on the Eastern Front in ugly battles like Stalingrad. He wore the Knight's Cross with Oak Leaves and looked stern. But when Steinhoff spoke, his voice was calm like a storyteller's and his words were articulate. Steinhoff had studied the history of languages at the prestigious University of Jena, hoping to become a professor, but when he could not find a teaching job he had joined the Navy. Instead of making him a sailor, the Navy had trained him to fly then handed him to the Air Force when their plans for German aircraft carriers fell through.

Steinhoff had not flown with a mechanic in his plane that day. A tragic story from his past explained his unwillingness to lock a man within his fighter's inescapable storage compartment. Roedel had heard the legend, whispered only in wing leader circles, and later told it to Franz. In April of the previous year, while flying over the Soviet Union, Steinhoff and his wingman, Lieutenant Walter Krupinski, a colorful figure everyone called "the Count" (because of his love for women and wine), had entered a swirling dogfight against Soviet Yak fighters. Steinhoff was leading their group and had shot down two Yaks and damaged a third, blasting it from nose to tail. As it burned, the Yak flew straight and level. Steinhoff and the Count pulled up alongside the plane and saw its pilot banging against the canopy glass. He was trying to escape, wanting to jump, but his canopy was jammed. Flames spat from the engine like a blowtorch, and gray

---

* Steinhoff would write of the route to Sicily, "Columns of smoke from shot down aircraft marked our course."[5]

smoke billowed into his cockpit. The Soviet pilot's plane had become an oven. The pilot pressed his face against the canopy glass and looked at Steinhoff in terror. Steinhoff decided he needed to do something. The man was being cooked alive. He told the Count to depart and lead the unit back to base, where he would meet him later.

The Count watched Steinhoff drop back behind the Soviet fighter. The Soviet pilot sat back in his seat and looked at the Count. He knew what his enemy was about to do and why. The Soviet pilot nodded his head to the Count. The Count nodded in return and peeled away. The Count glanced back one final time toward the Yak. It had become a cloud of black smoke and falling pieces, destroyed by a blast of Steinhoff's cannon.

On the ground, the Count found Steinhoff behind the wing of his fighter, crying. For days afterward, Steinhoff avoided conversations with his friends other than to issue orders and fly missions. He never spoke of the incident other than to tell the Count, "If I am ever in that situation, please do the same."[6] The Count told Steinhoff that would never happen, but if it did, he would show him the same mercy. Those who knew Steinhoff before the incident and after said he was never the same. That one day over Russia made him old.

As Steinhoff surveyed the weary men and the destruction that surrounded him at Trapani Airfield, he said to Roedel, "It's a good day to be alive." His voice carried a tinge of optimism as if he knew something the others had forgotten.

A MONTH LATER, JUNE 10, 1943

Franz and Willi ate their dinners on the steps of the Squadron 6 alert shack. It was evening, around 6 P.M. From the door behind them hung a small wooden sign that read: LIEUTENANT WILLI KIENTSCH, SQUAD-RON CAPTAIN. Two weeks prior, Roedel had promoted Rudi Sinner and transferred him to Greece to oversee JG-27's expansion. In Sinner's place, Roedel made Willi the leader of Squadron 6 because he was next in line, rank-wise.

Schroer ran to the shack, looking worried. He told Franz and Willi that Olympus had just called him with a distress message from the Italians. A flight of their Macchi fighters had just been shot into the sea north of Pantelleria Island.

Franz and Willi knew Pantelleria. They had been in combat there earlier that afternoon, when Willi had shot down two Spitfires while Franz covered his tail. The island lay halfway between Africa and Sicily and was swarming with Allied planes. Three weeks earlier, the Afrika Korps had surrendered, handing over 275,000 P.O.W.s to the Allies. Now Pantelleria's Italian garrison was the last obstacle preventing an Allied seaborne invasion of Sicily.

Schroer said that an Italian seaplane was taking off any minute from Marsala, just down the coast, to rescue any survivors. Franz joked that they should send two seaplanes, one to rescue the Italians and another to rescue their seaplane. Willi agreed—the mission was suicidal. The Allies had been bombing and strafing Pantelleria for five days, sending so many planes that they were seen circling, waiting in line for a chance to attack.

Schroer removed his hat and scratched his head. Looking to Willi, he broke the news. "The Italians can only put up three fighters," he said, "so Squadron 6 is going with them." Willi cursed. Franz shook his head. He knew the Italians as the same pilots who once attacked a narrow island off the coast of Trapani, thinking it was an enemy submarine. Schroer explained that the orders were Roedel's, not his. Roedel had ordered a "rescue flight" of ten fighters to take the Italians to Pantelleria and back.

Willi complained to Schroer that he had already been there that day and was not in the mood to go back. "Then send your pilots who haven't seen the enemy," Schroer said. Franz set down his mess tin and began to stand. "No," Willi said, tugging Franz's pant leg.

Willi told Schroer he could give him six pilots who had not been in combat that day. Schroer said he would find four others and took off running. Willi looked sheepishly at Franz as he stood to get his roster. Two weeks prior, Willi had surpassed "magic 30," triggering his nomination for the Knight's Cross. Suddenly, he had something to live for. Fan mail. Girls. An inevitable celebration in Kisslegg. Knowing the Cross was coming made Willi more cautious. Franz had reason to be more careful, too. Three weeks earlier his G model had caught fire during a practice flight over Sicily. Franz had bailed out of the plane, slightly burned, and lost his second fighter of the war. For three weeks he was grounded to heal.

From the steps, Franz and Willi watched the ten pilots run to their planes. As they took off into the darkening skies, Franz told Willi he had a bad feeling. Half the pilots of the rescue flight had no victories. Their leader, Lieutenant Hans Lewes, was a fresh-faced kid himself. As the "greatest gun" among them, Lewes had just three victories.

"We should be with them," Franz said. Begrudgingly Willi stood and reached for his life preserver. Franz grabbed his. Together, they ran for their planes.

FORTY-FIVE MINUTES LATER

The purple night sky slowly smothered the orange sunset as a lone 109 flew low over the sea toward Sicily. A cloud of vapor trailed the plane's wake. Metal pieces tumbled from its wings and body in the wind. The plane was falling apart.

Behind the controls, Franz wrestled with the plane's shaking stick. Bullet holes dotted the cockpit around him. The bridge of Franz's nose bled from a tracer bullet that had pierced the canopy glass and grazed him. Franz clutched the broken stem of his pipe between his teeth. A bullet had exploded the pipe's bowl. Near his right knee, the Mediterranean Sea was visible through a fist-sized hole in the cockpit's skin.

In the distance, the Sicilian coast came into view, a gray smudge above the blue-green sea. Franz's eyes flared. He talked to the plane, urging her to keep going. His 109 bucked and groaned. Franz tapped the oil pressure gauge with his finger. Its quivering needle told him the plane was bleeding fluids and dying. Every minute she flew was three miles closer to land. Franz wanted to call Olympus, but .50-caliber bullets had punched holes in his radio. The holes matched those along his wings and through his tail and cowling.

Franz and Willi had caught up with the rescue flight just in time to experience disaster. They had spotted the seaplane by the bright red crosses on its wings. Ahead of the seaplane they found their comrades with the three Italian Macchi 202 fighters nestled behind them. The formation flew at wave top level—without a fighting chance.

Sixteen American P-40s were waiting, hoping someone would come looking for the Italians they had shot down earlier. The pilots of the 79th Fighter Group were said to have whooped, hollered, and rocked their wings when they saw the enemy formation. Then they flew with deadly seriousness. "What got the boys mad," their PR men would write, "was the way the three Italian fighters were hugging the German formation—as though their own safety was assured by the presence of the twelve Me-109s around them. Something had to be done about that. Something was done."[7]

The Germans and Italians would call the next ten minutes a "slaughter." The Americans would call the same event "one of the most spectacular air victories of the North African campaign."[8] The P-40s dove. Burning Italian fighters hit the water first. The 109s splashed into the sea, one by one. The seaplane joined them, hit by a trigger-happy P-40 driver. Franz's fighting ability was useless. Bullet after bullet hit his plane. Only his flying skill kept him alive. He last saw Willi and two 109s running for Sicily with P-40s on their tails. He gave chase but was unable to keep up.

Franz found himself flying alone. Glancing at the sea, he tugged his safety straps. He had decided he would ditch before he would jump again. Like every German pilot, Franz knew his parachute straps were made of hemp, which was known to often snap and drop a pilot to his death. The Air Force was said to be developing new nylon parachute harnesses.

Three miles from Sicily's shore, the engine of Franz's fighter gagged without oil. With a jolt, the engine quit. Franz felt strangely relieved. The engine's painful struggle had been fraying his nerves. He steered the dead, six-thousand-pound fighter down like a glider from his boyhood. The sea below resembled a grass pasture. As he neared the waves, he saw that the water was green and undulating.

Franz lifted the plane's nose to stall and hit the waves flat. The fighter slapped down. Instead of melting into the sea, the plane skipped from one wave to the next. As the plane lost speed, its nose grew heavy and it dove into the water. Franz's body slammed forward before his straps pulled him back. The canopy glass held. From six feet under water, Franz looked up and saw the waves above him.

The sea poured in through the hole by Franz's knee. Streams of water spouted from the instrument panel and the holes in the canopy. The fighter sank, still flying into the depths. Seven feet deep. Eight feet deep. Nine feet deep. Franz's ears popped. Water poured over his shoulders. Franz unhooked his seat belt and tossed off his parachute straps. He tugged a red knob on his left to release the canopy. Nothing happened. He tugged again without effect. Panicking, he stood and tried to push the canopy upward with his shoulder. The water pressure held it down. Franz had neglected to follow procedure and jettison the canopy before hitting the water.

The plane flew deeper. Light faded. The water in the cockpit climbed to Franz's chin. *The window!* The words screamed in Franz's mind. Grabbing the side window pane, he pulled it back toward him and inhaled a lungful of the cockpit's last oxygen. A deluge of water rushed in, equalizing the pressure. With one hand on his life raft and the other on the canopy's metal frame, Franz kicked from his seat and flipped the canopy open. The dark sea squeezed him with a cold grip. Franz pulled a tab on his life preserver to release its compressed CO_2.

The vest inflated instantly, its buoyancy hauling him up. Franz clawed for the surface. He kicked furiously in his heavy boots. Desperate for oxygen, his lungs constricted. Just when he was about to gasp and inhale the sea, Franz popped out from a wave and splashed back down.

He floated in the gentle swells, panting. Franz could see the shore and a beam from the lighthouse at Cape Granitola on the island's southwestern tip. He inflated his raft and slid inside.* Clinging to the raft, he remembered—*My rosary!* Franz patted his chest and found his pocket still buttoned. Opening the pocket, Franz pulled forth the black beads and silver cross. Clutching his rosary, he rolled onto his back.

The gently rocking raft drifted toward land. Franz looked up at the inky sky. He thought about Willi and his friends. He knew many of them were now blue and lifeless because he had seen so many 109s crash. Who had died he did not yet know. Seabirds flew for the island, slowing just to glance on him with pity.

———

BAREFOOT AND SOAKED, Franz dragged his raft onto Sicily's rough shoreline under the day's last light. A flight of 109s flew overhead toward Trapani. Franz knew they had been searching the seas for his comrades, a search that had to end with darkness. Franz wandered the shore until he discovered an old fisherman tying up his boats. He startled the old man but slowly convinced him to give him a ride back to his base. Franz rode to Trapani, sprawled on sacks of grain in the truck's bed. Two hours later, when the truck pulled up to the airfield, the gate guards were shocked when their flashlights shined on Franz. He looked more dead than alive.

At the operations shack, as his comrades helped him down from

---

* "Getting into the life raft was the hardest part. I inflated it, tried to climb into it and found I couldn't. I kept trying but every time the blasted thing would slip out from under me. Finally, when I was almost exhausted I had sense enough to partially deflate it. After that I climbed in easily and pumped it up again," Franz would remember.[9]

the truck's lift gate, Franz asked if Willi had made it. "Willi's okay," they said. He had crash-landed on the field and was in the infirmary.

Franz asked who else had made it back.

"So far, just you," someone said. Franz's comrades gave the fisherman cans of food in thanks.

The next morning dawned on the airfield revealing twelve empty pens where 109s once sat. No joking or laughter echoed from the squadron shacks. A truck delivered the body of Lieutenant Hans Lewes, who had washed up at Marsala. The men lowered him in a cloth bag into the Sicilian dirt. On Pantelleria, another pilot's corpse rolled onto the island that day, but the Italians would not report this for several days. They were busy laying out white sheets across the island to surrender to the Allied bombers above.

A WEEK LATER

Franz was reporting to the squadron shack after a flight when Willi approached him, grabbed his arm, and pulled him out of sight. Pushing Franz up against the shack's side wall, he told him in a hushed voice that the "Black Coats" were waiting inside. "They want words with you," Willi said. The Black Coats were the Gestapo.

Franz thought it was a joke until he saw Willi's eyes. They were genuine with fear. Everyone from a private to a general knew The Party's secret police force operated with unchecked authority and brutality. The Gestapo had initially come to the airfield looking for Franz's superiors, unaware that Roedel and Schroer worked from Olympus. Impatient, the Gestapo asked around and someone had pointed them to Willi.

"What did you get yourself into?" Willi asked. Franz said he had done nothing wrong. He thought back and admitted he had snuck into the Colosseum on a leave in Rome but nothing worse. Franz told Willi he would confront them. Even if he thought The Party was bullshit, he never said it in the wrong company.

Franz entered the shack with Willi behind him. Two Gestapo agents were waiting for him. They wore shoulder holsters although they dressed like accountants, in white shirts and ties. One was the rank equivalent of a captain (*Kriminalinspektor*) and the other was an enlisted man. The Gestapo captain ordered Willi to leave. Franz found himself alone with them. The captain said they were from a regional Gestapo office.

The door to the shack swung open. Steinhoff, the commander of JG-77, entered. The Gestapo captain asked him to leave, but Steinhoff asked for the captain's rank. "The last time I checked, a major outranks a captain," Steinhoff said.[10] Folding his arms, Steinhoff leaned against a wall behind Franz, his presence and dangling Knight's Cross adding weight to Franz's defense. Steinhoff and JG-77 had returned to Trapani a few days prior, on June 13, to relieve JG-27 so the unit could begin to rotate home. Willi had found Steinhoff and summoned him to Franz's aid.

Steinhoff had always hated The Party and had dealt with the Gestapo before. In Russia they brought their inquisition to his unit, then Fighter Wing 52 (JG-52), to investigate the supposed Jewish backgrounds of a few of his pilots. Steinhoff had declined to assist them and had said to the Gestapo leader, "You'll be lucky if you leave Russia alive." The man asked if the skies were that unsafe. Steinhoff said, "No, it's because you just made enemies of forty fighter pilots who have never added a Ju-52 to their victory list, and I think that's yours sitting on my runway."

The Gestapo captain told Franz what he already knew from the newspapers. Three months prior they had captured the White Rose group, an anti-Party cell of students in Munich. The White Rose men and women were young intellectuals who had spread leaflets spurring opposition to The Party. The arrest and execution of the White Rose group had sparked a Gestapo witch hunt for anyone who had spoken out against The Party in any manner at any time.

With Steinhoff present, the Gestapo men behaved in an unusually restrained manner. The captain asked Franz if he knew any of the White Rose members and read the names of the young people involved. Franz told them he had never heard of such people, because he truthfully had not. The captain asked if Franz had followed the church sermons of Cardinal von Faulhaber or Bishop von Galen or any of the clergy who had spoken out against The Party. Von Faulhaber and von Galen were leading anti-Party voices in Germany. Franz said everyone had read the writings of von Faulhaber and von Galen. This reply made the Gestapo agents glare. Von Faulhaber had authored "With Burning Concern" in 1937, and in 1941, von Galen had spoken out so vehemently against The Party and the Gestapo that the British had copied his sermons and dropped them from planes across Europe.* German soldiers, civilians, and occupied peoples read them, including the future Pope John Paul II, who found a flyer in Krakow, Poland.

The Gestapo captain reminded Franz to watch his words. Under The Party's 1938 "Subversion of the War Effort" law, any words or actions that the Gestapo deemed as "undermining military morale" could be punished by death. This included speaking out against The Party or even saying that Germany was losing the war. The Gestapo had convicted the White Rose members under this "Subversion Law" and killed them by guillotine.

The Gestapo assured Franz they had evidence that his brother was connected to known traitors and they had reason to suspect Franz was, too. A flurry of memories rushed through Franz's mind. He remembered the "With Burning Concern" letters he had found in August's room and his suspicions of August's wife, the cardinal's niece. Franz knew why the Gestapo agents were questioning him. Worse, they probably had good reason to connect him with people identified as traitors. Thinking quickly, Franz told the agents that his brother

---

* On July 13, 1941, from the pulpit of St. Lambert's Church in Münster, von Galen had said: "None of us is safe—and may he know that he [who] is the most loyal and conscientious of citizens . . . cannot be sure that he will not some day be deported from his home, deprived of his freedom and locked up in the cellars and concentration camps of the Gestapo."[11]

was long dead and he, personally, had nothing to do with the clergy or the Catholic Church itself. "I was excommunicated long ago," he told them. Franz knew this was only partially true. He still had his faith; he just had been banned from participation in his church.

Under Steinhoff's stare, the Gestapo agents accepted Franz's explanation.* After they had departed, Franz thanked Steinhoff, who nodded and departed as quietly as he had arrived. Franz knew Steinhoff had taken a great risk in siding with him—the man had never even asked if Franz was innocent or guilty, he had just waded into the fire. Franz vowed he would figure out exactly why the Gestapo had come looking for him, although he knew the answer lay close to home.

ONE MONTH LATER, JULY 30, 1943, SOUTHERN ITALY

The sun rose across the Adriatic Sea as Franz, Willi, and their comrades gathered with their bags over their shoulders along the small Italian airfield of San Vito. They watched their mechanics walk the flight line. The mechanics carried gray cloth tarps. The group had fewer than half of its fighters remaining, just seventeen. At each fighter, two mechanics stopped and draped a tarp over the plane's canopy.

The day before, with the swipe of his pen, newly promoted Major Roedel had relinquished the planes to the Ace of Spades Wing, JG-53. Franz and his comrades had tried to defend Sicily when the Allied invasion came two weeks prior, on July 9, but had been driven away by endless waves of Allied fighters. Franz had been shot down for the first time by Spitfires, but not before bagging one as a victory. He had bailed out and landed behind friendly lines, but had lost his fourth fighter of the war.

Before Franz and his comrades boarded the trucks that would take

---

* "They were finally convinced that I did not know anything, and they left. I never heard anything else about it," Franz would remember.[12]

them to their train for home, some JG-53 pilots showed them a memo that their commander had issued them. It was from *Reichsmarschall* Goering, a teletype sent from Berlin. It was addressed to all fighter pilots of the Mediterranean and read:

> *Together with the fighter pilots in France, Norway, and Russia, I can only regard you with contempt. I want an immediate improvement in fighting spirit. If this improvement is not forthcoming, flying personnel from the commander down must expect to be remanded to the ranks and transferred to the eastern front to serve on the ground.*
>
> —Goering, Reichsmarschall[13]

When Roedel came to say his good-byes, he told Franz and his comrades that he was not going home with them. Instead, he was heading to Greece to oversee the formation of JG-27 with its new IV Group. Roedel must have thrown Goering's angry memo in the trash, because he never issued it to his men. Roedel knew Goering, the leader who wore a red toga at his home in the Alps and smoked from a huge porcelain pipe that touched the ground. Goering, the violent morphine addict who painted his fingernails. Goering, who recorded his rants against his pilots on records that he shipped to his men on the front lines so they could hear his rage. In Roedel's eyes, the Allies weren't "the enemy." They were merely "the opponent." On that day, Roedel knew who "the enemy" was. He resided in Berlin and something had to be done about him.

As Franz and his comrades rode the rails north, their spirits improved with each passing mile. From a knee, Willi led the others in singing songs to Italian girls in the cars around them. He had scored twenty-four victories in the campaign, the most of the group's three squadrons. Willi was certain his hometown would throw a party for him, his own Oktoberfest. Franz promised he would attend.

Franz was in a mellow frame of mind. He had registered just two victories during the Sicilian campaign, bringing his total to nineteen, although he had downed other planes without witnesses. Leaving the Mediterranean alive after two bail-outs and a crash into the sea was good enough for him. All he wanted was a sound night's sleep in Germany.

At a train stop, Franz picked up a German Army newspaper from an Italian paperboy. The headlines made his eyes open wide. Willi picked up a paper and became mesmerized. Another pilot grabbed a paper, then another did, until the whole platform was filled with pilots with their noses in papers. In northern Germany, British bombers were systematically incinerating the city of Hamburg with firebombs, night after night, while the Americans dropped iron bombs on the city's factories by day. The paper tried to put a heroic spin on the tragic news, calling a one-sided catastrophe "the Battle of Hamburg." They refused to mention that the bombs had produced a thousand-foot-high tornado of fire that had swirled and swallowed eight square miles of the city. They neglected to describe that the tornado had melted the city's streets and sucked the air from bomb shelters, killing, in one week, forty-two thousand men, women, and children.* Franz and Willi looked up from their papers and at each other with dismay. In Africa and Sicily they had fought for nothing, for meaningless sand and sea. Now with the front lines over their own soil, it suddenly struck them. They were going home to fight for everything.

---

* Sir Arthur Harris, the leader of the British Bomber Command, considered the bombing of Hamburg as payback for the German "Blitz" bombing of British cities that had cost the lives of forty thousand Britons. Hitler's minister of armaments, Albert Speer, would write in his memoirs: "Hamburg had suffered the fate Hitler and Goering conceived for London in 1940."[14] Hitler refused to ever visit Hamburg after it was destroyed.

10

THE BERLIN BEAR

TWO DAYS LATER, AUGUST 1, 1943, REGENSBURG TRAIN STATION

WHEN FRANZ JUMPED from the train, he saw other servicemen greeted by their sweethearts on the platform. But when they cleared out, no one stood waiting for him. He hired a driver to bring him home to Amberg. On the front steps of his home he did a double take when his mother opened the door. Her hair had turned gray, and she seemed to have aged twenty years in the five months since he had last seen her. Franz knew the hardships of wartime life, of losing a son, and the poor quality of rationed food had done this to her. Franz's father was away, but Franz had expected this. The Army had drafted his father to train horses. Due to fuel shortages the Army needed horses more than ever to pull equipment. Franz thought it ridiculous to call a sixty-four-year-old WWI veteran back into service, but he knew his father had had no say in the matter. Franz's mother showed him a recent photo of his father, who also looked much older than Franz remembered. His father tried to hide this by cropping his hair high above his ears and trimming his mustache short.

That night, as his mother drank her evening beer, Franz asked her why the Gestapo had come to question him. She said the Gestapo had come to see her, too, because of August's involvement in the anti-Party movement.* Franz's mother suspected that his name had been found among old letters and correspondence of other suspects the Gestapo had recently captured. The fact that August was long dead did not matter, as the Gestapo investigated his next of kin.

Franz shook his head in disbelief. He told his mother that August would have told him if he was involved. They shared everything.

"You were flying the world," Franz's mother said. "How do you know what he was doing?"

Franz admitted he had found the "With Burning Concern" letters in August's room but said he was certain the letters had come from someone else.

"What makes you think he was afraid to take a stand, quietly?" Franz's mother said.

"Because he was Air Force," Franz said.

"Did he have a choice?" Franz's mother asked. "Did your father? Did you?"

Franz looked away.

"They made your brother fight," Franz's mother said, "but he was master of his own decisions."

A WEEK LATER, THE TOWN OF WIESBADEN, WESTERN GERMANY

Franz, Willi, and the pilots of Squadron 6 clung to the fence of the Wiesbaden town pool as they watched adults and children laugh, shout, and dive into the cool waters. Franz and his comrades stood with towels around their necks in mismatched bathing trunks. Willi

---

* Asked about the personalities in Bavaria's anti-Nazi movement, Franz would remember, "I did not know any of those people, but my brother did know some of them to some degree. He was very anti-Nazi, as was my family. He had been one of the first anti-Nazis as a young man."[1]

held a basket full of bottled beer. Franz and the others were sweating, but the pool manager shook his head and folded his arms. He said he had nothing against the pilots but could not let them swim because they had brought their bear. He looked at Franz as he said this. Franz held the leash that encircled the neck of a three-hundred-pound black bear named Bobbi.

"We need to take him swimming," Franz said to the manager. "Look at him in that heavy coat. He's hotter than us." Bobbi panted, confirming Franz's sentiments. Germany was wrapped in a heat wave, the same one that had dried out Hamburg and made it burn from the bombing raids unlike any city before.

"He'll bite someone," the manager insisted.

But Franz and the others assured him that Bobbi would not bite because he had been raised by pilots and loved people. Willi explained that Bobbi was a gift from the Berlin Zoo to his squadron.

"How do you know he can swim?" the manager asked.

Franz promised him that Bobbi swam at the zoo. The manager knew the pilots flew from the airfield just two miles east of town, so close it was almost an extension of the town. Wiesbaden had not yet been heavily bombed, and if it stayed that way, he knew it would be thanks to the young pilots before him.

Some children came to the fence to see the bear. Franz let Bobbi walk up to them. The children reeled back in fear. Franz promised them the bear did not bite, "He only licks." One little boy stuck his fingers through the fence and squealed when Bobbi nuzzled them. Seeing this, the manager laughed, shrugged, and from that day onward the pilots and the Squadron 6 bear were allowed to swim.

The pool water seemed to turn the pilots into kids again. They shouted to their friends before jumping from the diving board. Willi and others talked to girls at the pool's edge. They all smoked. A few pilots drank beer while floating on their backs in inner tubes. Bobbi swam around as children laughed and paddled away from him. Everyone who encountered Bobbi became a fan.

Franz had met Bobbi when he reported to the squadron. Before Franz arrived, Bobbi lived in a pen at night. But then Franz saw him being bitten by flies, so Franz allowed Bobbi to move into his apartment with him. As squadron commander, Willi authorized this. He wanted Franz to care for the squadron mascot so he could be free to chase girls. Caring for the bear gave Franz something to do while his leave, the thirty-day gift of life from the Air Force, wound downward.

Franz set his beer aside and scampered up the platform to the diving board. From the board he whistled to Bobbi who followed him, gingerly climbing the same steps, paw after paw. Before Bobbi could step onto the board, Franz ran and jumped, pulling his knees into a cannonball. Treading water, Franz looked up and saw Bobbi gallop off the board. In a massive splash, Bobbi landed a foot from Franz's head.* Willi and the others laughed when they realized Franz had almost been squashed. The pilots, their girls, and the townspeople applauded as Bobbi swam, his nose in the air. The sight made Franz melancholy and put a thought in his mind.

How long can this last?

A WEEK LATER, MID-AUGUST 1943

When Squadron 6 began combat operations, every day at dawn a truck would pick up Franz and his comrades at their apartments in Wiesbaden. During their commute the truck would stop at a deli, where the men bought horse-meat sausages and filled their canteens with coffee. Bobbi always rode to work with them. The trucks carried them past the farm fields that surrounded the airstrip at odd angles, their crops planted in rows of varying colors that from the air appeared to zigzag and camouflage the airfield's one, long runway. On most

---

* "Bobbi never cleared the landing zone (before jumping)," Franz would remember.

mornings the ground was covered by a ghostly mist, a thin ground fog or frost that sparkled in the sun.

Bobbi always jumped from the truck first and ran ahead to the briefing room. Wiesbaden Airfield seemed new and clean. Straight white sidewalks lay between the tower and the squadron buildings. Fresh leafy trees bordered the sidewalks. The hangars were spotless and gently curved around a half moon of concrete where the squadron parked its planes. Even the 109s were factory-fresh G-6 models. Each plane wore the latest camouflage scheme, with wavy, dark green paint on top so the fighters would blend in with Germany's forests if seen from above. The planes' bellies were painted gray-blue to meld with the clouds if seen from below. Willi had claimed *Yellow 1* and Franz had taken *Yellow 2*. The pilots called the new G-6 "the Bulge" because the plane had bulging metal blisters on either side of its nose, just ahead of the cockpit. Behind the blisters were heavier machine guns and beneath the guns were superchargers, added to help the fighters fly faster at higher altitudes.

Every other day the routine was the same. Franz and his comrades would soar up to thirty-six thousand feet above the earth, to battle the Four Motors that flew from England. When the squadron was airborne, Bobbi would stay with the mechanics, riding around in their trucks. When Franz and the others returned, the bear became excitable and would lean its mud-covered paws on them. During Willi's debriefings in the squadron room, when female Air Force orderlies walked past, Bobbi would bolt after them because the swishing sound of their synthetic stockings drove him wild. Bobbi would chase the women until they climbed onto tables, screaming. Willi loved when Bobbi did this, because it allowed him to be a hero and rescue the women.

Bobbi was a lighthearted distraction from the harrowing new mission facing Franz and his comrades. They saw their job as simple, to stop the bombs from dropping and killing the German people. And never could Franz have imagined that such a simple mission would soon pit him against his nation.

11

THE FARM BOY

THE B-17's OLIVE-DRAB paint blended with the lush green mountains as the bomber flew at two thousand feet. The plane rattled as it
bounced in the turbulence from warm air rising off the mountains.
Two young men sat at the bomber's controls. They could have been
mistaken for teenagers who had stolen the plane had they not been
wearing olive flight suits with silver wings on their chests and garrison
caps on their heads with radio headsets overtop. The young men had
opened the cockpit's side windows and their clothes flapped in the
breeze. On their left shoulders sat the blue circular patch of the American Army Air Forces, a white star with a red center and bright yellow
wings sprouting from it.

The plane's pilot sat in the left seat. Although he was only twenty
years old, he wore the gold bar of a second lieutenant on his tan shirt
collar. His face was square and his brown eyes gazed up beneath short,
flat eyebrows. His name was Charlie Brown. Charlie's eyes looked
worried, although a smile spanned his thin lips. He always looked this

way, even when things were going well. His looks were ordinary, his build thin to average, but Charlie was a thinker. For his age, he was emotionally deep and quite happy to talk silently to himself, the best companion he had ever known.

Charlie's smile reflected his rough and humble upbringing on a West Virginia farm like those below his wings. Down there, he had milked the cows before school and lived without electricity. Down there, he had never missed a day of school and had worked as the janitor at the local elementary school every night. On the weekends he had served in the National Guard to earn money for his family. After high school Charlie had transferred to the full-time Army, where he found himself behind the controls of a B-17.

Charlie gripped the W-shaped control yoke while his newly assigned copilot, in the right seat, ignored his yoke to study a map. Charlie's copilot wore gold-rimmed aviator sunglasses that looked small on his round, full face. He was a second lieutenant named Spencer "Pinky" Luke. Behind his glasses' green lenses, Pinky's eyes appeared small and closely set. Pinky was from Ward County, in desolate West Texas, where he had been a mechanic before the war. He and Charlie were still getting to know each other, but Pinky refused to say where he had picked up such an unflattering nickname. Charlie guessed it stemmed from Pinky having a goofy demeanor and growing up in hardened cowboy country. Somehow the name followed him to flight school.

Pinky clicked a white button on the yoke's handhold to talk over the plane's intercom. His throat microphone, like a rubber collar, picked up his voice and beamed it to Charlie's earphones over the cacophony of aircraft noise. Pinky gave Charlie a new heading that would turn them away from their easterly course. Instead they would head south, directly toward Charlie's hometown of Weston, West Virginia. The detour was Charlie's idea. The flight that day was the final mission of B-17 training school for him and Pinky. Their instructors at their base in Columbus, Ohio, had assigned their final training flight with one stipulation—stay in the air for seven hours to simulate a mission over the Pacific or Germany. As a reward, they let the pilots plan the route.

Charlie turned his B-17 toward the new heading. He had been flying for five hours already, but nervous energy kept him sharp. Through the cockpit's side window he watched the fifty-foot wing tilt upward. Two massive round Wright Cyclone engines spun black propellers just feet from his face. Ahead, the B-17's nose looked stubby to Charlie because most of the plane sat behind him. She was a B-17 F model, seventy-five feet long nose to tail. After this mission, Charlie would fly to Texas with Pinky to pick up the other eight men of his crew. There, they would mount eleven machine guns in the bomber, turning her into a "Flying Fortress." Until that day, Charlie liked to think of the gentle plane by her other nickname: "the Queen of the Skies."

Charlie leveled the bomber with the horizon. Through his windshield he saw the West Fork River gleaming in the sun. He knew the river's bends would lead him home. Charlie's eyebrows lifted when he looked west of the river and out Pinky's window. There, a collection of lifeless green barns bordered a grass airstrip. "That's the state 4H camp," Charlie told Pinky. "Beyond it is the airstrip where I took my first airplane ride." Charlie explained that when he was young, a Ford trimotor airplane stopped there while touring the country, offering rides for a fee. He lacked the money to buy a ride, but the pilots took sympathy and made him a deal: if he washed the plane, they would pay him with a free flight.

"Is that how you got hooked on flying?" Pinky asked.

"Not quite," Charlie said. He told Pinky that he had originally been a soldier in the 7th Infantry Division at Fort Ord in Monterey, California. As a form of self-improvement, he had entered the base's boxing tournament in the lightweight class.

"That's where I met the opponent who changed my life," Charlie said. He told Pinky that a skinny old soldier had stepped into the ring to fight him, a man with gray hair and arms so spindly his boxing gloves looked cartoonish. Charlie said he had planned to go easy on the old-timer, to pull his punches, and had even smiled at the man to let him know he would not hurt him. "The referee had barely blown the whistle when, all of a sudden, he slapped me upside the head two or three times," Charlie said. "I didn't even see his arms move!"

Pinky looked unsure if he should laugh or groan.

"The old-timer was actually an old pro," Charlie said. "I knew then and there that I was in the wrong place at the wrong time."

Charlie told Pinky that the man had knocked him out of the fight in the first round then visited him at his stool. The old-timer said something he would never forget. "You're too nice a kid for this army. Check out the Air Corps."

Charlie turned to Pinky, grinning.

"I did check out the Air Corps, and he was right," Charlie said. "Flying fits my personality far better than fighting."

Pinky laughed. Charlie secretly knew that Pinky fashioned himself a fighter, although he was really the nonconfrontational type. He had told Charlie that he wanted to fly fighters and had only accepted B-17s with reluctance. Charlie thought bombers suited Pinky's personality, too, but did not want to say so.

A small town came into view with buildings on both sides of the teal-colored river. Charlie banked the aircraft and orbited over a flat gray bridge. He told Pinky that he was looking at Weston, his hometown. Pinky looked intrigued. The town was tiny. The bulk of its brick buildings sat east of the river, and none were larger than two stories.

Charlie pointed out east of the town to the town's glassware factories, which he said made a third of the country's glassware. He showed Pinky the Trans-Allegheny Lunatic Asylum on the west side of the river. The asylum resembled a haunted mansion. Charlie said that during his stint in the National Guard he had guarded patients there after the asylum caught fire and needed to be evacuated.

Charlie tipped the bomber's right wing toward a gray bridge over the river that ran through town. Old men sat and fished from the bridge, hoping to catch bass hiding under its shade.

"I was almost killed on that bridge down there," Charlie said. He told Pinky that he had been riding in a car driven by his older sister, one of his five older siblings, when another car hit them, head-on. He had flown face-first into the dashboard and broken his nose badly. "That's why I get nosebleeds," Charlie said. Pinky nodded, having witnessed Charlie's nose bleed during high-altitude flights. Charlie knew he was lucky that Pinky had told no one about his nosebleeds, or else their instructors would have banned him from flying.

In the town's center Weston's citizens walked from their shops and homes to congregate in the streets and marvel at the sight of the world's most advanced aircraft circling their town. Children jumped and pointed, amazed that such a large airplane could fly.

Steering the bomber south, Charlie told Pinky he had one last site to show him. He followed the curving river several miles until veering east, over farm fields. Charlie drew Pinky's attention forward. There, on Pinky's side of the plane, was a rundown house with a gray tin roof on a small farm.

"Is your family down there?" Pinky asked as they flew past the farmhouse.

"Nope," Charlie said. "But that was my home for most of my life. We moved out after my mother died."

Charlie explained that he was twelve when his mother, Myrtle, had died from illness. She had been the family's guiding light. Her loss crippled his father, who fell into a depression, and they moved to a smaller house. It took years for his father to recover, but he did. While Charlie was in the Army, his father was elected as the local justice of the peace.

Charlie turned the bomber westward, back toward the river and on course for their base. Pinky asked Charlie if his dad was still living. Charlie said he was.

"Do you think he's ever seen you fly?" Pinky asked.

Charlie admitted he had no clue. He said he had tried calling his dad but could not reach him. Secretly, Charlie wanted his father and everyone else in Weston to see him and know he was no longer the farm boy bringing in the cows, no longer the janitor scrubbing toilets, no longer a PFC in the back ranks of the local Guard unit. He was a B-17 pilot.

With an eager grin, Pinky asked, "What do you think about buzzing the town?" Charlie said it was a good idea and a bad one. They both were aware of the Army's rule that forbids flying beneath fifteen hundred feet over a city. But Charlie also knew Pinky had always wanted to fly a fighter plane, until the Air Corps shot down his dream. Despite carrying a grudge against the brass, Pinky never resented Charlie for sitting in the "lucky seat."

Charlie knew the town's layout like the back of his hand. He also knew if they flew fast enough people would be unable to discern the call letters on the bomber's flanks. Without catching their letters, no one would be able to call the Army and report them.

Charlie rotated the control yoke to the right and steered the plane north, locking once again onto the river as a course. He smiled to Pinky and told him to close his eyes so he could deny witnessing anything illegal. Pinky jokingly held his hands over his eyes, just for a second, then leaned forward in his seat.

With his right hand, Charlie pushed the four throttles forward. The bomber surged with power. The wind whipped faster through his side window, trying to swipe away his cap. Charlie pushed the control column forward, and the bomber dove toward the river, where he leveled off, just feet above the teal water.

Outside Charlie's window, the trees on the riverbank blew past in a green blur. The bomber thundered over fishermen in their canoes, who ducked with terror. Without the weight of bombs or a crew, the bomber raced along at 250 miles per hour. Pinky smiled with delight at flying like a fighter would. The control yoke vibrated in Charlie's hands. Ahead, he spotted his target, the flat gray bridge at the center of the town, where the old men fished.

The fishermen must have seen the bomber racing toward them. They ran shouting. Other citizens looked toward the bridge. One man had never left the sidewalk from the moment the bomber had first been heard overhead. He was a short man with gray hair, and his black judge's robe hung from his frail shoulders. He had been waiting, hoping the bomber would reappear. He knew Weston had a lot of boys in the service, but only one was flying B-17s. He was Charlie's father, Charles Miller Brown, and he knew his son was looking down on him.

Charlie jerked the yoke back, just enough to lift the bomber's nose above the bridge. The plane blasted over the bridge with a thunderous roar. The small brick town flashed past Pinky's window, and he waved at the town's startled residents. Outside Charlie's window, the asylum's white clock tower whipped by his window.* The force of the blast blew the river water over its banks and billowed the dust in Weston's dry streets.

"Who is that crazy son of a bitch?" a man in the street shouted while leaning around a corner to confirm that the bomber was gone.

Charlie's father heard this, clenched his fists, and walked up to the man. "You can't talk about my son that way!" he said.

The man shirked away.

Charlie and Pinky were so busy looking over their shoulders at the effects of their low pass that when Charlie's eyes turned forward they bulged with alarm. A towering green mass filled the bomber's windscreen. He had forgotten about the mountains north of town. The bomber's blistering speed made everything come closer more quickly. With both hands, Charlie and Pinky gripped their control yokes and pulled them toward their stomachs. The B-17 lifted skyward as the g-forces slid their maps and bags back along the floor. Only after

---

* "I was so low that I was level with the clock," Charlie would remember. "Looking back, it was an incredibly stupid move."

the blue sky filled the windscreen did Charlie and Pinky push the yokes forward and level out. Together, they pulled the throttles back. Charlie breathed a sigh of relief. Pinky panted and swept beads of sweat from his forehead. Charlie turned the bomber west for Ohio and asked Pinky if he still wanted to fly fighters. "I'm happy right where I am," Pinky chuckled. Charlie smiled in agreement.

12

THE QUIET ONES

SEVERAL MONTHS LATER, SEPTEMBER 1943, WEST TEXAS

UNDER THE BURNING late-day sun, a rider sat atop a horse on a dry desert hilltop. His horse began to whine and stir. The rider grabbed his wide-brimmed hat and doubled his grip on the reins. The crusty soil below the horse's hooves reverberated. The rider looked upward as a B-17 thundered over him, its landing gear hanging down, its prop blast swirling the dust around him. Downhill from the rider, the bomber drifted onto the runway of the sprawling Army air base called Pyote Field, a place known through the Army Air Forces as "Rattlesnake Bomber Base." The rider galloped away.*

The bomber's tires hit the runway with a *chirp, chirp*. The plane rolled and slowed. Its engines blew a cloud of tan dust from the white runway. The bomber taxied behind a seemingly endless line of B-17s

---

* Charlie would remember, "It was a true cowboy town and people on horseback used to come out to watch us fly as if they sensed some strange kinship between their horses and ours."

parked wingtip to wingtip, opposite five hangars with elegantly arcing roofs.

At the bomber's controls, Charlie leaned his head from his side window. Ground crewmen guided him with hand motions. The B-17 spun ninety degrees to park alongside the other bombers. Ground crewmen pulled up in two trucks with opens beds. They parked one truck at the bomber's nose and another at its tail to pick up its crew. The mechanical ticking sound of hot metal echoed from beneath the plane's wings. A hatch swung down beneath the bomber's nose, the officers' quarters. A canvas flight bag fell to the ground, followed by a parachute in its olive-colored padded pack. An officer in a green flying suit, his sleeves rolled back, dropped from the hatch, his heavy brown boots landing with a thud. He wore sunglasses and a crush cap with a gold eagle on the front. His cap was crumpled like a veteran's even though the man had not yet been in combat. He was Charlie's new navigator, Second Lieutenant Al "Doc" Sadok. Doc hailed from New York, although he looked like a Texan, with the face of the Marlboro man—a strong jaw, small nose, and permanent squint. Doc had been to college, unlike anyone else on the crew, and was well spoken and sometimes cocky. He rode in the nose of the bomber with the bombardier, Second Lieutenant Robert "Andy" Andrews, who dropped to the ground next.

Andy was a lanky kid from Alabama, with a narrow face, pointy ears, and slender dark eyes that sloped downward, giving him an analytical look. He followed Doc everywhere, although the two could not have been more different. Andy spoke with a soft Southern drawl, never drank, and never swore. Doc spoke with a Yankee twang and did not mind drinking and swearing. Andy was sensitive and Doc headstrong. But together in the bomber's nose, they made a balanced team.

Charlie and Pinky were the last to swing from the hatch. At the rear of the bomber, Charlie's gunners carried their machine guns and handed them up to ground crewmen who stood in a nearby truck bed.

Charlie had received his crew at Pyote two months earlier and had flown training missions with them every day since.

The mission that day had been like so many others. Charlie had followed Doc's course out to the base's thirteen-thousand-acre range, where Andy dropped practice bombs on white Xs that had been painted on the desert floor. All the while, the plane's gunners shot at wooden targets that stood on bluffs.

Charlie's top turret gunner, Sergeant Bertrund "Frenchy" Coulombe, approached him. Frenchy looked like a boxer, with eyebrows that hung low over his eyes, a small flat nose, and a square chin. Quiet and tough, Frenchy was from Massachusetts but often broke into a Creole-style French accent to amuse the crew. He doubled as the bomber's flight engineer, the expert in the plane's vital systems. He was also the gunners' spokesman. Frenchy reported that the men were loaded up and ready to depart. Charlie gave his permission for them to leave.

By the plane's nose, Doc and Andy waited in the truck. They helped Pinky aboard. Before Charlie could reach for a hand, a noise stopped him, the sputtering of engines twice as angry as those of his B-17. A green, cigar-shaped bomber on tricycle landing gear pulled up and parked alongside his B-17. The plane was a twin-engine B-26, the hot rod of all bombers. Charlie grinned. He had long wanted to fly a B-26.

The B-26's massive four-blade prop wound to a halt. Charlie saw the short, stubby wings that made the B-26 dangerous to fly but capable of fighter-like speed. Her pilots referred to the B-26 by a variety of nicknames: "the Widow Maker," "the Flying Prostitute," "the B-Dash Crash," and "the Baltimore Whore." The Army preferred to call her "the Marauder."

A pilot dropped from the B-26's belly. He wore a seat-pack parachute and an unusual white flight helmet and blue coveralls. Charlie walked toward the B-26 to talk with him, then stopped in his tracks, jaw dropping. When the bomber's pilot removed "his" helmet, shoulder-length brown hair with curls tumbled forth. The pilot was a lady and a pretty one.*

Charlie turned mid step and scurried back to the truck. Leaning over the side railing, he asked his officers if they had seen what he had seen. They nodded eagerly. Charlie asked Pinky to come with him to talk to the girl. With a look of dread, Pinky shook his head. Charlie turned to Andy.

"No way, I'll screw it up," Andy said, unblinking. Andy and Pinky looked to Doc.

"Sure," Doc said to Charlie. Charlie faked a smile. He had never planned on asking Doc. Charlie had heard Doc tell stories about his girlfriends. It seemed he had a few on every base he visited.

Sweat dripped from Charlie's cap as he approached the female pilot. At his side, Doc chewed a toothpick. The female pilot turned to greet them with a friendly smile on her bright red lips. Her face was oval, her nose turned upward, and her dark eyes almost disappeared as she squinted.

"That's a beautiful aircraft," Charlie said. The girl asked Charlie and Doc if the B-17 was theirs. With a reluctant tone Charlie said it was.

"There's nothing wrong with the Fortress," the girl said cheerily. Looking back at her plane, she added, "The Marauder is no prize. With its small wing surface it has a tendency to drop out of the sky. On approach you've got to land really hot." Charlie nodded, his eyes fixated on the enthusiasm that poured from her face.

"This is our skipper, Charlie Brown," Doc said, introducing Charlie. Charlie chuckled, having forgotten such pleasantries. The girl wiped her hand on her flying suit then shook Charlie's hand and Doc's. She introduced herself as Marjorie Ketcham. She was a WASP based out of Romulus Army Air Field in Detroit. Charlie said he had

---

* "It was a strange-looking pilot—a very attractive female!" Charlie would remember, "It sort of shocked me, but was a very pleasant shock."

heard of the WASPs, the Women's Air Force Service Pilots. They were the girls who flew planes from factories to training units and deployment points to free up male pilots for combat. Marjorie was a graduate of the first WASP class, "the trail blazers."

Charlie asked Marjorie what planes were her favorites. She said she flew whatever the Ferry Command gave her but enjoyed big planes like C-47 transports and B-24 bombers. "The best part about flying them," she said, "are the looks I get from my copilots when they discover they have to fly with a woman! Usually it's a stare that says, 'Oh my gosh, don't tell me she is my pilot!'"

Charlie was about to ask how long Marjorie had been flying, when Doc cut in. He reminded Charlie that the crew was waiting and suggested that Charlie and Marjorie continue their chat at the officer's club. Charlie agreed and looked to Marjorie.

"I'd enjoy that," she said, smiling. She and Charlie made plans to meet that night.

As Charlie and Doc walked to the truck, Doc whispered, "You did good but you've got to hold something back to keep them coming back." Charlie nodded but had no idea what Doc was talking about. At the truck Charlie climbed in first and gave Doc a hand up. Andy and Pinky tried to act like they had not been watching the two Casanovas. As the truck carried them away, Charlie looked back and saw Marjorie shoulder her parachute and walk toward a separate truck. Charlie could not stop smiling. He was very shy and a date was a rare thing for him. "Thanks Doc," Charlie said. Doc just gave Charlie a nod then pulled his crush cap down over his eyes.

———

CHARLIE AND MARJORIE sat at a table in the center of the dimly lit officer's club. Charlie wore his green dress blazer and Marjorie a rich blue skirt and jacket with a gold pin affixed to either collar that spelled WASP. A row of pilots conversed loudly at the bar. Every time Charlie looked their way, he caught sets of eyes looking at Marjorie.

Over drinks, Charlie told Marjorie how nice she looked. She said with a laugh that her uniform had cost her a fortune. Charlie looked confused. "Doesn't the military equip you?" he asked. Marjorie explained that WASPs were considered civil service employees and were required to buy their own uniforms. "If I die in a crash, my fellow WASPs will have to pass the hat to pay for my funeral," Marjorie said. "Since I'm outside of the military, my coffin can't even have an American flag on it."

Charlie shook his head in disbelief. Marjorie said that some people considered WASPs to be expendable. "When I pick up a plane from a factory, it's supposed to have been checked out and flown for fifteen minutes by a test pilot," she said. "But due to the high volume of aircraft production, some test pilots just run the plane for fifteen minutes on the ground and log that as flight time. When we fly a new plane, often it's for the very first time."

Marjorie asked Charlie about himself, how old he was and where he was from. He said he was from Weston and told a white lie, that he was twenty-four. Marjorie groaned and said she was twenty-five. Charlie tried to look nonchalant. Really, he knew he could not tell her his true age or she would walk out. He was twenty. When he had been introduced to his crew, he had padded his age so his men would not panic at the notion of flying under a pilot so young. Now he had to stick to that story.

Charlie told Marjorie about his crew, whom he called his adopted family. He never made his men salute him on the ground, but in the air he made certain they knew who was in charge. "The other crews call us 'the Quiet Ones,' because we've never been caught doing anything out of line," Charlie said. Marjorie told Charlie about her pilot class. Each of the twenty-three girls had been a civilian pilot with an average of one thousand hours of flight time before enlisting.

Charlie and Marjorie lost track of time until a waiter interrupted them and handed Charlie a folded note. Marjorie looked at Charlie with concern. He read the note aloud: "Crew in trouble—need help.

At the front door. Ecky." Ecky was his tail gunner. Charlie cursed his luck. Marjorie faked a smile and told him to go look after his men. Charlie reluctantly stood to leave. He knew Marjorie would be laying over at Pyote for three more days, bringing the B-26's new crew up to speed on the plane before returning to her base. He asked her if she would meet him at the O-Club the next night, at the same time.

"Yes," she said with a good-natured grin. "If you get going!"

———

OUTSIDE, UNDER THE stars, Charlie found Sergeant Hugh "Ecky" Eckenrode pacing back and forth. Ecky was the crew's shortest and quietest gunner, with a face that looked sad even when he was happy. Charlie and the rest of the crew loved Ecky, a simple kid from the hills of central Pennsylvania.

Ecky apologized for spoiling Charlie's date but said that two of the crew—Blackie and Russian—had gotten into a brawl in town. The MPs were questioning them and going to lock them up. Charlie suspected Ecky was involved, because liquid drenched the front of his shirt and tie.

Ecky led Charlie toward an idling jeep. Charlie's left waist gunner, Sergeant Lloyd Jennings, sat in the passenger's seat, his head leaned back. He hopped from the vehicle and saluted when Charlie arrived. Of "the Quiet Ones," Jennings took the prize for silence. His face was square and his chin thin. His tiny lips seldom parted, and when they did, he spoke in a proper, polite manner, as if he were British. Charlie saw that Jennings's lip was bleeding and knew he must have caught a stray punch, because Jennings was a teetotaler and, like Ecky, the last person to fight back. "Lloyd, go get some ice on that," Charlie told Jennings as he steered him out of his way. Jennings nodded and wandered off.

Charlie jumped in the passenger's seat. Sergeant Dick Pechout, Charlie's radio operator, sat behind the wheel. Pechout was from Connecticut and had a slender face and small but plump lips that defined his face. "Drive!" Charlie ordered. Pechout raced toward Pyote, just minutes north of the field. Along the way, he tried to apologize for disturbing Charlie's date. Charlie cut him off. "Dick, I know you weren't involved, so don't bother." Charlie knew Pechout was a techie from Connecticut who loved his radio so much he would have preferred to stay in the barracks examining its tubes and transformers rather than go hell-raising on the town.

Pyote resembled the set of a western film. The main street held a dozen buildings, each separated by vast empty lots. The buildings all had covered walkways and railings where horses could be tied. Charlie imagined that cowboys once rode down the center of the street, shooting up the place. Now servicemen stumbled between saloons, steadied by their buddies.

Charlie spotted a bar with two MP jeeps parked out front at odd angles, as if they had been parked in a hurry. Charlie hopped out and told Ecky to stay and Pechout to keep the jeep running. He bolted onto the porch outside the bar and stood aside as an MP barreled out the door, leading an airman who held a raw steak over half his face. A sobbing girl followed the injured man.

Inside, Charlie hacked from the gray cloud of cigarette smoke that rickety fans pushed down from a high ceiling. He spotted two MPs questioning Blackie and Russian in a corner. Nearby, a flipped table rested on edge.

Charlie was not surprised to see Blackie sitting there smirking, even as the MPs questioned him. Sergeant Sam "Blackie" Blackford was Charlie's ball turret gunner, a talkative Kentuckian whose face was always scrunched by a mischievous grin. Thanks to his backwoods upbringing, Blackie was a Davy Crockett type, as rough and tough as he was personable. No one wanted Blackie's job—to operate the twin guns slung in a metal ball beneath the bomber's belly—except Blackie. But everyone wanted Blackie down there because his dark eyes were the sharpest among the crew.

Charlie pushed his way through the crowd and stepped cautiously over broken glass. When Blackie saw Charlie approaching, his eyes lit up. When Russian saw him coming, he leaned his head back against the wall and stared at the ceiling.

Charlie knew Russian was better than such behavior, and Russian knew it, too. Sergeant Alex "Russian" Yelesanko was a tall, burly kid from Pennsylvania whose Russian-looking features reflected his ancestry—a sharp downturned nose, a strong chin, and big balled-up cheeks. Russian looked like a grown man compared to the others and was the crew's right waist gunner, probably because the waist was the only spot in the bomber big enough to hold him. The crew liked Russian because he was tough but kind. Charlie liked him because he was usually mature.

Charlie approached the two uniformed MPs and tapped the seniormost MP, the one with a sergeant's stripes, on the shoulder. The MP and Charlie saluted each other. Standing ramrod straight, Charlie said in his most authoritative tone, "I'm placing these men under arrest!" The MPs looked at each other, confused, having never heard of a pilot apprehending his own crew. Before the MPs could object, Charlie shook a finger at Blackie and Russian and in his most enraged tone snapped, "Exit this facility, immediately!" Blackie and Russian quickly stood up and left the bar, while looking back to see if Charlie was joking.

Turning to the MPs, Charlie said, "Thank you, gentlemen." He then spun and walked away. The MPs watched him leave as their minds tried to catch up to what had just transpired.

Outside the bar, Charlie pushed Blackie and Russian toward the jeep's backseat. Jumping into the passenger's seat, Charlie shouted to Pechout, "Drive!" As Pechout put the jeep in gear, Charlie purposely did not look back, in case the MPs had changed their minds and followed him out. Blackie and Russian rode in silence while Ecky held on to Russian to keep from falling out.

During the drive, Charlie asked the men, "Was it over a girl?" He was waiting for them to say yes and was prepared to pounce on them with a lecture about how their "skirt chasing" cost him his date.

"Yes and no," Blackie said.

Charlie turned, perturbed, his glare asking for a straight story.

"Ecky went to the bar for a beer and made the mistake of standing near two drunks showing off for their girls," Blackie spouted. "One of them spilled half his beer on Ecky and he came back all wet." Charlie looked to Ecky, who nodded.

"It wasn't that they spilled it on him," Russian said. "It was that they didn't apologize or buy Ecky a beer."

"So we made 'em apologize," Blackie said with a grin.

Charlie turned forward to hide a smirk. He asked the men what happened to Jennings.

"Jennings helped us, sir," Russian said.

Charlie smiled in the darkness as the jeep pulled through the airfield's gate.[*] The perfect record of "the Quiet Ones" was still intact.

———

CHARLIE AND MARJORIE met the next night and spent much of the ensuing two days together whenever Charlie was not flying. They grabbed lunch, went on walks, and met for drinks in the O-Club.[†]

On their last night together, Charlie walked Marjorie to her quarters. On the porch of her barracks, under a light that swarmed with bugs, Marjorie handed Charlie an empty matchbook. Looking inside, Charlie saw she had written her address at Romulus Army Air Field. She asked Charlie to write to her, so they could see each other again

———

[*] "In fighting for one man, they were really sticking up for the entire crew's honor," Charlie would remember. "I couldn't condone that behavior and give them the wrong idea, but I was proud of them."

[†] "I was a gentleman and didn't try to get her in bed or anything like that," Charlie would remember. "It was really a pleasant, old-fashioned relationship."

someday. Charlie grinned and promised he would have his first letter in the mail before her wheels touched down in Detroit. They kissed, and Charlie walked away into the dark.

A MONTH LATER, LATE OCTOBER 1943, CHICAGO

From the train car on the tracks of the train yard, Charlie and his officers peered through a window. Eerie street lamps lined the deserted platform. Charlie and Pinky sat across from Doc and Andy. They all held Cokes in bottles. Their enlisted men sat in cars farther back on the tracks. In his pocket, Charlie carried his crew's orders to a staging camp in New Jersey called Camp Kilmer. From there, he and his officers assumed they would sail by ship to Europe.

A whistle tooted. Steam rose up outside their window. The men knew the train was aiming eastward, but only when the train's pistons began pumping and its wheels cranking did they celebrate.

"Europe!" they shouted, backslapping one another. No bomber crews wanted to go west to the Pacific, where too much water lay between tiny island airfields. Charlie, in particular, feared the Japanese, after hearing stories of the atrocities they committed against captured airmen.

Charlie and his crew debated their ultimate destination. Charlie hoped they were headed to England and to the unit from the newsreels—the 8th Air Force. Pinky hoped they were headed to the Mediterranean, where the Allies had recently invaded Italy.

"There's plenty of Germans to bomb there," Pinky said, "And the best part is you don't have to fly over Germany to do it." The men debated Italian wine versus English beer, London versus Salerno, Italian mud versus English fog.

The debate abruptly ended when someone said, "What about Black Thursday?" The men grew silent. They had all heard the rumors leaking from bases in England. Only weeks prior, on Thursday,

October 14, the 8th Air Force had lost sixty bombers—six hundred men—in one raid over Schweinfurt, Germany. It was the first battle that the 8th Air Force had acknowledged they lost.

"Okay, Italy it is," Charlie and his officers agreed, clanging bottles in cheers to the mud of the Mediterranean.

13

THE LIVES OF NINE

TWO MONTHS LATER, DECEMBER 20, 1943, CENTRAL ENGLAND

IN HIS CORNER bunk at the end of the long metal hut, Charlie tossed and turned. From the cracks in the windows' blackout paper, he guessed it was the middle of the night, maybe 3 A.M. He knew he needed to get back to sleep. His second combat run to Germany was a sunrise away. A week earlier he had flown his first mission as a new member of the 379th Bomb Group. He had flown with another crew then, as copilot to a veteran pilot. This "introductory mission" was meant to acclimate a pilot to combat before he embarked over Germany with his own crew. During the mission, German fighters had passed above the formation Charlie flew in and beat up those behind him. The B-17 Charlie rode in bombed the submarine pens at the German port city of Bremen and came back without a scratch. The mission prompted Charlie to think, *Maybe this bombing gig isn't all that bad.*

Charlie pulled his blanket up to his chin. The room was freezing with an arched ceiling that seemed to trap the cold. Pinky snored in the bunk next to him, and other officers could be heard in their bunks throughout the hut. Engines belched in the distance as mechanics worked throughout the night to ensure that every plane was ready for the mission. Other men laughed as they walked by the hut, their voices traveling through the thin steel walls, probably the cooks on their way to fire up the mess hall. Charlie heard the squeaking brakes of trucks hauling bombs to their planes. Every sound kept Charlie from returning to sleep. The door to the hut creaked open. Footsteps followed.

"Sir," a voice said, directed at Charlie. Charlie did not reply.

"Sir," the voice said again. The orb of a flashlight shined against Charlie's closed eyes. A hand shook his shoulder. Charlie's eyes shot open. He squinted. The man was a sergeant tasked with waking up officers before a combat mission. Charlie sat upright and apologized for having overslept. The orderly told Charlie the time—4:30 A.M. He reminded Charlie that breakfast was at five and the briefing at six. The orderly roused Pinky from his slumber.

Charlie swung his feet onto the cold concrete floor. The fire in the building's kerosene stove had died during the night. The bitter cold of the English winter made Charlie shiver. Snapping open the footlocker at the bottom of his cot, he removed his toiletries and the uniform he had neatly folded the night before. He set his green boxer shorts on his bed and his blue "bunny suit," a pair of long johns with wires snaking through its quilted pads. An electric plug dangled from the suit that a crewman would click into an outlet on the bomber. Alongside his suit, Charlie tossed his olive slacks and shirt. He set his belt and tie on the pile and slid his polished oxford shoes from under his bed. He left his heavy flying pants and boots under his bunk to pick up later.

Pinky greeted Charlie with a whisper. Charlie nervously faked a smile. After getting a mission under his belt, Charlie was no longer apprehensive of combat. But this time he knew he would be flying as the aircraft's commander. He was worried, not of dying, but of messing up and taking nine other men's lives with him. Another thought crept into his mind and propelled him forward. No man in the Army Air

Forces was forced to fly in combat. He had volunteered for this. With that came extra pay and a sense of something intangible: pride. When Charlie reported to the 8th, he had landed himself in a unit that would lose more men in the war than the U.S. Marine Corps.

Charlie grabbed a towel, his toiletries, and shuffled off to the showers in a building behind the hut. December 20 was a Monday. It was time to get to work.

THE AIR WAS stinging cold as Charlie and other airmen hurried through the darkness toward the mess hall, their hands tucked into pockets of their leather jackets. Some carried flashlights because the base was still blacked out. The flashlights' bobbing beams revealed curved Nissen huts, the prefabricated dwellings that looked like half-buried cans and served as barracks, offices, and storage containers. The men passed the base flagpole and message board, which read: "Welcome to Kimbolton, home of the 379th Bombardment Group." Other men rode past Charlie on bicycles, dodging the neat white wooden blocks that lined the gravel streets like reflectors. A tiny light sat between the handlebars of each bike. In the darkness the lights sparkled as they converged from all directions on the long mess hall with the arched roof.

The tin ceiling above the rafters of the mess hall reflected the clatter of mess trays and silverware. Cooks sparingly ladled eggs and ham onto the trays of the bomber crewmen, knowing that most men had little appetite. The meal was primarily a formality. Most of the pilots and crews congregated around barrels of coffee and filled their mugs and thermoses.

Charlie sat with his officers, Pinky, Doc, and Andy. Andy looked meeker and more analytical than usual, and Doc tried to look cool although his eyes darted to and fro. Doc and Andy barely touched their plates. Instead they watched Charlie pick at his food and drink cup after cup of coffee. Pinky stuffed his cheeks with ham and eggs, too inexperienced to have butterflies. The breakfast was designed to avoid serving foods with fiber. Anything that could produce gas in a man could give him the bends at altitude. They made small talk about the base's holiday dance scheduled for that night, one that promised "Coke, beer, and women."

When Charlie stood, his men stood with him. He led them to the briefing hut. They found the room crowded with other officers and grabbed folding metal chairs near the front. Above a small stage were two large wooden doors that hid a vast map of Europe. Lights dangled from the ceiling, upside down cones that ran from the room's front to back. "The room has a man smell," a navigator would write, ". . . leather from our jackets, tobacco, sweat, a little fear, which has its own distinctive sharpness."[1]

Around Charlie and his crew, other pilots wore their hats cocked farther than usual. The veterans' jackets had dark, broken-in folds and whiskey stains. They tossed their white scarves as they joked and planned which pub they were going to hit after the mission. They were pros at hiding shakiness. Charlie saw colorful painted art on the backs of their jackets that glorified their planes' names: *Nine Yanks and a Rebel, Anita Marie, Sons of Satan*, and others. Small painted bombs in neat rows spanned the back of nearly every jacket, one bomb for every mission its wearer had flown. Every man in that room was trying to reach mission twenty-five and the end of his tour. Of the 379th's original thirty-six crews, not one had completed its tour with all ten men unharmed.

A pilot tapped the back of Charlie's shoulder. Charlie turned and saw the jug ears and toothy smile of his flight leader, Second Lieutenant Walter Reichold, who took a seat behind him. Walt was the most popular pilot in the 379th due to his snappy New England charm. Charlie was glad he'd wound up in the 527th Bomb Squadron, the same as Walt. Walt was from Winsted, Connecticut, and in college had been the president of his fraternity, a swimmer, diver, skier, and actor, all while studying Aeronautical Engineering, something he looked forward to resuming after the war. Walt's jacket was bare, like Charlie's, although Walt had flown twenty-two missions. Walt was superstitious. He was unwilling to jinx his tour by painting his jacket or even talking about his tour's end, which Charlie and everyone knew was just three missions from being complete.

"How'd you sleep?" Walt asked Charlie.

"Logged a few hours," Charlie said.

Walt was surprised Charlie had slept at all. Sleeping was hardest at the start of a pilot's tour and at the end. Walt offered Charlie his flask but Charlie refused. Coming from moonshine country, he had seen how alcohol compounded people's woes. Walt took a belt for himself and another that he said was "for Charlie." Then he passed the flask to his officers.

The hubbub ended as Colonel Maurice "Mighty Mo" Preston, the 379th Group commander, entered the rear of the room. A captain shouted, "Ten hut." The men sprang to their feet. Preston strode through the center aisle, already dressed head to toe in his leather flying gear, his jaw lowered like a linebacker's. Charlie felt the air move as Preston passed by him.

Preston took his place before the mission board with an actor's precision. He knew that in a way he was doing exactly that—acting. His job was to be larger than life to inspire the boys. It helped that he had a square jaw, thick blond hair, and that, as one officer put it, "his shoulders were square and wide as the front end of a jeep."[2]

Preston ordered the men to be at ease and seated. With a tight grin, he surveyed the room. Inspiration beamed from his eyes. Preston loved the war because he was good at it.* He was more than a hard-nosed commander. He was innovative. Under his leadership, the 379th had become the first group to fly in smaller, more maneuverable twelve-plane formations and the first to do multiple runs over a target

---

* Preston would remember, "I enjoyed in WWII the biggest success I have had in my day, in my time, in my life. One always enjoys what he is successful at."[3]

if bad weather covered the aiming point. After every mission, Preston passed out feedback forms to his pilots. He welcomed any ideas they had to improve tactics or remedy problems. With his encouragement his men even went so far as to take apart their bombsights to tweak the factory-programmed calibrations and improve the sights' accuracy. Preston encouraged his men to have girlfriends and to live with vigor, hoping they would fly and fight that way, too. Before the war's end, the 379th would prove him right.

Preston nodded to his operations officer. The officer fanned open the doors and revealed the map. The mission's course was marked with red yarn that led east across the North Sea, straight to the German city of Bremen. From there, the yarn shot ninety degrees upward into the sea before turning west and straight back to England. The men were silent. They would only groan if the target was new or deep in Germany. They knew Bremen too well, having gone there three times in the past eight days.

A grin crept across Preston's face. "It's nice to see no one objects to where we're going," he said. The men chuckled. When Preston looked at Charlie, Charlie squirmed. He wondered if Preston could sense his anxiety. The veterans around him turned silent and serious.

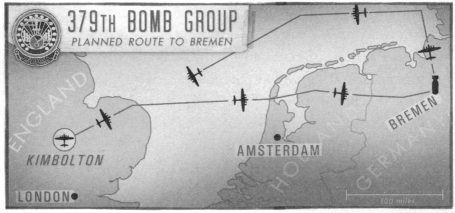

BRYAN MAKOS

"The target for today," Preston said, "is the FW-190 plant on the city's outskirts." Preston explained that nearly all of the 8th Air Force's bomb groups were on the mission roster, 475 B-17s and B-24s. At the time, there were twenty-six bomb groups operational in England and twenty-three of them were going to Bremen. Friendly fighter cover had been pledged for both the road to the Reich and home. Preston warned the men that in addition to P-38 Lightnings and P-47 Thunderbolts, they might see the new P-51 Mustangs and to not shoot them down, even if they looked like Messerschmitts.

Preston stepped aside as a young intelligence officer with spectacles jumped to his feet to explain the mission's nuts and bolts. He warned them to expect a greeting from German fighters, "maybe five hundred bandits or more." He was careful to call them "bandits." No one who had been in combat called the enemy "Krauts" or "Jerries," out of an odd, fearful respect.

The intelligence officer reviewed the escape and evasion plan and told the men that if they were shot down over Germany to move toward the coast. "Try to commandeer a fishing boat there, and sail for home." The veterans laughed at the notion of rowing three hundred miles across the turbulent North Sea. Preston did not stop their laughter—he, too, fought a smirk. He reminded the men that there would be no sailing to Sweden either. "If you have power to get to Sweden, you have power to try to get to England," he told the men.

This time, no one laughed. Sweden was actually far closer to Germany than England. But on Preston's map, Sweden, like Switzerland, had a big black X through it. Both were neutral countries where a bomber crew could land and receive sanctuary if their plane was badly damaged, although the crew would be interned for the duration of the war. Preston hated the idea of the safe havens and had announced that after the war he would court-martial any crew that had fled to a neutral country.

The intel captain resumed his briefing and pulled the map aside, revealing a blackboard that showed where everyone would be flying in the twenty-one-plane battle formation. Charlie took notes before his pencil stopped when he realized he was to fly "Purple Heart Corner," in the lowest spot in the formation and on the outside edge. Everyone knew the Germans loved to attack that spot—on the fringe—instead of barreling into the formation's heart. Charlie had expected this—he knew his rookie crew would have to earn their way to the top.

Using a pointer, the captain made circles on the map, showing the men the flak zones and warning them that the city of Bremen was guarded by 250 flak guns and manned by "the OCS [Officer Candidate School] of flak gunners." In other words, the men shooting at them would be the best of the best.

Someone snapped off the lights and flicked on a projector in the back of the room. The intel captain pulled down a screen and showed the men the FW-190 plant that they would bomb from twenty-seven thousand feet. He pointed out the railroad tracks that flowed into the factory.

For the next thirty minutes, Charlie watched Doc scribbling notes furiously, even though he would receive a typed sheet of notes at the briefing's end. Charlie found himself writing the takeoff time in pen on his left palm—7:30 A.M.—and the weather—"restricted," with a low ceiling. Charlie knew that meant a hazardous, spiraling climb through dark clouds to reach the assembly point.

The lights flickered on. Preston stood up, looking "twenty feet tall," as one man put it. He had saved the best news for last. Charlie expected him to mention the dance that night. "Today, gentlemen," Preston said, "we will be leading the entire 8th Air Force—it's a big honor for the Group and you earned it."

Charlie saw the others grinning, so he grinned, too.

"Keep the formation tight," Preston added. "I'll meet you on the taxiway."

The briefing was over. Charlie and the others snapped to attention as Mighty Mo stormed out the same way he had entered.

AFTER VISITING THE equipment shack, Charlie and his crew gathered outside the briefing hall, each man fully dressed in his leather gear. The sky was still deep with night, so the men stood beneath a streetlight to make their final preparations. The gunners wore their leather flight helmets, having forgotten that they were still an hour from takeoff. On the sidewalk beside them sat their parachutes and their yellow life preservers. In a nearby parking lot, a dozen deuce-and-a-half GI trucks idled, each waiting for crews to climb aboard for a ride to the planes.

Charlie chuckled at the thought: *"The Quiet Ones" have never been this quiet.* Each of the wiry boys looked a hundred pounds heavier in his heavy leather pants and jackets. The officers' chestnut-brown jackets were crisp and looked thin next to the gunners' thick jackets with puffy fleece collars. Charlie had heard that Blackie had wanted to paint his jacket before the mission.

"What will you put on it?" one of the gunners had asked him. "We don't even have a regular plane."

"The Quiet Ones," Blackie had said. The gunners had burst out in laughter. Only Ecky, the short, sad-faced tail gunner shared Blackie's sentiment. When he showed up to fly that morning, Ecky was the only one among "The Quiet Ones" with his jacket painted. In lieu of a plane's name, someone had painted "Eckey" for him, in tall, white, scrolly letters, across his jacket's shoulders.

Pinky handed out escape kits to the crew. Each kit contained a small waterproof bag with a map of Europe, a button-sized compass, and French money. Frenchy's face lit up at the sight of French currency and the idea that if they were shot down on the way to Germany, the Army wanted him to aim for France to seek out the French Resistance. Pinky handed each of the guys a Mars candy bar. Ecky said that if anyone did not want his bar, he would like it. The men, except for Pinky, piled Ecky's arms with candy. None of them had the stomach for sweets. Pinky frowned; he could have eaten it all. Charlie had slipped his chocolate bar into his front pocket but pulled it out and tossed it to Ecky.

As a crew, they waddled to the trucks, each man carrying his cumbersome gear. Charlie saw his flight leader, Walt, waiting to board. Walt invited Charlie to hitch a ride with his crew. Walt's crewmen boarded first then helped pull each man of Charlie's crew up and over the lift gate.

In the dim gloom of 6:45 A.M., the truck drove the crews past B-17s that sat atop concrete parking clusters, each shaped like a three-leaf clover. One plane sat on each leaf. Frost covered the bombers' noses. Large green tents lay outside each clover. Dark smoke piped from the tents and light glowed from within. Inside, mechanics lingered over coal stoves to keep warm. The mechanics had been on the job, working to get more than twenty planes ready by daylight. Now their work was almost through.

The truck stopped, and both Charlie's and Walt's crews hopped to the frozen earth. Looking past the cold, dead wheat fields, Charlie could have sworn the ocean lay just over the next hill. All of England felt like the coast to him, the way the clouds billowed up from the horizon. Often he swore he could smell the ocean, even though Kimbolton lay forty-five miles inland. Charlie turned his attention to his "lady," the B-17 with tall red Gothic letters with white outlines that announced her name: YE OLDE PUB. Charlie affectionately nicknamed her *The Pub*. She sat quietly next to Walt's plane, which lacked nose art.

"Sorry about giving you Purple Heart Corner," Walt told Charlie. "But don't worry. Just stick close to your wingman." Charlie promised he would. He and Walt shook hands, and Charlie went to say "Good luck," but Walt cut him off mid-sentence. "We never say that," he said. Charlie apologized. "Go get 'em," Charlie said awkwardly, searching for words. "That's better," Walt chuckled. "Never say 'good-bye'—it's bad luck."

Charlie saw the light from his crew's flashlights bobbing toward the bombers' hatches then disappearing within. The men were heading inside the plane to stow their chutes, inspect their guns, and check their ammo.

The bomber's crew chief, Master Sergeant "Shack" Ashcraft, approached Charlie. One of the 379th's original crew chiefs, Shack was twice Charlie's age and had a tough, lean face and a head that looked to be shaved beneath his olive-colored skull cap.

"How's she doing, Chief?" Charlie asked.

"Good enough, sir," Shack said. He warned Charlie that engine four was acting up when they started it. "She seems okay now, but I'd watch her," he added.

Shack seemed a bit distant, and Charlie suspected why. Rumor had it that Shack had lost three planes so far—three crews. Shack said the bomber was new to the group, a transfer from another unit, and that he was just learning her quirks. His words struck Charlie like a waiver.

Charlie began his walk-around inspection of the $330,000 aircraft. He beamed his flashlight on her patches from past bullet holes and felt comfort in knowing she was a veteran who had been "there" before. "There" was five miles up, a place without oxygen and devoid of the earth's warmth. There, her living crew would fly and fight in a netherworld of clouds and stranded ghosts.

Satisfied that *The Pub* was secure, Charlie placed his life preserver over his head and clipped it around his waist and under his leg. He approached the nose hatch and stopped. He knew that pilots were supposed to swing up and into the hatch, as he had seen veterans do. It took muscle and guts to enter the bomber from that direction. If a man lost his grip and fell, it would be a painful backward tumble, headfirst onto the tarmac. Entering the bomber that way was showy— "raunchy" as the veterans called it.

Toting his parachute, Charlie ducked under the nose and kept walking all the way to the rear door on the right side of the plane, just ahead of the tail. There, he entered the bomber, like a gunner would.

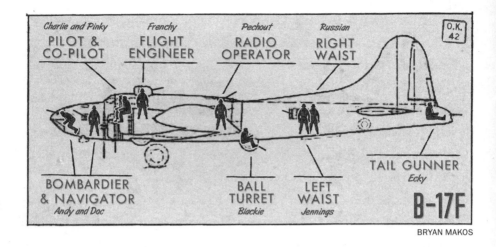

PILOT & CO-PILOT — Charlie and Pinky
FLIGHT ENGINEER — Frenchy
RADIO OPERATOR — Pechout
RIGHT WAIST — Russian
O.K. 42
TAIL GUNNER — Ecky
BOMBARDIER & NAVIGATOR — Andy and Doc
BALL TURRET — Blackie
LEFT WAIST — Jennings
B-17F

BRYAN MAKOS

Inside the plane, Charlie shined his flashlight down the narrow corridor toward the tail guns. The light's beam revealed Ecky crawling toward him. Ecky smiled like a raccoon caught in a spotlight.

"Guns and oxygen okay back there?" Charlie asked Ecky. Ecky nodded. When Ecky smiled, it seemed he needed to work hard to lift his hangdog cheeks.

Charlie walked past the waist windows where Russian and Jennings worked the bolts and checked the breeches of their machine guns. They leaned their guns skyward and stood aside like soldiers on review as Charlie slipped between them.

Charlie dodged the ball turret and its support pole that ran from floor to ceiling. He found its gunner, Blackie, checking the ammo in the radio room where the men always stored it during takeoff to keep weight over the wings. Blackie was writing his name in chalk on some of the boxes, marking them as his. He was known to have a heavy trigger. Once airborne, he and the other gunners would claim their ammo to lock and load. Blackie would lower himself into his ball turret, known as "the morgue," and the radio man, Pechout, would seal him inside. Gunners feared assignment to the ball turret, although time would prove it was actually the safest gun position.

Charlie passed Pechout, who pursed his lips as he listened to a headphone. Pechout tuned the glowing radio dials and tapped the Morse code button as a test.

Moving forward to the bomb bay, Charlie eyed the twelve five-hundred-pound bombs that hung in their racks. The bombs looked thick and harmless. Charlie stopped while Andy shook a bomb to ensure that it had been hung securely. Andy counted the steel pins that kept the arming propeller at the tail of the bombs from spinning. They were all there. Once under way over the Channel, Andy would pull the pins and arm the bombs. Charlie found it amusing that such a meek man controlled so much destruction. Andy gave him a thumbs-up and departed to his place in the nose.

Charlie shimmied sideways along the catwalk, past the bombs and out of the bomb bay. He entered "the office" of the bomber, the cockpit. Passing beneath Frenchy's top turret, Charlie saw Frenchy ahead of him, performing his flight engineer duties and checking the five yellow oxygen tanks on the wall behind the pilot's seat. Those bottles were the crew's lifeblood at high altitude, along with three behind Pinky's seat, seven under the cockpit, and three in the floor of the radio room. Each man would plug his mask into that one system and only use portable bottles when he had to move about.

Instead of getting in Frenchy's way, Charlie went to check on the boys in the nose. He lowered his feet down through the hatch in the cockpit floor and crawled on his knees up to the nose compartment.

Against the left bulkhead, Doc huddled over his desk and checked his compass beneath the light of a metal lamp. Seeing Charlie, he gave him a hand-sketched map he had made of the approximate headings and distances that Charlie should fly, just in case the intercom conked out. As a navigator, Doc was meticulous. He also kept the crew's logbook and doubled as a gunner. His .50-caliber stuck out from a window ahead of his desk, and a cord dangled from the ceiling to hold its grips level.

Andy fiddled with a gun of his own opposite Doc's. A third gun dangled in the Plexiglas nose blister, a smaller, .30-caliber weapon that the mechanics had added as a field modification. Charlie knew Doc would claim that gun, too, and Andy would not object. Andy was a trained bombardier, but aboard *The Pub* he lacked a bombsight. Not all bombers had one, usually just the lead planes. When the lead bombardier dropped, the others behind him knew to drop. Andy's role in "precision, daylight bombing" was that simple. "Precision" was actually a loose term. When one plane aimed and the others dropped blindly, bombs could fall only so "precisely." The 8th Air Force measured error in hundreds of yards and even miles.* The Germans on the ground measured that same error in city blocks and civilian casualties. At that time in the war, 54 percent of the 8th Air Force's bombs were landing within five city blocks of their targets. The other 46 percent fell where they were not supposed to. But one thing could be said for the American bombing method. The 8th Air Force always aimed at military targets, even if that target was nestled in the midst of a city. The 8th Air Force's commander, General Ira Eaker, had said, "We must never allow the record of this war to convict us of throwing the strategic bomber at the man in the street."[5] Error and all, the American bombing method could not have been more different from the common British bombing method. Due to the unrestricted manner in which the British and Germans bombed each other, British Bomber Command often practiced "area bombing," or scattering their bombs across swaths of German cities. This destroyed more than just German war production. Sir Arthur Harris, Bomber Command's leader, once explained the difference: "When you [the 8th Air Force] destroy a fighter factory it takes the Germans six weeks to replace it. When I kill a workman it takes twenty-one years to replace him."[6]

---

* Eighth Air Force historians Philip Kaplan and Rex Smith would describe precision daylight bombing with this comparison: "Consider that trying to drop bombs into a 2,000-foot circle while speeding past at an altitude of 25,000 feet in a bomber under fire was much like trying to drop grains of rice into a teacup while riding past on a bicycle."[4]

Charlie settled into his seat, the place he would remain for seven to eight hours or more, depending on head or tail winds. He found Pinky waiting for him, munching his candy bar. Charlie suspected that Pinky probably had a few extra squirreled away for the ride home. On Charlie's "introductory mission," the veteran pilot had told him to always take a "panic pee" prior to boarding, because there was seldom an opportunity to use the relief tube in the bomb bay that funneled urine outside the plane. That day, Charlie had been so full of nervous energy he'd forgotten the veteran's advice.

In the other planes in the cloverleaf, Charlie knew their crews were strapping in. The sun was rising, and he could see the goggles on the foreheads of the other pilots who studied their instruments.

Charlie and Pinky ran through their checklist until a sound drew their attention to the end of the field. Preston's bomber was cranking over, coming to life, telling everyone, "Gentlemen, start your engines." In no particular order, the bombers began lighting up their engines, creating a patchwork of sound that sprung from random cloverleafs. The cacophony was powerful. The air buzzed with electricity. Pinky squirmed in his seat. Charlie tried not to smile. He had been training for two years for this moment. He had a crew he trusted, a bullet-proof commander named Mighty Mo, and after his introductory mission he had come to believe that the air war was not half as scary as his imagination.

"Clear left," Charlie said, having peeked out his left window to make sure the ground crewmen were standing away from the prop. Pinky looked out his window and announced, "Clear right." They turned a selector switch to "Engine 1" and energized the first engine. While Pinky held the starter button and pumped primer gas into the engine, Charlie turned a switch and the Pratt & Whitney came to life with a *wheeze, cough, cough, cough* as all cylinders began popping. A white cloud sputtered from the engine, and the propeller blew it beneath the wing and across silver grass that the prop wash flattened.

Charlie and Pinky ignited the other three engines, adding their share to the combined noise of eighty-four engines that promised to wake every soul across the English isle.

Just as the head mechanic, Shack, had warned him, Charlie saw engine four running rough, the needles wobbling in the oil and manifold pressure gauges. Charlie looked past Pinky and along the right wing, where engine four sat at the far end. As if Charlie had caught it misbehaving, the engine settled into a rhythm under his watchful glare. Charlie throttled up the RPMs on the engines, one at a time, the prop blast flattening the grass behind the bomber's tail. Satisfied, he backed off on the throttle. Looking at the other clovers around the field, Charlie could barely see the bombers' outlines in the partial darkness and floating smoke. Their engines' exhaust flames burned blue.

As the throbbing plane warmed up, Charlie silently prayed or, as he referred to it, conducted a "short briefing with my Third Pilot." Beneath the layers of his life vest and parachute harnesses he patted the chest pocket of his leather jacket, assuring himself that his Bible was still there. Charlie was a Methodist, and just as he had never missed a day of school, he never missed a Sunday service. "God's on our side, right, Pinky?" Charlie asked.

"He better be," Pinky replied.

Bombers began taxiing past, so Charlie opened his window and motioned for the ground crewmen to slip away the wheel chocks so his bomber could move. Walt's bomber rolled from the clover and merged onto the taxiway behind the others. After the other bomber from the clover squeaked past *The Pub*, Pinky released the brakes and the bomber's bulging tires turned forward. With each start and squealing stop, the smell of gasoline and exhaust filled the cockpit.

Turning the plane onto the taxiway, Charlie saw endless upright tails ahead, each rudder waving the group's mark, a black K inside a white triangle. He glanced out his side window and saw the bomber's wings draped over the narrow taxiway. Because *The Pub* had been slotted for Purple Heart Corner, Charlie found himself twentieth in line to take off, one position away from last in line. Preston's bomber swung onto the runway and set itself for launch.

From the top rail of the control tower, the operations officer studied his wristwatch, while around him the group's staff watched the impressive panorama of twenty-one B-17s snaking around the heart-shaped field. Officers scrambled up the stairs to the control tower, their ears telling them they had not yet missed the big show.

When the operations officer's watch clicked to 7:30 A.M., he raised a flare gun and fired one green flare and then another. Charlie saw the flares arc through the fog. That was the signal to take off, a silent message because the Germans were monitoring the radio channels.

Preston's bomber lurched forward. It rolled, then barreled, then blasted down the runway before lifting up from the concrete with a wing wobble from the plane's weight. Thirty seconds passed before the next bomber launched. Thirty seconds later another followed. Then another. Then another. Bombers named *London Avenger*, *The Old Fox*, *Judy*, and *Damdifino*.

Ten minutes later, it was *The Pub*'s turn. Charlie pushed all four throttles forward. The bomber vibrated, fighting her brakes. She shook like a jackhammer from nose to tail, wanting to run. Pinky kept his eyes on his watch. He raised his hand. When thirty seconds had passed, he dropped his hand. Charlie lifted his feet from the brakes and let the bomber loose. With a roar she tilted her nose slowly downward as she ran.

Charlie felt the vibrations from the wings course through the ribs of the fuselage and through his seat. He had never flown a bomber so heavy or felt the runway so rough through his foot pedals. The engines roared louder. The props bit the air. Charlie knew that when he pulled back on the yoke, the lives of nine men would be in his hands.

The Pub raced past the fields and past the fire truck and ambulance that waited halfway down the strip. When the bomber's nose broke one hundred miles per hour, Charlie slowly pulled the control column toward his chest, until an invisible gust of air rushed beneath the wings and broke the suction of the earth, lifting the bomber into the sky. In an instant, Charlie felt the machine calm from vibrating to humming. With the bomber's propeller blades clawing for altitude, Charlie tapped the brakes to clench the wheels and stop their spinning. A glimpse out his window revealed the balloon tires were unmoving.

"Gear up," he ordered.

Pinky toggled the gear up, right side first, then left. The voice of one of the waist gunners crackled over the radio, "Tail wheel, up." Charlie swore he could feel his gunners' footsteps through the controls as they left their takeoff positions in the radio room to man their stations. Charlie banked into a gentle turn to follow the plane ahead of him. By 7:45 A.M. the quietness of a winter's morning had again descended on the base.

ABOVE KIMBOLTON, THE bombers of the 379th corkscrewed upward through dark clouds. Their plane blanketed in the haze, Charlie and Pinky gripped the control yokes tightly, although only Charlie steered. Pinky kept an eye out for the tail guns of the bomber in front of him. Charlie focused on his instruments, flying by blind faith. He feared ascents like this, the perfect setup for a midair collision.

From twenty-three bases across the breadth of England, nearly 475 bombers climbed through the clouds. Making matters more harrowing, as part of the "Round the Clock" strategy, the Americans were going out at the same time the British bombers were coming home from their night raids. *It's a sky full of terror*, Charlie thought.

Through a cloud, Charlie saw the bomber ahead of him appear briefly then disappear. The mist around his canopy parted, and *The Pub* popped into the clear air at eight thousand feet. Above him, Charlie saw the planes of the 379th spiraling upward. They seemed to fly around an invisible pole. Glancing across England, Charlie saw other bomb groups popping from the cloud's orange roofs, leaving purple holes in their wakes.

From one end of the sky to another, the bombers' radiomen fired flares from their rooftop hatches, signaling the groups to assemble into combat boxes. Colonel Preston flew onward, straight and steady, trusting everyone to follow him. In a B-17 there was no rearview mirror, just the tail gunner's voice.

As the 379th bombers slid into formation, the 303rd and 384th bomb groups latched on behind them. Together, the three groups comprised the wing that would lead the other wings of the 8th Air Force. In the lead, Preston steered gently to avoid a column of magnificent clouds. Slowly, the other wings fell into formation behind Preston's, forming a stream of bombers. From the forefront, Charlie looked out his side window during the turn. Behind him, he saw the long string of nearly five hundred bombers, which made him smile in awe.

At the tip of the spear, Preston's navigator set a new course as the flock of bombers turned toward Germany.

Climbing steadily through twelve thousand feet, Charlie and his crew donned their oxygen masks. A little rubber bag like a tiny lung dangled from each man's mask. The lung expanded and contracted with each breath. Charlie addressed the crew and ordered an oxygen check. Each man wore a throat mic, and to talk, all he needed to do was squeeze a button on a clicker that was wired to a wall outlet. One by one the crew checked in, each confirming that his mask was working. If flak severed a man's oxygen line, he would become sleepy and drunk before he passed out from "anoxia," as it was known. Charlie had heard stories that more than a few gunners had bailed out of perfectly good planes, drunk with anoxia. Waist gunners under anoxia were once found singing and toasting each other in the back of the plane, thinking they were already at the bar.

At twenty thousand feet, Charlie plugged his heated suit into the outlet by his left thigh and ordered his men to plug in as well. The frost on his window told Charlie that the temperature outside had plummeted far below freezing. He piped over the intercom a reminder for the men to keep their gloves on. The aluminum that separated them from the open sky was only a few millimeters thick and so cold that if they touched the metal with bare skin, they would stick.

Passing through twenty-four thousand feet, the stream of bombers crossed over the English coastline above the town of Great Yarmouth and departed friendly territory. Charlie felt a sinking feeling in his gut when he realized that the freezing North Sea lay below his feet.

Charlie told the gunners they were free to test their weapons. Charlie heard the burst of their .50-calibers from over his shoulder as the noise traveled up the centerline of the bomber and into the cockpit. He knew that behind them, his men were firing with vigor toward the sea, a cathartic outpouring of angst. He smelled the acrid odor of gun smoke when Doc and Andy fired from the nose.

"Permission to arm the bombs?" Andy asked from the nose.

"Granted," Charlie replied.

Andy carried a yellow portable oxygen tank back to the narrow catwalk and crossed the bomb bay like a tightrope walker. Delicately he pulled the arming pins and brought the bombs to life. After returning to the nose, he reported to Charlie, "Bombs armed."

Ye Olde Pub was off to war.

14

THE BOXER

EVER SINCE TAKEOFF, bombers all around Charlie had been turning home for mechanical reasons. Three of the seven planes in his flight had departed, an unusually high number considering that a 10 percent abort rate was normal. Charlie's flight leader, Walt, got on his radio. "Goldsmith two-zero," he said, using Charlie's call signal. "Close up on my left wing."

Charlie eased the bomber into her new slot tight to Walt's plane. Together, they glided at twenty-seven thousand feet above the icy sea.

A white fleck fell onto the brown sleeve of Charlie's jacket. Then another fell and another. He risked a glance upward. Frost had formed and spread across the ceiling. The moisture that had been in the plane on the ground had now risen. He ran his gloved hand across the ceiling. White flakes cascaded like snow inside the cockpit. "Well how about that," he said with awe.

"It's going to be a white Christmas after all," Pinky joked, smiling behind his mask.

Charlie chuckled. He knew Pinky and the crew had been looking forward to the Christmas party that the group would be hosting for the children of Kimbolton Village the next day. Despite his hangdog demeanor, Ecky was actually looking forward to Christmas the most. All the chocolate bars he'd been scrounging and hoarding weren't actually for him. Blackie had told Charlie that Ecky had been saving the chocolate rations for weeks, wrapping them up as presents for the kids at the party. Christmas itself was on a Saturday, just four days distant.

The bombers passed over the coastline and onto the European continent. A swatch of cold gray-green fields appeared below. "That's Germany below, boys," Charlie told his crew. "Keep your eyes peeled for fighters." Preston kept the 379th on its southeasterly path. They had thirty miles to go before the turn toward Bremen followed by a thirty-mile bomb run.

It was 11:05 A.M. Charlie knew that if he could see Germany, then German radar and ground spotters could also see him. At that very moment enemy soldiers were calculating the bombers' speed, course, and altitude and feeding it to flak gunners ahead. Even up so high, Charlie could feel their weighty stare.

"Little friends at two o'clock," Frenchy radioed from the top turret. The brown specks out Pinky's window were P-47s, their fighter cover. The fighters flew parallel to the bombers and were easy to see with visibility ranging ten miles and scattered clouds below. The P-38s and P-51s that Preston had promised were nowhere in sight, but Charlie knew they could be anywhere along the eighty-mile-long bomber stream.

"Bandits!" Ecky called out. "High and distant, on our six."

"How many, Ecky?" Charlie asked.

"Can't tell," he replied. "But they're jumping somebody back there."

"More of them to port," the left waist gunner, Jennings, said. "Eleven o'clock."

"Our fighters are moving to intercept," Frenchy announced with relief as the P-47s crossed over the formation to chase the enemy.

"Keep an eye on them," Charlie told the crew.

Preston's bomber gradually banked left and so did the others. Doc told Charlie and the crew what they already knew, that they were turning onto the Initial Point, the start of the bomb run. Seeing the bombers operate in unison, Charlie felt a warm, safe feeling, knowing that the others were there to "share the misery."

Charlie looked at his watch and saw it was 11:32 A.M. They were thirty miles from the target and "on rails," locked into flying a straight course for ten long minutes.

Through his windscreen, Charlie saw an oily black puff of smoke. Then another. Then another. Quickly the sky frothed with a man-made storm. Far below, the 250 flak gunners had begun pulling the lanyards of their 88mm cannons while their comrades cranked handles that traversed the guns, tracking the bombers between earsplitting blasts. Every three seconds the cannons kicked, sending twenty-pound shells skyward. Each gun and its crew operated in a four-cannon battery that fired together to create a "kill zone"—each shell fused to explode at a slightly different altitude in order to embrace a target.

From the lowest position in the lead formation, Charlie had an unobstructed view ahead. He saw the black flak cloud hover like fog along a country road. That "fog" marked his path through the open sky, a trail where angry shells lit the way.

The flak puffs floated past Charlie's window, mesmerizing him.

A flash of orange lit up the cockpit and shook his gaze. Then another. The veteran pilot had told Charlie not to worry about the black smoke puffs but to be afraid if he saw the red flash of a bursting shell. The explosions came closer. They now had color to them and reminded Charlie of "black orchids with vivid crimson centers." At once, four separate explosions burst like lightning just ahead of The Pub, on Pinky's side. Charlie heard the smack of shrapnel and felt the yoke go momentarily limp as the bomber bucked upward then settled down hard. He saw that Walt's bomber, too, had been tossed by the blast and was bobbing for stability.

"We're hit!" Andy yelled through his throat mic, his voice overlapping Doc's cursing.

"There's a big hole!" Andy reported, "We're hit in the nose!"

"Feels like a hurricane in here!" Doc shouted.

Up front, flak had sheared away a large swath of the bomber's Plexiglas nose, allowing subzero wind to howl in through the jagged hole. The two-hundred-mile-per-hour gale pushed the interior temperature down to seventy degrees below zero Fahrenheit. But Doc and Andy knew they were lucky. The nose of a B-17 had little structural support. It was a delicate part of the plane, and if hit hard enough, it was prone to falling off.

"We're losing oil pressure on number two!" Pinky told Charlie, his eyes fixed on the engine's gauges. Glancing out the window to his left, Charlie saw the inboard engine smoking, punctured by shrapnel. He told Pinky to shut the engine down. Pinky reached to his left and pulled back on the turbocharger and throttle levers for the damaged engine. Charlie knew Andy and Doc were watching because he heard their excited voices lowering as if synchronized with the turning propeller as it revolved slower and slower. The propeller and their voices stopped together in silence. Pinky flipped a switch and "feathered" the propeller, turning it knife edge against the onrushing air to minimize drag.

Reduced to flying on three engines, Charlie kept pressure on the control yoke, pulling back ever so slightly to hold the bomber up and in position. To his right, he saw smoke trailing from the outboard engine of Walt's bomber, a result of the same flak bursts that had hit *The Pub*.

"Doc!" Charlie said. "How far to the drop?"

"One minute," Doc replied.

"Oh shit," Pinky muttered, pressing his face to his window. "A shell passed clean through the wing! It didn't explode, but we got a helluva hole!" Charlie leaned against his straps but saw nothing, so he asked if they were streaming fuel. Pinky told him somehow the shell had missed the fuel tanks.

Another burst of orange rocked the bomber. At the end of the right wing, engine four began running wild, accelerating as if the throttle controls had been severed. On the ground, Shack had warned Charlie about this finicky engine.

"She's going to rip right out of the wing!" Pinky shouted.

Charlie told Pinky to begin the shut-down procedures but not to go all the way or else the engine might not restart. Pinky began to shut down the engine while Charlie gripped the yoke tightly to hold the bomber level as shrapnel rattled like hail. Charlie normally liked the sound of hail and thought it comforting, a reminder of his boyhood when he would lie in his bed at night, listening to hail strike the roof of his family's farmhouse. But that type of hail wouldn't punch through the ceiling.

"Bomb bay doors opening," Andy said.

Pinky restarted engine four just before its prop stopped spinning. The engine returned to life and hummed steadily. Charlie told Pinky to keep an eye on the engine and to repeat the procedure if necessary.

"Pilot, hold her steady," Andy said. "Steady. Steady. Steady."

Charlie saw the first bombs tumble from Preston's plane far ahead, and then, like heavy acorns shaken from a tree, bombs showered from the other planes.

"Bombs away!" Andy shouted as he clicked the bomb-release button. He and Doc turned to each other and shook hands, as they always had on the practice range. With a *click, click, click*, the twelve five-hundred-pound bombs were released from their shackles in the bomb bay behind Charlie, each falling a millisecond apart to prevent them from colliding. A fading whistle howled as the bombs plummeted toward the Focke-Wulf plant five miles below. *The Pub* leapt skyward as if overjoyed to have shed three tons of unwanted cargo.

From the ball turret, Blackie turned his guns downward to watch the bombs blossom in bursts across the landscape like a malevolent string of firecrackers.

Their duty fulfilled, Preston led the group in a left bank away from the target, leveling his wings to the north. The strategy was to escape Germany as quickly as possible. Behind them, the 379th had deposited their share of the 2.6 million pounds of iron that the 8th Air Force would drop that month, the first month that the 8th Air Force out-bombed the British Bomber Command.

Like the men in every other plane, the crew of *The Pub* began scanning the skies for enemy aircraft and their own fighter cover. But neither could be seen. They did not know it, but their friendly fighters had departed early, "because of excessive headwinds they had to buck on the way home," the group's lead navigator would note.

At a horrible time for anything to go wrong, the bomber's engine four began running wild again. Pinky renewed the restart process, but with engine two silent and four winding down, the bomber lost speed and slipped behind the group. *The Pub* was not alone. Walt's bomber was also wounded, and bleeding fluids from its left wing. Walt dropped from formation and stayed on Charlie's wing. Under reduced power, Charlie and Walt watched helplessly as the silhouettes of their buddies' planes shrunk and converged in the distance. Slowly, the rest of the 8th Air Force passed overhead, their shadows darkening Charlie's cockpit. Charlie knew that gunners on the other bombers were looking on his plane and Walt's with pity. They had become stragglers.

Charlie followed Walt as he steered onto a course that would take them out of Germany. Pinky tugged Charlie's arm, drawing his attention to Walt's plane. Smoke trailed from both engines on the left wing, those closest to *The Pub*. The smoke grew thicker by the second.

Charlie heard Walt radio a distress call as his bomber lost speed and height. Charlie leaned forward, tracking the bomber as it slipped back past Pinky's window.

"Keep your eye on her," Charlie told his men.

In the ball turret, Blackie had a ringside seat. His ever-present grin faded as he watched Walt's plane dive in an effort to extinguish its burning engines. The plane faded into a cloud bank just behind *The Pub*. Walt's radio cries rang out. Fighters were attacking him. Charlie looked frantically around.

Then Charlie heard Walt shout, "Everybody, bail out!"*

In the ball turret, Blackie saw an orange flash through a gap in the clouds. "Something bad just happened!" Blackie reported to Charlie. Charlie knew this was true because silence had replaced Walt's radio cries. Charlie held the bomber on course and gazed out the windscreen at the empty sky where Walt's plane had been.

"Bandits!" Ecky cried from the tail. He reported five 109s leaping from below and behind *The Pub*, the same clouds where Walt had disappeared and where Blackie had seen the flash.

Charlie's heart raced. He tried to look out his side window to see backward, forgetting it offered no rearward visibility. From the nose, Andy cried, "Bandits! Twelve o'clock high!" Charlie looked up and above the instrument panel. There he saw a flock of eight German fighters climbing far ahead in trail formation. They blocked *The Pub*'s path to the North Sea. Charlie squinted and saw they were Focke-Wulf 190s, each with a big, rounded nose and a sharply angled dark gray body that flowed into a rounded tail. Each wore a yellow number on its fuselage and a yellow band just ahead of the tail, the markings of Fighter Wing 11 (JG-11). Charlie saw them lingering at a distance, as if trying to decide who got the honor of attacking first, them or their friends behind the wounded bomber.

I'm in the wrong place at the wrong time, Charlie thought.

Charlie yelled to Doc to give him a course out of Germany. With the arctic wind blowing through the nose and tossing his navigation

---

* His B-17 on fire and under fighter attack, Walt held the plane steady so his crew could attempt to bail out. His radio operator and both waist gunners escaped before the bomber fell into a spin then exploded. Walt and six of his crewmen were killed.

charts, Doc tried to work.* Stopping for a moment, Doc unzipped his jacket. Despite the subzero temperatures, he found himself sweating.

At the controls, Charlie longed for the safety of the formation. When huddled in formation, a bomber could absorb little bites of damage, each plane taking its fair share. But now *The Pub* was alone. Charlie knew that if an enemy fighter poured even a two-second burst into her, he and his crew would be finished. Then he remembered something from his attempt at boxing. He had underestimated the old-timer who had pummeled him and worse—he had stood still and "taken it." Charlie decided to do something radical. "Let me know when they start their attack!" Charlie told his crew.

Barely seconds had passed when Frenchy radioed from his turret, "Here they come!"

Ducking to see beneath the lip of the roof ahead of him, Charlie spotted two 190s diving straight for the cockpit. The Germans' approach revealed that they knew the fastest way to remove a Fortress from a fight. They were gunning for its pilots or the controls, in either order.†

Biting his lip, Charlie hauled back on the yoke and climbed directly up and into the path of the two enemy fighters. Pinky realized what Charlie was doing and braced his arms on the instrument panel, his eyes wide with disbelief. Charlie held the course. Instead of giving the enemy a flat target with wide wings and a long body, Charlie was presenting the bomber at her narrowest, increasing the closing speed. He was playing Chicken.

The maneuver caught the first enemy fighter pilot by surprise. He opened fire from a distance, his bullets glancing off the bomber, biting metal but failing to deliver a knockout blow. Frenchy remained cool in

---

* Doc would remember, "I felt like a one-armed paper hanger trying to figure out the safest heading home which would not take us over many flak areas."

† "When the first two fighters came at me and opened fire and I saw the twinkling lights, I knew I had made a mistake by volunteering," Charlie would remember.

the top turret and waited to return fire. When Frenchy opened up with his twin .50s, their muzzles belched fire just above the thin, sheet-metal ceiling that separated Charlie's head from the sky. Charlie flinched. Shrinking in his seat, he struggled to hold his climb. Frenchy's heavy slugs found their mark and hammered the 190 in its gaping mouth before it could break away. The 190 coughed flames across its fuselage and bled smoke as it zoomed past, out of the fight.

Charlie stomped the rudder and swerved the bomber left toward the next onrushing 190. "Here he comes, Doc!" Charlie shouted. But in the nose, Doc's gun hung idle in its mount. Instead of firing, Doc was feverishly using his gloved fingers to scrape away frost from the glass. "Get him, Doc!" Charlie urged.

Doc swung his gun toward the fighter and fired. The heavy machine gun bucked and spewed brass casings that clattered to the floor. The 190 fired back, its wing guns blinking. The fighter scored hits, its slugs rattling the bomber's skin, but Charlie's maneuver had reduced its firing time. Snap-rolling, the 190 tried to dive away but revealed its belly in the process. Doc stitched it with a string of bullets. He failed to follow the plane to watch it crash because he became distracted by his shaking knees.

***

Charlie scanned the skies, keeping an eye on the other enemy fighters that circled ahead. "What the hell are they waiting for?" he said aloud to Pinky. Charlie allowed a moment of hubris to run through his mind: *Are they afraid?*

Pinky noticed that the needle in the RPM gauge for engine three was quivering backward. He tapped the gauge. The needle dropped farther. Pinky slapped Charlie on the arm and pointed to the gauge. "Don't tell me . . ." Charlie muttered. Surveying the engine just outside his window, Pinky reported that bullets had shredded the skin around it. Charlie pushed the throttle forward, but the engine did not speed up. He looked at Pinky, who did not blink. Charlie pulled back on the throttle, but the engine did not power down. "The controls are shot out," Charlie said. Engine three was frozen at half power. With one engine out, one irregular, and now one at half power, Charlie knew they were on the verge of a complete disaster.

Ecky called out from the tail, "Fighters attacking, six o'clock level!"

Charlie suddenly realized why the 190s were orbiting above—they weren't afraid; they were giving their comrades a crack at the B-17 from a new direction.

From behind, five 109s bore in on the bomber. Their spinners were black and their bodies a ghoulish gray on top and pale blue on the bottom. They, too, were from Fighter Wing 11, a unit that was slowly replacing its 109s with newer 190s.

Charlie expected to hear the noise of Ecky's guns but instead heard Ecky shout, "Get them, somebody! My guns are jammed!"

Blackie swiveled his ball turret rearward to cover Ecky. He saw the 109s motoring in, fixed in their purpose. He pressed his thumb triggers. But his guns did not bark. *Did I forget to turn the gun selector switches on?* Blackie thought. *Did I overlook putting a round into each of the chambers?* Horrified, he leaned forward against his straps and saw the problem. "My God!" he shouted so everyone could hear. "My guns are frozen!" A half inch of ice encircled the barrels of his twin .50s.

Blackie knew the 109 pilots could see him and knew they would be watching his barrels, so he did the only thing he could. He tracked them with his frozen guns—as a bluff.

Charlie asked Blackie if he could clear his guns, but Blackie screamed, "Jesus, they're firing at me!" Hearing this, Charlie threw the bomber into a bank. Blackie shielded his face with his hand as bullets ricocheted off the bomber's frozen belly and clanged against his turret, cracking its glass but not penetrating.

Up front, Charlie felt the controls grow sluggish and knew the enemy had landed some jabs. Where, he did not know. In reality, half the rudder had been shot away, but none of his gunners were in a vantage point to see it. More reports came through the intercom, all claiming frozen guns. Andy on the right nose gun, Jennings and Russian on the waist guns, and Pechout in the radio room—all reported that their weapons had been welded shut by ice. Of the bomber's eleven guns, only three were operational: Doc's up front and those in Frenchy's top turret.*

After the enemy fighters' first two passes failed to knock the bomber from the sky, they attacked the twisting and weaving bomber haphazardly, every man for himself. Their bullets and cannon shells slowly dismembered *The Pub*.

Spinning 360 degrees in his turret, Blackie tracked the fighters. The gunners' shouts overlapped on the intercom. Desperate for assistance, Charlie told Pechout to patch him into the friendly fighter radio frequency.

"Denver 1, Denver 1," he said. "Mayday, mayday, mayday! This is Goldsmith two-zero, under attack south of Wilhelmshaven. I need assistance!"

The only response was the lonely sound of static.

"Keep trying to get us some help!" Charlie told Pechout.

Charlie felt liquid trickling over his lips, inside his oxygen mask. Pulling the mask from his face he discovered he had a nosebleed, brought about by the thin atmospheric pressure. The blood was freezing inside his mask and stood to block the hole that supplied his oxygen. Charlie took a deep breath and held it. Removing the mask, he blew into it, spraying clear the accumulated blood. Pinky's eyes went wide and he panicked. He shouted for Frenchy to bring a first-aid kit, screaming, "Charlie's been shot in the head!"

"It's just a nosebleed!" Charlie assured Pinky and his startled crew.

Pinky shook his head, having forgotten about Charlie's chronic nosebleeds. Charlie resumed flying. *The Pub* was still responsive as he

---

* The problem of the frozen guns, Charlie believed, was due to the guns being too lightly oiled before the mission or because they had been given a coating of contaminated oil that the crew, on their first mission, had not noticed.

banked, dove, and racked the bomber around on a knife's edge to meet each new threat that his gunners called out. The maneuvers slashed the Germans' firing times and spoiled their aims. The enemy pilots did not know how to react. They had never seen a "target" attack them.

Despite *The Pub*'s resilience, her thin, sheet-metal walls were not enough to shield her crew. A fighter's 20mm cannon shell tore through the bomber's right waist gun position and exploded. The shell's concussion threw Jennings and Russian to the floor. The shell fragments blasted the bomber's skin outward. Both gunners' flak vests had shielded their vitals from shoulder to groin but the vests had not covered everything. When Jennings sat up he saw Russian holding his left thigh skyward, groaning through his mask. His lower leg hung by just a few strips of tendon. The stump of his thigh gushed blood.

"Russian's hit!" Jennings yelled into his mic as he rose wobbly to his knees. Jennings grabbed a nearby first aid kit and knelt over Russian with a pain-relieving morphine syrette in his hand. He fumbled to pry open Russian's flight gear to find a place to stick the needle.

At the bomber's rear, Ecky reported with uncharacteristic alarm, "FW-190 attacking from nine o'clock level!"

Up front, Doc heard Ecky's cry and braced for the impact. *Prepare to meet your destiny*, Doc thought. But Charlie had heard Ecky, too, and threw the bomber into a wild bank. The FW-190's shells flew wildly, missing the bomber's waist and striking the tail instead. Down in the ball turret, Blackie saw sparks and metal cascade from the tail. He expected Ecky to say something. He heard only silence.

His guns worthless, Blackie retracted the ball turret, pulled his mic from the intercom, and flipped open the hatch. Disconnecting from the oxygen system, he crawled out and tried to stand but fell to his knees. His feet were frozen because the heating wires in his boots had shorted out. Blackie needed oxygen. He crawled for a nearby yellow "walk-around" oxygen tank and clawed his way up the bomber's metal ribs to pull the tank from the wall. Plugging in, he twisted the knob. Oxygen flowed into his face before he could pass out. Blackie saw that Jennings had pulled down a corner of Russian's pants and was sticking him again and again with the morphine as Russian convulsed with pain. *What the hell?* Blackie wondered. He crawled to Jennings, who told him the morphine had gelled due to the cold and would not flow.

"Slip the tube inside your glove and try to warm it up!" Blackie shouted.

Staggering to the rear, his feet like bricks, Blackie assumed Ecky's intercom had been knocked out. Crawling through the narrow tunnel under the rudder, Blackie saw Ecky sitting in his seat, his shoulders hunched over his guns, the painted name "Eckey" facing the ceiling. He was not moving. Blackie slapped the back of Ecky's jacket, but Ecky did not raise his head. Crawling closer, Blackie saw that the tail gun position had been destroyed; the glass was gone, and the metal walls had been hacked open to the sky. A cold breeze blew from one side to the other. Only direct hits from several cannon shells could have done this. Blackie turned Ecky by a shoulder then reeled back in fright. Ecky's head had been nearly severed and dangled onto his chest. His guns pointed silently earthward.

Blackie backpedaled out of the tunnel in terror. Returning to the waist, he found Jennings clinging to his gun mount while holding Russian as the plane tossed around. The morphine had worked and Russian was asleep, but now Jennings fought to keep his friend from flying out the waist window. Plugging into Russian's intercom port while holding on for dear life, Blackie told the crew: "Ecky's dead!" In disbelief, Charlie and the others asked for clarification, but Blackie stopped mid-sentence as a flash erupted in the plane's midsection. Blackie saw sparks, smoke, and papers floating in the radio room.

Walking slowly in a living nightmare, Blackie stumbled past Jennings and Russian and toward the radio room. Entering the compartment, he saw Pechout hunched over his desk. The room resembled "the inside of a cheese grater" to Blackie after the destruction from several 20mm shells. Blackie was terrified to inspect Pechout after what he had seen with Ecky, so he waited a second and saw Pechout moving. Blackie put a hand on Pechout's shoulder. Pechout ignored him. Pechout was intensely focused on his radio that had been blown into pieces. He was in shock and had removed his gloves to try to reassemble the radio, to obey Charlie's last order to keep calling for help. Blackie assured Pechout he had done his duty. He gently lifted his friend from his seat and set him on the floor. Blood trickled from one of Pechout's eyes where a tiny steel shell fragment was imbedded. His fingers were frostbitten and bleeding, missing skin from handling the frozen metal radio. Blackie found Pechout's gloves and slid them back over the wounded man's hands.

In the cockpit, Charlie frantically scanned the skies through his narrow windows. With the radio and intercom dead, he knew he could only defend against enemy planes he and Pinky could see. Blinded in a sense, Charlie's maneuvers became more radical in his attempts to dodge a knockout blow.*

Inside the bomber's frozen nose, Doc kept firing. The plane was gyrating so wildly and the 20mm shells were blasting so frequently that Doc found himself looking over his shoulder, to confirm that Andy was still there. He saw Andy hugging the floor. *Are we the last ones living?* Doc thought.†

Behind the controls, Charlie was flailing, flying by survival instinct. He racked the bomber into a near vertical turn of eighty degrees, slamming his crewmen and their gear in a landslide against their compartments' walls. In the waist, Jennings held Russian back from falling out the window. Charlie aimed at any fighters he saw coming in, knowing it was better to duel head-on than have them

---

* Charlie would remember, "I became angry and forgot that many of the crew were not held in place by belts and, in the case of the waist gunners, they could be thrown or could fall from the aircraft through the open windows."

† "The silence on the intercom was more terrifying than the sounds of the exploding shells," Doc would remember.

hanging on his tail. For nearly ten minutes, *The Pub* had stayed on her feet after a pummeling. But the punch-drunk bomber's turns grew sluggish.

In the nose, Doc's gun stopped rattling, its ammo spent. One of Frenchy's twin .50s jammed. The bomber was down to one operational gun in Frenchy's turret. In sheer desperation, Charlie flew in circles, pulling tighter and tighter. He was flying in a near-vertical bank with the bomber's left wing pointed toward the earth when bullets ripped through the cockpit's ceiling. In a shower of glass and sparks the bullets passed between Charlie and Pinky and punctured the oxygen tanks behind their seats. A bullet fragment ricocheted and embedded itself against Charlie's left shoulder blade. He ignored the sting and gripped the yoke tighter. With a violent hiss the bomber's oxygen system vented a white cloud that Charlie felt behind his seat back.

The Pub shook from the tail forward, almost breaking Charlie's turn. Charlie knew an enemy plane was behind him, chewing up his tail section; he could feel it. But he did not know that a fighter had just shot off his left horizontal stabilizer, leaving just a three-foot stub from what had been a sixteen-foot rear wing.

Charlie clutched his mask as the oxygen slowed its flow. Gasping, he said to Pinky, "We gotta reverse the circle or they're going to nail us!" Charlie rolled the bomber violently to the right, turning the left wing upward from the earth to the horizon then to the sky. But the bomber did not stop rolling. With a stabilizer shot off, the left wing kept tipping until the bomber flipped and entered a slow, upside-down, flat spin. Through his groggy eyes, Charlie saw Pinky hanging upside down by his straps, unconscious. The world outside his window spun. Charlie's mask stopped feeding him oxygen and he pulled it down around his neck. He gulped for air but only an oxygen-poor chill filled his lungs. As Charlie's eyes faded, his head went limp. Through the cockpit ceiling window above him, he saw German farm fields orbiting five miles below. Then he, too, closed his eyes as *The Pub* spiraled toward the patchwork earth.

AT THE SAME TIME, THIRTY MILES NORTH

From above, the gray 109 with a dark green spine blended with the pine trees as it approached the air base at Jever, Germany. The plane drifted downward, landed on the gray concrete runway, and taxied up to ground crewmen in heavy parkas who directed the plane to park on a slab of concrete. The base had circular parking spaces nestled among the trees, but ground crewmen knew this fighter was not one of theirs—it wore the red Berlin Bear of JG-27's II Group—so they guessed its owner was dropping in for a pit stop like others had before from the fighting over Bremen.

The 109's white spinner had barely stopped whirling when the ground men swarmed the plane, connecting a hose from it to a fitting in the concrete that led to an underground fuel tank. Others pulled up with a *kettenkrad*, a small vehicle that was half-motorcycle in the front and half-tank in the back. Wooden ammo boxes filled the *kettenkrad*'s rear bed. The crewmen could see that they were dealing with an ace, because the plane's rudder wore twenty-two white victory marks and a low number on its flanks, *Yellow 2*.

As he slid from the wing in his black leather flight gear, Franz's thick black boots stomped the earth. He knew Jever from his flight instructor days, when the field had been a training school for bomber pilots. It lay on a peninsula northwest of Bremen, just ten miles from the North Sea. The lead ground crewman, a portly sergeant with his hood pulled over his cap, approached Franz and saluted. Franz had been promoted a month earlier and now wore the rank of a lieutenant on the shoulders of his jacket.

"Any luck, sir?" the sergeant asked. Franz shook his head and explained that he thought he had knocked down a B-17 just northwest of Bremen, but he had lost sight of it before it crashed. The sergeant asked Franz how he had attacked it, but instead of answering Franz just smiled and pointed to the man's clipboard. Remembering his duty, the sergeant handed Franz the clipboard and Franz signed off with his hand still shaking, authorizing the ground crewmen to start the fuel and ammo flowing into the 109. The time was 12:30 P.M. With wounded bombers limping across Germany, Franz was impatient to get back into the fight.

He needed one more bomber victory. Since arriving at Wiesbaden, Franz had shot down three bombers, raising the score on his rudder to twenty-two victories. However, his rudder did not reflect the bonus points for victories over bombers. With bonus points added, his score was 27.* One more bomber victory would push him through "magic 30" and qualify him for the Knight's Cross.

Willi had scored a bomber that day, a B-24, but did not need the points. A month before, Schroer had hung the Knight's Cross around Willi's neck. When Willi told Franz he was leading the squadron home, Franz said to proceed without him. Willi was miffed. He knew it was unlike Franz to push his luck. Franz had always been the cautious one in their duo. Alone, Franz landed to rearm, refuel, and keep fighting.

Meandering from his plane, Franz lit a cigarette in a nearby blast pen to steady his hand. It was bitterly cold although no snow had fallen. Over the speaker system, the Air Defense radio channel blared across the field, announcing the location of bombers over Germany, along with the packs of American fighters that were trying to shepherd them home. Every time the rumble of an engine or the sound of a diving plane echoed from behind the treetops, Franz and the ground crewmen scanned the skies.

Alarmed, the portly sergeant ran to Franz and reported that they had found an American .50-caliber slug in his plane's radiator. The sergeant suggested they wheel the fighter in for repair, but Franz forbid him to, insisting he was going back up. The sergeant looked at Franz

---

* One of Franz's three bomber victories had counted as only two points, instead of the usual three points because another pilot had wounded the plane before Franz destroyed it. This is why he had the equivalent of 27 victories, not 28.

as if he was crazy. He had just given the pilot an "out," a reason to stay on the ground and a guarantee that he could live to see another day—but instead, the pilot wanted to go back up into the shooting gallery of a cold hell. The sergeant returned to his men and shook his head, unable to understand Franz's obsession. But to Franz, the Knight's Cross was more than a bragging right. It was a sign of honor that he had done something good for his people. Franz had seen things the sergeant had not. Franz had seen Hamburg from above—eight blackened miles of city where people had once lived. He had seen small villages flattened as if they had mistakenly fallen in the footsteps of a giant. To Franz, his duty was to the people below whom he could never see but who were looking up to him. If he stopped a heavy bomber from reaching England and coming back to bomb his people, it would be a personal triumph. If they gave him the Knight's Cross for doing so, the victory would be all the sweeter. As the ground crewmen topped off his fighter, Franz watched the skies and listened to the radio, knowing he needed just three more points, one more bomber.

15

A HIGHER CALL

MEANWHILE, ABOVE OLDENBURG, GERMANY

THE PUB DROPPED from the sky in a spin, accelerating as she passed through twenty-two thousand feet . . . twenty thousand . . . eighteen thousand. . . .

In the cockpit, gravity pulled Pinky's limp body against the wall and Charlie across the gap between their seats.

The fall continued to sixteen thousand feet . . . fourteen thousand . . . twelve thousand. . . .

Some twenty seconds later the bomber spun through ten thousand feet, where its spiral broke into a nosedive. The plane plunged straight down. At low altitude, the cockpit began to flow with oxygen-rich air. Charlie regained consciousness. Shaking his head he saw the German landscape through his windscreen, rushing closer by the second. The ground was barely a mile below. Pressed back into his seat, Charlie strained for the controls. He gripped them and hauled back.

"Pinky!" Charlie yelled to his unconscious copilot. Pinky still wore his oxygen mask, one that ironically now prevented him from breathing. Charlie reached over and tore the mask from Pinky's face.

"Damn it, wake up!" Charlie shouted. Pinky began to breathe but remained unconscious.

Charlie toggled the bomber's flaps to create drag and slow the plunge. Vibrations rattled the bomber, threatening to shake it to pieces. Ahead, Charlie saw that he was diving straight toward a German city.

The altimeter wound backward: 7,000 feet . . . 6,000 . . . 5,000 . . . Charlie strained with all his might. The trees and homes of the suburbs of Oldenburg came into focus. At three thousand feet, *The Pub* did something that no B-17 missing a stabilizer should have done. She stopped diving. For reasons inexplicable, her wings began to flutter. The plane flirted with the idea of lift.

Charlie dug his heels into the rudder pedals and pulled back on the yoke with his whole body. The bomber's wings took bigger bites of the air and surged at the taste. Passing beneath two thousand feet, after falling nearly five miles, the bomber's wings began flying again. But the plane was still dropping. Charlie's arms shook.

Just when Charlie was sure *The Pub* was going to scrape the houses below, her nose lifted to the horizon and she leveled out, blowing leaves from trees and shingles from homes. Charlie had not flown so low over a town since buzzing Weston. The German people below him gazed up in awe, forgetting to run from the green bomber that thundered overhead, rattling their windows.

Charlie took a deep breath and looked over at Pinky. Pinky held his head and glanced out the window at the treetops passing beneath him. "Are we in England?" he asked, groggily.

"Germany," Charlie said, uninterested in explaining what Pinky had missed. Charlie scanned the skies around the bomber for enemy fighters, expecting them to have followed him down. He saw only emptiness. *They're probably at the bar lifting steins of beer and singing,*

Charlie thought.* With trepidation, Charlie raised the flaps, afraid the bomber would drop out of the sky without their lift. But she surprised him and kept flying.

Charlie called into his throat mic, "Pilot to navigator." Then he remembered the mics were out. "Get Doc," Charlie told Pinky. Pinky unstrapped himself, leaned into the tunnel that ran under the cockpit floor, and shouted for Doc.

Doc emerged in the cockpit. Charlie told him to figure out where they were and establish a course for home. As Doc departed, Charlie shouted behind him, telling him to fetch Andy. Charlie shouted for Frenchy.

Frenchy slowly dropped from his turret and poked his head into the cockpit. He moved shakily and held a gloved hand over his temple where he had smashed his head against his gun butts. Because Frenchy was the plane's fix-it guy, Charlie had a job for him. "I need a damage report," Charlie told him.

Frenchy disappeared to check on the plane as Andy climbed into the cockpit. Charlie told Andy to check on the crew.

Frenchy returned shortly. "We're chewed to pieces," he said. "The left stabilizer is all but gone. The hydraulics are bleeding from the wings. There's holes in the fuselage big enough to climb through, and up front the nose is open to the sky. I don't know how Doc can work with his charts whipping all over the place." Charlie saw Frenchy wincing and barely able to stand, so he told him to go lie down in the waist with the others. Frenchy insisted on staying near his guns. He sat down against a bulkhead beneath his turret.

---

* The Germans did claim the bomber as destroyed and gave credit for the victory to Lieutenant Ernst Suess, a sixty-seven-victory ace. That morning Suess had picked up his pregnant wife at the train station in Oldenburg so they could spend Christmas together. During his attack on *The Pub*, his plane was damaged and Suess bailed out. According to his comrade, Viktor Widmaier, Suess's parachute failed to open and his comrades found him, dead, in a field west of Bremen.

Doc came up from below and handed Charlie a map. Pointing, Doc showed Charlie that they were northwest of Oldenburg. The fastest way out of Germany, he explained, was to fly north thirty-five miles to the sea. Charlie looked up and saw turbulent, billowing clouds rising ahead, where Doc's map said the coast should lie. Doc had drawn the course in red pencil. The route was fine by Charlie, but he saw a new problem. Along the coastline, the map showed countless concentric red rings, each identifying a flak battery. They were strung along the entire coast.

"Is there any gap through the guns?" Charlie asked.

"Nope, they overlap," Doc said. "It's one of the heaviest-defended flak zones in all of Germany."

The Germans had given a name to their fortified coastline that stretched from France to Germany then up to Norway: "the Atlantic Wall." Its defenses were especially strong where they guarded the homeland, to prevent an amphibious assault. Charlie shook his head. On one good engine, two rough ones, and a nose full of drag, the bomber was lucky to be pulling 135 miles per hour, just above its stall speed.

As Doc departed, Charlie stopped him. "Tighten your chute," Charlie said. Doc nodded.

Andy found Jennings seated against the fuselage wall by the left waist gun, cradling Russian in his lap with Pechout at his side. Russian's eyes were closed. His mangled lower leg jutted at a right angle to his thigh. Blood was everywhere on the walls and covering the floor.

"Is he dead?" Andy asked.

"No, the freezing air stopped the bleeding," Jennings said. "But I need help putting a tourniquet on him."

Andy saw the pine trees of northern Germany through holes in the right fuselage wall, where the shells had entered that hit Russian.

Andy knelt by Pechout, who muttered an incoherent greeting.

"Where's Blackie?" Andy asked.

Jennings said that Blackie was back in his turret, checking if his guns had thawed.

Andy moved toward the rear of the bomber.

"Don't go there," Jennings told him. "Ecky's dead."

Andy heeded his advice. Wheeling, he hurried to the cockpit to report to Charlie.

"It's like an operating room back there," Andy said, as he described the casualties. "Everyone's out of it."

Charlie instructed Andy to go back and ensure that the others were wearing flak jackets, helmets, and parachutes. Andy looked confused. "We're approaching the coastal flak," Charlie told him. "We're going to try to barrel through it." Andy started to say something, but no words came out. Pinky's cheeks could not have sagged further with a look of dread. Andy hurried from the cockpit to retrieve his flak vest.

But there was an error in Doc's course that neither he nor Charlie had spotted. When Doc drew their course on the violently convulsing map, he was so fixated on the flak rings that he had failed to see that the course he drew would dodge the village of Jever, but not its German airfield.

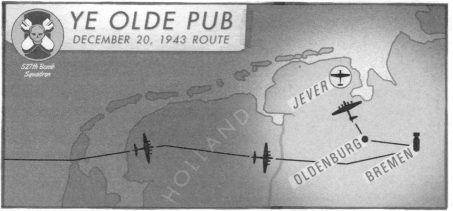

BRYAN MAKOS

FRANZ HEARD THE bomber before he saw it. The ground crewmen had just strapped in a fresh belt of 20mm cannon shells and slammed shut his fighter's engine cowling when a low drone emanated from south of the field, drawing everyone's attention. There, several miles away, a B-17 flew toward them, so slow and so low it looked like it was coming in to land. The drone grew louder and deeper, like the thundering of a thousand bass drums. The sergeant's eyes lit up. Franz flicked away his cigarette and climbed up the wing into his plane. The ground crewmen yanked the fuel lines. Tossing on his straps, Franz made a twirling motion with an outstretched finger, and two crewmen cranked the engine over. As the revolutions climbed, Franz tugged the starter lever and ignited his fighter's engine.

Franz and the others watched, their mouths agape, as the bomber skirted the base and disappeared behind the trees. Franz knew the bullet was in his radiator and could have caused the engine to overheat at any minute. He did not care. Franz throttled forward and the ground crew scrambled out of his way. Franz saluted the portly sergeant. Without stopping for clearance from the tower, Franz fast-taxied to the runway and blasted off toward the bomber, in pursuit of his Knight's Cross.

PINKY HAD BEEN stewing ever since Charlie told Andy to gather parachutes for the men. Finally, Pinky blurted, "You know we're never going to make it!" Charlie focused impassively on the horizon. He knew Pinky was right. One hit from a flak shell or even a near miss would shake the bomber from the sky.

"Should we jump?" Pinky asked.

"Russian won't survive if he lands in the woods," Charlie said.

Pinky nodded.

"There's another option," Charlie said. "Go deliver a message to the men. I'm going to try to fly back to England but anyone who wants to bail out has my permission."

Pinky agreed. Charlie and Pinky both knew that a P.O.W. camp would be preferable to being blown apart by flak or ditching in an icy sea. As Pinky departed, Charlie put a hand onto his copilot's shoulder. "I'm going to give us some altitude," Charlie said. "If anyone wants to jump, it needs to be right now."

Pinky departed as Charlie pulled back on the stick to climb. *The Pub* resisted at first, content to fly level and low. Charlie tugged harder. The bomber climbed, slowly, straining through two thousand feet, where Charlie felt the plane begin to shake. Leveling off, he saw the cold, gray coastline in the distance.

Charlie knew his odds had been better down along the treetops. At least there the flak gunners would have had a tougher time aiming at him. But he had made his choice, to sacrifice himself and Russian if need be, to allow seven men to jump.

Charlie held the bomber steady and waited for his men to hit the silk. To Charlie his decision was not heroic—it was his job as their leader. In his mind, the rest of his men still had a chance to live.

―――――――

BEHIND *THE PUB*, Franz's 109 appeared, a small black speck racing above the forests. Climbing up from the treetops, Franz began his attack run.

In his ball turret, curled around his guns, Blackie eyed the coast ahead, a finish line and invisible fence he longed to clear. He never considered that a firing squad of flak guns lay there. Nor did Blackie have any idea that his buddies in the fuselage above him were debating whether or not to bail out. Instead, he worked the triggers of his frozen guns, squeezing them, hoping the guns would thaw. They made a dull clicking sound.

Remembering his duty, Blackie spun his turret to watch for enemy fighters. He planned to bluff them if they attacked. He stopped his spin when his guns faced the tail.

"Dear Jesus," he muttered. There, a mile away, a 109 was climbing straight for him.* Soon the 109 had climbed above Blackie's line of sight. Blackie wanted to shout, but his microphone was dead. He wanted to slap his turret to summon his buddies' attention, but no one would have heard him. He was alone.

Franz saw the bomber's ball turret aim toward him so he climbed even with the bomber's tail, above the ball turret's line of sight. Because the bomber was alone, without the overlapping guns of a formation to protect it, Franz decided to attack it from behind. He throttled back to steady his approach and avoid overflying the slow, wounded machine. He worked the rudder and settled his *Revi* gun sight on the bomber's tail, where he knew a tail gunner sat with two guns aiming back at him. He hovered his gloved index finger ahead of the trigger. Whoever fired first and straightest, Franz decided, was the man meant to live.

Franz squinted and aimed through his gun sight. He lowered his finger onto the trigger, a pound of pressure away from igniting the guns. When the bomber's thin wings spread past the ring of his gun sight, Franz narrowed his eyes on the tail gun position, looking for the blink of his opponent's guns. But nothing happened.

Something's wrong, Franz thought when he saw the tail guns pointing lifelessly to earth. His eyes fixed on the bomber's left stabilizer. He realized it had been shot away. "My God," he muttered. "How are you still flying?" When the bomber's wings filled his windscreen, Franz knew it was time to shoot. His finger arched on the trigger, ready to squeeze. But still the tail guns pointed silently downward.

From a hundred yards away, Franz saw the tail gunner's position and knew why the nearly four-foot-long guns had never been raised. Shell fragments had obliterated the compartment. The glass was missing from its windows. Nursing his throttle back to match the bomber's

---

* Blackie would remember, "My guns were frozen up and I had my barrels pointed at him. He kept closing and I couldn't shoot."

speed, Franz settled in behind the tail. He saw fist-sized holes on one side of the tail gunner's position where 20mm shells had entered. On the other side, he saw where they had burst, peeling the bomber's skin outward.

Then Franz spotted him, the tail gunner. With the rudder's frayed fabric silently flapping overhead, Franz saw the gunner's fleece collar red with blood. Inching closer to a plane's length from the bomber, Franz saw the gunner's blood frozen in icicles where it had streamed down the barrels. Franz lifted his finger from the trigger.

There, floating behind the B-17, Franz looked at the bomber with the curiosity of his boyhood, a time when he would run from his house at the sound of an airplane. In a rush of long-dormant emotions, Franz forgot he was a German fighter pilot.

Franz had seen planes come back from battle shot to pieces. But he had never seen anything like this. Every foot of the bomber's metal had silver holes where the bullets had entered and flaked away the paint. Franz became entranced with wonder. Pushing the rudder pedal and nudging the throttle forward a bit, Franz swung his 109 past the tail and flew along the bomber's right side, parallel to the fuselage.

Franz scanned the craft for guns that the bomber's crew could still turn on him. He saw that the waist gun was missing, blasted from its mount. He saw that the top turret was empty and that the radio room had been blown apart. He flew just high enough that he was beyond the elevation of the ball turret. Then, alongside the bomber, Franz saw something troubling. Exploding shells had stripped away its skin in the waist. Through the plane's exposed ribs he saw its crew, huddled over one another, caring for their wounded. Moving forward, Franz settled his 109 into position above the bomber's right wingtip. He could see that the bomber's nose was blown away. The bomber flew as if held up by an invisible string.

What now? Franz thought.

Suddenly, movement beneath the bomber drew his eyes. Franz

watched as the ball turret gunner swiveled his guns toward him. *You'd shoot me if you could*, Franz thought. He knew the turret lacked the elevation to aim at him.

From his turret, Blackie looked in shock at the 109 pilot. A minute before, Blackie had prepared to die, expecting the 109 pilot to shoot him from the sky after disappearing behind the tail. But the pilot had never fired. Now, instead, the German fighter pilot flew formation with the American bomber.* Blackie abandoned his efforts to clear his guns. Instead, he folded his hands. "What are you waiting for?" Blackie said quietly as the German's eyes met his.

The Franz Stigler who went to Africa to avenge his brother's death would have had an answer. He would have destroyed the bomber and killed its crew. But there, in the desert, and over ancient Sicily, the last of Europe's Knights had taught Franz Stigler a new code. Their code said to fight with fearlessness and restraint, to celebrate victories not death, and to know when it was time to answer a higher call.

Franz gazed at the men in the waist tending one another's wounds. He looked into the ashen face of the ball turret gunner. He thought about what his brother August would have done.

A gear clicked in Franz's soul. He laid a hand over the pocket of his jacket and felt his rosary beads within. *This will be no victory for me*, Franz decided. *I will not have this on my conscience for the rest of my life.*[1]

Franz saw the coast a few miles ahead. There he knew alarms were blaring and soldiers were running to their guns. Any second explosions would ring out, showering the bomber in a rain of steel. Franz had chosen to spare the bomber's crew from his own guns, a gesture that would have been enough for most men. But Franz decided he would try something more.

Looking along the wing and into the cockpit he saw that the copi-

---

* Blackie would remember, "He came up on our right wing, so close that his wing actually overlapped ours. I kept my dead guns trained on him. We looked directly at each other."

lot was absent. Through the shadows he saw the pilot in the left seat, his hands gripping the controls. Franz waved, trying to get the pilot's attention, but the man stared straight ahead. Franz remained on the bomber's wing, the machine's laboring engines drowning out his 109's purr. He wanted to shout to the pilot, to tell him that time was running out.

———

INSIDE THE BOMBER'S cockpit, Charlie's eyes alternated between his instruments and the white coastline that filled the windshield. He knew the flak guns would start popping any second. He hoped Pinky and the others had jumped.

Charlie leaned forward to check the gauges, watching for any signs of trouble from engine four, his problem child. Glancing out the copilot's window at the engine, Charlie saw a sight that made his heart freeze for a second.

A gray 109 with a green spine bobbed in the turbulence, three feet from *The Pub*'s right wingtip.*

Charlie shut his eyes and shook his head, thinking he had slipped into a bad dream. But when he opened his eyes, the 109 was still there.

In the nose, Doc caught a glimpse of the same dark shape through Andy's window. He locked his eyes on the 109 and witnessed something unbelievable.

The German pilot nodded to the American pilot.

Charlie saw the German nod at him but thought he was seeing things. Instead of nodding back, Charlie just kept staring. In the nose, Doc remained glued to Andy's window.

Pinky climbed into the cockpit and took his seat beside Charlie. "We're staying," he said. "The guys all decided—you're gonna need help to fly this girl home."

---

* "I look out and there's the world's worst nightmare sitting on my wing," Charlie would remember. "That little sucker looked like he owned me and belonged there."

Pinky expected Charlie to grin or object. Charlie stared past him. Pinky followed Charlie's eyes out the window.

"My, God, this is a nightmare," Pinky said.

Unblinking, Charlie said to Pinky, "He's going to destroy us."

FROM HIS PERCH on the bomber's wing, Franz saw the two pilots staring at him. He saw shock and fear in their eyes. They knew they were helpless.

With his left hand, Franz pointed down to the ground, motioning for the pilots to land in Germany. He knew it was preferable to be a P.O.W. than to have one's life snuffed out in a flak burst. But the American pilots shook their heads. Franz cursed in frustration. He knew he could be shot for letting the bomber go. That alone was treason. But Franz also knew that leaving the bomber now would be no different than shooting it down.

Kicking the rudder, Franz moved a few feet away from the bomber's wing so his silhouette could be seen from above and below. He knew that if another German fighter came along it would not interfere with him there. He reasoned the same for the boys on the ground. Germany's flak gunners were the best in the world and would know the silhouette of a 109 by heart. If they spotted him they would know he was one of theirs. But when they saw the bomber on his wing, would they hold their fire?

THE SOLDIERS SCURRIED between flak guns along the concrete embattlements of the Atlantic Wall. Nestled in their concrete gun pits, the flak gunners of the German Air Force watched the fighter and bomber flying toward them. Side by side, the two planes looked like a small sparrow and a large gull.

The gunners had been watching the planes with field glasses ever since they first appeared as two black crosses on the southern horizon.

Something was unusual about the approaching planes. It was their formation. The battery commander and his spotters studied the formation through their field glasses. Seeing the two planes flying in unison flipped a switch in their minds.

Whenever a bomber flew over them as a straggler, it was always alone—smoking, limping, and fleeing as fast as it could. But the approaching fighter and bomber had purpose and deliberation to their flight. They flew low and slow in unison, as if they had nothing to hide.

"It's one of ours!" they saw and shouted.

"It's one of theirs!" they realized as well.

No one knew what to do, not even the battery commander. Everyone in the German Air Force knew they had B-17s of their own, shot down planes that had been rebuilt to fly clandestine operations or be used in training, so fighter pilots could practice flying against the plane they would meet in combat. The battery commander knew there could be any number of explanations, but one thing was certain: there was a Messerschmitt 109 about to fly over him and he could not fire on one of his own.

"Hold your fire!" he shouted. One by one the gunners stepped back from their long-barreled cannons. The ammo bearers set down their shells. They tipped up the rims of their helmets, marveling as the fighter and bomber flew overhead. Side by side the 109 and the B-17 soared over the soldiers defending the Atlantic Wall then over the beach obstacles and the crashing surf.

The sight was a beautiful one, the little fighter protecting the big bomber. They flew together out over the gray sea as if they were leaving one world for another. The gunners watched, their hands shading their eyes, squinting as the two planes flew away and shrunk in the distance. No one said it, but it looked like the 109 was taking the bomber home.

BEHIND THE CONTROLS, Charlie was so fixated on the nightmare flying alongside his right wing that he had totally forgotten about the Atlantic Wall. It was not until he looked down and saw only the sea that he realized that dry land and one of Germany's most tightly defended flak zones were behind him. Not a shot had been fired. But Charlie had not yet connected the dots. When he looked at the German pilot on his wing, he saw the enemy pilot as a threat, probably one of the same fighters who had shot his plane to pieces earlier, now toying with them, planning to finish them off over the sea.

Charlie felt a new emotion—despair. He wanted always to have the answers for his crew or a plan. This was the leader's job, he believed, the reason he'd always pretended to be older than he was and had never told his crew otherwise. But now, with the German 109 stuck on his wing, he had no idea what to do next.

Unlike Charlie, Franz had a plan. He had seen the bomber's wounds and knew the bomber's damage better than its pilots. He knew what they needed to do. Franz waved to get the pilots' attention. When they looked his way, Franz pointed across his body, motioning to the east.

"Sweden!" he mouthed to them. "Sweden!"

Franz knew that neutral Sweden was just a thirty-minute flight away. He saw the Americans slowly turning west and knew they were going to attempt a two-hour flight across the sea to England. All they needed to do was fly to Sweden, land, and be interned. There, doctors could care for their wounded and together the crew could all outlive the war in peace and quiet.

Franz pointed again, with greater vigor and mouthed, "Sweden!"

The American copilot just shrugged.

Flying over the sea was a scary prospect for Franz in his small fighter. He could not imagine what the bomber pilots were thinking in their plane that was slowly falling apart. "Sit out the war!" he wanted to shout to them. "It's better than a watery grave!" But the B-17 copilot just looked at him, perplexed.

Franz knew he was not getting anywhere with the copilot, so he decided that the pilot was perhaps a more sensible man. Gently nudging his rudder, Franz leapfrogged the bomber, his shadow passing over the cockpit. Hovering above the left wing, Franz saw long brown oil stains creeping backward from the bomber's knocked-out engine. Now he was absolutely certain. They needed to turn to Sweden or they would never make it home alive. When the bomber's pilot looked at Franz, he did so with resignation, as if he had hoped that the German had left him for good when he departed the right wing. Again, Franz pointed toward Sweden and mouthed the word, "Sweden!" But the bomber's pilot shook his head, confused.

What a dumb guy, Franz thought.*

Inside the cockpit, Charlie asked Pinky, "What is he getting at?" Pinky had no idea. Charlie's mind was so frayed from having passed out earlier that he never considered Sweden as an option.

Charlie shouted for Frenchy, who crept into the cockpit, having fallen asleep. Frenchy could not believe his eyes. "Look how relaxed he is," Pinky marveled.

"Audacious SOB, huh?" Charlie said.

Frenchy was at a loss for words. Charlie told Frenchy the German was probably one of the ones who had shot them up earlier and was now out of ammo or else he would have shot them down. "He's just curious," Charlie concluded.

Pinky told Frenchy the German was pointing, trying to tell them something.

"He probably wants you to turn and fly back to Germany," Frenchy said. Charlie's face grew serious at the thought. His nerves were already stretched. The thought that the German could be a threat to his crew was the final straw.

---

* "He ignored my signals," Franz would remember. "He and his crew needed doctors. I kept motioning to him but he kept going, both arms wrapped tightly around the controls. The bomber, I believed, was doomed to crash in the sea. All aboard would be killed."[2]

"He's not taking us anywhere," Charlie promised Frenchy. Charlie asked if Frenchy's guns were working. Frenchy said they were.

"Get up in your turret and swing toward him," Charlie ordered. "See if you can chase this crazy bastard away."

FRANZ HAD SEEN the third airman appear in the cockpit and look at him wide-eyed, then disappear. He knew the Americans were puzzled and scared and wasn't surprised when he saw movement in the top turret. A crewman poked his head between the turret's guns, confirmed that Franz was still there, and began to revolve the turret toward Franz's fighter.

Franz knew what was coming. Taking one last look at the American pilot, he did the only thing that came to mind. He saluted him.

The American pilot stared back with a genuine look of surprise.

"Good luck, you're in God's hands," Franz said. Banking his fighter, Franz peeled up and over the bomber then dove away, leveling out in the direction of Germany.

WHEN BLACKIE REGAINED his composure, he emerged from his turret and entered the cockpit to tell Charlie what he had seen. He found Doc already there, jabbering with Charlie and Pinky about their 109 escort.

"What do you think he was trying to say?" Pinky asked.

"He was looking for the string so he could cut us out of the sky," Charlie quipped.

"I think he flew up to salute us," Blackie said. "To say, 'I gave you my best and you survived.'"

"What do you think, Doc?" Charlie asked.

"Pretty damn brazen," Doc said. "Shades of Eddie Rickenbacker." Doc was referring to Rickenbacker, America's top WWI ace and most chivalrous pilot. The legend went that Rickenbacker was so overjoyed when WWI ended that he flew over the trenches to watch the soldiers from both sides meet in no-man's-land to celebrate their survival.

Charlie nodded in agreement. He and the German had flown side by side for fewer than ten minutes, never exchanging a word. But the image of the pilot's salute was frozen in Charlie's mind. Charlie did not know the German's name or what he wanted, but he was certain of one thing: whoever he was, his enemy was a good man.

16

THE THIRD PILOT

THAT SAME AFTERNOON, OVER THE NORTH SEA

WITH THEIR GERMAN escort now departed, Charlie saw the murky North Sea below him, swirling with the promise of an icy death. The bomber's slight but steady descent terrified him. The plane seemed to be swimming laboriously through the heavy air, falling a few feet every minute due to drag from the hole in her nose, a dead engine, and her frayed skin. She was overweight for the two and a half engines that were pushing her, and Charlie found the only way to keep her flying straight was to drop the left wing by a few degrees.

A quarter of the way home, engine four shook any confidence that had surged in Charlie. "It's running away again!" Pinky shouted. By then Pinky knew the routine too well and launched the shut-down procedures, praying the troublesome engine would restart. It did, but the momentary loss of power cost the bomber two hundred feet of altitude. Charlie wondered if they had enough altitude to cross all three hundred miles of ocean at the rate their height was bleeding away. He knew the answer: *No way.*

Charlie called for Frenchy, who stumbled in from his turret. "Spread the word, have the men toss everything that's not nailed down," Charlie said. Frenchy nodded. "My guns, too?" he asked. Charlie thought about it. They would be truly defenseless without Frenchy's guns. But that German pilot's strangely uneventful escort had given Charlie a sense of hope that they were going to make it home. "Dump 'em," Charlie said.

The crew roamed the length of the plane, gathering anything they could expel. From the waist windows they tossed machine guns, flak vests, and oxygen bottles. Belts of bullets trailed through the sky. The men got on their hands and knees and scooped brass shell casings into helmets and shoveled them out to sea. Pechout amazed the others when he appeared at the waist, a bandage over his eye, his beloved radio set in his arms. He heaved out the black box. Frenchy suggested removing Ecky's guns, but Blackie warned him not to go back there.

Frenchy returned to the cockpit and told Charlie it was done. "All we can do now is pray," Charlie said. Frenchy draped his arms over the seat backs of Charlie and Pinky as if he was afraid to be alone. Although battered beyond the endurance of most aircraft, *The Pub* continued to claw at the stormy sky through scattered, misty clouds.

Halfway home, with the sea still spanning the horizon, the needle on the altimeter slowly ticked backward as the bomber slipped beneath one thousand feet of altitude. Blackie appeared in the cockpit, grinning like he always did. Charlie asked how his feet were feeling, and Blackie said he couldn't feel a thing below his knees. Charlie asked if Russian was stable. "The morphine has him in la-la land," Blackie said. Blackie stopped talking when he noticed the altimeter. Frantically he looked out both windows to see the altitude for himself. "Yup, we're dropping," Charlie said. Blackie suggested he was going back to go hit the morphine himself.

Thirty minutes later the bomber dipped below five hundred feet.* They were three-fourths of the way home, but the ocean still filled the horizon. Pinky trembled, his arms shaking the yoke. Each time Charlie felt *The Pub* shudder and drop a few feet, he touched the Bible in his pocket like a transmitter on a microphone hoping it would beam his prayers up faster. He asked his "Third Pilot" to stay close.

A short time later, two green flashes streaked from behind the bomber and ripped past Charlie's window with a roar. Startled, Charlie ducked his neck into his shoulders. "Fighters!" he shouted in alarm, assuming the worst. Pinky leaned forward, wide-eyed, to catch a glimpse. Frenchy turned to run for his turret, then stopped when he remembered he had tossed his guns. He returned to the pilots' seatbacks and ducked behind them.

The fighters held their course, racing ahead of the bomber. Charlie could not tell whose side they were on because their markings were hidden from behind. Then Charlie saw the fighters crossing in front of the bomber, their olive-colored flanks and wings revealing big white stars set within the blue circles of the American Army Air Forces.

"Little friends!" Frenchy screamed into Charlie's ear. Charlie turned, perturbed until he saw a wide grin on Frenchy's tough face and his deep-set eyes alight like a kid's. Charlie realized Frenchy was still deaf from his own gunfire.

The fighters were P-47 Thunderbolts of the 8th Air Force. They circled and disappeared from Charlie's sight. The next time he saw them they had pulled up on his left wing, where they flew formation with him.

The planes had sharp spines that led from the cockpit to the tail and gave them another nickname, "Razorbacks." Their white noses were dirty from oil that streaked their gray bellies and dotted the tall

---

* "The lower we dropped," Charlie would remember, "the more ominous the North Sea appeared with its dull gray mantle, interspersed with large whitecaps indicating strong wind and high waves."

white unit letters on their flanks. Silver metal peeked from weathered spots in the planes' olive skin. Charlie had never seen such beautiful machines. Through the canopy, Charlie saw the closest pilot smiling. His goggles were tipped up on his forehead and his oxygen mask dangled below his chin. He waved confidently. Afraid to let go of the yoke, Charlie unlocked his left hand, finger by finger, and waved quickly, forcing a timid smile. Charlie grabbed the yoke again as fast as he had let go. Pinky waved, too, with two hands.

The P-47 pilot pointed to his headset, a signal to ask if Charlie had radio communications. Charlie shook his head. The P-47 pilot understood and flashed Charlie a thumbs-up. The fighter pilot looked forward. Turning back to Charlie, he pointed ahead. Charlie looked through the windshield and his jaw dropped. He squinted and leaned forward. There, in the center of the horizon, was a small swath of land catching sun through a break in the clouds. It looked like a small island. Slowly the island seemed to stretch wider and wider as the clouds above it spread open, allowing more sun to reveal the beautiful green pastures of England. Pinky grinned. Frenchy clutched Charlie's and Pinky's shoulders. Charlie tapped his Bible in thanks.

The P-47 pilot saluted Charlie and raced ahead with his wingman. Minutes later, *The Pub* passed over the rugged, stony English coastline at 250 feet, rumbling low enough over a fishing village to see sailors lowering their sails and men in the cobblestone streets headed for drinks after a day at sea.

Inside the bomber's cockpit, Charlie began to breathe again. But the bomber was still sinking. As it passed through two hundred feet, Charlie told Frenchy to get Doc out of the nose and to tell the others to prepare to crash-land. Frenchy departed as Charlie looked for a soft field. Every field he saw seemed small and laced with stone fences. Frenchy emerged from the nose and said that Doc had refused to leave and was going to find them an airfield. Charlie told Frenchy there was no time for that. Then he saw them. The two P-47s were ahead and to his left, circling at one thousand feet.

"Are they trying to tell us something?" Charlie asked aloud. He did not wait for Frenchy's or Pinky's reply. Charlie muscled the sluggish controls and turned toward the fighters. Passing just above a thick grove of trees, he saw what the circling fighters were trying to show him. Below them, lay the smooth gray runway of an airfield.

"Flash them the landing lights!" he told Pinky. He knew the P-47 pilots were watching. Charlie focused on the two-thousand-foot runway, just three miles out to the southwest. Banking to line up his approach, Charlie reached forward and flipped the toggle for the landing gear. He looked to the instrument that showed the silhouette of the bomber and waited for three green lights to appear. But the bulbs remained clear. Charlie tried to lower the flaps, too, but they were frozen. Charlie knew the hydraulics had bled out. Frenchy saw what was happening. "I'm on it," he said, and departed to crank the gear and flaps down by hand.

Charlie told Pinky to cut engine four just before touchdown so it would not run wild and careen the plane out of control. The aim was to try to land a four-motor plane on an engine and a half. Charlie slipped off his gloves to better grip the yoke. Ahead the runway seemed to swell. From his window, he watched the left landing gear slowly descend and lock down. Frenchy popped back into the cockpit to report that the gear on both sides was down but the flaps were frozen. Charlie told Frenchy to fire the emergency flare and then get everyone into the radio room to brace for a crash.

———

AT THE AMERICAN air base of Seething, the airmen of the 448th Bomb Group formed a crowd around the tower. They had poured from their quarters and hangouts when they heard the P-47s circling overhead. Now they watched the damaged B-17 shakily descending from the distance.

The men of the 448th had been in eastern England just a month and had yet to enter combat. Their green B-24s ringed the base in hardstands where mechanics stopped their work and stood atop the planes' high-mounted wings. Alerted by the P-47s' radio calls, the base's fire trucks and "Meat Wagon" ambulances pulled up along the runway. Everyone was somber and quiet as they listened to the bomber laboring toward the earth.

FROM THE CEILING window in the radio room, Frenchy fired red flares, alerting the emergency responders that the bomber contained wounded men. *The Pub* wobbled, drifting faster with her gear down, passing below seventy-five feet then fifty feet. Charlie told Pinky "Now!" and Pinky cut engine four. Charlie gently pulled on the yoke, keeping the bomber's nose up as she settled to earth.

The bomber flared then stalled as her front tires kissed the concrete with a breath of smoke. *The Pub* raced along the runway, her tail up and wings level with the ground, as if trying to show the onlookers that she had landed on her own accord and undefeated. Finally the bomber's tail wheel dropped to earth and slowed her roll. The emergency vehicles chased the bomber. From the tower, airmen and officers boarded jeeps and raced after the ambulances.

Charlie and Pinky mashed the plane's spongy brakes, and *The Pub* graciously complied, coasting to a slow stop, her propellers still wheeling. Charlie and Pinky pulled back the throttle and turbocharger levers. They flicked off the fuel switches and the engines stopped. Charlie leaned back and put a hand over his Bible. Pinky leaned forward and buried his head on the yoke. Frenchy entered the cockpit and saw the pilots sitting in silence. He left them alone. It was nearly 3:30 P.M. The crew and *The Pub* had completed their first mission together.

PINKY DEPARTED THE bomber first, swinging his feet through the hatch in the nose. Charlie followed him. The seasoned pilot who dropped down to the tarmac was different from the nervous boy who had boarded *The Pub* that morning. Charlie's hair was matted and his eyes were glassy. Blood from his nosebleed covered his mouth and yellow life preserver. He looked ten years older.

When Charlie's feet hit the concrete, he found that his legs were wobbly. Unable to support his own weight, Charlie staggered a few steps and collapsed under the bomber's nose. Seething smelled like the nearby ocean, and he sat on the tarmac, breathing in the cool sea air. Charlie knew his men were being cared for. He had seen dozens of people congregating around the bomber's rear door. His mind turned fuzzy. His eyes focused ahead, but he saw nothing. A tall, lanky second lieutenant who resembled a young Gary Cooper approached and knelt at Charlie's level. He wore a leather jacket like a pilot's, but he was not a flyer. His name was Second Lieutenant Bob Harper and he was the base's assistant intelligence officer.

"Lieutenant? You okay?" Harper asked, shaking Charlie's arm.

Charlie turned to face Harper. "What a hell of a way to start a war," Charlie said.

Harper nodded.

"What a hell of a way to start a war," Charlie repeated.

Harper hollered for a medic. When the medic came, Harper moved rearward to help the more seriously wounded men. Pinky and Frenchy stood behind the medic, concerned about Charlie. The medic wanted Charlie to lie on a stretcher, but he protested.

Shaking himself from his stupor, Charlie wiped the blood from his face and slowly stood to convince the medic he was not wounded. He told the medic he had been hit by fatigue, nothing more.

The medic noticed the blood on Charlie's shoulder from the bullet fragment. Charlie knew the rule that a wound meant he would be grounded for at least three days. Pinky and Frenchy knew it, too, and realized they might get stuck flying with a lesser pilot if Charlie acknowledged his wound.

"It's just a scratch," Charlie told the medic. But the medic insisted he could see a hole in Charlie's jacket. Charlie cut him off and told him to go look after the crew. Pinky and Frenchy grinned with relief. Charlie whispered that one of them would have to help fish out the bullet shard later.

His strength renewed, Charlie stumbled under the bomber's nose and back toward its rear exit. He stayed out of the way as medics steadied Pechout and Blackie and helped them into the back of an ambulance that whisked them away. Four airmen carried Russian out on a stretcher and slid him onto the floor of another ambulance. Charlie looked inside and saw that Russian was unconscious. "Will he make it?" Charlie asked a medic who hunched over the gunner. The medic made no promises but indicated that they had stabilized him.

At the bomber's rear door, airmen reverently passed the stretcher containing Ecky's body to waiting hands outside the plane. A blanket covered Ecky, but not his small flying boots that pointed skyward. The stretcher bearers loaded Ecky into the ambulance with Russian then slammed the vehicle's double doors. Charlie watched the ambulance drive away.

One of the stretcher bearers wore a leather pilot's jacket and wiped his bloody hands on his pants as he approached Charlie. He was an older man with silver hair and a small mustache that gave his strong face a dashing quality. He introduced himself as the 448th's commander, Colonel Jim Thompson. Thompson asked Charlie if he was the pilot, and Charlie said he was. The colonel laid a hand on Charlie's shoulder. "Son, your men are okay, you did your job. What can we do for you?"

Charlie saw Pinky, Frenchy, and the others tossing their flight gear into jeeps. He knew he had to call Kimbolton and probably attend a debriefing. But something more important was on his mind.

"Sir, I'd just like to use the bathroom," Charlie said. "I've been holding it for eight hours."

ACROSS THE NORTH SEA, JEVER AIRFIELD

Some twenty minutes after his encounter with the B-17, Franz landed at Bremen Airport to have his radiator changed. He wanted to get home to Wiesbaden but also knew he could not risk catastrophic engine failure on the flight there. He had chosen Bremen Airport over Jever Field to avoid questions about his encounter with the American bomber. Franz knew from the moment he had peeled away from the bomber that he had committed a dangerous act. He could not tell anyone the truth—he had helped the enemy escape. If anyone pinned him to that act, he knew he would face a firing squad. People in Germany had been killed for far less. The prior June, a woman had been executed for telling a joke during a break from work at a munitions factory. Her crime was to say:

"Hitler and Goering are standing atop the Berlin radio tower. Hitler says he wants to do something to put a smile on Berliners' faces. So Goering says: 'Why don't you jump?'"

That was it. Someone overheard her tell that joke and turned her in. The fact that the woman was a war widow made no difference. Hitler's "Blood Judge," Roland Freisler, ordered her to be killed for violating the Subversion Law. [1]

Franz wanted to get as far from the scene of his crime as possible. He asked a mechanic to get to work on his plane so he could fly home that night.

"You won't be going anywhere," the mechanic said. "This will take hours." Reluctantly, Franz prepared to stay the night. If the Gestapo came looking for a pilot who had let a B-17 escape, Franz would play dumb and pray for the best. His fate, he knew, was in God's hands.

Franz headed for the tower to call Wiesbaden. On the way he saw a small Fieseler Storch observation plane in a hangar, its high wing and ungainly long landing gear giving it the look of an insect. Franz was eager to escape the base, even for a few hours. After reporting his

status to Wiesbaden, he got permission from the Storch's pilot to borrow the plane. He lifted off and flew northwest of Bremen. There, he
scanned the countryside, looking for the crash site of the B-17 he was
sure he had downed earlier. He spotted the bomber in a farmer's field.
Franz wondered what had happened to the pilots—did the farmer
have them in his barn waiting for the military to pick them up? Or
worse, had he called the Gestapo? Franz decided to investigate, to ensure that the men had been treated with civility.

Franz knew the Storch could operate from rough, unfinished air-
strips, so he assumed the farmer's field would be no problem. He eased
the plane down toward the earth, aiming to land alongside the crashed
B-17. But Franz's mind was back at Jever, wondering if the Gestapo
would be waiting for him when he returned to the base. He failed to
notice that the farmer's field was deeply furrowed. The Storch touched
down, caught a furrow, and nosed over, its wooden propeller snapping
away. Franz emerged unhurt and shook his head as he looked over the
wrecked plane, cursing his luck.

The farmer who owned the field ran to his aid. He informed Franz
that the entire crew had been taken prisoner by the German Air Force.
Franz breathed a sigh of relief. He knew the Air Force would treat the
American pilots fairly. A captive Allied airman made a tempting candidate for a lynching by mobs of civilians displaced from their cities,
or German farmers if their livestock had been strafed by fighters.
Worst of all were the SS, whose capacity for mercy was epitomized by
the death's head insignia on their black caps.

In seeking out his enemy to guarantee their safe conduct, Franz's
actions were not exceptional. Somehow, even during the destruction of
their homeland, many pilots of the German Air Force continued a
style of chivalry similar to that of the desert. No longer did they seek
out their downed opponents to talk with them; now they sought them
out to save their lives. Since German pilots often did battle over their
bases, they would often land, grab a driver, and hurry to locate their

downed opponents to ensure their protection before their countrymen could reach them.*

Using the Storch's radio, Franz called Jever Field for a ride. Franz explored the downed B-17 as he waited for his lift. As Franz sat on the wing of the downed bomber, his thoughts raced to the bomber he had escorted out of Germany. He wondered if its crew were alive, kissing the tarmac and hugging one another in relief. Or were they floating in a raft in the North Sea, or on the bottom of the ocean in their Four Motor tomb? Their fate mattered to him. He could not get the thought out of his mind: *Was it worth it?*

AT THE SAME TIME, SEETHING AIRFIELD

After a bathroom break and nap in the tower, Charlie asked Colonel Thompson for permission to visit *The Pub*. Thompson agreed. He told Charlie he had notified Kimbolton of the crew's predicament. The 379th was sending a B-17 in an hour or two to take them home.

The sun was setting behind withered trees when Thompson drove Charlie west across the field to a hardstand where ground personnel had towed the bomber. Airmen milled around the plane, examining its damage with awe, some snapping pictures. Charlie and Thompson circled the bomber, marveling in the same way. In the soft, waning glow of the sun behind her, *The Pub* looked defiant as she stood on her own legs.

A mechanic walking the plane's wing drew Charlie and Thompson's attention to the number three engine. He had made a discovery. A 20mm round had blown off the top of the fuel tank but never ignited the fuel. At the tip of the right wing, Charlie looked up through

---

* Author's note: Decades later, when I talked with American bomber crewmen who had been taken prisoner, almost to a man they would admit, "I was never so glad to see the Luftwaffe" when a German pilot showed up to take them prisoner, as opposed to the alternative, who often wanted their heads.

the hole where the 88 shell had passed through, leaving a gap the size of a softball. Charlie and Thompson stopped at the tail section. Someone had draped a tarp across it to hide the sight of the deceased gunner's blood. Charlie told Thompson that his gunner, Ecky, had been looking forward to the base Christmas party that night.

Circling farther, Charlie saw the stub of the horizontal stabilizer and shook his head. Looking up at the remaining half of the rudder, he saw that all but one of the rudder's control cables had been severed.*

Their inspection completed, Thompson told Charlie he was going to recommend medals for the entire crew, including Charlie.

He said he had one last question.

"Why didn't you hit the silk over Germany?"

"Sir, I had a man who was too injured to jump."

"So you and your crew stayed for just one man?"

"Yes, sir," Charlie said and nodded. To him it was that simple. They had fought for one another from a Texas bar to the skies of Bremen. They knew they were stronger together than apart.

—————

THOMPSON DROVE CHARLIE to Lieutenant Harper's office, a brick building south of the tower. There, Harper was set to debrief Charlie. Charlie and Thompson shook hands and parted alongside Thompson's jeep. Charlie had come to quickly admire Thompson, who was fatherly in his leadership style, compared to Preston, who was more like a big brother or a big man on campus.[†]

———————————

* "When I saw the condition of the airplane, it frightened me more than anything in the air did," Charlie would remember. "It seemed as if a hand had been holding us up in the air, and it wasn't mine."

† Some three months later Colonel James McKenzie Thompson led his group over Germany on April 1, 1944. Of the twenty-one planes dispatched, five did not return, including Thompson's. His B-24 hit heavy headwinds on the flight home and ran out of fuel over France. Only he and one other man from his crew bailed out. Thompson's parachute failed to open.

Harper welcomed Charlie into his cozy office. The room's brick walls had been freshly painted white, and the windows had been covered with tan paper to block light from escaping. A potbelly stove sat in the room's corner. From the ceiling hung small black airplane models that Harper said he used in teaching aircraft recognition to bomber and anti-aircraft gunners.

Harper sat behind his desk and motioned for Charlie to sit across from him. He opened a file and admitted that the interrogation would be his first, since his unit had yet to see battle. Charlie asked if Harper would be calling in the others, and Harper said there was no time because their ride was due shortly. "You can speak for your crew," he told Charlie.

Charlie felt like a mess. His hair was stringy and his body felt sticky from sweat. A debriefing was the last thing he wanted. He also knew that now was the time to see his crew's bravery recognized. Like a testimony under oath, the story he gave Harper would become the official record.

Harper unlocked a drawer in his desk and removed a bottle of Vat 69 whiskey and two shot glasses. He uncorked the bottle while explaining that policy permitted him to give each crewman a shot to loosen his tongue before reviewing a tough mission. He poured Charlie a glass. That morning Charlie had turned down a drink from Walt, but now that moment seemed like another lifetime. Charlie slugged the whiskey in a stinging gulp. Harper kept holding the bottle at an angle. "No one's counting here," he said. Charlie accepted another shot.

Charlie walked Harper through the mission. He explained how Frenchy and Doc had downed enemy fighters, how Ecky and Blackie had remained at their useless guns to call out fighter attacks, how Pechout had refused to leave his radio, and how Jennings and Andy had saved Russian from bleeding to death. Harper scribbled notes, hanging on every word.

Charlie told him of the spin, of pulling out over Oldenburg, and of racing for the coast. "Then the last 109 parked on our wingtip," Charlie said, "and I thought it was all for nothing."

Harper stopped Charlie. "The last 109?"

Charlie clarified, "Yeah, the one who flew with us."

Charlie described their bizarre encounter with the German pilot who had escorted them out to sea and said good-bye with a salute.

Harper cocked his head and stared at Charlie as if he was joking. "He flew with you?" Harper said, leaning across his desk, incredulous.

"He was probably out of ammo," Charlie said. "But he took us out of Germany."

Harper slapped his desk. "I thought I had heard it all," he said. Harper closed his notes. Charlie interrupted him to ask how he could nominate his crew for awards. He wanted a Distinguished Flying Cross (DFC) for each man as well as a Bronze Star for Ecky. Harper told Charlie he might want to think bigger.

"They'll take one look at that plane of yours and every one of you will be wearing the Bronze Star," Harper said. Charlie knew his request for DFCs for his crew was not asking much. The DFC was a modest medal given routinely to bomber pilots who flew twenty-five missions or to fighter pilots after fifty missions.

Harper promised Charlie he would forward his report to his counterpart at Kimbolton.

It was around 5:30 P.M. when Harper walked Charlie to the base officer's club. Harper and Charlie found Pinky, Doc, and Andy sitting in plush chairs and eating sandwiches. A painted mural decorated the wall above a nearby fireplace. When Harper saw Charlie admiring it, he admitted he had painted it. The mural featured a creature with the body of a lion and the head and wings of an eagle jumping through the center of a massive blue American star. It was supposed to be a patriotic mural representing the bomb group on attack. Harper said painting was his hobby. Someday he hoped to be an artist. Doc and Andy covered their mouths with their arms and coughed, fighting not to break out in laughter. They found Harper's artistic rendition to be hilarious.

Harper excused himself to call his superiors at 8th Air Force head-quarters. He had told Charlie on their walk to the club that he saw tremendous PR value in the story of a miracle plane and the crew that stayed together to stay in the war. He departed with a wave. Charlie told his officers about Harper's reaction. They grinned at the thought of how Harper would paint them as heroes.

———

CHARLIE AND HIS officers heard the B-17 land at 6:30 P.M., even before the orderly stuck his head into the club. The orderly informed them of a hitch. The B-17 had developed an engine problem and would need to be grounded for a while before its flight back to Kimbolton. The me-chanics were working on it. Doc grumbled something about missing the dance.

Three hours and many Cokes and sandwiches later, the orderly returned. The bomber was ready to fly again. As Charlie and his men donned their jackets, Harper entered the club with a wild look of con-cern. He was glad to have caught them before they left. Harper pulled Charlie to a nearby table and asked him to sit down.

Charlie told his men to board the plane and that he'd catch up.

"I told them your story, just as you told me," Harper said. "But when I mentioned the part about the German they went berserk!"

Charlie sighed with relief. He thought Harper had come to deliver bad news about Russian.

Harper explained that 8th Air Force headquarters had given him orders to pass along. "When you see your crew, you are to instruct them not to discuss the mission with anyone."

Charlie raised an eyebrow.

"Here's the worst part," Harper said. "Forget about any medals for your crew."

"That's bullshit!" Charlie said, standing.

Harper rose to Charlie's level. "I tried as hard as I could. I know what headquarters is thinking. If your men get medals, people will ask how they got them. Then if your men tell the story, they'll mention the Kraut pilot."

Charlie shook his head in disbelief.

"The brass wants you to forget this day ever happened," Harper said. "Those are the orders."

Three words crossed Charlie's mind: *Go to hell*. But he held his tongue, tossed on his jacket, and started for the door.

Harper caught Charlie by an arm and leaned in with a sudden whisper. "Listen—suppose another of our planes gets in a similar fix. And suppose our gunners hold their fire just as a 109 swoops in because they heard some story about how he's going to 'fly with them.' Now suppose this Kraut isn't as nice as yours and blows our boys out of the sky?"

Charlie thrust his hands in his pockets. Harper had a point.

"What am I supposed to tell my men?" Charlie asked.

"You tell them they did what they came here to do," Harper said. "Bomb Germany, fly home, and go back to do it again."

Charlie gave a terse nod. He and his crew weren't in it for the medals. Surviving a horrendous attack was just doing what they had volunteered to do. He looked straight at Harper. "What about Ecky? Would you at least help me nominate my tail gunner for a commendation? For his family's sake."

"Write it up, and I'll grease the wheels," Harper said.

IN THE DIM light of a quarter moon, Charlie jogged toward the tower. His ride to Kimbolton lay idling behind the tower. Peering across the field, Charlie looked for *The Pub* but couldn't see her. He passed the tower and approached his ride to Kimbolton from the tail. Blue exhaust flames spit from beneath the bomber's engines. Charlie removed his crush cap and tucked it under his arm as he crossed through the prop wash. A crew chief waited with a flashlight near the bomber's rear door. For a moment, Charlie hesitated before he entered the plane.

The crew chief had barely shut the door when the pilots gunned the engines, hurrying to make the thirty-minute hop to Kimbolton, seventy-seven miles west. Charlie found Pinky, Doc, Andy, Frenchy, and Jennings in the radio room. Charlie apologized for not wanting to sit with them and explained that he was curious to see what England looked like at night, from the plane's nose.

The pilots swung the bomber around onto the main runway as Charlie took his seat in the nose. The pilots gunned the throttles. The bomber barreled along the runway and had just lifted off when Charlie heard a popping sound from the left wing followed by sputtering. The bomber had an engine problem again, this time a blown supercharger. The pilots lowered the plane back toward the earth and touched down. They slammed on the brakes and Charlie thought he heard an unusual squeal. The bomber veered left and ran off the concrete, just before the end of the runway.

As the bomber's wheels dug into the mud, the sudden stop threw Charlie forward, into the Plexigas nose cone. Ammo cans, clipboards, and pencils from the navigator's desk cascaded around him. Lying with his head in the tip of the cone, Charlie trembled. The bomber, somehow, managed to stay on its gear.*

Charlie followed the pilots out the nose hatch and found his men behind the plane. The bomber had crashed just across the runway from *The Pub*. The bomber's pilots examined the blown engine with flashlights. Frenchy looked at his luminescent watch. It was 9:47 P.M. "I think we're gonna miss the dance," he joked.

"I should have bailed out over Germany," Doc said.

Charlie knew he still had to break the news to Doc and the others that their heroism was being swept under the rug. He was dreading

---

* "As I sat there in the darkness, I reflected that it had been a very long and rather tiring day for a thoroughly frightened, confused, and totally misplaced West Virginia farm boy," Charlie would remember. *The Pub* would sit at Seething until March, when the men of the 2nd Strategic Air Depot would repair her over twenty-three days. *The Pub* was then flown back to America and later scrapped.

the letter he had to write to Ecky's parents and the question he knew they would ask him, "How did he die?" Looking at the wrecked bomber that should have been their ride home and *The Pub* sitting proudly, as if ready for another trip to Germany, Charlie said what each man in his crew was thinking: "Why did I volunteer for this?"

17

PRIDE

CHARLIE SLOWLY SULKED up to the door of his Nissen hut dragging his canvas kit bag. Forty-eight hours after his traumatic flight over Germany, Charlie still wore his same heavy flying uniform. The 379th had sent a hapless truck driver to Seething to retrieve Charlie and his crew. The driver took all of December 21 just to reach them. He arrived at Seething wearing a ball cap too big for his head and said he had been lost because the English had taken down their road signs to confuse a German invasion. On the drive back to Kimbolton, he had crisscrossed the back roads of eastern England all night while Charlie and his crew bounced around in the rear of the truck. Only a flap of canvas separated them from the freezing cold. Following a twenty-hour-drive, they fell from the truck's lift gate at Kimbolton, sick from diesel exhaust.

His eyes half-shut, Charlie slowly opened the door to his hut. He had not bothered to check in at the squadron headquarters like Pinky and the others had.. He only wanted to drop to his bunk to sleep. Charlie saw that fellow officers were straightening their ties and slicking back their hair for dinner dates. They stared at Charlie in the doorway then ran to him, slapping him on the back.

"Back from the grave!" someone yelled. Charlie grinned wearily. His good friend, Second Lieutenant Dale Killion, broke through the crowd beaming a wide grin. Dale was a rookie pilot, too, and a simple farm kid from Iowa who resembled film star Ronald Reagan. Dale was twenty-two years old, so Charlie looked up to him, although Dale's "gee whiz" mannerisms made him seem younger.

"We were told you went missing over Germany!" Dale said. Charlie told Dale and the others he had phoned from Seething. "Somebody didn't get the message," another pilot said. One by one the men hurried to their footlockers and returned, piling Charlie's arms with his cologne, his comics, his socks, and his broken watch. Dale handed Charlie a stack of perfumed letters from Marjorie. "Glad I held off on burning these," he said. Charlie shook his head in disbelief. He knew the Air Force's standard practice was to remove the possessions of a downed crewman as soon as possible for morale purposes. They would always give the missing man's buddies the chance to sort through his belongings and remove anything embarrassing before the man's effects were sent home to his family. By tradition, the missing man's buddies were allowed to keep useful items, like books or toothpaste or hair pomade. Dale advised Charlie to hurry over to the Operations Office before they mailed the rest of his belongings home to West Virginia.

Glancing toward the corner of the hut, Charlie saw a man sprawled out in the bunk Charlie had claimed. The man's feet were crossed and his nose was in a book. "What the hell?" Charlie muttered. Charlie approached the man and stood at the foot of the bunk, his shadow blocking the man's light. "I think you have the wrong bunk," Charlie said.

The man looked up from his book. Charlie knew the man was a replacement. The wings on his shirt revealed that he was a navigator. The navigator had already hung pinup girls on the wall above his head and sat his shoes on the footlocker that had been Charlie's. "They assigned this to me," he said flatly.

"They wrongfully assigned it to you because they thought I was dead," Charlie explained.

"It was empty," the navigator said. "Just grab another one." The other officers in the hut looked up from their grooming. Dale lingered silently a few paces behind Charlie.

Charlie looked around. The hut was full. Charlie saw with relief that no one had disturbed Pinky's bunk—yet. "That's not going to work," Charlie said.

"Then move to another hut," the navigator said.

Charlie's face turned red. He had lived in that hut for two months and had grown used to his friends' snoring and nightmares. That cold, lousy hut was "home."

Charlie set his kit bag on the concrete floor and dumped his belongings from his arms into the bag. He thrust a hand into the bag, fished around, and pulled out his .45 pistol. "You're going to leave one way or another," Charlie told the navigator.

"You're goddamn crazy!" the navigator said sitting up in bed.

"I'm going to fire one round through the ceiling," Charlie said. "The next round will be through your leg." The man scowled but did not move. Charlie leaned in close and whispered something inaudible. The navigator saw the pistol wobbling in Charlie's shaking hand. He got up, grabbed his shoes, and left the hut without his coat.*

As Charlie's adrenaline dissipated, he sat down on Pinky's bunk. No one had raided Pinky's goods, because the replacement navigator had chosen Charlie's corner bunk instead. Dale called the other officers to help him gather the navigator's belongings. In a minute, they cleaned out the man's footlocker and departed, carrying his uniforms and effects in sloppy bundles to the squadron headquarters. Charlie flopped onto his cot and fell fast asleep.

---

* "I told him that I was combat certified—war weary—and could get away with it," Charlie would remember.

TWO NIGHTS LATER, WIESBADEN, GERMANY

The smoky pub was filled with pilots on Christmas Eve. The party was rowdy and coarse because the married men were away with their wives. Franz was in the center of it with Bobbi. Normally, Franz liked to be in the middle of the party but not the center of attention. With Bobbi at his side, this was impossible. Willi was drunk and telling jokes, his Knight's Cross dangling proudly.

When Franz had returned from Jever, he told Willi he had found the B-17 he downed in the farmer's field but had no witnesses to confirm the victory. He never mentioned the bomber he let escape over the sea. "You won't get anywhere by not claiming victories—I'll confirm it for you," Willi had said. "Your word is good enough."

Franz had never been closer to the Knight's Cross. But to him, the Cross had taken on new meaning. He had seen the eyes of the wounded bomber crew, young men no different than the ones he had been killing for two years. He knew the Cross stood for bravery. But Franz now realized it also represented a man's success at his most corrupted service to the world—his prowess at killing other men. Franz knew he could not stop fighting. The war would not let him. But never again would he celebrate his job as a fighter pilot, the role he had volunteered for. On December 20, 1943, he had given up on the Knight's Cross for good. "Don't bother," he had told Willi. "Let's go get drunk."

Because Christmas Eve was a special occasion, the pilots bought Bobbi a beer. The bear loved the taste. So the men found him a bowl and filled it high with beer, then refilled it again and again, each pilot pouring the beer from his tall mug. The men got drunk with their mascot. Franz finally stopped his comrades from giving Bobbi any more beer by insisting that they would need to help carry Bobbi home if he became too inebriated to walk.

The pilots sang obscene songs to one another but changed their tunes when the local girls trickled in after midnight Mass. At some point, they began singing Christmas carols, including a sad rendition of "Silent Night," a German song by tradition.* Franz stumbled out into the cobblestone street with Bobbi. Drunkenly, man and mascot plodded to their apartment. With the voices of his comrades still singing in the background, Franz smiled, unaware that their time together was coming to an end.

ELEVEN DAYS LATER, JANUARY 4, 1944, KIMBOLTON AIRFIELD

Charlie and his officers ate their lunches in silence in the nearly deserted mess hall. Dark circles sagged beneath their eyes. Instead of talking with one another, they looked around at other crews, at the swinging doors, at every sound outside the windows. They picked at their food and dropped their silverware, jittery.

That morning they had been assigned spare gunners and a temporary B-17 called *Anita Marie*. Soon after takeoff they had lost an engine and returned to base. Now the group was away, bombing the German ports at Kiel, without them.

Charlie and his officers had just wanted to log another mission to put December 20 behind them. Charlie had broken the news to them about their heroics being quashed. The men couldn't care less. Russian and Pechout had survived and were going home. Rumor had it that Blackie was coming back. What bothered them was that they had been stuck in limbo for fourteen days. Three times they had gone to bed expecting to fly the next day. Three times they had tossed and turned all night only to wake up beneath the orderly's flashlight beam and to hear his voice: "Sorry, sir, mission's scrubbed."

Now, instead of talking with one another, they talked to themselves and thought themselves in circles, pondering the odds against

---

* Franz would remember, "At that time religion wasn't the highest thing in Germany, but that did not stop us."

AIRCRAFT OF "A HIGHER CALL"

He-72

"Pupil" glider

Bf-109F and Ju-88

Jorg Czypionka

Bundesarchiv, Bild 101I-439-1286-26

Spitfire

Hurricane

P-40

Imperial War Museum

B-17 Flying Fortress and B-24 Liberator

P-38 Lightning

Fw-190

P-47 Thunderbolt

Me-262

P-51 Mustang

Above: August Stigler and the "Pupil" glider.
Below: August, pictured here in 1939

Franz Stigler Collection

Above: The Stigler family during the 1930s.
Front: Franz's mother, Anna, and Franz.
Rear: August and the boys' father, Franz.

Franz Stigler Collection

Above: Franz Stigler, fall 1944.

Left: August alongside his Ju-88
bomber in France, summer 1940.

Franz Stigler Collection

Right: Franz in his 109, White 12, at Martuba, Libya, spring 1942.

Above left: Franz in a vehicle with Sgt. Erwin Swallisch (center) and Lt. Ferdinand Voegl (far left). **Above right:** Lt. Werner Schroer **Below left:** Franz's mentor, Gustav Roedel. **Below right:** Roedel (wearing shorts), in Greece during August 1943, as commander of JG-27.

Above: Cpl. Mathew "Matthias" Letuku, POW and Marseille's friend.

Right: 1st Lt. Hans-Joachim Marseille, the 22-year-old "Star of Africa," in May 1942.

Above: Capt. "Edu" Neumann, JG-27's inspirational leader in the desert.

The Voegl Flight photo session at Quotaifiya, Egypt, on August 15, 1942. L to R: Franz, Voegl, Swallisch, and Bendert.

Right: A mechanic services a 109 at Trapani airfield, Sicily.

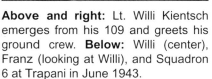

Above and right: Lt. Willi Kientsch emerges from his 109 and greets his ground crew. **Below:** Willi (center), Franz (looking at Willi), and Squadron 6 at Trapani in June 1943.

Above: A flight of P-38s over the Mediterranean.

Right: Franz emerges from his 109 at Trapani, cigarette in hand, after a convoy escort to Africa.

Franz Stigler Collection

Franz Stigler Collection

Above left: Adolf Galland, a general, at age 31. **Above right:** Galland and Col. Gunther Luetzow during their inspection of Trapani airfield. **Below:** A 109G over the Mediterranean.

Bundesarchiv, Bild 1011-529-2385-17

Above: A 109 with Mt. Erice in the background. **Below:** Lt. Hans Lewes.

Above: Maj. Johannes "Macky" Steinhoff in Sicily. **Below:** Reichsmarschall Hermann Goering, commander of the German Air Force.

Robert Forsyth

GOERING
HERMANN
3IG 350013
22 JUNE 1945

GOERING
HERMANN
3IG 350013
22 JUNE 1945

Above: The crew of "Ye Olde Pub." Kneeling, L to R: Charlie, Pinky, Doc, and Andy. Standing, L to R: Frenchy, Russian, Pechout, Jennings, Ecky, and Blackie. **Left:** Charlie Brown in 1944.

Above: WASP Marjorie Ketcham at Romulus Army Air Base, Michigan.

Left: Sam "Blackie" Blackford alongside his ball turret, at Kimbolton Army Air Station, England.

Below:
The 379th commander,
Col. Maurice Preston.

Above: "Ecky" Eckenrode follows Dick Pechout through the enlisted mess at Kimbolton.

Above: The 1939 college yearbook photo of 2nd Lt. Walter Reichold.

Above: A briefing before a mission over Europe. **Below:** A B-17F prepares to take off.

Above and Right: Flak explodes amid B-17s along the "road to the Reich."

Above: A bomber's gunner grips his .50 caliber machine gun.

Right: Eight FW-190s, like this, attacked "the Pub" on December 20, 1943.

Above: John D. Shaw's painting "A Higher Call" depicts the December 20 encounter.

Above (L to R): Col. James Thompson, 2nd Lt. Bob Harper (standing on right), 2nd Lt. Dale Killion.

Right: The Brown crew with replacements at Kimbolton, spring 1944. Front, L to R: Paige, Miller, Blackie, Doc, and Frenchy. Rear, L to R: Liddle, Charlie, Andy, and Pinky.

Right: His final mission completed, Charlie Brown enjoys a bottle of whiskey and a cigar at Kimbolton on April 11, 1944.

Above: Franz and his pilots at Graz after their victory over the B-24s. Mellman and Sonntag are the pilots standing on the far left.

Eva poses in Franz's 109.

In bombed-out Potsdam, Franz met the Greisse family.

At Dresden, October 1944, Franz (center) endures the antics of his adjutant, Sgt. Alfred Stueckler. The faces of Franz's young pilots at left, reflect the gravity of the times.

"FLORIDA," on Lake Tegernsee.

Munich airport in ruins.

Col. Hannes Trautloft.

Eric Hohagen as a first lieutenant.

Walter "the Count" Krupinski as a first lieutenant.

Robert Forsyth

Above: To conserve jet fuel, Kettenkrads were often used as "runway tugs" to pull 262s.

Robert Forsyth

Right: At JV-44's alert shack, Steinhoff takes a call from the orphanage. Behind him (L to R) are the Count, Hohagen, and Luetzow.

Robert Forsyth

Above: Maj. Gerd Barkhorn. **Left:** At the orphanage, Luetzow (center) confers with Col. Gunther von Maltzahn (left) and Trautloft (right).

Robert Forsyth

Above: Steinhoff's burnt 262.

Right: One of the last photos of Luetzow and Galland.

Robert Forsyth

Right: JV-44's senior staff, late April 1945. Franz (far right) wears sunglasses, and Hohagen (foreground) shields his eyes. Joining them are the commanders from the KG-51 bomber unit (far left) and the jet training wing at Lechfeld (center).

Robert Forsyth

At the war's end, a Me-262, the world's most advanced aircraft, lies abandoned in Austria.

their survival. They imagined what they could do to improve their chances, like sitting on a flak vest, finding a new lucky charm, or going to the chapel more. They had become mentally rattled or what the combat crews called "flak happy."

Colonel Preston's policies had failed to help the Quiet Ones. Whenever Preston knew a crew had come back from a bad mission, he tried to put them back into the air as soon as possible. Preston had learned to do this from an earlier mistake. Several months prior a crew had come back with wounded and dead men aboard. Preston gave them a week off at a rest home to calm their nerves. A 379th navigator would remember what happened: "They had used their week off to mull over their collective past and unpromising future. On their return they announced their unanimous decision to quit the war."[1] After that crew resigned from flying duty, Preston and the group's flight surgeon instituted a new policy to get a flak happy crew back into the air and off the ground. But even Preston could not un-scrub a mission or prevent an abort.

Looking at his men, Charlie wondered if they were having nightmares like he had. Every night he had been dreaming of the red flak orchids and of German pilots flying along his wingtips like devils. After December 20, Charlie had come to conclude that his survival rested not in his hands, but in the hands of his enemy. Had the German flak gunner paid attention in gunnery school? Had he miscalculated the wind? Had the enemy fighter pilot been drinking the night before? Had his girlfriend visited him? To Charlie, this realization was devastating.

Someone whistled a tune that echoed throughout the mess hall. The sound floated from behind the buffet, where cooks wore white aprons as they scrubbed pans. Charlie and his officers looked at one another. They all had heard the story of the cook, Snuffy, who was so happy to be in the mess hall that he whistled all the time. Snuffy had been a gunner once. The legend went that Snuffy was so certain his "number was up" that he had declared one day, "I ain't a'flying anymore,"[2] and tore off his sergeant stripes. He volunteered to work in the kitchen, and Colonel Preston allowed this.

When Charlie dumped his tray in the trash, he looked across the buffet for Snuffy, but the whistling had stopped. Instead, all he saw were cooks who all looked the same, with healthy faces and rosy cheeks. Charlie did not want to ask which man was Snuffy because he knew that to know Snuffy was to know defeat. Snuffy's whistling was a horrible siren, a lure to an airman to quit flying and follow him. Snuffy's only promise was the guarantee of life.

ONE DAY LATER, JANUARY 5, 1944, AROUND 5:15 A.M.

Charlie's breath fogged up the mirror as he tried to shave in the freezing cold latrine. He wore a T-shirt and a towel around his waist. Down a hallway behind him, showers poured hot steam that swirled against the door's cold draft. Every time Charlie splashed the sink's freezing water against his cheeks he grimaced. He hated shaving but knew it was necessary to ensure a good seal of his oxygen mask against his face. Charlie saw his likeness in the mirror. His face was pale and his eyes hung sad. He could not smile. Sixteen days after December 20th he knew he had to get back over Germany or throw in the towel.

Dale greeted Charlie as he stepped up to a sink a few mirrors over. Charlie grunted a greeting between swipes of the razor. Dale seemed alert, as if he had been up for hours. Charlie marveled at his happy-go-lucky attitude.

"Shoot!" Dale said, pulling his razor away. Charlie glanced over and saw a crimson splotch through the shaving cream on Dale's cheek. When Dale placed the razor back to his face, Charlie saw his hand trembling. Dale nicked himself again. He looked over at Charlie with just his eyes, without turning his head. Charlie looked away.

Dale was to fly his fourth mission that day, and the prevailing rumor was that an airman stood a 25 percent chance of completing his tour. By those odds, after mission five, every flight was on borrowed time.

Charlie wanted to shout to Dale, *Why are we doing this to ourselves?* But he said nothing.* Charlie knew that no pilot wanted to fly tight formation with someone rattled, shaky, or flak happy. The third time Dale nicked himself, Charlie could not take it anymore and departed, pretending he'd never noticed.

Inside the officer's mess, amid the smells of fried SPAM and coffee, Charlie followed Dale through the chow line. Scrawled across the back of Dale's jacket was the name of his plane, *Rikki-Tikki-Tavi II*, in jungle leaf letters. Below the letters, someone had painted a likeness of the smiling black mongoose, Rikki-Tikki-Tavi, a character from Rudyard Kipling's *The Jungle Book*. In the book, Rikki-Tikki-Tavi defends a British family from two poisonous cobras, at great risk and suffering to himself. Alongside the mongoose on Dale's jacket, someone had painted three yellow bombs that signified Dale's completed missions, his commitment to his tour. The back of Charlie's jacket, like those of his remaining crew, was blank.

A cook behind the chow line, maybe Snuffy himself, ladled eggs onto Charlie's plate. The man grinned politely. Before a mission, the ground personnel restrained their smiles, projecting quiet respect until the flyboys were in the air. They never whistled or joked or said "Go get 'em." Most of the cooks could imagine where the airmen were headed, a place Snuffy knew too well. *Why did I volunteer for this?* Charlie thought, as he looked from the cook in his dirty apron to the scared pilot ahead of him, his face nicked up, and the mongoose Rikki-Tikki-Tavi beckoning: "Follow me."

---

* "There was no way that you could express that you made a mistake in volunteering," Charlie would remember. "There was nobody that I could talk to. I couldn't tell my copilot, any of my crew, or even the other pilots. I could not do anything that indicated any weakness."

———————

THE B-17S TAXIED one behind the other through the ground fog, the lights in the bombers' wings glowing like lanterns on a ship's bow. Every time a bomber launched down the main runway, the others rolled forward a plane length, then stopped.

Far back in the snaking line, Charlie and Pinky sat behind the controls of another borrowed B-17, this one named *Duffy's Tavern*. Charlie steered the bomber while Pinky leaned outside his window and shouted corrections to him so Charlie could keep the plane on the narrow taxiway. Charlie squinted at the two small white taillights of the bomber ahead, trying to maintain a safe distance while trusting the pilot behind him to do the same.

It was 7:45 A.M., but a sinister dark fog had turned morning at Kimbolton Air Base into night. The chilly fog floated in through Pinky's window. A few degrees colder and it would have snowed. The runway lights passed by like tiny lighthouses on a foggy coastline. Bombers named *Lakanuki*, *Deacon's Sinners*, and *Polly* launched one after another toward the northwest, their red and green wingtip lights streaking through the fog. "This is idiotic," Pinky said as he watched. Instead of agreeing, Charlie gripped the yoke more tightly, his eyes darting with intensity. He was certain that nothing would stop him from logging this mission, another to Kiel, Germany.

Soon just a few planes sat between Charlie's bomber and the right-hand turn onto the runway. Through Pinky's side window, Charlie saw a bomber launch and disappear into the fog at the runway's halfway point. Suddenly, a yellow flash cut through the fog followed by the sound of a thunderclap.

"Oh shit!" Pinky said as he recoiled. Charlie stomped on the plane's brakes. Flashes blinked from the end of the runway, each followed by an explosion like two fogbound ships trading broadside cannon bursts.

"Dear Lord!" Charlie said. He knew that one of their planes had just crashed on takeoff. The bomber ahead of them sat still. The radio was silent. Pinky said halfheartedly that the mission would be scrubbed now. Then the shortwave radio squawked with a call from the tower and a terse message: "Continue takeoff sequence." Pinky looked at Charlie with alarm. "What about the wreckage?" he asked. Charlie just shook his head, his fists trembling on the controls.

The bomber ahead of them moved up a spot, and Charlie knew another plane had launched. Charlie released the brakes and let his bomber crawl a few steps. He and Pinky could see the orange glow of the wreckage but had no sense of depth or distance.

Two planes ahead of Charlie, *Rikki-Tikki-Tavi II* turned onto the runway with Dale at the controls. The bomber revved its engines, sucking the fog around its body and blowing gray wisps from its tail. The lights of the bomber behind it lit *Rikki-Tikki-Tavi II*'s tail as it rolled forward and launched, vanishing like the others into the fog.

After the bomber ahead of them had begun its takeoff roll, Charlie revved the engines on the left wing and began swinging his plane onto the runway. It was his turn—finally. He leaned forward, trying to see the white marks of the runway's centerline. An explosion, a bigger one, erupted in the sky ahead. Its orange tentacles of fire curled among the clouds.

"Holy shit!" Pinky yelled.

"That has to be another one of ours!" Charlie said, his eyes fixed on the orange glow as it fell through the clouds to earth.

"There goes another midair collision," someone said calmly over the radio.

A heavy *thump, thump, thump* drew Charlie's attention forward. His eyes widened as his bomber rolled off the runway and onto the grass. Distracted, he had forgotten to complete the turn. He stomped on the brakes and cursed. Gunning the engine, Charlie tried to swing the bomber back onto the concrete, but it had dug into the soggy ground and would not budge.

Charlie ripped off his headphones and slapped them against the instrument panel. His cursing increased when he felt his bomber shake as the planes behind him took off, leaving him and his crew behind.

Pinky leaned back in his seat and held his face in his hands. He looked like he wanted to cry.

"Is everything okay up there?" a crewman's shaky voice asked over the intercom.

Charlie slumped over the control yoke in disbelief. Pinky turned to Charlie and asked if he should call for the aircraft's evacuation.

"No—we're flying this goddamn mission!" Charlie shouted, his eyes turning wild. He pushed the throttles full forward. The bomber's wheels trembled but would not budge. When Charlie pulled back on the throttles, the plane seemed to rock back on its heels. Revving the engines again, Charlie cursed like a madman. Pinky shouted, imploring him to stop, telling Charlie the bomber would never move with a full bomb load. The bomber shook from the engine's fury. Its wheels vibrated, wanting to break free of the mud. Pinky reached and pulled the throttles back, shouting, "Let's wait for the ground crew!" Charlie shoved Pinky's hand away and pushed the throttles forward. The bomber trembled then broke free. Its tires rolled up and over the troughs in the mud then onto the concrete runway. Charlie pulled the throttles back to align the bomber's nose with the centerline then rammed the throttles forward again. The bomber roared down the runway and leapt into the skies, soaring over the first burning bomber that had crashed in the field beyond the runway and over two others that had collided barely three miles from the runway. Charlie flew the bomber blindly up through the clouds, looking for the group.

Ten minutes later, Charlie flew in the clear, above the clouds. He was still over England when Doc told him over the intercom that they stood no chance of catching up with the formation. "We either turn back or go to Germany alone," Doc said.

Charlie scowled as he stared ahead as if he could see Germany. Pinky turned to Charlie, with fear in his eyes, and said, "For God's sake, don't." Charlie's scowl softened and dropped into a look of defeat as he banked the control yoke left and turned back for Kimbolton. He flew tight-lipped, without asking Doc for a heading. Charlie knew the fires on the ground would guide him home.

THAT SAME MORNING, AN HOUR LATER

In the quiet warmth of the officer's club, Charlie sat at a square cocktail table and sipped from a glass of Scotch. Two shot glasses sat before him, empty. On a sign above the club's door, red letters spelled, DUFFY'S TAVERN, the club's nickname. The B-17 Charlie had flown that day had been named in the club's honor. A few officers sat around the bar and drank bloody Marys beneath a red-and-white striped awning that gave the bar a poolside flare. Someone had painted a beautiful blonde in a white bathing suit on the bar, and another reclining, with her back turned, over the club's entrance.

Charlie glanced at his watch with glassy eyes, following the group's progress in his mind. He knew they were approaching the German coast. When anyone entered the club, Charlie looked up at them with guilt. With two aborts in a row on his record, he knew he had become what the pilots called an outcast—a "pariah." The real reasons behind the aborts—a bad engine and getting mired in the mud—didn't matter. What mattered was that he had done it twice. Every pilot knew that one abort was common because B-17s were complex machines that often broke. But two aborts in a row was a pattern that would give rise to suspicions of cowardice. The officers ignored Charlie. Instead, they ordered coffee and sat down around him to read newspapers. With the group gone, word of Charlie's abort had not yet traveled back, so the officers did not yet know that they had a pariah in their midst.

Charlie was not the only pariah in Duffy's Tavern. The club's manager was a major who had been a pilot in the group until he covered his eyes during a German fighter attack. Preston had grounded the major but allowed him to run the officer's club. Ashamed for letting the group down, the major now managed the club with vigor, turning it into a contender for the best-stocked bar in England. The other pilots had come to respect the major once again because they no longer had to fly with him.

Between drinks, Charlie reached inside of his brown jacket and unfolded a letter from Marjorie. Since December 20 he had fast become a drinker and justified it, telling himself it was medication for his nerves.* Charlie had carried Marjorie's letter with him that morning as a good luck charm. Now he read the letter with cold eyes. As a joke, Marjorie had written that she wanted to apply to be his copilot. She also made Charlie grit his teeth when she asked: "Is it as bad as you thought it would be?"

Charlie wanted to tell her so much. He wanted to tell her about watching Dale Killion's hand shaking as he shaved that morning. He wanted to tell her about how Ecky's chubby little boots pointed up from the stretcher. He wanted to tell her that he had just watched thirty young men die an hour prior. Their lives ended in a series of flashes. They were young men who had spent twenty or twenty-two years on earth, growing and learning and living, just to die fewer than three lousy miles from their base, planted into an English field. Charlie crumpled Marjorie's letter. He wanted to ask her, *Would you have wanted to be the copilot on any of those planes?*

Charlie was angry at Marjorie only because he was angry with himself. He had realized that morning that his fate rested not in the hands of his enemy. The enemy had not killed the thirty men that morning. The odds had killed them. Charlie had decided that the odds were going to get him, too—if he kept flying.

Shuffling toward his barracks, Charlie passed the squadron opera-

---

* "For combat people, self-medicating is a big part of their reason for drinking," Charlie would remember. "I only had two men on my crew who were not heavy drinkers, and both men ended up with psychological problems."

tions hut. He knew all he had to do was walk into the hut, fill out a form, and his flying days could be over. The clerk who worked there had once been a waist gunner. Rather than resign from combat duties, the man had taken his gloves off at high altitude and held his hands out in the slipstream until his fingers were severely frostbitten. Charlie knew he didn't have to freeze his fingers to achieve the same result. He could do it with the swipe of a pen. He knew shame. He had grown up a poor farm kid unable to afford a comic book at the local drugstore. He could live with it.

Then, Charlie saw him. A man was walking toward Charlie's hut with a brown box between his arms. Charlie knew the man, the orderly who gutted men's footlockers when they went missing. The man opened the hut's door and slipped inside. Charlie's eyes bulged with alarm. He ran across the field after him.

Charlie entered the hut and found the orderly walking from bunk to bunk looking for someone's footlocker.

"Can I help you?" Charlie asked, defensively.

"No, sir, I don't mean to be a bother," the orderly said as he opened a footlocker, sorted through some papers, and shut it. Charlie folded his arms.

Turning to Charlie, he asked, "Sir, maybe you can help me. Do you know which locker is Lieutenant Killion's?"

Charlie's face turned white. He dropped his arms.

"Why?" Charlie asked.

"Lieutenant Dale Killion and his crew were killed this morning," the orderly said, shaking his head. "The midair." Charlie sat heavily on the edge of a nearby cot as the orderly gave him the details.

Dale's plane had collided with a B-17 from the 303rd Bomb Group. Charlie knew the 303rd was based just six miles to the northwest, at Molesworth—the flash he had seen in the clouds had been Dale's death.[*]

---

[*] The official accident report would declare that no one was responsible because "it is impossible to avoid such accidents with so many aircraft in the same vicinity."

Seeing Charlie's face twist with emotion, the orderly apologized for bearing such news. Without a word, Charlie pointed to the bunk opposite his. The orderly knelt and opened the footlocker. He told Charlie he had to empty the lieutenant's locker of his belongings. "It's a shitty job, sir," he said. "And I've got nine more to go."

Charlie nodded, afraid to speak for fear of breaking down. The orderly gave Charlie permission to sort through Lieutenant Killion's belongings first, if he wished.

Charlie thanked him. He knelt and sifted through the box as the orderly stood back. Charlie held Dale's *Guide to Understanding England* book, and Dale's postcards of California, where he said he planned to live after the war. Stuck to the lid of the box with tape, Charlie saw photos of Dale with his farm family and a photo of him standing proudly in front of his B-17, his hands on his hips. Charlie's frown lifted slightly as the thought struck him. He and Dale had gone from being farmhands to captains of B-17s.

Charlie suddenly remembered the pride of flying a B-17. He remembered how the gunners waved when he formed up on another bomber's wing. He remembered seeing white American stars on the flanks of bombers that stacked up to the heavens. He remembered looking across the frozen gap between cockpits and seeing a pilot like Dale or Walt look back at him and nod. The other pilots were just as scared to die as he was, but up there, Charlie knew they had mastered their fears by keeping the formation tight and sticking together. After two weeks away from the formation, Charlie had forgotten his pride. Looking at Dale's photos, he remembered why he would not back out of the brotherhood he had volunteered for.

Charlie stepped from the footlocker and backed toward his bunk. The orderly scooped Dale's belongings into his cardboard box, nodded to Charlie, and departed, the box between his arms. Charlie sat on his bunk in the empty barracks and looked across the aisle to where Dale's footlocker sat empty. He suddenly knew what he had to do.

THAT SAME NIGHT

Charlie opened his footlocker and removed his leather jacket. With the jacket folded over his arm he entered the enlisted gunner's hut. The gunners stood to salute, but Charlie told them to relax. Charlie approached a group of gunners huddled in the hut's center around one man who was striking something with a clanging noise. When they saw Charlie, the gunners stood and backed away.

The man at the center turned and looked up at Charlie with a grin. Charlie could not help but smile when he saw that the rumors were true—Sam Blackford had returned. Charlie squatted next to Blackie and discovered he had laid a small sheet of metal on the floor over which he had piled wood shavings and sticks. Blackie held a flint clip in one hand and a square of steel in the other. With a smirk he explained that he was giving a Boy Scout lesson to his buddies.

"Back home, they call me Sour Dough Sam on the trail," he said proudly. Charlie told Blackie he was not a bit surprised. Blackie noticed that Charlie carried his jacket.

"Do you still want to paint your jacket?" Charlie asked Blackie.

Blackie nodded, his grin growing.

"Will you paint mine, too?" Charlie asked.

"Sure," Blackie said. "What do you want on there?"

"Two bombs," Charlie said. "One for each mission and leave room for more."

"How about I paint all the guys' jackets?" Blackie asked.

"Good idea," Charlie told him. "Paint 'em up."

On his way out the door, Charlie stopped, having forgotten something.

"Blackie, can you paint the word 'Bremen' on the bombs?" he asked. "When we get home," Charlie said, "we'll want to tell everyone where we've been."

TWO DAYS LATER, JANUARY 7, 1944

In the dimness of the hut Charlie dropped Marjorie's letter into his footlocker and shut the locker's lid. He had decided to write to her only after he had completed his tour, when he had something worth saying.*

On the airfield, a truck pulled up alongside the B-17 *The Celestial Siren*. Charlie and his crew—Pinky, Doc, Andy, Frenchy, Jennings, and Blackie—jumped from the lift gate along with three replacement crewmembers named Liddle, Miller, and Paige. War paint covered all of their jackets. Blackie had painted the squadron patch, a skull and crossed bombs, on the front breast of some and "The Quiet Ones" across the upper backs of others. On the jackets of the men who had flown on December 20, he had painted two swastikas, one for each fighter that the crew had shot down, and a bomb with the word "Bremen" written across it. On each man's jacket read the words "379th Bomb Group."

Charlie looked at his watch and declared, "All right, let's get on with it." The gunners sauntered around the plane to enter from the rear door. Charlie waited while Doc, Andy, and Pinky swung up through the hatch beneath the nose. The tired old crew chief, Shack, and his ground crew stood watching. Charlie tossed his kit bag through the hatch. He reached up and with an underhand grip seized the bar that ran across the hatch. In one smooth motion he curled his legs and swung up and into the bomber. His hand reached back down and slammed the hatch shut.

———————

THAT DAY, CHARLIE flew the Quiet Ones to Ludwigshaven, Germany, and safely back. In the days that followed, the Quiet Ones would be

———————

* Charlie would write to Marjorie, months later. When he did write, his letter would come back: "Undeliverable."

issued a bomber of their own, a B-17G named *Carol Dawn*. They would fly their next twenty-six missions together. They would survive a mission to Brunswick when the bombers on their right and left wings would be shot from the sky, and the ride home from Berlin when they would lose two engines simultaneously over the sea. They would return from Frankfurt when a massive headwind slowed them to a crawl over a flak zone. During those moments of terror, Charlie would have flashbacks and glance at the bomber's right wing tip expecting to see the German pilot there, flying with him.

On April 11, 1944, Charlie and his original crew would complete their twenty-eighth and final mission after an eleven-hour flight to Sorau, Germany. Beneath their bomber's nose, Charlie would smoke a cigar and drink from a bottle of whiskey that he would pass between Pinky, Doc, Andy, Frenchy, and Blackie. Even Jennings would break his rule and take a sip. They had survived their tour and more. By the war's end, they and other young men like them would have helped the 379th earn the title "the Grand Slam Group" for flying more missions, dropping more bombs, achieving higher bombing accuracy, and suffering fewer losses than any other group in the 8th Air Force. By war's end, the 379th would be the best in the bombing business.

On that day when Charlie would watch his men toast their survival, in the back of his mind he would wonder about the German pilot who had escorted them out of hell. *Who was he and why did he let us go?* Charlie would look to the eastern horizon and secretly hope that his enemy would survive the war.

18

STICK CLOSE TO ME

LIGHT FLURRIES FELL from the gray clouds across the grass airfield as Franz knelt on the wing of the 109. Behind him, the wind blew across the city of Graz from the snowy blue mountains to the north. It was 1:00 P.M., but the winter weather made the day feel later. Franz leaned in close to the rookie pilot who sat strapped into the plane, his face long, pale, and harmless.

"We hit hard, hit first, then get the hell out of there," Franz told the pilot, a young corporal named Heinz Mellman. Mellman nodded rapidly with fear. Today would be his first combat mission. Mellman looked like a teenager compared to Franz, now twenty-nine years old. Franz's face had grown leaner, his jaw stronger, and his nose sharper. Flying three hundred combat missions had turned him into a grown man. Franz and the rookie wore the new flight uniform: all gray leather with a black velvet collar. The rookie wore the other new fashion, a forage cap, a boxy ball cap with a long brim that kept falling snow from one's eyes. Franz didn't like the forage caps and instead kept his gray officer's crush cap that was crumpled and worn in spots.

Franz gazed south across the airfield and saw three squadrons, some thirty-six fighters, scattered about. Graz Airfield was an earthen strip set almost within the city's southern limits. On some days the grass runway wore a blanket of snow. On either side of Franz and Mellman sat ten other pilots in their 109s, each waiting for a flare to arc across the field and tell them to start their engines, the sign that the Four Motors were near. The ground crewmen in their dirty black coveralls kept their distance out of respect for the aviators.

Two months earlier, Roedel had taken Franz from Bobbi, Willi, and his comrades in Squadron 6 and shipped him to Yugoslavia. Roedel had promoted Franz and made him the leader of JG-27's Squadron 12. Eleven pilots came under Franz's care. Bobbi had to remain with Squadron 6 because he was their mascot, but before Franz and Willi parted, Willi had promised Franz, "Don't worry, I'll look after the bear."

Just three days prior, Franz had led Squadron 12 to its new home at Graz. At Graz, new faces appeared—rookie replacement pilots. Within the batch of rookies were Mellman and another youngster, Sergeant Gerhard Sonntag, both assigned to Franz. Both of the young men were in their early twenties, but neither had flown combat yet. That day Franz had scheduled them to fly as his wingmen on their first mission. He knew if they survived a week's worth of missions they might just make it as pilots.

Franz thrust a hand into his thigh pocket and scooped out a handful of roasted coffee beans. He chewed a few, savoring the caffeine kick. Franz offered some to Mellman, who declined. The days were gone when replacements were veterans of Spain or the Channel Front. What veterans the Air Force still had left were scattered at all ends of the continent, dropping one by one, leaving rookies like Mellman to take their place.* When Franz looked at Mellman, he knew he was looking at Germany's great tragedy—a generation of innocents too young to have seen the rise of Hitler or The Party who now were forced to pay for their leaders' sins.

Franz looked to the tower but still saw no flares. He knew the bombers were on the way. The early reports said three hundred American heavies had departed Italy and were heading north. At that moment, German Air Force spotter girls were sitting in the mountains of Italy and Yugoslavia, tracking the bombers with binoculars and calling in their progress to JG-27. The lower half of Italy had become the Allies' newest base after their conquest of Sicily. Everyone knew the invasion of France would come next, giving the Allies new airfields, even closer ones.

"If you're hit, bail out away from the bombers," Franz reminded Mellman. "Float through a bomber formation and the gunners will shoot you." The rookie nodded, gulping.

Seeing the ill effect of his warning so close to takeoff, Franz slapped the rookie on his back and assured him, "Stick close to me and you'll come home alive." Mellman managed a smile. Franz never was cocky before, but now he exuded a forced confidence to bolster the spirits of the younger guys.

Franz slid from the wing and walked to the fighter of his other rookie, Sonntag, to give him the same talk. Franz stopped and shouted back to Mellman, "If you're going to get sick, do it now, outside your plane!" The ground crewmen thanked Franz with a chuckle.

After talking with Sonntag, Franz settled into his fighter. He still flew his old *Yellow 2*, only now the plane's rudder was painted white, the mark of a squadron leader. The Berlin Bear crest had been wiped

---

* "I really worried about these kids and along with most responsible squadron commanders tried to bring them along slowly but the war would not always wait," Franz would remember. "I can remember that terrible feeling I got when I was forced to have them fly combat before they were anywhere near ready, for I well recall how green I was during my first combat and I had several thousand hours of flying time."[1]

from the plane's nose and Franz had not bothered to add an edelweiss flower, the crest of his new parent unit, IV Group. Sealing the canopy, Franz relaxed within the familiar aroma of oil, gun powder, and sweat-drenched leather. Franz rapidly cycled his black rosary beads through his fingers. The black paint had begun to fleck from the beads, revealing their true color, a pale purple. His prayers had changed lately. He now prayed that he would lead others well. He no longer prayed for himself or for his safety. He had long given up on the idea of surviving the war. Franz had been away from Squadron 6 for only two weeks when a sergeant came looking for him on his base in Yugoslavia. The sergeant nervously told Franz that the wing commander—Roedel—was on the phone in the tower, waiting to talk with him. The sergeant thought Franz was in trouble, not knowing that Franz and Roedel were protégé and mentor. The date was January 29 and Roedel was calling from his headquarters near Vienna. He sounded disturbed. The day's casualty report, a teletype, had come across his desk. Willi was dead.

Willi had led his squadron against eight hundred bombers that had bombed Frankfurt. The bombers' P-38 escorts had chased Willi down to earth, where the clouds were low and foggy. Disoriented, Willi had flown into the ground. Franz could not believe it. Willi was gone, at twenty-two years old, planted into the earth fifty miles west of Wiesbaden, near the town of Wurrich. All Roedel could say was that he was sorry. Franz heard defeat in Roedel's voice. When he hung up, Franz buried his face in his hands. For a few days he beat himself up over the thought that he could have saved Willi, because they had once handled a dozen P-38s—just the two of them.

A red flare shot across the field. Dropping his rosary into his chest pocket, Franz signaled his ground crewman to crank over the engine. Franz and his pilots ignited their fighters' snarling V-12s. The spinners of planes belonging to their sister squadrons—Squadrons 10 and 11—also spun to life around the field. Franz looked to his left and right to confirm that all his pilots' engines were humming. White smoke belched from their exhaust ports. When green flares arced across the field, Franz flashed a half salute to his crew chief and taxied away. His two young wingmen and the others followed him into the skies.

Franz had not shot down a plane since encountering the wounded B-17 over Bremen on December 20. Since that encounter Franz's priorities had changed. He no longer strove for victories. Now his mission was to get his boys home. With the arrival of 1944, the benchmark for the Knight's Cross had been raised to "magic 40." Franz couldn't care less.

TWENTY MINUTES LATER, FORTY MILES SOUTHWEST OF GRAZ

From his perch at twenty-nine thousand feet, Franz and his squadron mates circled. Franz smiled through his oxygen mask. Some ten thousand feet beneath him flew thirty-five B-24 Liberators without fighter escort. The B-24s looked like mustardy brown Ts against the thick winter clouds. Several miles behind the bomber formation Franz saw a second batch of B-24s that looked to be even fewer in number.

Checking his wingtips, Franz told his rookies to tighten up. Mellman flew on his left wing and Sonntag on his right. The old days of staggered formations were gone. Now, with so many rookies in the ranks, the new German formation was to fly side by side so the flight leader could keep an eye on his wingmen.

The B-24s kept motoring northward, their gunners undoubtedly watching the 109s, waiting for them to attack. His heart pounding, Franz scanned the skies for their escort fighters. He saw none. This never happened over Germany. Franz was accustomed to raids of five hundred bombers and had heard that the 8th Air Force was now sending thousand-bomber raids, since February 20, a milestone the Americans called "Big Week." What Franz saw below him seemed too good to be true.

"Keep your eyes peeled for escorts!" Franz's group leader snapped over the radio. The group leader was talking to him. "Yes, sir," Franz replied. Franz's squadron was on "high patrol," and their job was to watch for escort fighters and cover the other squadrons so they could attack the bombers. Below, Franz could see the group leader as he led the unit's other two squadrons.

Franz scanned the skies, again, but was certain that the bombers had come without escorts. "Sir, you're clear to attack," he radioed the group leader. But something was wrong. The group leader was not attacking. Instead, he led his twenty-four fighters in an orbit beyond the range of the B-24s' guns.

"Sir, no enemy escorts in sight," Franz said again.

"Keep looking!" the group leader replied tersely.

Franz saw the B-24s turning northeast. Franz's heart sunk. The bombers were aiming for a target near Graz, maybe one in the city itself.

"Sir, what are you waiting for?" Franz asked the group leader, alarmed.

"Shut up!" the group leader retorted. "I'm watching for their escorts!"

Franz had seen some leaders, after they had won the Knight's Cross, grow cautious and weary of combat, as if their incentive to fight had waned, but this group leader had no Knight's Cross and half the victories that Franz had. Still, he was in command.

As the B-24s curved right, toward Graz, their American crews marveled at the sight of so many 109s doing nothing. In the lead plane a navigator of the 450th Bomb Group would report: "From the lack of aggressiveness displayed it was evident that the enemy aircraft were trailing our formation waiting for stragglers damaged by flak."

Angry, Franz radioed the group leader and told him they needed to attack at once. He could see they were headed for Graz, the city of all cities that they were to protect. The group leader did not reply.

The first thirty-five bombers got away. Franz could see them, turning onto their bomb run. Flashes blinked through the gaps in the

clouds over Graz and told Franz the bombers had dropped their payload. Franz saw the second formation of nineteen bombers now passing beneath him. Franz radioed the group leader and asked permission
for Squadron 12 to attack the bombers below.

"Hold position!" the group leader replied. The second flight of
bombers slowly slipped away. Franz had heard that Roedel was in the
air with planes from I Group and III Group, patrolling northwest of
Graz. But summoning him would require an act of mutiny.

Switching radio channels, Franz called the radio operator back at
the air base. A female voice replied. Franz told the woman to alert
Roedel's flight that the heavies were approaching Graz from the south.
A few minutes later, the female controller reported back that Roedel
was near Graz and preparing to attack.

Relieved and emboldened, Franz radioed his squadron, "Follow me!"

In defiance of his leader, Franz throttled forward and engaged the
superchargers hidden beneath his fighter's bulges.* His 109 surged.
Franz felt the torque build through the stick. With his squadron behind him, Franz raced north to catch up to the heavies. Far ahead,
Franz saw a swarm of 109s—Roedel and his pilots—diving and attacking the bombers. Franz wanted to cheer.

Minutes later, Franz caught up to the B-24s. On the tops and sides
of the bombers' tails were two white circles, one containing a black
number 1 and the other a black diamond, the markings of the 454th
Bomb Group. Franz told his rookie wingmen to wait a few seconds
then follow him. He radioed his men, "Let's get them!" and unleashed
his squadron. Breaking from flights into solo elements, they dove on
their prey. Franz pulled up and over and dove toward the B-24s from
an almost vertical angle.

---

* "Finally, after repeated calls to my commander, and furious because we were allowing
a prize opportunity to slip through our fingers, I initiated the attack," Franz would
remember.[2]

A screaming plummet from the heavens had become Franz's attack method of choice against bombers. He aimed just ahead of the rearmost bomber. As his altimeter wound backward, Franz had no time to look back to see if his wingmen were there. He knew that of any attack, this eye-watering test of courage was their best chance at survival. Through his gun sight Franz saw his target from above and at its widest. He knew the bomber was also at its weakest. Only its top turret gunner could fire at him, but to shoot the gunner had to aim straight up into the sky.

Franz's cheeks sucked back against his oxygen mask. His fighter's wings quivered. The 109 raced toward the earth like a bolt from the blue. Franz's control yoke and rudder grew heavy from the terrifying speed. As Franz neared his target, time seemed to accelerate. As the bomber flew faster, its wings seemed to stretch and swell. The B-24 grew vivid in color, sharper in detail. Suddenly it filled Franz's windscreen. Franz mashed his triggers, awakening his fighter's machine guns and cannon. His guns belched their mechanical rage for a split second, stitching the bomber between its wings. Franz twisted his fighter and dove past the bomber's double tail, barely missing it. He felt his fighter shake from the bomber's wake. Franz did not know if the rookies had fired their guns, nor did he care.

"You did it, now head for home!" Franz ordered Mellman and Sonntag as they pulled up behind him. In Franz's mind, his purpose had been served, to get them through the first pass. Now he was fighting for the people of Graz. With his rookies disengaged, Franz used the speed from the dive to climb back up and dive again. In his second dive, another B-24 fell, and then another fell on his third pass. Each time as he dove through the formation, the bombers' gunners stopped firing, afraid to hit other bombers.

Of the two breeds of Four Motors, B-24s were easier to shoot down than B-17s. B-24s were faster due to their thin, high-mounted wing, but also more fragile. Their wings would fold if hit at the spot where they conjoined, and Liberators had fuel lines leading into the bomb bay that could be easily ignited. When they caught fire, they would quickly burn the plane from the center out.

Roedel's fighters kept pummeling the formation. Soon eight plumes of black smoke rose from crashed bombers in a path along the road to Graz. But Graz would not be unscathed. The first formation of bombers that the group leader let escape had dropped 105 tons of bombs on a factory in the city and across the south side of the town, as their after-action report would record.

Only half the bombers of the second formation would bomb Graz. They would later report, "Formation was attacked by 40–50 Me 109s and Fw 190s. These made aggressive attacks. After attacking, they peeled under formation, reformed and attacked again." Thirty minutes after Roedel had sparked the battle, Franz knocked down his fourth B-24 then turned for home. What bombers remained limped over the horizon. Of the first formation, all thirty-five B-24s would return home to Italy. Of the second formation, only nine out of nineteen would make it back to their base.

Franz would never fully know the horror that he and his pilots had inflicted. The first B-24 they attacked, the one in the rear of the formation, was named *Hot Rocks*. It was one of the earliest bombers to fall. The men crewing *Hot Rocks* were superstitious and had expected bad luck before they got to Graz. They had borrowed *Hot Rocks* from another crew because their usual plane was under repair. Making matters worse, the crew had taken on a stranger, a replacement gunner named Sergeant Michael Buffalino, and the mission was their thirteenth. When *Hot Rocks* lost an engine for no reason on the run to Graz, the bomber straggled behind the others. The crew was convinced they were cursed. Then the fighters came. A gunner in a bomber alongside *Hot Rocks* reported seeing a 109 pour "a burst of cannon shells" into the plane at the start of the battle, lighting her on fire. Seconds later, a second 109 blasted *Hot Rocks* in the tail but she struggled onward.

Inside *Hot Rocks*, the right waist gunner, Sergeant Lyle Taylor, saw the tail turret explode behind him from a fighter's cannon shells. The explosion tossed the new gunner, Buffalino, into the plane's waist. In pain, Buffalino pounded the bomber's wooden floor with his fists. Blood poured from the seams of his oxygen mask. Taylor ran to Buffalino and hooked him up to an oxygen tank. Buffalino tore away his mask and revealed his badly mangled face.

Taylor looked toward the bomb bay and saw the silhouettes of the other crewmen scrambling toward him. A fiery inferno followed them as flames spewed from the bomb bay. There was now only one way out of the Liberator, a hatch by the tail. The gunners ran for it while Taylor cared for Buffalino. The parachute of one of the gunners must have been on fire, because when he jumped it never opened. From lack of oxygen, Taylor passed out. The fire's heat on his face woke him. Through stinging eyes he looked for Buffalino, but he was gone. Buffalino had chosen to jump without a chute rather than perish in the flames. Taylor looked around, found his chute, slipped it on, then rolled through the hatch and into the open sky.

In the nose of *Hot Rocks*, the bombardier, Second Lieutenant William Reichle, was suffering through a personal hell. Twenty-two-year-old Reichle, a former Ohio State college baseball star, was holding his best buddy, Francis Zygmant, trying to plug his bleeding bullet wounds with his gloved fingers. Zygmant was a Polish-American kid from New Jersey. When Zygmant breathed his last, Reichle returned to his guns and called out fighters over the intercom, his dark eyes bulging wildly with shock.

Reichle was not aware that the intercom was dead, nor had he heard the pilot and copilot ring the bail-out bell. Reichle only knew that he was in trouble when the flight engineer came into the bomber's nose carrying a heavy box of ammo. He screamed to Reichle that they were riding in an empty plane and a fire had blocked the path to the rear escape hatch. The flight engineer thought quickly, then dragged the ammo box to the spot where the nose wheel retracted up into the plane. He lifted the box above his head and slammed it through the door that held the nosewheel up. The door fell away, leaving a hole. The flight engineer wiggled through his makeshift escape hatch. Reichle slipped his bulky parachute over his back and dove after him. Taylor and Reichle would survive and become P.O.W.s, but their crew lost three men that day, including Buffalino, whose mother would write to the survivors for years to ask what happened to her son. None could ever tell her the truth.

Franz was already flying home for Graz when the group leader radioed, "Stigler! Return to base immediately!" His adrenaline flowing, Franz snapped back, "Yes, sir, it's time to refuel anyway!" Franz knew the group leader had never attacked and instead had orbited above the whole battle. Only a few brave pilots from the other squadrons had broken orders and followed Franz's lead.

As he flew home toward the smoke that rose from Graz, Franz realized he could be tried for insubordination and possibly stripped of his command. His fears were confirmed when his radio crackled to life. The group leader must have landed because the unit's radio operator, a woman, called Franz and told him to report to the command center as soon as he had landed.

The instant Franz's boots hit the ground, he raced to the headquarters to plead his case. As Franz walked down the hallway to the group leader's office, he heard a voice booming, angrily telling someone what Franz had done. At the entrance to the office, Franz saw Roedel leaning on the commander's desk, his arms crossed. The group leader turned to Franz, his face red. Franz saluted Roedel, who saluted back with a thin smile. Roedel had landed with the pilots of his staff, to rearm and refuel in case more bombers came. He told Franz he had heard the claims against him and now he wanted to hear Franz's defense. Franz told his story. Content, Roedel reminded the group leader that everyone was tired and urged him to get some rest. Roedel departed the office and told Franz to come with him. Franz took one look at the group leader and saw the man fuming, having been politely told by Roedel that he was in the wrong.

Franz and Roedel lit up cigarettes outside. They watched the mountains turn colder—a snowstorm was brewing. Whenever possible Roedel smoked American cigarettes, which he obtained by trading food with captured bomber crews. He was going to leave to fly back to Vienna with his staff before they got stuck at Graz. Roedel had claimed two bombers of the twenty that JG-27's pilots would claim to have shot down within thirty minutes. Roedel asked how many bombers Franz had downed. "Four, with help," Franz said. Roedel smiled and nodded in approval. He knew four victories was incredible but not impossible. He had been flying on the September day in Africa when Marseille had claimed seventeen victories, several of which Roedel had himself witnessed.

After Roedel departed, Franz found Mellman and Sonntag in the squadron lounge. He told them to come with him to claim victories. The young pilots assumed that Franz wanted them to sign off as witnesses to his victories. Instead of filling out forms himself, Franz pushed a pile of papers in front of each rookie. He said he was pretty sure they each had knocked down a B-24. The rookies looked at him with surprise. They admitted they had been too afraid to look back.

"You fired, didn't you?" Franz asked them.

They both nodded.

"I saw bombers fall," Franz said. "They were yours."

With a swipe of his pen, he put his signature onto their papers.[*]

In the local pub that night, Mellman and Sonntag would rehash the battle using their hands in place of planes while Franz watched quietly from a distance. Willi had told Franz he would never get a Knight's Cross by not claiming victories. If only Willi could have seen him now, giving away victories. Franz knew the rookies would write

---

[*] Franz would remember what he did with the victory claims: "I spread them all out. I know I had four but I couldn't care less. We shot them down, that was the important thing. We were quite elated of course. The crashes were all in Austria, so no one could say you didn't shoot them down, because the wreckages were there. The boys were on their first mission. That's the reason why I did it."

home of their victories to their parents. Their parents would tell friends and neighbors. But looking at them, Franz felt a wave of sadness. He knew the odds, and the odds said they would not survive the war. He would be right. Four months later, Heinz Mellman and Gerhard Sonntag would both be dead.

A WEEK LATER

When Franz and his squadron entered the banquet hall in Graz, each man wore his dress uniform and had brought a date, gathered from the ample supply of the town's lonely girls. The entire citizenry of Graz, it seemed, had turned out to honor the pilots. Because Franz and the others had knocked down so many B-24s, the townspeople overlooked the bombs that had fallen and threw a party instead.

Beneath the banquet hall's high ceiling, tables of hot food awaited the men while an oompah band played lively tunes, its members wearing tiny fedoras with feathers. Franz dismissed his squadron and told them to have a good time. The townspeople handed them glasses of hot red wine.

Franz's date hugged his arm. She was an eighteen-year-old girl who studied at the local university. Her name was Eva. Franz had met her through a friend who knew he needed a date for the dance. Eva was an aspiring actress and was as beautiful as a film starlet. Her curly hair was dark brown, her face was wide with prominent cheeks, and she wore a heavy dark jacket with a leopard-print collar. Beneath that was a fancy dress with real lace, probably a gift from a prior suitor.

Eva asked Franz to dance, but he said he preferred to watch. The merriment around him troubled him. No one danced cheek to cheek. Hitler had called that "kitsch," or distasteful, and had outlawed it along with music such as swing, jazz, and the blues. Yet still the people danced and smiled. Franz envied their optimism and knew it would change when the Allies' invasion landed. But Eva's personality was strong and charismatic; she would not give up. "It's just a dance," she laughed. Franz knew he was in trouble from the moment he drank his wine in a gulp and let the intoxicating girl lead him to the dance floor. The girl was charming and tenacious, with a personality that overwhelmed even Franz's stubborn nature. When they parted that night, Franz knew he had met his match.

A few days later, Franz gathered with Mellman, Sonntag, and the others around his fighter. Just ahead of the cockpit they looked at the new nose art that Franz had drunkenly asked a mechanic to paint during the night of the dance. The mechanic had painted a cartoon of a red apple with a green snake weaving through it, an allusion to the Garden of Eden. Alongside the cartoon were scrawled letters that spelled "Eva." "What was I thinking?" Franz wondered aloud as the others grinned. They had seen their leader, like them, three sheets to the wind.

In the days that followed, Franz would not have time to second-guess himself. An orderly greeted him one day with a telegram and tragic news. Franz's father had been killed, kicked by a horse while shoeing it for the Army. At sixty-five years old, the aged veteran had paid a final price for his service. As Franz flew his fighter home for the funeral, he flew with a face of stone. The war had taken his brother and now his father. He mourned the most for his mother. He knew that for the rest of her days when she sat down to drink her nightly beer, she would be drinking alone.

19

THE DOWNFALL

THE DAYS AND nights had blended into a blur to Franz as he led his squadron in taxiing along the edge of the pine forest to park. Beyond his right wingtip, he saw the ground crewmen congregating at the tree line. They waited for the 109s to shut down so they could push the fighters back under the trees to keep them safe from prowling Allied fighters. Franz's 109 still wore the "Eva" nose art. He and Eva had continued dating ever since the party at Graz, but Franz had kept his distance so things would not become serious. In the months since his time at Graz, Roedel had shifted Franz around to lead Squadron 8, Squadron 11, and even all of III Group for a short time. Now, Franz led Squadron 11 at Grossenhain Airfield in Eastern Germany.

Franz gunned his plane's engine, stomped the rudder, and swung the plane's nose toward the grass runway so his tail faced the pines to make the ground crew's job easier. His 109 was a new G-14 model. Its spinner was black and had a swirling white streak painted through it that produced a hypnotic effect as it spun, a paint trick meant to fixate the eyes of a bomber's gunners. The plane's rudder bore twenty-seven victory marks, three new white bars since Graz that represented victories over a P-38, a P-51, and a Spitfire. Franz knew Roedel disapproved of this, but he thought the marks would inspire his rookie pilots. These days they needed all the confidence they could get.

Franz cut his engine and popped his canopy. A burly mechanic climbed the wing of the plane and helped him remove his straps. One by one the other planes' engines wound to stillness. All of their canopies opened except for one fighter a few planes over from Franz. The mechanic helped lift Franz to his feet and steadied him on the wing. Franz looked pale and moved gingerly. He had flown three missions that day, as he had every day for months. He walked down the wing and was met by two other mechanics who helped him stand on solid ground. As they showed Franz to a waiting *kuebelwagen*, Franz saw the 109 with the canopy still closed.

"He's asleep," Franz told the mechanics. "Wake him gently."

THAT EVENING, FRANZ hunched over the table in his office to write a letter, as he did most nights. He was not writing to Eva—the frown on his face revealed that much. With a brown bottle of cognac and a glass at his side, he took sips of the golden liquid between dips of his pen in an ink vial. Every so often Franz looked at his door, anticipating the knock that he knew was coming.

That summer and fall, Franz had witnessed the slaughter of the Air Force. Now, at their new station north of Dresden, where Franz had once trained cadets, the Air Force had grown weak and thin. He and his comrades were still flying the old 109 because Goering gave them nothing better. Rookies now came to his squadrons with only ten flights in 109s, not the seventy-five flights Franz had made before deploying to Africa. The novice pilots now outnumbered the veterans in his squadron by three to one.

In an attempt to reverse the tide of the war after four years of his bad decisions, Goering had decided to drive the tired veterans like Franz harder. Now, on Goering's orders, pilots had to attack until out of ammo, land, rearm, refuel, and go up to attack again and again, until the bombers had all departed German airspace. Goering's new rule succeeded best in breaking men, causing them to lose their nerve and pass out in their cockpits to the hum of their engines. Pilots began to fly drunk. In Fighter Wing 26, a squadron leader even shot himself in his cockpit with a handgun.*

That night at the base, like most nights late in the war, Franz wrote to the parents of a young pilot who had been killed in action. He always told the parents that their son had died a hero, because the truth was too terrible to tell. The best the rookie knew was to "target fly"—straight and level—until an Allied fighter came along to claim him as a victory. "What can you do with kids like that?" Franz often lamented to his fellow veterans when they got drunk at night. By the time he finished the letter his bottle of cognac would be half-empty. When Franz splashed water on his face and looked in the mirror, he realized that he was penning the same kind of hollow letter that his brother's squadron leader had written to him when August died.

The knock always came in the evening. Franz knew it was coming that night; his group of forty pilots had lost nine of their men the week before. And so it happened. A light rapping on his heavy door. Then a heavier knocking. When Franz opened the door, he wanted to throw up his arms. He saw a new pilot standing there, a teenager, maybe seventeen years old. The new rookies these days were always lowly corporals. The boy reported for duty and gave Franz his name, but Franz tried to forget it just as quickly, to keep his own sanity. The boy's face was white and devoid of lines. He made Franz's rookies from Graz look like grown men.

The rookie clicked his heels and tried to look brave as he gave The

---

* "We were being beaten both physically and psychologically, literally hammered to destruction," Franz would remember.[1]

Party's stiff-armed salute. Franz returned the salute the old way, with a hand to his eyebrow. So much had changed since July 20, when a former Afrika Korps officer, Colonel Claus von Stauffenberg, had tried to assassinate Hitler. Stauffenberg was a Bavarian Catholic opposed to Hitler and had tried to kill him with a briefcase bomb that only wounded the dictator. In the aftermath, Hitler and The Party arrested five thousand suspected "conspirators" and executed two hundred of them. The Party turned paranoid. Suddenly they viewed the "old military" style of salute as a form of resistance, so they made their stiff arm salute mandatory. But Franz was too tired to adapt. The new salute was like the new award Berlin had given Franz on October 1. It was called "the German Cross," although it was not even a cross. It was Hitler's invention—a black swastika wrapped in a circular laurel wreath. It was worn on the tunic, below the right breast. The German Cross fell below the Knight's Cross in prestige and was awarded for six or more acts of bravery. Franz found it insulting and amusing that after four hundred combat missions someone thought he had finally managed six brave acts. He had to wear this "cross," no questions allowed.

Franz ushered the rookie into his office, sat him down, and welcomed him to Squadron 11 with a drink. He faked a smile and told the boy that he was lucky; he had joined "the best squadron in the Air Force." Franz told every new pilot this to bolster his spirits. He knew that no squadron in the Air Force was half of what he had known in the desert. There, he had served in a squadron of experts. Those days now seemed a mirage.

As DAWN CRACKED across the frozen horizon, Franz found himself suited up and watching the sky. He always prayed that the weather would be foul—preferably sleet or blinding snow—anything to keep his squadron from flying. He knew the rookies had to fly that day, possibly two, three, or four missions. He wanted them to have another day of life. More often than not, snow did not fall.

Franz and his pilots waited in chairs beneath the trees behind their planes. Mechanics had camouflaged the planes with black tarps that ran from the cockpit to the wings and with pine branches layered across the wings. A nearby radio speaker broadcast the air defense channel that announced when Allied fighters had entered German airspace. These days the Allied fighters were always spotted before the bombers. They would fly ahead of the bombers in a new strategy to kill the German fighters as they formed up, before they could attack the bombers. The strategy was devastatingly successful.

Franz looked at his nervous pilots around him and saw the rawest form of bravery. They were to go up against impossible odds. His enemies saw the same bravery. A B-17 pilot, Joseph Deichl, remembered, "When we did see the German fighters queuing up and start making their passes at us, we always thought they must have been on drugs or something because they were absolutely fearless, coming through the formation."[2] Goering, however, attributed his pilots' inability to stop the bombing raids as "cowardice." Their grievous losses did not matter to him. He accused his own pilots of sabotaging fuel depots so they wouldn't have fuel to fly. He told the general of fighters, Galland, that his wing and group commanders would rather "play with themselves on the ground" than fight. Goering told JG-77's leader, Steinhoff, "The fighter force is going to give battle to the last man. If it does not, it can go and join the infantry."[3] Goering even transmitted a message to group commanders authorizing them to court-martial pilots who had been seen to "run from a fight." If any pilots were found guilty, Goering wanted them shot in front of their comrades.

The fighter pilots' "problem," Goering decided, stemmed from their lack of National Socialist spirit, so he sent political agents into the squadrons. Some agents arrived undercover as typists or clerks whose job was to listen for anti-Party rhetoric. Other political officers were announced to the units as "inspirational officers," who led the squadrons in daily readings from Hitler's book, *Mein Kampf.* The pilots' reactions to the political officers were similar. "Nobody took kindly to being spied upon," one pilot wrote. "We all loathed these Commissar types and considered their presence among us to be an insult."[4]

When the radio blared out a warning that Allied fighters had crossed into German skies, Franz and his comrades turned toward the speaker. This alert served to warn student pilots and transport pilots to return to earth immediately. Franz's young pilots looked to him. They knew this was also their signal to launch—the announcement of Allied bombers would follow shortly. Franz looked back at the young men in his care. They were barely able to fly by instruments and only capable of simple aerobatics. Fuel shortages from Allied bombings had cut short their training. Since the spring, Germany's aviation fuel production was down from 175,000 tons per month to just 5,000 tons, and combat units, not training units, took every drop. At this point in the war, the average British pilot began combat after 450 flight hours of training. An American went into combat with 600 hours. Franz's rookies came to him with fewer than 150 hours of flying time.[*]

Franz stood. "Stick close to me," he reminded his boys, then walked to his fighter. He no longer told them, ". . . and you'll come home alive," because he knew it was no longer true. He had seen too many veterans die when trying to rescue rookies from hopeless predicaments. Since Graz, Franz himself had been shot down more times than he could count. In seven months, he had bailed out four times and belly-landed his fighter just as much. Franz still checked his rosary before every flight. The beads were now more purple than black. They were getting worn out, too. Still, off Franz went with the men and boys of Squadron 11 into the skies that others fled.

---

[*] Franz would remember, "My instincts told me to protect them [the rookies] as best I could. Many of them were lost the first time they went up. They would simply freeze and just sit there while P-51s and P-47s shot them to pieces. They didn't know what to do."[5]

SEVERAL DAYS LATER, OCTOBER 26, 1944

Franz's 109 taxied slowly to a halt along the trees. Its engine shut down, but the canopy did not open. The ground crewmen saw this and ran to the plane. The first to climb the wing popped the canopy open and saw that the windshield's glass had cracked like a white web. In the center was a hole the diameter of a man's pinky finger.

Grabbing Franz's shoulders, the crewman pulled his body toward him. Franz fell limply to the canopy rail, his head flopping like a ragdoll. The crewman gasped. Red blood surrounded a black hole of dried blood in Franz's forehead. A bullet had pierced the windscreen's supposedly bulletproof glass. The crewman looked at the back of Franz's head and checked for an exit wound, but there was none. He saw that Franz was still breathing. The crewmen lifted Franz from the fighter. On the ground, Franz slowly regained his senses and opened his eyes. The men were startled—they were certain that a bullet had pierced his brain. Franz opened the palm of his hand. In it was an inch-long copper bullet, its point mashed and coated with blood. The crewmen were in awe. Somehow Franz had managed to stay conscious long enough to land. They remembered to call for the medics only when Franz's eyes closed and he passed out again.

That evening the flight doctor cleaned and placed a bandadge on Franz's wound. The .50-caliber slug, which had come from a B-17's gun, had not pierced Franz's skull, although it had caused a nasty dent in his head. Franz stood to leave, but the doctor stopped him. The doctor knew Franz's skull was weakened, maybe fragmented.

Franz tried to pretend that he had not seen flashes of light. He denied having headaches. But the doctor knew better. Franz insisted he was not going to leave his young pilots, but the doctor told him otherwise. The doctor explained to Franz that he probably had brain trauma from the impact, problems that would be compounded by high altitude and stress. "You're grounded," he said, as if handing Franz a gift. But Franz begged him not to report his condition to the higher-ups. The doctor shook his head. He had to. He handed Franz a medical waiver that recorded that he had suffered brain damage, which could trigger "adverse behavior." The form said Franz "should not be held responsible for his actions." Franz reluctantly took the waiver and walked away, steadying himself against the wall.

A day later, Roedel called. Franz promised Roedel he could still fly, but Roedel knew better. He told Franz to take a leave of absence to the fighter pilot's rest home. Franz had heard of the resort on the banks of Lake Tegernsee, at the foot of the Alps below Munich. There sat a tall white, Alpine-style chalet, with the resort's name, FLORIDA, in bold letters over its wide, double doors. Pilots' weddings and Knight's Cross award parties were often held there. It was a place of levity where a tired pilot could check in with his commander's consent to enjoy good food, alcohol, a warm bed with feather comforter, views of the lake, and a place to repair his mind. A pilot could stay there weeks or months. If he claimed his nerves were no better, he could sit out the rest of the war. To placate Roedel, Franz agreed to check into Florida. As Franz packed his bags, sadness struck him when he looked at his tan JG-27 cuff band that said AFRIKA. He had been with JG-27 for two years and seven months before a lone bullet took him down. The men of the legendary "Desert Wing" had become the only friends he had left, and now he was leaving them.

At a time when Germany needed every fighter pilot, Franz Stigler was out of the war.

SEVERAL WEEKS LATER, NOVEMBER 1944

Franz was amazed at the destruction around him as he sat in a train that chugged through the suburbs of Berlin. The train passed by buildings that looked like cutaways, whole walls sheared off and their insides gutted. Stairways in apartments climbed up to floors that had fallen through. Children played among the rubble in the streets. Other children watched from the sidelines, some on crutches, others missing limbs. Sixteen RAF firebomb raids had likely caused this ruination. The 8th Air Force had hit Berlin the prior March, before shifting focus to bomb targets in France in preparation for D-Day.

The people who sat in front of and behind Franz were silent and depressed. Their clothes were worn and tattered. Everyone wore the same weary frown. Franz had heard how the British had sent a few speedy Mosquito bombers over Berlin every night, just enough to trigger the air raid sirens and send people stumbling outside to the bomb shelters, a form of psychological warfare to deny the populace sleep. It worked.

Now their tired eyes glanced at Franz in his black leather jacket and gray riding pants. They saw that his black gloves had all their fingers intact. They looked at his thick cheeks and knew he was healthy, while their faces were lean and gaunt from substitute "ersatz" foods. Their "coffee" was made from oats and barley and tinted with an extract taken from coal tar. Their "meat" and "fish" were really just rice cakes flavored with animal fat or fish oil. Their "bread" was made of flour from ground chestnuts. In some cases, the people expanded their rations with pet rabbits and house cats.

Shouldn't you be flying? their eyes seemed to ask Franz with sarcasm. His officer's cap obscured the bandage on his forehead. He looked away, knowing he could never explain what he had seen. After his medical expulsion from JG-27, Franz had gone home and found his mother cold and hungry, alone in their empty house. Father Josef checked on her when he could but had told Franz that his father's war pension and death benefits had stopped flowing. His mother had no income to rely on. Father Josef's letters to the old soldier's office had gone unanswered. So Franz decided to travel to Berlin, a three-day train ride through bombed-out train yards, to find out where his father's pension had gone. Only after his mother had been cared for would Franz allow himself to report to Florida.

Walking the streets of Berlin, Franz saw that they were dotted with piles of black rubble, the result of the citizens' daily cleanings. In craters that had been buildings he saw rats drinking where pipes had burst. Franz entered the tall "old soldier's" office, its white façade now pitted by bombs. There, Franz sat across from a bureaucrat who supervised pensions, a balding man with a round face, glasses, and sagging cheeks. The man introduced himself as Mr. Greisse. He wore a round, red National Socialist swastika pin over his breast.

Mr. Greisse made small talk, asking Franz about his unit. Franz told him he was "in between outfits," but reporting to Lake Tegernsee next. Mr. Greisse asked Franz what unit was there, so Franz told him about the Florida resort. Mr. Greisse said he admired fighter pilots and would have permitted his eldest daughter to date one if her mother had not forbidden it. Franz smiled at the backhanded compliment, well aware that fighter pilots had gone from heroes to villains in the eyes of the German people due to Goering's slander.

Getting down to business, Mr. Greisse told Franz it was heartwarming to see a young man travel so far to look after his mother. But then to Franz's surprise he said, "Only you can care for your mother these days." Franz's father's pension and death benefits, Mr. Greisse explained, had dried up like those of every other old soldier to meet the needs of the war.

Franz eyed Mr. Greisse's swastika pin with contempt. "You don't like me because I'm in The Party?" Mr. Greisse asked him. Franz replied that he had nothing against him personally but that he represented the people who had put his mother in a bad fix. Mr. Greisse leaned forward and in whispers told Franz that some jobs required Party membership—he had worked in veterans affairs before the National Socialists took over his office, as they had the post office, the transportation authority, and every facet of government. Franz nodded that he understood.

"Where are you staying?" Mr. Greisse asked him. Franz said he was taking a train home that night. Mr. Greisse warned Franz that he might be stuck on the platform in the cold, if there was an air raid.

He asked Franz to come with him to his home in Potsdam, a short train ride southwest to the suburbs of Berlin. Franz trusted the man's smile and agreed.

Hours later, Franz arrived at the tall, stately Greisse home in Potsdam. He was amazed upon entering to see heavy blankets dangling in place of a front door. Inside, the home's windows had been blown out. Wooden boards had been hammered up in their place. Still, a grandfather clock stood untouched in the hallway and Mr. Greisse bragged that the house's pipes had not yet burst.

Mr. Greisse introduced Franz to his wife, who was preparing a meager meal. His eldest daughter was out and about, but he introduced Franz to his little daughter, Helga, a short thirteen-year-old girl with strawberry-blond hair. The little girl called herself "Hiya" and was not afraid of Franz or fighter pilots because her sister had brought one home before. Hiya showed Franz to her room, where she kept her bomb shard collection. She handed him one and explained that she would trade the pieces with her friends, swapping unique shapes for bigger ones. Franz saw how the rough edges of the shards reflected light like a prism.

Franz left Hiya and went to talk with her father. Later, around the dinner table, Hiya arrived wearing her Indian costume. She had made a headdress out of cardboard that she'd colored. She had frayed her pants to look like tattered buckskin. Her mother wanted her to take her costume off, but she let her keep it on throughout dinner when Franz acted impressed.

During the meal, Hiya showed Franz how to behave in a bomb shelter. She put both thumbs in her ears and opened her mouth. Franz knew this but pretended to learn. He knew this was done so the bombs' concussion would not rupture one's eardrums.

That night, Franz saw Hiya leave the dinner table without a word and run outside. Her parents did not follow her and Franz thought this odd. Her mother started sobbing. Mr. Greisse comforted his wife while explaining to Franz how hard it was as parents to have to wake Hiya up night after night, to grab her backpack, their suitcases, and run to a bomb shelter. He asked Franz, "What do you say when she asks, 'Papa, in America are their kids getting up now, too?'"

Franz looked down at the table. After a few moments of silence he asked Mr. Greisse if he could go check on Hiya. Mr. Greisse nodded while hugging his wife.

Franz stepped through the blankets in the doorway and found Hiya standing in the cold looking up to the sky. Franz kneeled next to her and looked up, too.

"If you see the stars," she told him, "it means the bombers won't be coming." Franz nodded. He knew this might have been true in the early war, when the bombers avoided clear skies because the flak gunners could see their silhoutettes, but now nothing stopped them.

"What do you see tonight?" Franz asked her. Looking up, he saw the sky was clear. Hiya turned to him and said with a smile, "Tonight we can sleep." Franz smiled gently at the little girl, although his eyes were sad.

THE NEXT MORNING, Mr. Greisse walked with Franz to the train station. The platform was crowded with people sleeping on benches and others waiting in long lines, staring at their toes while facing the empty tracks. Soldiers milled about checking papers.

Mr. Greisse was bound for Berlin and Franz was headed home to Amberg. Mr. Greisse apologized for not being able to help Franz's mother. Franz reassured him that she would be fine because he would send her his pilot's salary.

Mr. Greisse shook Franz's hand and said, "Good luck wherever you end up." Franz felt his medical excuse in his pocket. He was days away from an easy chair in Florida's opulent bar while the rest of Germany suffered in the cold. But Franz now had a problem with that notion. He had seen a little girl living in fear, without sleep, collecting bomb shards for toys. He knew the government of the 44 percent had long abandoned her. He would not join them. His sense of duty had never been to Hitler or The Party or Goering, it was always to Germany. But now, in the war's last days, Germany had a new face, that of a little girl.

"I won't be at Tegernsee long," Franz told Mr. Greisse. Mr. Greisse smiled because he knew what Franz meant.

"Be careful up there," he said. Then he turned and walked away, vanishing among the weary, shuffling crowd.

NEARLY TWO MONTHS LATER, EARLY JANUARY 1945

The snow crunched beneath the tires of the long black staff car as it pulled up and parked at the small hunting lodge on Lake Wannsee, southwest of Berlin.* A small sports car and then a *kuebelwagen* with its top up followed the staff car. In long coats, men scurried from the vehicles, stopping only to glimpse the gray, icy lake that blended with the evening winter sky. Inside the lodge, dangerous words were spoken, words that could carry fatal consequences after von Stauffenberg's attempt to assassinate Hitler.[6]

"We are convinced that we can put a stop to this devastation from the air and save the lives of innocent people," said one voice.

"We must examine the reality of our situation. Hitler needs to go, we all know that, but Goering must go first," said another.

"Treason is the only way you can explain what we are discussing."

"Exactly."

---

* Two years earlier, at a villa on Wannsee, SS general Reinhard Heydrich had gathered fourteen top Party and government officials to outlay his plan for the Holocaust. But the Holocaust was not only Heydrich's brainchild. In 1941, Goering had ordered Heydrich to formulate a plan for, in his words, the "final solution of the Jewish question."

Through snow flurries, the black boots of five of the bravest men in the German Air Force marched up the snowy steps to the "House of Flyers," as the Air Force club was known. The snow and the late afternoon light cast an eerie blue glow over the empty streets and the men in their long coats. The House of Flyers loomed with its tall marble columns and ornate carvings set into the building's façade. The men had legendary names among Germany's fighter forces: Roedel, Neumann, Luetzow, Steinhoff, and a colonel named Hannes Trautloft. They had all gathered for the most dangerous mission of their lives. They glanced anxiously over their shoulders as chauffeurs drove their staff cars away. They knew there was no turning back.

Roedel had proposed they shoot Goering that day, but the others talked him out of it, aware of an awful truth: killing Goering would not solve their problem. They needed him to step down. Stauffenberg could have shot Hitler but instead used a bomb because he knew that Hitler could be replaced by someone equally evil from his entourage. The same rule applied to Goering. Instead of killing him, the fighter leaders decided they would stare down the second most powerful man in the Reich and tell him it was time for him to go. They wanted Galland to take his place, reasoning that maybe he could do something to stop the bombing of Germany and, after consolidating power, maybe he could stand up to Hitler.

The fighter leaders entered a conference room with dark wood walls and paintings of Air Force heroes, including Goering. There they waited for Goering on their side of a wide table. The radiator blasted hot air that filled the room with the scent of old cigars. The men began to sweat. A stoic intensity clouded Luetzow's face as he clutched his chair, his mind elsewhere. He had lost his brother, Werner, at sea, a year prior. He knew his wife, Gisela, his four-year-old son, Hans-Ulrich, and his two-year-old daughter, Carola, were suffering under the same bombs as millions of other innocents, waking up three or four times a night to hurry to air raid shelters. The Man of Ice's "easy charm" had vanished—he had flipped the switch and frozen his emotions, just like when he flew. Steinhoff lingered by the door like a bodyguard, while Roedel lounged at the table in a thick, padded leather seat, smoking cigarette after cigarette. Neumann nervously peeked from a snow-streaked window, watching for Goering's arrival. Trautloft, the inspector of Germany's day fighters, sat and stirred a cup of coffee, staring at the table. Trautloft's thin lips tightened and his low-hanging eyelids had narrowed over his light blue eyes, causing them to almost disappear. He worried how Goering would react when he saw him there. The *Reichsmarschall* had no idea that Trautloft had cast his lot with "the Outcasts."

Trautloft's friends in that room had all fallen from favor with Goering long before that day. They had been heroes of the Air Force until Goering demoted them the prior November and December. Goering's plan to "Restore the Air Force" through greater National Socialist spirit also meant purging opposition. Goering had sacked Galland, the general of fighters, and replaced him with Colonel Gordon Gollob, a Party member. Goering had booted Roedel from command of JG-27 and Steinhoff from his new wing, JG-7. Goering had demoted Luetzow and sent him to oversee a flying school. Goering had already relegated Neumann to obscurity, assigning him to lead Italian pilots in Verona, Italy.

Two weeks earlier Luetzow had summoned these men, his fellow Outcasts, to gather in secret. They had met clandestinely at Trautloft's lodge on Lake Wannsee. There they agreed that Goering's inept leadership had resulted in the destruction of their cities and the slaughter of their young pilots. When a solution emerged that could save Germany's cities, Goering had squandered it. That solution was a wonder weapon, the Me-262 jet fighter, the only plane capable of sprinting past the Allied fighters to shoot down bombers. But Goering and Hitler had a lust for vengeance that blinded them to reason. Instead of giving the Me-262 to the fighter pilots, they had turned the jet into a bomber, a weapon of retaliation.

There at Trautloft's cabin, Luetzow and the Outcasts decided to act before not a brick was left standing in Germany. So Luetzow called the meeting with Goering under harmless pretenses, a confrontation that would later be called "the Fighter Pilots' Mutiny."

Goering's long, bulletproof limo screeched to a halt in the club's turnaround. He climbed out, flanked by his bodyguards. He knew full well what awaited him. Word of the mutiny had already leaked. It had not come from Galland; the mutineers were careful not to invite him because they knew the SS were watching him, investigating Galland for violations of the "Subversion Law" because Galland had angered them by opposing their proposal for an SS jet wing. Galland knew of the "mutiny," however, and wanted to follow the confrontation. He had Trautloft call him from the conference room and leave the phone off the hook on a table in the back, so he could hear everything.

Goering learned about the pending mutiny from General Karl Koller, his chief of staff, a man the Outcasts had approached seeking his support.

Later, it would be discovered that Koller had written in his diary:[7]

13 January 1945, 14.45 hours

Have just heard that the Fighter Force is in the throes of a major crisis of confidence regarding its supreme commander.

Some very bad feeling indeed. The most impossible ideas being thrown around. Occurrences similar to those of 20 July [Von Stauffenberg] must be avoided. . . . Talk of forcing a supreme commander to resign his post amounts to mutiny.

The conference room's doors swung swiftly open. Steinhoff spun and found himself staring into Goering's blue eyes, the eyes of the second most powerful man in Germany. Goering's face was tired and swollen. On his cheeks he wore pink blush that looked as garish as his pale blue uniform, which he had designed for himself. Its lapels were made of white silk and its collars piped with gold at every seam. He wore gold rings and his nails were painted with a clear coat.

Goering, "the Colossus," took his seat at the head of the table. Steinhoff and the others saluted. Goering offered a halfhearted salute in return. His entourage of officers, including General Koller, took their seats flanking him. Luetzow's comrades sat at his sides.

Luetzow broke the silence with a calm voice. "Herr *Reichsmarschall*, we are grateful to you for agreeing to listen to our problems. I must ask you, however, to hear me out to the end. If you interrupt me, sir, I believe there will be little point to this discussion."[8]

Goering's eyes seemed to frost over. He glared at Luetzow then at each of the young men who sat with him. The men who opposed Goering were all half his age, in their thirties. Goering's entourage stared at the table, afraid to breathe or move, bracing for his outburst.

Luetzow knew he had only the ruse of strength with which to bully the bully. With the men at his sides, Luetzow hoped to bluff Goering into thinking that the fighter forces were behind them. In actuality, only the men at the table and a few confidants, like Galland, knew of the plot.

Any other man would have melted under Goering's stare. In brawling to bring Hitler to power, Goering had once been jailed. Behind bars he was deemed so violent that he had been kept separate from the other prisoners for their safety. A former morphine addict, Goering now wielded the power of life and death with the snap of his fingers. But instead of backing down, Luetzow upped his bluff. He slid a typed list across the table, his "Points of Discussion." Goering pushed the list aside to Koller.

"There is still time, sir, to prevent every city in Germany from being reduced to rubble and ashes," Luetzow said. He told Goering that Galland needed to be reinstated and the 262s taken from the bomber forces and released immediately for fighter missions. Luetzow cited a quartermaster's report that listed sixty 262s operational for combat operations, fifty-two of which belonged to the bomber forces. Another two hundred of the precious jets were sitting in bombed-out rail yards, stranded, because someone had decided to ship them by rail to save fuel.

Goering interrupted Luetzow and reminded him sarcastically that the fighter forces were in a "deplorable state." Goering told Luetzow with a smirk that in touring the bomber units he saw greater spirit and discipline. The bomber pilots, he said, were healthier and contained more veterans than the fighter forces.

Luetzow cut Goering off. "So you have told us time and time again," Luetzow said. "But you forget that we fighter pilots have been flying missions daily for over five years now. Our young pilots survive a maximum of two or three Reich Defense missions before they're killed."

Red with rage, Goering shouted, "As if the head of the Air Force was not aware of that!"

Luetzow did not break his stone-face composure. So Goering reverted to taunting. He told Luetzow that the real problem was the fighter pilots' cowardice. Germany needs braver men, he said, "eager for a crack at the enemy," to challenge the bombers nose to nose.

Luetzow retorted, "And you, sir, have simply ignored the existence of four-engined bombers completely. You've given us no new aircraft, no new weapons."

"Enough!" Goering screamed. The sting of Luetzow's words cut deeply. Goering had ignored the bomber threat and once said that the Americans were best at making razor blades, not airplanes. Goering had kept his Air Force flying decade-old 109s, and when the newer FW-190 fighters arrived, he sent most of them to the Eastern Front to fly ground attack missions. More than any one man's, Goering's foolhardy decisions had led to the devastation of Germany's cities.

Steinhoff spoke up. He agreed with Luetzow's points. Roedel,

Trautloft, and Neumann added their voices to the chorus. Steinhoff asserted that the 262 was Germany's last hope to make a difference in the air war.

Goering told Steinhoff to keep dreaming because the 262 was not going to him or the fighter pilots. "I'm giving it to the people who know what to do with it," Goering said with a defiant pout.

Luetzow had heard enough. He raised an outstretched finger, ready to tell Goering that compromise was obviously hopeless and that for Germany's good Goering needed to step down. He never got to utter his words.

Goering stood, quaking with rage. "What you're presenting me with here, gentlemen, is treason! What are you after, Luetzow—do you want to get rid of me? What you've schemed up here is a full-scale mutiny!"

Goering pounded the table and began cursing irrationally. Foam filled the corners of his mouth. Sweat poured from his brow. His eyes and the veins of his neck bulged as if he was about to explode.

Goering turned to Steinhoff and screamed, "Your career is over and so is Galland's—that coward would not even face me!"

Turning to Luetzow, his lip quivering, he added, "And you, Luetzow—I'm going to have you shot!"

Neumann looked at Roedel. They both knew they were watching Goering in the throes of a nervous breakdown.[9]

Swiping Luetzow's "Points of Discussion" to the floor, Goering stormed from the room with heavy footsteps, his entourage following him, casting sinister glances over their shoulders.

"Galland will be shot first to set the example!" Goering shouted from the hallway.

Silence settled in the room. Luetzow and the others stood around, hesitant to speak. Steinhoff looked to the window, where snow melted as it struck the glass. The room suddenly seemed tighter and hotter. He tugged his collar. The thought hit him. *I feel like I'm in prison already.*

Trautloft gingerly picked up the phone he had left off the hook in the back of the room. Galland was still on the line and gave Trautloft a message for the others.

"Adolf thinks we should save time as he did and get measured for our coffins now," Trautloft said. "He did his before Christmas."[10]

Trautloft hung up the phone. No one spoke.

"What now?" Steinhoff asked.

The men looked to Luetzow, whose eyes remained stern. Reaching for his coat, he told the others: "Oh well, let's go and get something to eat."

GOERING WANTED TO shoot Galland, Luetzow, and Steinhoff but needed time to assemble a case because each man was a national hero. He needed evidence more treasonous than just their act of defiance against him. He needed proof of treachery against the German people. As promised, Goering focused his rage on Galland first. He had Galland confined to his home on the Czech border and sent the Gestapo to dig for dirt on him, something Goering could use in a trial. The Gestapo arrested Galland's adjutant, bugged his phones, and stole his BMW sports car. With both the Gestapo and the SS investigating him, Galland told his girlfriend, an artist named Monica, that he was flattered—they could just as easily have assassinated him.

Eager to remove the mutineers from German soil, Goering banished Luetzow to a desk job in Italy with Roedel and Neumann. He fired Trautloft and assigned him to run a flying school. To spite Steinhoff, Goering banned him from all airfields and contact with the other mutineers. When Steinhoff was caught trying to visit Luetzow in Italy, he was sent back to Germany under guard.

With the mutiny a failure, Galland and Luetzow were certain that Germany was doomed. They also knew it was only a matter of time until they would hear a knock on the door and find the Gestapo waiting to drag them to a firing squad. A deep depression fell over both men. They were Prussians, professional soldiers bound by an ancient code that valued honor and service above one's life. Now they found themselves dishonored and effectively without careers. The war had already estranged Luetzow from his wife, who did not understand his devotion to the Air Force. To protect her and his children, Luetzow broke contact with them. Galland considered defecting to the Allies but worried that The Party would kill his parents in retaliation. He confided in his girlfriend that he had a plan to spoil Goering's pleasure. That night, his girlfriend saw Galland cleaning his pistol.

20

THE FLYING SANATORIUM

BENEATH THE HANGING lights in a vast wooden hangar, Franz sat in the cockpit of a 262, but one not attached to an aircraft. Instead, it was just a mock cockpit that sat on wheels. An instructor leaned over him with a checklist, testing Franz, who practiced emergency procedures with blinding speed, his hands flipping inoperative switches, pulling dummy levers, and calling out numbers from fake gauges. Other pilots in other mock cockpits sat around Franz, undergoing the same training.

Located in Southern Germany, Lechfeld was the hub of Germany's jet training because Messerschmitt's headquarters lay in the nearby town of Augsburg. Instead of retiring to Florida, Franz had landed a slot in jet school after pestering Roedel, who secured him the appointment, one that long lines of pilots desired. But jet school was not what Franz had expected. Three weeks into the eight-week course, he had not even sat in a real 262 and instead had flown just two hours of refresher flights in old twin-engine planes.

Almost hourly, sleek 262s would rip past the hangar on takeoff, their twin engines blasting like rockets strapped to their wings. To their instructor's annoyance, Franz and his fellow students would forget their exercises to stop and stare. Some called the jet "the Swallow" and others "the Stormbird," but whenever they saw it buzz the field at 575 miles per hour, faster than anything else in the skies, they knew the 262 was Germany's last hope.

An instructor stopped the class and shouted for the students to gather around. The instructor read Franz and the others a teletype sent from Goering to all Air Force units. It said that Galland, the general of fighters, had stepped down due to health problems. Franz scowled, having heard rumors that said Goering had sacked Galland.

Goering had written the announcement weeks prior but had held it, waiting for the Gestapo to bring him evidence against Galland. Now they'd found witnesses who would testify that Galland had admitted "the war is lost." These words, coming from a general, constituted treachery under the Subversion Law. Goering knew that Galland would kill himself rather than face the shame of a trial, so he sent the notice to the fighter forces to prepare them for the general's death.

While the words of Goering's memo were still swirling in Franz's mind, across Germany, Galland was loading his pistol. He had told his girlfriend, "Tonight will be the night," and she fled his house. Galland spent the rest of the day pondering how Goering and The Party's propaganda machine would spin his death. When they forced "the Desert Fox," Rommel, to kill himself, they said he died of an embolism. When Goering pushed General Ernst Udet, Germany's top surviving WWI ace, to kill himself, they said he died in a plane crash. When General Hans Jeschonnek, Goering's chief of staff, shot himself, they said it was from fatigue.

That night, before Galland could pull the trigger, his phone rang. Galland picked up. The caller was the chief of the Gestapo, who begged Galland not to shoot himself. Hitler had learned of Galland's intentions via his girlfriend's pleas, and now Hitler was enraged at

Goering. Hitler was certain that the fallout from Galland's death would destroy the Air Force in its fragile state. The dictator had ordered Goering to stop Galland's suicide, so Goering had ordered the Gestapo to intervene. The Gestapo chief told Galland that Hitler and Goering had a proposal he needed to hear.

SEVERAL DAYS LATER

Galland stepped from his sports car at Goering's country estate, called Carinhall, that lay east of Berlin. Goering was suspiciously gracious as he showed Galland to a great room, its walls lined with the mounted heads of wild game. He invited Galland to sit on a couch and talked with him like an old friend. Goering took credit for intervening to prevent Galland's suicide and dismissed any rumors of treason charges. Goering gleefully explained that Hitler had authorized him to give Galland a squadron of his own, ". . . so you can prove what you've always said about the 262's great potential." Galland's dark eyes sparkled. Goering said the squadron could fly and fight in the manner of Galland's choosing as long as he did not interfere with other units. "You can recruit anyone you want," Goering added, "provided that my office approves of them." Galland nodded in agreement.

"Take that 'sad sack' Steinhoff," Goering said with a grin, "and Luetzow, too."[1]

Galland left Goering's estate as happy as the *Reichsmarschall*. He knew why Goering and Hitler were being so generous: they wanted him and his "traitors" to again take to the skies, where they would surely die in combat.

Galland had admitted that the war was lost, and he did not want to see it prolonged. But he also knew the Allied heavy bombers would not stop coming until Germany had surrendered, a day that seemed far away with the madmen—Hitler and Goering—at the helm. Goering had told the people of Germany that the fighter pilots had abandoned them, but Galland departed that day determined to prove that Goering was wrong.

TWO MONTHS LATER, MARCH 17, 1945

In the hangar at Lechfeld, a dozen pilots huddled around Franz as he gave a lesson about a jet engine that sat on a mount in front of him. One of the pilots asked if Franz could show them the engine's insides. "I wish," Franz said, "but there are parts you're not allowed to see." The students groaned. Franz sympathized with them.

After graduation from jet training, the school's instructors had kept Franz on the roster to teach because he had mastered the 262 so quickly. Franz owed his success to his airline days, where he flew multi-engine craft, unlike the average fighter pilot who had only single-engine training. Upon graduation Franz had hoped to join a jet fighter unit, but only the jet bomber units, who had Goering's favor, possessed planes, fuel, and openings for pilots. Rather than join them, Franz begrudgingly stayed as an instructor and waited.

Unlike his earlier days in flight instructing, Franz's students were no longer cadets. Now they were veteran fighter and bomber pilots. Franz explained to the pilots that the 262's revolutionary Junkers-built Jumo 004 engines were both the jet's gift and its curse. They provided incredible thrust, but they were finicky. "Keep your hands off the throttle whenever possible," Franz told the pilots, "especially at high altitude." The men looked at him with confusion—every pilot knew the importance of using the throttle in a dogfight. Franz explained that dramatic changes in the engine's internal speed could cause it to snuff out like a candle. When the pilots asked Franz why this happened, he said that he was forbidden from telling them how the engine actually worked. "It's secret," he said mockingly. The pilots laughed.

Really, Franz knew the engines were as fragile as china because they were made from low-grade materials due to mineral shortages.* A brand-new engine had a life-span of just twenty-eight hours, and re-furbished engines were good for just ten hours between overhauls.

That night in the Lechfeld officer's club, Franz was talking and drinking with his students. One of them was a new pilot who had been trained to fly bombers but had never entered combat. "What's it really like out there?" he asked Franz. Franz told him candidly what he had seen the prior fall when he was stationed near Dresden. "Be thankful for this training," Franz told the young pilot. "It takes eight weeks to teach you what you could learn in an hour." The pilots laughed in agreement. Franz was taking another drink when it hit him. "Here we are studying engine manuals while our comrades are being slaugh-tered," he said. The veterans nodded in sad agreement.

Just as the political officers made their way into front-line squad-rons, they also were imbedded in jet school. The following morning Franz found himself standing at attention in his commander's office. The new pilot Franz had been talking to the night before had secretly been a political officer. Without a choice, Franz's commander expelled him from the school.

Outside his commander's office, Franz looked at his doctor's waiver, his ticket to Florida. Then he remembered the whispers he had heard among his fellow instructors. They had heard that Galland and his mutineers were forming a 262 squadron at Brandenburg Air Base, west of Berlin. The instructors jokingly called the unit "the Flying Sanatorium" and "Galland's Circus." But Franz knew Galland, the man behind the unit, and knew there was nothing funny about him. In the school's office, Franz called Brandenburg and eventually reached Galland. He asked the general if he could join his squadron.

* Some of the 262's parts were actually made by slave laborers in underground factories, a Third Reich crime against the workers that also put the pilots of such jets in danger of fly-ing a sabotaged or poorly constructed machine.

"Yes, we'd be glad to have you," Galland said. He explained a catch—Goering had given him authority to build a squadron but gave him too few aircraft to succeed. "Just bring a jet with you," Galland told Franz. Franz's heart sunk. He knew it was impossible to procure a jet without orders. Thinking quickly, Franz asked Galland if his unit had a name. "JV-44," Galland told him.* Franz told the general he would try to join him, somehow.

Franz had an enlisted man drive him from Lechfeld to the town of Leipheim, an hour west. Leipheim was nestled around a factory that churned out 262s and had its own airfield. In the factory's parking lot, Franz suited up in his flight gear. Smoke billowed from the factory following a raid that morning by B-24s of the 467th Bomb Group.†

Inside, on the production line, he saw only one intact 262 sitting on its gear. The jet's smooth body was painted gray like a shark, and white putty filled its seams. Hastily painted black crosses decorated its flanks and wings. The factory foreman approached Franz and asked if he could assist him. "I'm here on orders to collect an aircraft for Galland's unit, JV-44," Franz said. Puzzled, the foreman checked his lists. He said he had no such transfer orders and had never heard of "JV-44." Seeing that his bluff was not working, Franz admitted the truth to the foreman, that he had no orders or papers. Franz told the foreman that Galland was forming a squadron of aces who had volunteered to fly against the bombers.

The foreman scratched his chin, pondering Franz's admission. Seeing his opportunity fading, Franz asked the foreman, "What would

---

* No one knows exactly why Galland chose the designation "Jagdverband 44/JV-44" or Fighter Band 44, although many suggest it was his tongue-in-cheek reference to the year 1944, when Goering had destroyed the fighter forces.

† The bomb group's PR officer would write of the raid: "It's daily more apparent that the Luftwaffe's last stand relies on racy jet-propelled fighters. The surest place to smash them is in the incubator. . . . That's why the attack on Leipheim, assembly and testing center for Me-262s, represents a gigantic air battle won before the breathless Jerry could swing his saved-up Sunday punch."

be better, letting me take this into the sky or seeing it destroyed, here, in the next raid?" The foreman looked at the beautiful machine and the smoldering plant behind it.

"I think I found your paperwork," he said with a smile. Franz called Brandenburg and reached JV-44 to ask the weather and tell them he was coming.

Bulldozers were repairing the factory's runway as Franz taxied the gray jet between bomb craters. With a roar, Franz blasted off in the machine with the pulsing engines, the craft said to be Germany's last hope. He steered northeast to join the Flying Sanatorium.

FORTY-FIVE MINUTES LATER, OVER BRANDENBURG AIR BASE

From above, Franz admired the circular flak towers that surrounded the airfield, spires that kept away enemy fighters. When his wheels touched down, he taxied toward the control tower and hangars, where dozens of 262s sat parked in lines.

But the air traffic controllers radioed him to say he was heading to the wrong place—JV-44 was across the field. So Franz cut across the runway and motored toward the distant tree line, where ten or so 262s sat parked in front of a small one-story office. Franz shut down his jet and slid from the wing. Half the jets around him were missing engines. The flight line looked more like a boneyard.

"I'm in the wrong place," Franz said to the first crewman who approached him. "Where's JV-44?"

"You're in the right place, sir," the man replied. "This is JV-44."

Confused, Franz asked where Galland was, but the crewman just shrugged.

A man emerged from the ops office and approached Franz. He wore flying boots and black pilot's pants but oddly also a knit sweater and skullcap. The man's arms dangled and he walked with a lean. Franz thought he looked like a sailor navigating a tossing deck.

When the man came closer, Franz saw that long strands of blond hair shot from beneath the man's skullcap, covering his eyes. Franz became certain the man was a sailor.

"Beautiful machine!" the man said. He flashed a large grin across his strong, deep jaw. He wore the rank of a major.

"An hour old," Franz said proudly, saluting.

The man saluted with gusto and introduced himself as Major Eric Hohagen, JV-44's technical officer. Franz knew the technical officer was effectively third in command and in charge of keeping the aircraft operational.

Franz had heard of Hohagen. He was an Air Force legend. As Hohagen patted Franz's 262 like a horse, Franz saw for himself that the stories about Hohagen were true. His right eyebrow arched higher than his left one, giving his face a permanent quizzical expression. Hohagen had been shot down in '43, and in the crash his head had hit his gun sight, shattering his skull. With no other options, doctors had replaced his broken skull pieces with Plexiglas before sewing him back up, leaving his face forever uneven.

Hohagen asked Franz how he had come to join the unit. Franz explained that he knew Galland from Sicily and recently got booted from jet school courtesy of a political officer.

"So you don't sleep well with The Party?" Hohagen asked. Franz laughed. Hohagen asked how he was to know Franz was not a political officer himself. Franz shrugged. Hohagen told Franz a joke that he called "the political officer test."

"Hitler, Goering, Himmler, and all of their friends are out on a boat at sea," Hohagen said. "There's a big storm and their boat sinks! Who's saved?" Hohagen's mouth remained agape as if he wanted to give the answer himself.

Franz knew the joke. "Germany."

Hohagen roared with approval. He explained that no political officer would have the stomach to finish the joke. Franz chuckled at the irony that the man he had thought was a sailor had told him a joke about the sea. Throughout the Air Force, Hohagen was known for his colorful spirit, for flying in a yellow leather coat with a fox fur collar, and for wearing boots topped with fur. Hohagen was anything but a clown in the air and had fifty-odd victories to his name.

Unsettled by the paltry image of JV-44 around him, Franz asked where everyone was. Hohagen explained that JV-44 was off to a slow start. The unit had about a dozen pilots. A third of their jets were broken because they had been drawing refurbished planes from factory repair lines. They had no base housing and lived in private homes. Their motor pool was Galland's BMW sports car, Steinhoff's DKW motorcycle, and a few *kuebelwagens*.

"Can you draw support from JG-7?" Franz asked, having seen Fighter Wing 7, one of the few jet fighter outfits, across the field. Hohagen explained that he had served under Steinhoff in JG-7 until Steinhoff was fired. Hohagen said that he, personally, had led III Group across the field, but the man who took his job, Rudi Sinner, could do nothing to help—they had already asked. Goering had forbidden anyone from assisting JV-44, "the Mutineers." Franz's ears perked up. He told Hohagen he knew Sinner from Africa.

"You can go over there," Hohagen told Franz. "But I cannot."

Franz was confused. Hohagen explained that he had been so angry when Steinhoff was fired that he trashed his office, destroying the place in protest. Before he could be arrested, he called the flight doctor and told him to hurry quickly, because his head wounds were making him crazy. Instead of a court-martial, he was banished to the hospital, from which Galland and Steinhoff retrieved him for JV-44. What Hohagen failed to mention was that to protest Goering's treatment of Steinhoff he also stopped wearing his Knight's Cross that day except for photos.

Franz removed his cap and showed Hohagen the dent in his forehead. Hohagen removed his cap and showed Franz the massive scar in his. They compared their doctor's certificates and instantly bonded.

Later that afternoon, a BMW sports car pulled up to the office.

Galland and Steinhoff emerged from the car, grumbling from a fruit-less trip in search of pilots. Galland had chosen Steinhoff as his number two man, the operations officer who would oversee training and recruiting when not leading missions.

"You must have pissed someone off!" Galland said when he saw Franz. Franz smiled guiltily as he saluted. Galland explained that he had wired Franz's name to Berlin, and no one protested his attempt to join the unit. Galland said that Goering was blocking many of his pilot requests and only allowing men to stay with JV-44 if they had run afoul of him or The Party. Goering wanted the Mutineers to fly long enough to die, not to consume the Air Force's last veterans and precious aircraft.

Franz asked Galland, "Will your brother be joining us?"

"No, he's dead," Galland said. Franz remembered from their meeting in Sicily that Galland had lost one brother but had another who was still flying fighters.

"No, the other one, who was flying 190s," Franz said.

"They're both dead," Galland said as calmly as if he were ordering a cup of tea. "Wutz joined Paul in the afterlife more than a year ago."

Franz apologized, but Galland cut him off. "Don't apologize when you're coming from the same place." Franz realized that Galland had remembered his stories of August from their conversation in Sicily. At that moment, Franz's doubts of the meager unit vanished. Regardless of JV-44's strength or success, he knew that they were all fighting for the same thing. Not for the Reich. For their brothers.

———

DURING HIS FIRST week in the unit, Franz and the others waited around Brandenburg. Galland departed one morning in his sports car, motoring south. Steinhoff said the general had gone to find JV-44 a new base as far from Berlin as possible. The American and Soviet armies were driving to link up and separate the top half of Germany from the bottom half. Galland wanted his unit to be on the American side, not the Soviet side, when the curtain came down.

Franz watched as ground crewmen painted his naked fighter a wavy, mottled green that covered the black Air Force crosses on its flanks. In place of each black cross, they painted the white outline of a cross and on both of the plane's flanks they painted a white number 3.

One night Franz snuck across the airfield to visit Sinner, who welcomed him into his office. Franz was astounded that Sinner, in the nearly two years since he had seen him in Sicily, had never earned the Knight's Cross. Sinner, who always called himself "just an ordinary soldier," laughed it off. Franz knew Sinner was anything but "ordinary." He had nearly forty victories and had been shot down eleven times.

"So sad about the bear, isn't it?" Sinner said. Franz fell back in his seat. He knew Sinner was talking about Bobbi, the Squadron 6 mascot.

Sinner told Franz that he had heard their old squadron had been so torn up in the fighting that during their retreat to central Germany they needed to leave the bear behind. They could not release the bear into the wild, because he had been raised by humans and did not know how to hunt. Since the bear had come to weigh four hundred pounds, he was too heavy to transport. When the zoo would not take the bear back, the squadron had no other options. The squadron pilots and ground crew could not bring themselves to do what had to be done. Franz looked away, afraid to hear the rest.

"They handed the bear to a neighboring unit that led it into the woods and shot it," Sinner said. Franz sat, unmoving and unblinking. Sinner saw this and put a sympathetic hand on his shoulder. Franz would later think how silly it must have looked, a grown man grieving over an animal. But to Franz, the killing of his bear was symbolic of so much more than just one death. As he had once told the pool manager in Wiesbaden, the bear never bit anyone.

BRYAN MAKO

SEVERAL DAYS LATER, MARCH 31, 1945

Beginning at dawn, Steinhoff led JV-44 into the air for the unit's first mission en masse. Galland had found them a new base at the Munich airport, far from Berlin. Franz and eight other pilots followed Steinhoff south.

As the autobahn passed beneath his jet's wings, Franz saw that the elegant roadways were strangely empty. German civilians lacked gasoline. Most fighter units had disintegrated, too, from lack of fuel, and their personnel were transferred to the infantry. Franz knew, however, that the forests bordering the highway still contained life. There, the last of the Air Force operated. Units now parked their fighters and even four-engine bombers under the pine trees. Side roads served as taxiways, the autobahn as a runway. Mechanics repaired engines on wood benches, and fighters hid beneath underpasses between takeoffs. The once-gentlemanly, black-tie Air Force now operated like partisans. Racing from Berlin to escape the Allies and the grasp of The Party, the men of JV-44 felt a rush of freedom. They sensed that they were the last squadron of the Air Force, the last knights in a crumbling realm.

When the flights arrived over Munich, they steered east to the airfield. From the air, the field looked like an oval racetrack for horses. At the north end, the terminal and hangars curved like a reviewing stand around a concrete parking area for aircraft. A vast oval of grass ran east to west where planes would take off. Franz knew this field from his airline days. As he flew lower, he saw that the white terminal's classical architecture had been marred. Franz could see through the roof's burned beams to pools of water where passengers once had sat. The control tower still stood from the second story of the terminal, but its glass had been shattered.

Franz landed and taxied to a halt in a line with the others in front of the field's two damaged hangars. The pilots anxiously scanned the skies, expecting to see the Allied fighters that now flew from bases in France and Belgium. With endless numbers and fuel, the P-38s, P-47s, Spitfires, and plentiful P-51s orbited over Germany, their shadows challenging any German pilot to come up to fight. Galland greeted his men and assured them they were safe at Munich because no one knew they were there—yet.

The next morning, April 1, 1945, dawned with optimism as Franz and his comrades reported to the unit's new headquarters, a tall, castle-like building two miles south of the field. The vacated building had been an orphanage once, but the children were long gone—now tucked away in safer territories. The pilots hung their pistols side by side on coat racks and ate breakfast together in a long dining hall beneath chandeliers. An outline on the wall marked where a large crucifix had once hung. At their morning meal together, the men sat wherever they wished, sergeant next to general. Galland had returned to his old charisma and Steinhoff toasted the unit, "a forlorn little troop of the outcast and condemned."[2] The prior night the pilots had settled into the village of Feldkirchen, just east of the airfield, where German families loaned bedrooms to them. Galland had chosen quarters more befitting a general, on the fringe of town, where he moved into an Alpine-style lodge.

The men of JV-44 wasted no time preparing for battle. They set up their headquarters in the abandoned orphanage and spread a large war map across a table in the center of the room. Over the map they laid a sheet of glass with grids. The map showed Southern Germany and northern Austria, the areas that Galland intended JV-44 to defend. A red line on the map showed the shrinking front lines. The Americans would reach Southern Germany first. They were now gaining fifty miles of territory per day.

On the airfield grounds, the pilots found an old shed in the northeast corner that they turned into an alert shack where they could gather between missions. Technicians strung a telephone line from the alert shack to the orphanage in order to coordinate flights. In the fresh light of spring, the men draped green camouflage netting over the shack's roof. They arranged white lawn chairs and small circular tables on the side of the shack that faced the airfield. Between the shack and the terminal were blast pens. For easy access, the pilots taxied their jets up to the pens and shut down their engines. Hopping out, they helped their mechanics push the jets backward into the earthen half-moon enclosures.

A long-nosed FW-190D fighter landed on the field as the men worked. The 190D taxied to the empty terminal. Nicknamed "the Dora," the 190D had an elegant profile and a long in-line engine where a fat radial had once sat. At the empty terminal, the plane stopped, the pilot unsure where to go. The plane then turned around and taxied across the field, stopping at the alert shack. The Dora's pilot climbed out and glanced around, clearly disoriented. He wore a long, black leather coat and a forage cap. The men laughed until they realized who he was. He was Colonel Trautloft. The colonel walked closer and greeted his fellow outcasts and Mutineers. Galland drove over from the orphanage to greet Trautloft, who slipped the general a list of places where he could find the supplies he needed to build JV-44. As quickly as he had arrived, Trautloft hopped in his Dora and flew away to work for Galland in secret.

Galland and Steinhoff looked at the list. They knew that jets and supplies were useless without pilots. Their recruiting efforts had floundered thus far due to Goering's interference. So they decided to take more drastic measures. That evening they drove to the fighter pilot's rest home—Florida. They had heard rumors that one of Germany's top pilots was recuperating there, a man with 195 victories to his name.

The next morning that pilot took a seat at the unit's table during breakfast. He was Captain Walter "the Count" Krupinski. He had been Steinhoff's wingman on the Eastern Front. The Count looked more Polish than German, having been born near the Polish border. His forehead was wide, his chin was strong, and his brown eyes were round and friendly. He wore riding pants with wide flares to play up to his nickname, one given by his comrades because he had expensive taste in wine but came from humble origins. He was actually the son of a soldier.

Though the Count had a loud reputation, the ace who took his seat at JV-44's table was a quieter version of himself. He had checked into Florida to recover from burns sustained the prior August and to mourn. Five months earlier, his younger brother, Paul, had died in a U-boat off the Norwegian coast. Ever since he lost his brother, the Count's eyes no longer flickered with mischief. "He loved life itself," a German propaganda postcard had once boasted of him, the aristocratic hero of the common folk who now wore the Knight's Cross. Before his brother had been killed, the Count had loved wine, women, and song. A year prior he and Germany's top ace, Lieutenant Erich "Bubi" Hartmann, had been summoned to Berchtesgaden in southeastern Germany, to receive decorations from Hitler. Hartmann's comrades called him "Bubi" or "Little Boy," because he had a childlike face, bright blue eyes, and thick blond hair. The night before the ceremony, the Count and Hartmann celebrated their momentary freedom from the war by drinking champagne and mixing it with cognac. The next day, drunk on their feet, they reported to Hitler. When the dictator dangled new Knight's Crosses with Oak Leaves around their necks, the pilots wobbled, unable to stand rigid. The Count had trouble clicking his heels to greet Hitler because he was fighting the urge to vomit. Hitler stopped momentarily when he smelled the booze seeping from the Count's pores. After they had received their awards, the Count thought a cigarette would settle him down. He forgot that Hitler did not drink or smoke and pulled out his silver cigarette case to light up. Hitler saw this and told him to stop his "disgusting" habit. Instead of punishing his drunken pilots, Hitler regaled them with his plans to reverse the losing tide on the Eastern Front. After the Count and Hartmann left the ceremony, they both needed another drink. "He's a raving lunatic!" the Count had said of Hitler. Hartmann chided him: "I told you so, I told you so!"[3]

When Franz met the Count that morning, he knew that behind the legendary pilot's relaxed demeanor he carried a heavy secret. Roedel had told Franz how the Count had watched Steinhoff dispatch the Soviet pilot trapped in his burning fighter and had agreed to Steinhoff's request to shoot him if he was ever in a similar predicament. All pilots feared a fiery death. Franz had been burned in Sicily. The Count had been burned in a crash the prior August. But Franz wondered if the Count knew of the 262's reputation for burning. He doubted the Count knew that the jet's fuel was made from kerosene derived from coal, fuel housed in tanks in front of, behind, and below the pilot's seat. Franz had heard Galland bragging to the men who had not flown the 262, "It's as if angels are pushing you!" Franz knew that he and the pilots around him had outlived their nine lives. On the eve of battle, a new question troubled Franz. *What happens when the angels stop pushing?*

THE NEXT MORNING, APRIL 2, 1945

The pilots of JV-44 stood high on a blast pen surrounding the 262 on the ground. They looked down and marveled that the slender jet looked wider and shorter from above. There were twenty of them, all the pilots in JV-44. Only nine were officers like Franz. Each had flown a lifetime in combat hours, but some, like the Count, had never even sat in a jet. By unspoken agreement, they all wore the same classic black leather jackets and flying pants to summon all the machismo as they could muster.

In the blast pen beneath his pilots, Galland leaned against the wall, his arms folded. In his place, Steinhoff, Franz, and Hohagen taught the lesson. While Franz and Hohagen stood along the leading edge of the 262's wing, Steinhoff paced back and forth atop the wing with a pointer stick. Even those pilots who had flown the 262 listened, because the 262 was a dangerous machine that a pilot could never fully master.

Steinhoff told the men that landing the 262 was the most dangerous moment of a flight. In the 262, a pilot had to commit to the approach and stick with it. Due to the engine's tendency to snuff out with quick throttle movements, a pilot could not "pour on the coals" to recover from a bad approach. Instead, he had to anticipate any speed changes far in advance.

Having instructed in the 262, Franz knew the engines better than anyone. In jet school, the rules had forbidden him from telling his students anything about the engine's inner workings. Now, with his comrades listening intently, Franz revealed the engine's secret flaw. He told them the engine's fan blades were made from inferior metals that could not resist heat the way they should. Germany could no longer access minerals like cobalt and nickel to make strong blades. If a pilot throttled forward too quickly, heat would build in the engine and melt the blades. "It won't always kill you," Franz said. "It will kill the next guy." He explained that the blades would cool and crack after the engine cooled down, usually once on the ground. On the next flight the blades would be primed to shatter, resulting in catastrophic engine failure. Franz's comrades nodded. Franz knew he, Steinhoff, and Hohagen were trying to teach in a day what he had usually taught in eight weeks of jet school. But the men standing above him were no ordinary pilots.

THE SIGHT OF his pilots standing on the blast pen inspired Galland to take Trautloft's list and go to work. Goering and Hitler often derogatorily called Galland "the actor," but like a movie star with far-reaching connections, Galland shined up his charm and called in favors, siphoning supplies from the Air Force to JV-44. He-111 bombers arrived from factories in northern Germany and unloaded experimental under-wing rockets. Trucks pulled up and dumped crates of Jumo 004 jet engines. Near the hangars, tanker trucks filled the airfield's underground fuel tank with kerosene jet fuel. Galland sent his pilots to factories, and they flew back in refurbished 262s.

The Count's name on JV-44's roster helped Steinhoff's recruiting. Whispers began floating among Germany's remaining fighter squadrons that the Count had cast his lot with the Mutineers. Pilots began sneaking away from their units to join JV-44, and combat-proven instructors in Trautloft's flying school asked to transfer to Galland. Trautloft obliged, secretly funneling them under Goering's nose. Franz remarked to Galland that Marseille would have joined the unit. Galland agreed but reminded Franz of Marseille's disregard for The Party and all things military. "He never would have lasted this long," Galland said. Franz nodded at Galland's compliment to Marseille. A rumor began that to join JV-44 a pilot had to wear the Knight's Cross. When Franz heard this, he laughed because only a black tie decorated his neck.

21

WE ARE THE AIR FORCE

THREE DAYS LATER, APRIL 5, 1945, 9:30 A.M.

THE COLD SUN seemed barely to rise above the airfield as Franz and his comrades lounged around the alert shed in their flight gear. The ground around them glittered with frost. The pilots nervously smoked cigarettes and leaned back in their straight-legged chairs, acting nonchalant. Hohagen stood along a window of the alert shack with his ear glued to a field phone. Unlike the others, he was not dressed to fly, because he was coordinating the day's operations. Every few minutes he relayed a message from the orphanage, the grid coordinates of the Four Motors, a countdown as the bombers neared Southern Germany.

Franz and his comrades knew that one thousand Four Motors and six hundred escort fighters were coming. The radar men had been tracking them since they departed England, and now spotter girls were monitoring them with field glasses.

Franz and the others were eager to fly on what would be JV-44's first combat mission in strength from its new base. It would not be the unit's baptism of fire, however. Three days earlier, just hours after he had learned to fly the 262, the Count had taken a jet to buzz Florida and show his friends he was back in the cockpit. During his flight, the orphanage radioed him to tell him to come home because P-38s had been spotted nearby. Instead, the Count had attacked the P-38s, thinking "it would be nice" to score on his first mission.[1] But he overestimated his speed, overshot the P-38s, and fired wildly, his shots missing.

Now the Count sat next to Franz, his knees bouncing. Other pilots paced. Franz felt the same anxiety, a new worry he had never faced in the war, the question of who would be chosen to fly. Out of the unit's eighteen planes, half sat without engines in the blast pens. Their engines were in nearby villages, at auto shops where mechanics repaired them with tools once used to fix cars. Only seven planes were flyable. When Galland and Steinhoff approached, dressed to fly, Franz saw them with relief. The waiting was over.

The pilots snapped to attention, but Galland told them to relax. Unfolding a map on a table, Galland told the men to gather around. Using his finger, he explained that the bomber stream had split into small elements to hit multiple targets across Southern Germany. He tapped the map. Steinhoff would take off first and lead a flight of the five most reliable jets to intercept the bombers east of Munich. Galland would lead a separate mission afterward, of whatever jets remained flightworthy.

Steinhoff announced the pilots who would fly with him. Count. Lieutenant Fahrmann. Lieutenant Stigler. Sergeant Nielinger. And that was all. Hohagen shouted new grid coordinates to Galland—the Four Motors were within range.

Galland reminded his pilots what they already knew. Hundreds of escort fighters would be waiting for them. He told them what they tried to forget, that jet pilots had become the Allied fighters' top targets, both in the air and in their parachutes.* Galland had just heard from Fighter Wing 7 that one of their pilots, Major Rudi Sinner, had been strafed the day before after bailing out. Mustangs had shot up Sinner's jet, and he was badly burned in the fire. After he had bailed out, he landed in a farmer's field, tangled in his chute. The Mustangs came back around and strafed him but missed. Sinner played dead until they left. He was injured but alive.

Someone lamented aloud, "So don't bail out, because they'll strafe you in your chute. But don't crash or they'll strafe you on the ground. What's a guy to do?"

"Don't get shot down," Franz said, half-joking. The other pilots chuckled. Galland did not laugh. His straight face killed the others' amusement. As general of fighters, he had seen the bodies of pilots who had been hit by .50-caliber bullets while floating down in their chutes. They landed weighing half the weight they had been when they jumped. During the Battle of Britain, Hitler had considered ordering German pilots to shoot their enemies in parachutes. Hitler asked Goering how he thought the order would go over, and Goering sought out Galland's opinion. "I should regard it as murder, Herr *Reichsmarschall*," Galland told Goering, and he promised to disobey such an order if it was ever issued. Goering smiled and said, "That is just the reply I had expected from you, Galland."[2] Due to Galland's steadfastness to his code, Hitler never issued the order.

Hohagen relayed word to Steinhoff—it was time to launch. Galland dismissed the pilots with a salute. Steinhoff called Franz and the others of his flight together. Steinhoff had once admitted that attacking the heavies "was something like controlled suicide." But now, he

---

* As the war wound down, American fighter pilots knew that any German pilot still flying had to be an expert. This awareness led some American pilots (a small, unknown percentage) to shoot German pilots in their parachutes or after landing. Their logic was pragmatic. They did not want a German expert returning to the skies to kill a ten-man bomber crew, a buddy, or them.

tried to inspire his men. He said he had been listening to the bombers on a radio at the orphanage and could hear their pilots talking between planes. They no longer bothered with radio silence, assuming that the German Air Force was finished. "Let's prove them wrong," Steinhoff said.

GREEN FLARES ARCED across the field. With the tower vacant this was the signal for ground personnel to clear the runway. From the cockpit of *White 3* through his headset Franz heard Steinhoff's voice telling him and the others to ignore the flares and wait until their engines were warm. Franz found himself looking over his shoulder, hoping enemy fighters did not swoop down on the field. He removed his gloves and passed his rosary beads between his fingers. Only specks of black paint remained on the pale purple beads.

After five minutes that seemed like five years, Steinhoff began his takeoff roll followed by the Count and the others. Franz dropped his rosary beads into his chest pocket and zipped it shut. He slipped on his gloves and gently pushed the throttle forward. Orange flames in the shape of cones throbbed from his engines' exhausts. *White 3* rolled along the runway's grass, leaving in its wake a hazy cloud that smelled like coal. The 262 shrieked like a banshee and built speed slowly, its three wheels spinning into a blur as the runway whipped past. Franz knew that the 262 required two thousand yards to reach its liftoff speed of 120 miles per hour, so he held the stick neutral to keep the nose down. Ahead, Franz saw the airfield's tree-lined perimeter growing closer. Beyond lay the steeples and rooftops of the village of Feldkirchen. Pulling back on the stick, Franz lifted the plane's nose. The jet hesitated, its nosewheel dragging through the air before the whole machine floated upward. Small trees whipped beneath the jet's spinning tires. With its gear sucked into its stomach, the jet began to sprint, sucking air into turbojets that heated the air and spit out thrust. Unlike the 109's engine torque, the 262's engines pushed together, resulting in straight speed.

The flight of five aimed toward the northeast and flew low to build their speed before climbing. The skies around them were empty. Franz suddenly believed what Steinhoff meant when he said, "We are the Air Force." Through his jet's plastic bubble canopy, Franz saw Bavaria around him. The countryside sparkled as the snow melted to reveal spring's green pastures. *An ugly war has never been fought in a more beautiful place*, he thought.

Blistering along at 475 miles per hour, the flight blasted over the female flak gunners who manned the guns around the airfield. The pilots called them "Fighter Dolls." The formation whistled over battered villages where women, children, and old men scurried to catch a glimpse. They passed over columns of German refugees, some of the nation's two million homeless who now camped in villages and alongside country roads. The flight ripped across the autobahn, their engines' thunder echoing along the concrete, calling out the beaten pilots and tired mechanics from beneath the trees where they waited to surrender. The men stepped to the road and stared wide-eyed at the jets that raced across the pines, trailing a snarling roar of defiance that quickened their hearts.

The people on the ground held their hands over their eyes, fixated at the sight of the five jets climbing toward the sun. Some wept with pride and others with sadness. Some shook their heads with scorn at such futile stubbornness. But everyone who watched the five jets knew they were going off to battle an overwhelming foe. They saw for themselves that Goering was wrong, the Air Force had never abandoned them. They had seen the Air Force and more, something that Goering had told them no longer existed in German skies: bravery.

32,000 FEET ABOVE THE EARTH

From his place at the right rear of the triangle formation, Franz heard Steinhoff call out the bombers with elation. Steinhoff banked the formation northward to the left, and Franz saw the heavies. They flew like a wispy silver cloud above the patchwork fields. His eyes lit up. The cloud of bombers was tiny, just thirty-odd planes, and appeared to be floating westward between the cities of Straubing and Inglostadt. Compared with the two-thousand-bomber raids the Americans had been sending, thirty bombers was nothing.

Steinhoff began his five-hundred-mile-per-hour charge. The attack method in the 262 had changed to compensate for the jet's blazing speed. The days of dive, hit, climb, and repeat had past. Now Franz knew to make a sprint for the bombers, hit them from the sides or behind, pull up, curve around, and repeat the attack. Franz flipped up the metal spoon that guarded the 262's thumb trigger. His gloved thumb rested on the brown button that would ignite the four 30mm heavy cannons in the jet's nose. Franz used to tell his students what he had been told, that the cannons could "chew through the wing of a B-17" with just five shells. He was ready to test the claim.

The bombers were still tiny and far beyond range when Franz looked up and saw a sight that made his eyes bulge. Flying straight toward him and his comrades, high above, was a flock of silver fighters. He knew the silhouette—long noses, straight wings, and narrow tails. He had shot one down the prior April. It was the fighter the Germans called "the Flying Cross," the one the Americans called "the Mustang." It was the P-51, and there were at least one hundred of them. Franz knew he was in trouble. In his calm professor-like voice, Steinhoff radioed: "Trouble above." A 262 could normally escape the P-51 and outrun it with ease. But if a P-51 was high above a 262, it could dive and pick up enough speed to briefly run with the jet. Looking up while shielding his eyes, Franz removed his finger from the trigger when he saw the P-51s diving.

Franz looked up again and saw three P-51s breaking from the diving gaggle, their noses pointed straight at him. He knew this was a battle he could not win, and the others knew this, too. The jets on Franz's left banked to the left, and Franz banked hard to the right.

Franz would never get close enough to the bombers that day to see that they wore tail markings he would have recognized, the triangle K of the 379th Bomb Group. Rolling inverted, he instinctively turned to the tactic that had saved his life for three years in 109s. He dove.

Aiming *White 3* at the earth, he let her run like a rocket blazing through the atmosphere. The speed pinned him to his seat. Franz glimpsed the P-51s behind him, racing to catch up. Other P-51s swarmed his comrades. Franz pushed the trembling control stick forward to deepen the dive. The needle in the airspeed indicator quivered. Franz felt the g-forces piling their weight on his sternum.

The voice of Lieutenant Fahrmann shouted over the radio, "Danube One, my horse is lame!" Franz knew the code for engine trouble and knew the P-51s had gotten Fahrmann. Seconds later, he heard Fahrmann say he was jumping.

White 3 raced faster and faster toward a layer of clouds at twenty thousand feet. Franz's eyes watered. His airspeed indicator wound past the 600-mile-per-hour mark. The jet's redline was painted on the dial at the 625-mile-per-hour mark. When the needle reached that point, the jet's controls would freeze and the craft could potentially break apart.

Franz knew he had left the P-51s behind when clouds whipped past his canopy, revealing his blinding speed. Thanks to gravity and the turbojets, his 262 had become a bullet, ripping through ten thousand feet in seconds. As he burst through the clouds, the wide, patchwork fields below spread across Franz's windscreen in all directions. Franz decided he was safe with the clouds separating him from the fighting above. He tried to pull up, but the flightstick was frozen, locked by "an evil spell."[3]

The cockpit turned silent. Only the sound of the wind howling across the wings told Franz he was alive. The speedometer's needle quivered at the 625-mile-per-hour mark. He had flown past the plane's limits. He had forgotten a rule of the 262, to never dive in a jet so fast it needed no help from gravity. Now, *White 3* was frozen in a death dive. Franz struggled to pull the control stick, but it felt as unbending as an iron bar. Pinned to his seat, Franz knew he could not bail out. He felt himself grow cold as the thought struck him. *I just killed myself.* Franz began to pray feverishly.

Kick the rudder! Franz thought he heard a voice. But his earphones were silent. Perhaps it was the voice of one of his instructors from jet school. Using the immovable control stick as leverage, Franz dug his heels into the rudder pedals. He pushed the left pedal forward with all his might. The jet shook from the tail. He pushed the right pedal. The jet shook again. Franz began kicking the rudder pedals, one then the other, until the jet's tail began to wag. Suddenly Franz felt the control stick move. The jet tore through ten thousand feet, then eight thousand feet. Franz saw the farm fields ahead tighten in clarity, with crop lines and roads appearing. He wanted to rip back the throttle but fought the urge. He kept kicking the rudder. He pulled back on the control stick, grunting and straining. He was certain the stick was about to snap.

Slowly, *White 3*'s nose twitched. Then it rose. Gritting his teeth and straining at the stick, Franz pulled the jet into a gentle arc. He saw the earth approaching, three thousand feet away, then two thousand, then one thousand. Franz knew it would be close, whether his pullout had enough arc to curve above the earth. He stopped breathing but kept pulling. Just before the jet's underslung engines could scoop the soil, *White 3*'s nose lifted upward and her engines' thrust blasted off the earth.

Regaining control, his altimeter at 0, as he flew along the field Franz glanced to his left and saw the shocked faces of a group of farmers standing even with him. Climbing and turning, he caught his breath. Then he saw something incredible. The farmers were stomping flames that had broken out among the hay they had been laying out for their animals. His engines had made the ground catch fire.

Franz flew past the farmers again and waved in apology. The farmers stopped and stared in wonder, too shocked to manage a reply. Their cows bolted from the jet's noise. The farmers returned to stomping. Turning for Munich, Franz flew past a plume of black smoke that rose from Ingolstadt, where the B-17s had struck an ordnance depot. He unzipped his black leather jacket. Sweating, Franz cursed himself for being so stupid. In the same breath, he thanked God for flying with him. His instructors had never warned him not to dive in the 262. No one could have experienced what he had and come back to warn of it.* Franz knew he had not pulled from that dive alone. Something had broken the evil spell, and it was a force more powerful than his muscles.

FOUR DAYS LATER, APRIL 9, 1945, AROUND 4:00 P.M.

Franz buried his shovel in the airfield's white, sandy soil and pitched the dirt aside. His foxhole was already four feet deep, but he kept digging. Next to him, *White 3* sat in the late day shadows on the other side of the blast pen's wall. Franz worked in his flying uniform because he knew he could be called to scramble at any moment.

Four days earlier, the Americans had found JV-44. When Franz flew home after barely recovering from his plane's death dive, he arrived over the field just after P-51s had strafed it. Everyone knew they would be back. The one-man foxholes were Galland's idea, so the men could reach cover immediately upon landing. At the other blast pens leading east to the alert shack, the other pilots—Galland included—were digging foxholes alongside the pens that housed their jets. Franz smirked at the irony that he was digging a "grave" like the one he called home in Africa.

A rapid, punctuated *thump* of machine guns froze Franz's foot to his shovel. Glancing west, he saw a P-51 burst over the trees then dive

---

* Franz would remember, "Later the next day we actually had a briefing on my experience. Remember that we were all still learning about these planes. This was a valuable lesson."[4]

to earth and race low toward the airfield. Another P-51 appeared. Then another. Black-and-yellow checkerboards covered their noses, the war paint of the 353rd Fighter Group. The fighters swept across the southern edge of the field, their guns puffing. Their bullets chewed along the dirt and strafed up and over the blast pens and anti-aircraft gun pits. A parked jet exploded in flames. Anti-aircraft gunners fell dead over their earthen pits. The P-51 pilots hugged the ground, the air scoops beneath their bellies almost swiping the grass. Across Germany, enemy fighters had declared open season on German airfields, continuing eight straight days of raids that would claim 1,697 German aircraft destroyed.

Sirens wailed as the field's flak guns came to life and threw up rapid black clouds. The P-51s seemed to fly faster than their engine noise, a guttural growl that echoed after they had cleared the field. The P-51 pilots kept running east after each strike, staying low, not climbing or banking. Franz could tell they knew their craft. The first wave had barely departed when a second wave of P-51s burst through the smoke at the field's southern edge. They ripped north across the field at 320 miles per hour and strafed the planes parked in front of the terminal. Each time, the P-51s came from a new direction to confuse the flak gunners.

For a moment, Franz stood still, his body frozen with alarm. The P-51s had hit everywhere except the flight line where he was standing. Men around Franz had jumped into their holes, ducked into blast pens, and sprinted for a bombed-out barn behind the alert shack. Franz found his feet, tossed his shovel aside, and jumped into his foxhole. Peering up at the sky, he saw ribbons of fire rip overhead. A shower of dirt told him he had moved just in time. A split second later Franz looked up and saw a flight of P-51s fly directly over his head. Their prop blast blew off his hat. He could smell their exhaust.

After the flak guns had chased the P-51s away, Franz slowly climbed out of his hole. Three of the unit's jets lay burning around him, and others had caught bullets. Franz ran to check on his comrades, but miraculously, none had been hit. When Galland came by, inspecting the damage, he lamented, "They would strafe a stray dog if they could."[5] Franz climbed onto *White 3*'s wings and walked from side to side. He smiled when he saw that she was unscathed.

A siren stopped Franz. He jumped from his plane and into his hole, certain the P-51s were back. The other men along the flight line hid in their holes. Only their heads showed as they nervously glanced skyward. Franz waited for an order to take off, but none came. He waited in his hole next to *White 3* until he heard a low rumble that he recognized from his time in Sicily—the droning of steel wasps. Franz saw them emerge from the clouds high above. Box after box of silver bombers motored from south to north. They were B-17s, two hundred planes strong.

The flak guns of the airfield and the city of Munich blasted out, rocketing shells thirty thousand feet up. Some of his comrades ran from their holes, but Franz stayed. He expected Galland to come running to tell him to evacuate *White 3*. When Franz heard the high-pitched whine of bombs, he knew that no such order was coming. Franz put his thumbs in his ears and opened his mouth just as the little girl had demonstrated in Potsdam. He squeezed his chest to his knees and huddled belowground as the earth shook. The pressure from each blast ripped over his hole and flung dirt down his back. His ears rang. His eyes watered. Each shock wave of pressure hit like an invisible foot on his back. Each blast sucked the breath from his lungs and stomped him deeper. Franz knew from the direction of the fury that the bombers were pounding the terminal and hangars where they expected JV-44 to live and operate. He heard glass shattering, fire sizzling, and walls slamming down. A bomber whined and spun toward the earth, but Franz never heard its crash over the chaos.*

---

* A JV-44 officer, Major Werner Roell, was in Munich and saw an airman parachute from the B-17. Roell found the airman in the hands of civilians and an SS officer. Before the SS officer could execute the airman, Roell chased the officer away and took the American to a hospital. "The man might have worn a different uniform but he was still a fellow human-being," Roell would remember.[6]

When the earth stopped shaking, Franz looked up from under his arm and saw the bombers turning west for home. He climbed from his hole and wiped his eyes. His comrades emerged, shaking the cobwebs from their heads. Across the airstrip, gray smoke rose from the terminal. The side of the tower had been chopped away and now it teetered. The bombers had dropped firebombs that had burned through the roofs of the hangars, from which black smoke poured. High explosive bombs had pitted the terminal's concrete parking area and the grass runway, leaving deep, white craters with a perfect dirt ring around each. Along the field's southern blast pens, jets were burning. When the air raid sirens stopped wailing, others cries could be heard—faint, muted sobs of pain from the south end of the field. There, fifty men and Fighter Dolls had been wounded. Six men had been killed. Franz saw the survivors limping among the burning jets. As he joined his comrades in a sprint to lend aid, Franz knew that without some glimmer of hope, JV-44 was going to fold before doing any good.

THE SQUADRON OF EXPERTS

A WEEK LATER, MID-APRIL 1945

FRANZ AND HIS comrades stood around the alert shack, eating sandwiches of bread and jam, as they did every day at noon. They ate in silence, tired from the British Mosquito bombers that had flown over Munich, triggering air raid sirens to deny them sleep. They were weary from cleaning up after the bombing and strafing raids that had not let up. They hardly noticed the pilot who entered their midst, the one with the shoulder boards of a major and the Knight's Cross around his neck. One of the pilots saw the stranger and did a double take. He recognized the man with the strong, simple face, who happened to have 301 victories, three and a half times the victory count of the Red Baron. The pilot asked: "Barkhorn?" The stranger chuckled and nodded.

Franz turned and saw the famous steel-blue eyes of his former flight cadet, Gerd Barkhorn. But Barkhorn was no longer just a cadet. After three and a half years of fighting, mostly on the Eastern Front, Barkhorn stood before Franz as history's second greatest ace. He was reporting to JV-44. Franz and Barkhorn embraced as the others crowded around them. Barkhorn bragged to everyone that Franz had not only saved his career but had shown him his first naked woman on the shores of Dresden's nudist colony.

Barkhorn said he had come from Florida to join the unit. He had seen the names on JV-44's roster and had wanted to visit but reasoned that if he came to visit, he might as well stay. He told Franz he had never flown the 262. Franz promised to teach his old student once again.

———————

SOON AFTER BARKHORN's arrival, Galland kept a seat empty on his side of JV-44's dinner table. Dinner at the orphanage was a formal affair served by waiters. Galland wanted to maintain the unit's professional spirit. He and his staff—Steinhoff, Hohagen, and a non-flyer or two—adjutants—sat on one side of a long table, like a wedding party. The pilots sat across the table facing them. Franz glanced at the empty chair repeatedly. Steinhoff sat to Galland's right. The empty seat was to Galland's left. Franz wondered whom the general was expecting. The double doors of the dining hall creaked open. An officer strolled quietly through, hung his long, gray leather trench coat on the wall, and approached the table. The men saw with surprise that Luetzow, the Man of Ice, had departed his Italian exile to join JV-44.

As he showed Luetzow to his seat, Galland beamed with the same smirk he always wore. Luetzow's frown seemed to lift as he took his place at the table. The morale of the pilots opposite him soared, marked by their grins. During the meal, Luetzow nodded to Franz, remembering him from Sicily.

Franz would learn that Luetzow had come because Galland had asked him, not because he wanted to join the unit. He had not flown combat for three years, let alone the 262. Galland had summoned Luetzow to serve as his right-hand man, to handle all logistics and operations so Steinhoff could focus on leading the flying. But Luetzow insisted that if he joined the unit, he would shoulder his share of the dangers. He, too, would fly.

With JV-44's table full, Steinhoff looked around and knew that never before had a unit existed with so many legends, "a body of young men in which everyone knew so much about everyone else."[1] Outside of JV-44's dining hall the pilots' peers would begin calling "the Flying Sanatorium" by a new name: "the Squadron of Experts."

THE NEXT MORNING

Beyond the tree line east of the field, the night sky began to warm into day. By flashlight, Franz led Barkhorn to *White 3*. Franz hurried, aware that when the sun rose, so might the P-51s. Franz was going to give Barkhorn his first lesson in the instruments of the 262. Farther along the flight line, a light shined from Steinhoff's plane, where he knelt on the wing over Luetzow, who sat in the cockpit.

"Where's your nose art?" Barkhorn asked Franz, shining his flashlight on *White 3*'s nose. Franz explained that everyone in JV-44 shared planes, so there was no sense in staking a claim. Even Galland abided by this rule and ended his tradition of painting Mickey Mouse on his plane. Barkhorn told Franz about his wife, Christl, and said he painted her name on every plane he flew, for luck. Franz cautioned Barkhorn to put his wife far from his mind if he wanted to see her again. Franz lifted the canopy for Barkhorn to take a seat. Shining his flashlight on the gauges, Franz told him not to be deceived by the 262's "sinister beauty." It was unforgiving. It flew so fast that a pilot needed to think faster than ever before, to anticipate every maneuver.

Franz remembered from flying school that Barkhorn's mind was his own worst enemy. Barkhorn himself had admitted that when he first entered combat he flew more than one hundred missions without a victory, until he settled down. Franz had also heard that Barkhorn's nerves, coupled with his physical wounds, had landed him in Florida.

Franz knew any man could succumb to strain. He almost had, if the B-17's gunner had not shot him first. Franz worried about Barkhorn because he knew he was a decent man who cared about his comrades, the real reason he had left Florida to join JV-44.*

Franz would have worried more about his former student if he had known a story about Barkhorn and his enemy. Sometime during Barkhorn's three and a half years of fighting over the Eastern Front, he had shot a Soviet fighter plane to pieces. The fighter was smoking and falling apart. Instead of finishing off the plane, Barkhorn pulled up alongside it. There he saw the Soviet pilot sitting in the cockpit, frozen in fear. The pilot looked at Barkhorn. Barkhorn gestured with his hand for the pilot to bail out. The Soviet pilot had given up on jumping, expecting to be shot if he stood to jump. With Barkhorn's encouragement, the man jettisoned his canopy, jumped, and floated by parachute to safety. Barkhorn's best friend, Erich "Bubi" Hartmann, who would trump him by fifty-one victories as history's top ace, had asked Barkhorn why he risked his life to fly alongside an enemy to convince him to bail out. Barkhorn had told Hartmann, "Bubi, you must remember that one day that Russian pilot was the baby son of a beautiful Russian girl. He has his right to life and love the same as we do."[2]

After his lesson with Barkhorn, Franz talked with Steinhoff, who had his own worries about Luetzow. Steinhoff said that Luetzow kept forgetting his lessons and was not grasping the new jet, as if his mind was screaming over his thoughts, trying to keep him away from the cockpit.

———

THE HAPPY SOUND of an accordion echoed through the orphanage after dinner, a bouncy tune reminiscent of an airline's theme song. The song was "Rhapsody in Blue," by American composer George

———

* Franz would remember, "He was tired, as were we all, and not exactly in love with the 262 either. It was the worst possible mix because the 262 couldn't care less how you felt."

Gershwin. Anyone new to the orphanage would have cocked an ear and thought, *Have the Americans arrived?* The song came from a sitting room that the pilots had turned into a bar where they gathered every night. There, Franz sat in the midst of his comrades and played an accordion he had borrowed from his host family.

The Count, Barkhorn, and others tapped their feet. They asked Franz to repeat some songs two or three times. Everyone kept a bottle of spirits close to hand. Franz played songs by Gershwin, his favorite composer, and the German love song "Lili Marlene," while his comrades sang along. Franz suddenly appreciated that his mother had made him take lessons as a child. Had there been an organ in the orphanage, he could have played that, too.

Franz stopped the music when Steinhoff, Luetzow, and their guest, Colonel Trautloft, entered the room. Franz and the others stood shakily to attention then collapsed into their seats. Trautloft was visiting to discuss JV-44's aircraft needs with Luetzow, after their recent losses.

Steinhoff encouraged Franz to resume his music. Trautloft asked someone to pass him a bottle. Trautloft had once been a fighter pilot, too. He had fifty-eight victories to his name. The men drank and drank, except for Luetzow, who remained sober and observant. Soon unable to hold a tune, Franz set the accordion down. Trautloft and Steinhoff told loud stories from the Eastern Front. One by one the other pilots excused themselves to quit for the night, until Franz found himself alone with Trautloft, Steinhoff, Luetzow, and one or two others.

"What are you going to do when it's all over?" Trautloft asked the men. Luetzow shrugged. As a professional military man, he knew his career would be over. He and the others assumed that after two world wars, the Allies would never allow another German Air Force. Steinhoff said he wanted to teach philology, the history of languages, if higher learning was permitted after the war. Franz said if he did not have his mother to care for, he would start over in Spain. The others looked at him with surprise. Franz explained that he had only known good times there.

Steinhoff nodded. Trautloft's eyes narrowed with seriousness. He said that if they were smart they would all follow Franz there. Lowering his voice to a whisper, Trautloft warned his comrades that every man in Germany would soon be branded for the crimes of a few.

"It's all true," Trautloft said. "The whispers."

Franz looked at Trautloft, confused. Trautloft revealed what he had seen in October 1944. He had been the inspector of the day fighters when a rumor had reached his desk of Allied airmen imprisoned by the SS in a labor camp.

Trautloft knew that the Geneva Convention made captured airmen the responsibility of the German Air Force, not the SS. Trautloft decided to personally investigate. Under the guise of inspecting bomb damage at a nearby factory, he asked the SS to show him and his adjutant around their labor camp called Buchenwald.

Inside the fences, the SS showed Trautloft only the camp's presentable aspects, the administration offices and the guard's barracks. The inmates, the SS told him, were all political prisoners who provided the workforce for a munitions factory within the camps' walls and other factories nearby.

Trautloft was about to leave when a man in a gray uniform with dark gray stripes shouted to him from behind a fence. The man spoke German but said he was an American officer. The SS tried to dissuade Trautloft from talking with him, but Trautloft pointed to his rank and made them stand back.

The American told Trautloft that he was one of more than 160 Allied airmen imprisoned there. He spoke German so perfect he must have learned the language before the war. He said that he and his fellow prisoners had been brought to Buchenwald because they had been captured while hiding with the French Resistance or trying to escape. Instead of treating them as prisoners of war, the Gestapo and SS had labeled them as "terror fliers," the equivalent of spies, and sent them to Buchenwald instead of an Air Force–run P.O.W. camp.

The American begged Trautloft to rescue him and his comrades.

He said that several men had already died of pneumonia and worse, that they suspected the SS had plans to kill them. The American said the SS were working people to death in the camp and killing others outright—children, Jews, priests, Soviet P.O.W.s, and more. The American pointed to the crematorium that he said burned their bodies.

Trautloft returned to Berlin deeply disturbed and worked quickly to arrange a transfer of the Allied airmen out of Buchenwald.*

Trautloft would later learn that he had rescued the Allied airmen seven days before their scheduled execution by the SS.† But his authority as an Air Force colonel only went so far. Trautloft was powerless to free the scores of other prisoners from Buchenwald, the camp where the SS would eventually work to death or outright murder fifty-six thousand people.

Franz and the others remained silent. Trautloft's testimony stunned them. Franz had been exposed to the idea of a "concentration camp" during the pre-war years. That's when The Party had advertised Dachau to the world and dangled the threat of imprisonment there over all of Germany. But not until hearing Trautloft's eyewitness account had Franz ever imagined that the camps had become like Buchenwald.

Shocked and dismayed, Franz did not doubt Trautloft. He had seen The Party turn Germany into a place where a person could be killed for telling a joke. Had The Party gone from incarcerating its opponents in 1934 to slaughtering them in 1944? The idea no longer

---

* Trautloft would remember, "After he told me about these things, my blood ran cold, I just could not believe it."[3]

† On October 19, trains carried the Allied airmen away from Buchenwald. Joe Mosher, an American P-38 pilot rescued by Trautloft, described the trip to a German Air Force (Luftwaffe) P.O.W. camp: "We were certain that conditions would be better where we were heading, particularly when we saw the disgust exhibited by the Luftwaffe officers on their visit [to Buchenwald]. It seems ironic now, but the Luftwaffe men who accompanied us as guards seemed our saviors. We wanted desperately to be free from the Gestapo and the SS and in the hands of men who still honored the brotherhood of fellow aviators."[4]

seemed far-fetched. Franz knew he could have ended up in a camp as punishment for his brother's actions. Steinhoff, Luetzow, and Trautloft could have been thrown into a camp after their mutiny's failure. Every man and woman in Germany had reason to fear the camps, where some 3.5 million Germans would eventually be incarcerated as "political enemies" of The Party. But never before had Franz heard what was actually happening in the camps and what could have happened *to him*.

Luetzow and Steinhoff seemed especially troubled by Trautloft's account. They had served on the Eastern Front, where they had heard whispers of a new type of camp that only SS eyes had seen. The camps were rumored to exist to exterminate The Party's enemies. As they did with most wartime rumors, they found the notion of "death camps" difficult to believe.* But now Trautloft's testimonial confirmed that the whispers of a greater evil could be true.† After the war, the evil would have a name, when the Allies opened the camps and lifted the SS's veil of secrecy. What the Allies revealed was a systematic slaughter of Jews and other innocent people called the Holocaust.

TWO DAYS LATER, APRIL 18, 1945, AROUND 1:00 P.M.

Inside the alert shack, where the pilots hung their parachutes, Franz suited up to fly. He slid his gloves over his hands. He zipped the cuffs

---

* The U.S. Holocaust Museum would write: "The psychological barriers to accepting the existence of the Nazi killing program were considerable. The Holocaust was unprecedented and irrational. It was inconceivable that an advanced industrial nation would mobilize its resources to kill millions of peaceful civilians. . . . In doing so, the Nazis often acted contrary to German economic and military interests."

† The SS put death camps into operation in 1942. These camps, such as Sobibor, Treblinka, and Auschwitz, existed for the "efficient mass murder" of Jews, Soviet P.O.W.s, Poles, Gypsies, and others. Unlike Dachau, the death camps were built in Poland, to hide them from the German citizenry and military. The SS kept the death camps so secret and left so little evidence of their crimes that Holocaust denial arose in postwar years.[5]

of his baggy leather pants over his heavy black boots. During the days prior, Franz had flown in combat against B-26 medium bombers. Now he was preparing for a different mission. Franz had agreed to test fly a jet that had had its engine changed, because he had the most familiarity with the 262's engines. Mechanics had started up the jet and were warming the motors. They and the machine waited not far from the alert shack.

The shack rattled. Franz glanced out and saw three jets launching, led by Galland. Steinhoff followed, leading another flight of three jets into takeoff position on the worn grass strip. They carried experimental rockets, a dozen under each wing. Steinhoff's jet stopped and idled, its engines throbbing. The Count pulled up behind Steinhoff's left wing and another pilot behind Steinhoff's right wing. Nearly three years prior, on one of his nine-hundred-plus missions, Steinhoff had destroyed the burning Soviet plane to spare its pilot from a painful death. The Count had been on his wing then and was again now.

The field was rough, with white patches where ground crewmen had filled in craters. They called the struggle "the battle between shovel and bomb." Steinhoff's jet lurched then rolled forward, gaining speed by the second. The others followed him. About three-fourths of the way along the runway he had nearly reached the required 120 miles per hour to liftoff, when his left tire exploded. His jet veered violently left into the Count's lane. The Count was lifting into the air as Steinhoff's left landing gear collapsed. Steinhoff's left engine and wing slapped the earth. His plane bounced into the air from the impact, flying momentarily on borrowed time.

Franz ran to the shack's doorway. He and the others saw Steinhoff's plane pitch into the air. They saw the nose of the Count's plane about to fly into the tail of Steinhoff's. But just before they could collide, Steinhoff's jet fell heavily downward. The wheels of the Count's jet skimmed just past Steinhoff's tail.

In the split second as his plane dropped, Steinhoff prepared to crash. He pulled hard on his shoulder straps, drawing his body into his seat. He knew that if he was knocked unconscious, he would burn to death. In front of the cockpit lay a fuel tank holding 198 sloshing gallons of kerosene. Behind him sat another 330 gallons. Below his feet rested a third tank of 37 gallons.

Steinhoff's jet slammed to earth. The impact stripped both of the jet's engines as the machine slid, leaving the engines behind. Steinhoff heard a *pop* as the craft ignited. It kept sliding, trailing a trough of fire, until grinding to a stop.

Around Steinhoff, the world turned red. In slow motion he saw a tire and parts of his plane tumble through the air, past his canopy. In all directions he saw fire and heard the flames' angry hiss.

The fuel tank beneath Steinhoff's feet burst, shooting flames up through the holes in the cockpit floor. Steinhoff's wrists began burning at the gaps between his gloves and jacket. With his gloves, pants, and feet on fire, he flung his straps from his shoulders.

The oxygen tanks behind him ruptured, blowing the flames like a blowtorch. The inferno swirled around the cockpit. Steinhoff could no longer see his plane's wingtips through the flames. It looked like he had been dropped into a burner barrel. The metal walls of the cockpit began to melt and drip.

Steinhoff flipped open the canopy and jumped onto the wing. The fire hit his exposed face, his eyes instantly swelling shut. Any other man would have dropped and died. But Steinhoff clawed at his burning face and ran along the wing, his screams drowned out by the blast furnace around him. The rockets ignited beneath his feet and launched, skipping along the earth before exploding. Steinhoff jumped blindly off the wing.

High above, Galland had heard the Count's frantic radio calls. He turned his jet and saw Steinhoff burst from the blaze, "a human torch." Galland wept, because he knew he was watching his friend die. Franz saw Steinhoff staggering, a "flaming figure."[6] Cannon shells ruptured behind him. Steinhoff fell to the ground and into a pool of burning jet fuel. He rolled through the flames in agony.

Franz frantically searched for a fire extinguisher but found none. He sprinted toward Steinhoff on the heels of two mechanics. The mechanics reached Steinhoff first and pulled him from the fire, their hands burning when they clung to his liquefied jacket. When they pulled him to safety, they gasped. Steinhoff's once lean and striking face had melted.

Franz stopped just yards from Steinhoff and pulled his hair in horror. Two other ground crewmen raced up in a *kettenkrad* used to tow the jets. Returning to his senses, Franz helped the mechanics lift Steinhoff into the bed of the vehicle. Franz hopped onto the ledge of the *kettenkrad* with the mechanics and together they held Steinhoff down, smoke rising from his body, as the driver sped away.

Franz told the driver to stop at the alert shack. He knew JV-44 had no ambulance or doctors, but he knew they had to do something quickly. Franz screamed for the men to bring cold water and dump it on Steinhoff. He ran to the phone and called Oberfoehring Military Hospital in Munich, just six miles away. The hospital operator said they would dispatch their ambulance.

When the water came, Franz had the others put Steinhoff on the ground. They poured bucket after bucket on him, and each time he moaned.

Franz and the others tried to strip Steinhoff of his clothes so water could reach his skin, but when they did they found his skin stuck to his uniform. They removed his flight helmet and found his helmet and scalp had become one. Steinhoff's fingers had fused into claws. The men needed to cut off his boots. They retched when they saw the muscles of Steinhoff's feet.[7]

Franz thought it might be more merciful to shoot his friend. Looking to his side for his pistol, he realized it was still hanging inside the shack. A calm voice shook his attention. It was Luetzow, who knelt next to Steinhoff. As buckets of water were dumped on his thrashing friend, Luetzow leaned close to Steinhoff's face, where his ear had been. Luetzow whispered something to Steinhoff that no one else could hear. Steinhoff grew still. Luetzow moved out of the way so the men could pour water, more gently now, on Steinhoff. Franz saw Luetzow turn away, hiding his face. He saw Luetzow, "the most stoic and disciplined man" he had ever known, start to cry, without sound, just tears. Franz began to cry. Everyone around him began to cry.[8]

Wiping his eyes with his ash-covered hands, Franz ran to the phone and called the hospital again, pleading with them to hurry. The ambulance had already left. It would take an hour for the medics to arrive, their progress delayed by roadblocks and destruction in the streets. All the while, Luetzow huddled close to Steinhoff, his hand on Steinhoff's shoulder, his face next to Steinhoff's charred body that smelled horrid and burned. Luetzow kept talking to him, repeating the name "Ursula," the name of Steinhoff's wife. Luetzow whispered to Steinhoff even as Franz and the medics lifted Steinhoff onto a stretcher and into the ambulance. When the ambulance raced away, Luetzow broke down and wandered away.

Minutes later, Galland and the others landed. Franz met Galland by his plane and told him where the ambulance had taken Steinhoff. Galland jumped into his BMW and raced to the hospital, alone. Farther down the flight line, the Count, in tears, asked his mechanic where they had laid Steinhoff's body. The mechanic said that Steinhoff was somehow still alive, which sent the Count into a frenzy. He sprinted for the alert shack, trembling at what he knew he needed to do. Franz had heard the story from Roedel, of the Count's promise to Steinhoff, and intercepted him at the shack. The Count demanded to know where they had taken Steinhoff. Before Franz could stop the others from revealing where Steinhoff had been taken, someone told the Count. Before the Count left for the hospital, Franz told him, "Luetzow says he's going to live." The Count looked at Franz with surprise and took off running, his pistol belt bobbing.

At the hospital, the doctors would not let the Count near Steinhoff, no matter how hard he pleaded. The Count saw Steinhoff through the glass of an operating room. He knew he could barge in and do what had to be done, but another thought fought within his mind, the notion that Steinhoff might yet live. The Count left the hospital, distraught, but with his holster sealed.

That night, Franz and his comrades gathered in the orphanage, their faces ashen. They toasted Steinhoff with cognac, bottled in the First World War. Then they drank another and another. Luetzow was absent, still missing. Franz and the others were certain Steinhoff would never survive. Barkhorn gathered Steinhoff's effects and his medals so his wife, Ursula, could one day receive them.[9]

Galland watched from the shadows. As the pilots departed, Galland called over Franz and Hohagen. Franz leaned drunkenly on Hohagen, who was sober, unwilling to drink after his head wound. Galland quietly reminded them that their work was not over until the war was over. Galland's face twitched with grief, but he kept his emotions from welling over by focusing on his duty. He told Hohagen that he had promoted him to assume Steinhoff's position as operations officer, effectively second in command, equal with Luetzow. Galland turned to Franz and said he was giving him Hohagen's job as technical officer. Franz nodded and tried to straighten up.

When Franz stumbled into the silent streets and plodded toward his adopted home, he was no longer just a pilot in the Squadron of Experts. He had become the fourth in command of the world's most elite flying squadron. At that moment, Franz would have been happy to have never worn an Air Force uniform if he could have avoided what he had seen that afternoon. Franz had heard that his brother had died without suffering. But if Steinhoff lived, Franz knew that the war had just turned the best man among them into a monster. *If he lives,* Franz thought, *Steinhoff will die over and over again, every day.* On the walk home, Franz stopped to vomit. Wiping his mouth with his sleeve, he hoped his host family would be asleep so they would not ask, "What's wrong?"

FOUR DAYS LATER, APRIL 22, 1945

Alone, Galland walked on a path to Goering's chalet on the snowy, muddy mountainside called the Obersalzberg. To his left, Galland saw the village of Berchtesgaden in the valley to the north. To the south loomed massive Kehlstein Mountain, where Hitler's Eagle's Nest retreat perched above the clouds like a small castle on the mountain's peak. Air Force soldiers with rifles emerged from Goering's home and hurried past Galland carrying large wooden boxes. Other soldiers, empty-handed, passed Galland and entered the chalet, avoiding eye contact.

Galland had expected the worst when he heard that Goering had summoned him. Two days prior, on Hitler's birthday, the dictator had all but announced his intention to die in Berlin. With Soviet armies fewer than ten miles from his bunker, Hitler had placed Goering in charge of Southern Germany and the armies of any southern territories still standing. Galland believed that Goering, who now wielded absolute power over him, had summoned him to have him killed. A bullet would do what JV-44 had failed to accomplish.

Inside Goering's home, where the *Reichsmarschall* had once smoked his tall pipe and paraded in togas and a hunter's lederhosen, Goering supervised the removal of his art collection. His men were whisking priceless paintings out the door and ushering them to a bunker in the forest. Galland had expected Goering to be foaming or sinister. Instead, the *Reichsmarschall* struck him as "deeply depressed." Goering received Galland with civility. He asked with genuine interest about JV-44's progress. Galland told Goering that two days prior the unit had launched its most jets—fifteen—on one mission. They had scored their most victories that day, shooting down three B-26 medium bombers and damaging seven others. Galland reluctantly told Goering about Steinhoff's crash.

Goering showed traces of sympathy. He told Galland why he had summoned him. He wished to acknowledge that he had been wrong.

He admitted that Galland had been right about the 262 when he said it belonged with the fighter pilots, not the bomber pilots. Then Galland's greatest enemy said, "I envy you, Galland, for going into action. I wish I were a few years younger and less bulky. If I were, I would gladly put myself under your command."[10]

Galland departed Goering's chalet smirking, eager to tell Luetzow that even though the war was lost, the Man of Ice and the Mutineers had won a battle.

TWO DAYS LATER, APRIL 24, 1945, EARLY AFTERNOON

The airfield had never been so busy. Jet after jet was landing on Munich's grass as planes and pilots poured in to join JV-44. Units were folding, and the Americans were closing in on Lechfeld, causing the jet pilots who remained to come running to the last intact squadron.

Franz walked the flight line with a clipboard. As technical officer his job was to review the battle-worthiness of each new batch of aircraft, to know how many hours their engines had logged and what quirks each possessed. Thirteen jets had arrived from Bomber Squadron KG-51. Sixteen flew in from the jet school at Lechfeld. Franz chuckled when the instructors and commander he had known reported to him, saluting, to brief him on the condition of their aircraft.

With forty jets now entrusted to him, Franz had his hands full. He was so busy that he had allowed another pilot to fly *White 3* on a mission that morning. Franz had downed as many as four bombers in *White 3* during the weeks prior, a B-17 or two and several B-26s. He no longer watched them crash to claim them as victories. In fact, Franz had not claimed a victory since the prior August. To him, his score no longer mattered. He wanted only to do his job.

A headache followed Franz around the field as he tried to work. The headache was a young, blond-haired lieutenant with a meek face. The boy had said his last name was Pirchan. He was an Austrian who had just come from jet school but brought no plane of his own. Hoha-gen had steered Pirchan to Franz. The youngster pestered Franz. He begged Franz to let him take a jet up just for one flight, so he could say he flew combat with JV-44 before the war ended.

"No chance," Franz said. "There's no time for glory flying. Be-sides, you don't want to go up there anyway." Pirchan dropped his arms. "It's for your own good," Franz added, dismissing Pirchan with a wave.

Around 2:00 P.M., the phone rang at the alert shack. The orphan-age was calling with a mission—American medium bombers had been spotted approaching Munich. Eager to escape the headaches of his new job, Franz convinced Hohagen to put him on the roster.

Franz reported to Luetzow's jet, where he found Luetzow, the Count, Barkhorn, and two others. Luetzow was to lead the mission in Galland's absence. Luetzow reviewed the flight plan with his pilots. Franz saw that the Man of Ice was in high spirits—not to the point of smiling, but at least he wasn't frowning. Fresh in Luetzow's mind was the news of the day. Galland had received a call from Hitler's bunker in Berlin. Hitler's minister of armaments, Albert Speer, wanted JV-44 to arrest Goering. More importantly, Speer's orders to Galland stipu-lated, "I ask you and your comrades to do everything as discussed to prevent Goering from flying anywhere." Deep within his bunker, Hit-ler and Speer had suspected Goering would try to represent Germany and negotiate the country's surrender to the Americans.

"What are you going to do?" Luetzow had asked Galland, nearly smiling.

"Ignore the order and stay with the unit," Galland laughed. Hear-ing this, Luetzow's frown had lifted.

As Luetzow briefed Franz and the others, hope flickered in his brown eyes. He knew the war was just days from its end. News had escaped Berlin that Hitler was staying in the doomed city to die as eight Soviet Armies tightened their noose of encirclement. The SS had arrested Goering because Galland had declined to do so. With his enemy Goering under arrest and Hitler surrounded by Soviet Red Stars, Luetzow felt a surge of optimism. All he wanted was to outlive the war, his honor intact. To him, this meant serving until the arrival of peace.

When Franz and the others followed Luetzow into the air, they flew over the charred wreckage of Steinhoff's jet, which had been dragged to the side of the field. Luetzow had been right about Steinhoff. Nearly a week after his crash Steinhoff was still alive. JV-44's ground officer, Major Roell, who had saved the American bomber crewman in Munich, had visited Steinhoff in the basement of a hospital. There beneath dangling lightbulbs, Steinhoff lay, bandaged head to toe with only holes for his eyes and mouth. But he was alert and his mind was functioning.

"How are you doing?" Roell had asked Steinhoff, in the hospital room.

"Fine," Steinhoff had replied. Roell knew this was Steinhoff's way of saying: "Miserable!"[11] Roell told Franz and the others that Steinhoff's eyelids were gone. He could not blink or shut his eyes.

The flight was just northwest of Munich at twenty thousand feet when one of the pilots radioed Luetzow to say he was turning back with mechanical troubles. Franz watched the man peel off, reducing the flight to five jets. A short while later, Franz saw a bank of *White 3's* gauges flickering. Looking to the right of his stick, he squinted at the two vertical columns of round, red-ringed gauges. The left column reflected the left engine's vitals and the right column the right engine's. All at once the gauges in the right column surged in unison and did not retreat. Certain that he was on the verge of catastrophic engine failure, Franz nursed the throttle back on the right engine.

"Sir, I think I'm losing an engine," Franz told Luetzow. Luetzow cautioned Franz not to take any chances and to return to base. Franz reluctantly peeled off and steered for Munich. With the flight reduced to four jets, Luetzow continued with the mission.

On the ride home, Franz heard Luetzow's flight call to the orphanage over the radio. The flight reported contact with enemy bombers some fifty miles northwest of Munich. The bombers were on course to strike one of the last remaining fuel depots in the woods near the town of Schrobenhausen.

Luetzow announced he was beginning his attack. He called out enemy fighters and told the others to "look up," because P-47s were diving on them. Franz had heard that the Man of Ice flew without emotion, and now believed it. Luetzow's tone never changed. Luetzow ordered the formation to split up. Someone shouted that he was being fired upon.

Franz found himself leaning forward and checking his tail even though he was far from the fight.

Franz heard someone say he was trying for another firing run. Someone said he was running for the clouds. Franz wanted to turn around to help his comrades. He tapped his gauges, but the surging needles did not subside.

Luetzow's voice cut across the radio. He was taking hits. Someone shouted for Luetzow to take evasive maneuvers.

Seconds of silence followed. The voice of the Count crackled and said they were turning for home. Franz leaned back with relief. If they had lost someone, Franz knew they would have been shouting to one another to look for a parachute. Seconds more passed. The Count called Luetzow. Luetzow did not reply. Franz heard the pilots talking among themselves. He knew Luetzow was with them. The others were able to see him on the far right edge of the formation, to the south.

"Sir, want to form up?" someone asked. Luetzow did not reply.

"Is there a problem, sir?" The Count asked. Still no reply came from Luetzow.

"Colonel Luetzow, want to form up?" someone asked again. No answer.

"Sir, if there is a problem with your radio, rock your wings," someone offered.

Luetzow continued to fly straight and level. "Something's wrong," someone stated. "But he's flying well enough," someone else said. "His radio must have taken a hit," the Count concluded.

The Count called the orphanage and asked if they were talking with Luetzow on another channel. The orphanage said no, but they would try calling him. Franz found himself holding his breath between transmissions. Seconds later the orphanage reported back. They had received no reply.

Luetzow's plane banked gracefully to the right. When it faced south toward the snowcapped Alps, its wings leveled.

The Count and the others called one another with alarm.

"Where is he going?" someone said. Beyond their right wingtips, they watched Luetzow's jet shrink until it was barely discernible.

"He's wounded," the Count decided.

Far away, Franz's heart sunk.

"Should we go get him?" someone asked.

"Stay in formation," the Count ordered with a trembling voice. They all knew their fuel was low, too low for detours.

The Count would later conclude that a P-47's bullets had hit Luetzow's jet, probably striking him and his radio behind him in the fuselage. When Luetzow was flying home alongside his comrades, he was probably bleeding to death.

Franz dropped his oxygen mask from his face and breathed in heavy gasps. He knew Luetzow had never wanted to join JV-44. But Luetzow was a religious man, of the Lutheran faith, who believed the rule that Marseille had once voiced: "We must only answer to God and our comrades." Like the others, Luetzow knew he had made a moral mistake by serving his country. He would answer to God for that. Luetzow had reported to JV-44 out of duty to his comrades.

The Count watched Luetzow until he vanished from sight. Far away in his cockpit, Luetzow must have known he was going to die and turned toward the mountains to die alone in peace. He was probably thinking about his wife, Gisela, and his son, Hans, and daughter, Carola. Luetzow had cried for Steinhoff but was not one to cry for himself. He was probably flying with a face of stone.

The Count kept glancing south, even after the silhouette of Luetzow's jet faded into the hazy distance. Far beyond the Count's vision, over the medieval town of Donauwoerth, two P-47s caught up to Luetzow and dove to finish him off. Luetzow must have seen them coming and decided to deny the enemy pilots the reward of killing him.

Twelve miles in the distance, the Count and the others spotted an orange flash, just above the tree line. When he regained his composure, the Count radioed the orphanage and said he had seen an explosion where Luetzow had been flying. No one replied. The men of JV-44 had crowded into the orphanage's map room. Everyone was listening. All were too stunned to speak. The radar operators called the orphanage. They had been tracking Luetzow as a white blip on their screens. The blip was now gone.

The P-47 pilots would later report Luetzow's final moments. He had nosed forward and dove straight down from the heavens. When he crashed, he entered a forest, vertically. Galland would send planes to look for Luetzow's crash site. They all would come back to report the same thing. Luetzow had vanished from the earth.

That night at JV-44's long dinner table, Franz found it torturous to look across at his comrades. After his promotion, Galland had moved Franz across the table to sit among Galland's staff. There, Franz had sat next to Luetzow, who sat on Galland's left. When Steinhoff was burned, the men kept his chair, to Galland's right, empty.

Listlessly, the pilots pushed their food around their plates. Franz could not bring himself to look over at Galland, who hung his head, knowing he had called Luetzow back from Italy and to his death. Galland sat alone that night, with Steinhoff's empty chair to his right and an empty seat to his left, where the Man of Ice once sat.

THE LAST OF THE
GERMAN FIGHTER PILOTS

A DAY LATER, APRIL 25, 1945

THE *KETTENKRAD* TOWED *White 3* from her blast pen toward the hangar. Franz chose not to walk and instead rode his jet's wing. At the former Lufthansa hangar he delivered his jet to the mechanics. The hangar had become their favorite place to work because it had already been bombed and was the last place the enemy bombers would attack again.

Inside the hangar a radio blared the same war news as the radio at the pilots' alert shack. Everyone kept an ear tuned, waiting to hear "It's done," so they could go home or surrender. After Luetzow's death, Galland had called the pilots together on the airfield and addressed the men as they stood in a line. "For us the war is over," he said. He would no longer order anyone to take off—they could only volunteer. "Whoever wants to go home may do so," he added. A few men thanked him and left. One cited his fiancée, another his sick parents. But someone else said, "We fight until the end." Galland's eyes twinkled and he replied, "I am proud to belong to the last fighter pilots of the German Air Force."[1]

Franz showed the mechanics his jet's problematic engine, the one that had taken him from the fight where Luetzow had been lost. The engine had never failed, but Franz wished it had, so he would not need to wonder if he could have made a difference. Even though the Soviets were in Vienna and the Americans were north of Munich, Franz had decided to stay with Galland and keep flying. He knew that he still had a duty as long as four-engine bombers were over Germany.

A defiant, bombastic voice boomed from the radio, a broadcast that had been repeated for days. The voice bounced between the hangar's brick walls, off its dirt-covered floor, and up through the burned rafters. It was the last broadcast of Joseph Goebbels, Hitler's propaganda minister, and it came from Hitler's besieged bunker in Berlin:

"I appeal in this hour to the defenders of Berlin, on behalf of the women and children of the Fatherland! Do not fear your enemy but destroy him without mercy! Every Berliner must defend his house or apartment! Those who hang a white flag are no longer entitled to protection and will be treated accordingly. They are like a bacteria on the body of our city! [2]

Every time Franz heard Goebbels's speech, he shook his head. Goebbels's broadcast had become the sinister soundtrack to the nightmare of Germany's last days.

MEANWHILE, WEST OF MUNICH

Low over the forest a pack of P-51s chased a 262 with a smoking right engine. Barkhorn was behind the 262's stick. He knew he could not fight the P-51s in his plane's stricken condition, or outfly them. He was afraid to bail out and risk being shot, and he decided only one option remained. He steered for a forest clearing to crash-land.

As his jet neared the ground, Barkhorn removed his straps. He had seen Steinhoff burn and planned to leap and run, even before the plane stopped moving. His jet touched down, skipped across the pasture, and slid. Barkhorn stood and lifted the hinged canopy. He waited for the jet to slow to a near stop, ready to leap to the wing. When his engines plowed into the dirt, the jet's nose pitched violently downward. The machine jarred to a halt. The momentum flung Barkhorn sideways, his head falling outside the cockpit. At the same time the canopy slammed down onto his neck. Somehow the canopy rail did not decapitate him, although it sliced into his neck, pinning him to the cockpit ledge.

Barkhorn watched the left engine sizzle, just beyond his face. He moved his legs and knew he was not paralyzed. His eyes followed the sound of the P-51s as they looped around to strafe him. He braced for the sound of gunfire that never erupted. Instead, the P-51s flew overhead, one after another, and departed. Barkhorn looked to the engine, waiting for the spark that would burn him alive, but the spark never flickered. People from a nearby village found Barkhorn alive, pinned to his jet in silence. They took him to the hospital, where he would outlive the war and see his wife, Christl, again.

A DAY LATER, APRIL 26, 1945

Franz and his comrades listened to the radio on a table at the alert shed as they ate their lunches. To the men, the radio was a beacon of hope, a squawking countdown to their surrender. In a twangy voice, the broadcaster read a statement from The Party meant to prepare the German people for news of another forced suicide. The pilots had come to know by then how The Party worked. The broadcast identified The Party's new target.

Reich Marshal Hermann Goering has been taken ill with his long-standing chronic heart condition, which has now entered an acute

stage. At a time when the efforts of all forces are required, he has there-
fore requested to be relieved of his command of the Luftwaffe and all
duties connected thereto. The Fuehrer has granted this request.[3]

A deep rumbling shook the radio on its table. Galland and his flight of six jets were in the air, but the men knew the sound was not the whine of turbines. It was a throaty grumble of massive American radial engines. A flight of four P-47 Thunderbolts ripped overhead with rockets slung beneath their wings. Their four-blade propellers blew a heavy gust as Franz and his comrades dove to earth. Hiding beneath tables and behind fallen chairs, Franz and the men looked up as the P-47s strafed and blasted the field.

To the west, a lone 262 flew through the cloud of gun smoke and explosions. Smoke trailed from its right engine and its wheels were down. Franz saw that it was *White 3*. He had loaned her to Galland to fly against B-26s. Over the field, Galland cut both engines and the jet touched down with a gentle whistle. Galland steered toward the alert shack as the P-47s flew over him without firing. The American pilots were struck speechless at the sight of such audacity.

In the middle of the field, *White 3*'s front tire deflated with each turn until it was flat. It had taken a bullet. Stranded, Galland hobbled from the jet, his right knee bloody. He had been hit by a bullet's fragments during his earlier attack on the bombers. Rockets burst behind him as the P-47s strafed from one direction then another. Galland dove into the first hole he reached. There the thought struck him how "wretched" it felt to jump from "the fastest fighter in the world and into a bomb crater."[4]

A mechanic raced toward Galland in a *kettenkrad*. Without stopping, the mechanic reached an arm out to Galland, who grabbed the mechanic's forearm and swung aboard the vehicle. The mechanic steered for the alert shack while Galland hung on. The P-47s' bullets tossed the dirt around the *kettenkrad* but missed both the mechanic and Galland, who both dove for cover when they reached the shack.

Franz saw *White 3* sitting alone on the field as the fighters ripped overhead shooting everything but her. Over the noise of gunfire and explosions, Franz shouted to Galland that he would never lend him a plane again.

"You don't play well with borrowed toys!" Franz joked. Galland looked back sheepishly.

A DAY LATER, APRIL 27, 1945

When Franz entered the hangar to check on *White 3*, the mechanics quickly turned down the radio. Franz knew they were listening to the enemy's broadcasts. Franz told the men not to worry and to turn the radio back up. He wanted to hear the truth just as they did. He wanted to know when to go home or attempt to surrender. They raised the volume. A German translation of a broadcast from London could be heard. "The forces of liberation have joined hand," the broadcaster asserted. The Americans and the Soviets had met at the Elbe River two days earlier, splitting Germany in half.

A mechanic brought Franz papers to sign. The mechanics had fixed *White 3* overnight after Galland had brought her back with a Thunderbolt's bullets in her right engine and bullet fragments in the cockpit, the same that had struck Galland's kneecap. Franz scribbled his signature. With Steinhoff and Luetzow gone and Galland's leg in a plaster cast, Franz had told Hohagen he was willing to lead what flights remained.

Franz turned to find Pirchan waiting for him. The youngster was dressed in his daily uniform, not his flying suit. He said he had come to say good-bye. He was leaving the unit and planned to surrender near his home at Graz. Franz said he knew Graz. He expected Pirchan to pester him, having seen *White 3* emerge fresh from repair. Instead, Pirchan turned to leave. "What will you do after the war?" Franz asked.

"Study engineering, I hope," Pirchan said.

Franz had considered doing the same thing, wanting to resume his studies. He wished Pirchan luck.

When Pirchan began to walk away, Franz realized he had truly come just to say good-bye.

"One flight," Franz shouted at Pirchan's back.

"Really?" Pirchan asked.

Franz nodded.*

Franz told Pirchan he could take *White 3* up for one combat mission with JV-44. But Franz had one condition. "You go up, circle a few times, and land," he told Pirchan. "I'll sign your logbook so it will count as a combat mission." The young Austrian could not stop nodding. Franz knew that the skies were safer than usual. The American heavies had stopped bombing Germany two days prior.

Pirchan suited up and sat in the cockpit. Franz reviewed the instruments to ensure Pirchan knew what he was doing. He seemed proficient. Franz watched him light up the engines and taxi from the hangar. Franz lit a cigarette at the edge of the Lufthansa terminal he had known in 1937. Inside the lounge where the laughter of travelers once echoed, Franz could only hear dripping water. Where radial engines had once rumbled, announcing arriving flights from exotic cities, he now heard the whine of *White 3*'s engines as Pirchan launched to the east.

Franz stood up quickly. He thought he saw the jet's engines flare, as if Pirchan had panicked and given her too much power too quickly. But when *White 3*'s landing gear sucked up into her belly, Franz sat down.

Pirchan banked the jet left toward the north and began to orbit the field. The young pilot had barely started turning when Franz

---

* Franz would remember, "I thought, *It's days before the war is over, why not?* He did not have a plane of his own."

THE LAST OF THE GERMAN FIGHTER PILOTS

heard *White 3*'s engines suddenly cut to silence. Franz watched the jet dip beneath the roof of the terminal. He tracked it between the roof beams and through the terminal's collapsed walls until *White 3* dove behind the rooftops and steeples of a village. A metallic crack echoed. Black smoke billowed. Franz stood, staring, his mouth agape. His cigarette smoldered all the way up to his fingers. When the cigarette burned him, he flicked it away and knew he was not dreaming.

A mechanic started a truck and Franz hopped in. They raced to the village of Oberweissenfeld, north of the airfield. Pirchan had crashed between two houses. The people had him out already, lying there on a mattress, right beside the airplane. Pirchan's head had slammed into the fighter's gun sight, and his brain was exposed. Franz held him as he thrashed with pain. Pirchan asked Franz to tell his mother and sister good-bye for him. Franz promised he would. He gave the young fighter pilot a shot of pain reliever and the boy died in his arms.

LATER THAT DAY

Franz entered Galland's lodge and found the general reclining in a chair, his whole right leg in plaster. Galland told Franz he had just missed it—the SS had just departed after coming to arrest him. The SS had said that a Catholic revolt had begun in Munich. The revolutionaries were broadcasting over the radio that their fellow Catholic, General Galland, was with them. Galland told Franz he was flattered but had been unaware of the uprising. The SS only left him alone, Galland explained, when they saw he was crippled. Galland planned to head south to a hospital at Lake Tegernsee where Steinhoff had been taken.

Franz reported Pirchan's death and told Galland he saw no further need to fly or fight now that the Americans had stopped their bombing campaign. "I'd like permission to leave the unit," Franz said. Galland told Franz he could leave but asked him to stay, one more day. Galland revealed that orders had come from Berlin even as the Soviets were fighting through the city's limits. Goering's successor wanted him to fly JV-44 to Prague, Czechoslovakia, to continue fighting. Galland said he would ignore the order.

The general lowered his voice to a whisper. He told Franz he was planning to deliver JV-44 to the Americans before the war ended. Franz knew this meant a defection and not just of one man, but of the whole unit. Galland was certain the Americans would soon be fighting the Soviets and would want the 262s to study the jets or use them in combat. Galland planned to surrender JV-44's aircraft, pilots, and operational knowledge to the Americans. He suggested that JV-44 could even fly for them.

Franz admired Galland's optimism but could not act enthusiastic. He had never wanted to fight for Germany, let alone another nation.

Galland saw Franz's disappointment and asked him to fly one more mission for him, as a comrade. Galland needed time to send a message to the Americans, but he worried that the jets would be destroyed on the ground before he could arrange the defection. He had decided to ask his pilots to ferry every flyable plane to Salzburg, Austria, the next morning, where they would be safer. Franz knew that if the SS caught wind of Galland's plan, they would execute every man in the unit as a collaborator.

"I'll go as far as Salzburg," Franz told Galland.

Galland smiled. "Then where will you go?"

Franz said he had no idea. Galland assured Franz that the Americans would be looking for him. Franz did not understand why they would want him. Galland reminded him, "They'll want you for what you have up here," he said, pointing to his head.

Galland saluted up at Franz and Franz saluted down at the seated general, much like their first meeting in Sicily. They both knew that JV-44 had succeeded if they had stopped bombs from destroying one more house or maiming one more child or killing one more mother in a factory. The unit had not failed. It had simply arrived too late.

"I put you in for the Knight's Cross weeks ago," Galland told Franz before he left. "If you stick around it may come through." The general laughed. He knew it was wishful thinking that a medal would come from Berlin. He also knew Franz's mind was made up. Franz smiled and walked away.

THE NEXT MORNING, APRIL 28, 1945, AUSTRIA

The instant Franz's boots landed on the tarmac at Salzburg Airport, he began to plot his escape. He opened a hatch in the jet's fuselage and shouldered a backpack filled with canned food. He brought no clothes other than the ones he flew in. He looked east, where the sun shined on the white hilltop castle Hohensalzburg. He knew that far beyond that were the Soviets.

Looking west, he saw tall gray mountains with snowy peaks that loomed over the airfield. Franz knew the mountain passes wound south toward Berchtesgaden, where Hitler and Goering once lived. That's where the Americans were headed. He decided he would rather be a prisoner of the Americans than the Soviets.

At the tower, Franz found Hohagen, the Count, and their comrades. Some of them planned to retreat to the mountains but most planned to stay. Before Franz left Munich, Galland had issued him his discharge papers and a pass authorizing him safe passage through checkpoints. Hohagen asked Franz where he planned to go. Franz said he had decided to walk into the mountains, find a cabin, and wait for the war to end. Hohagen warned Franz that SS soldiers were blocking roads and bridges.

"They're hanging deserters and anyone they think should be fighting," Hohagen said. He warned Franz that his papers might not protect him. "Stay with us and wait," Hohagen said. Franz knew Hohagen meant "wait for the unit's defection" but was hesitant to utter the words.* Franz told Hohagen that with Galland laid up the unit could yet be ordered to fly to Czechoslovakia. He was leaving.

"You're just going to walk?" Hohagen asked. Franz nodded. His plan was to head south a bit then cut west into the mountains. Then something caught Franz's eye. A *kettenkrad* clinked past while towing one of JV-44's twenty remaining jets into the woods along the airfield. Franz knew a *kettenkrad*, with its tank tracks, could go anywhere. Hohagen saw Franz eyeing the *kettenkrad*.

"Help yourself when they're not looking," Hohagen suggested. "I'll take the blame. If they give me hell, I can just point to my head." He and Franz chuckled.

Early the next morning, Franz and Hohagen snuck across the deserted, frost-covered field. Inside a hangar they found a *kettenkrad*, fully fueled. Franz started the vehicle. Over the rattling engine, he reached out his hand. Hohagen shook it with vigor. Franz clunked the vehicle into gear and drove away.

SIX DAYS LATER, MAY 4, 1945

Franz felt uncomfortably alone as he drove the *kettenkrad* west along the narrow, winding road deep within the Alps. The road flowed through a mountain pass, alongside a stream of icy, pale blue water. Clumps of snow clung to the road's fringes, where pine trees stood creaking in the wind. Every now and then, an abandoned car or truck

---

* Two days later, on May 1, Galland sent a pilot, Major Willi Herget, in a light plane to find American General Eisenhower. In Eisenhower's absence, General Pearson Menoher met with Herget. Herget delivered Galland's letter seeking to surrender JV-44. Menoher sent Herget back to tell Galland where to deliver the jets and to offer an 8th Air Force fighter escort. Galland received the message and dispatched Herget back to Menoher to clarify the plan. Herget never made it. American ground forces shot down his plane. He was injured, captured, and all means of communication between Galland and Menoher were lost.

lay in a roadside ditch, the victim of winter driving. Franz stopped to siphon gas from the wrecks' fuel tanks.

Franz had entered the Alps near Hallein, Austria, several days earlier and driven until he found a lodge where other wayward soldiers had congregated. Franz had joined them and lived off his canned food while waiting. On May 1, he and the others crowded around a radio that announced the news they had long expected: Hitler was dead. He had shot himself in his bunker. A day later, Germany's forces began surrendering, first in Berlin then in Italy, and finally, on May 4, in Bavaria. Having decided it was safe to surrender, Franz had left the lodge and steered his *kettenkrad* back onto the deserted road that led west to Berchtesgaden, where the Americans were rumored to be.

The *kettenkrad* sputtered. Its six tracked wheels ground slowly to a halt. Franz turned to the side of the road and stepped out. A glimpse of the gas gauge confirmed he was out of fuel. He lit a cigarette and grabbed his backpack. He pulled his black logbook from the pack and dropped it into the deep thigh pocket of his leather flying pants. The book was a prized possession of his that documented his 487 combat flights. He removed his holstered pistol from his belt and tossed it into the back of the *kettenkrad*. It could only get him in trouble. Leaving the pistol and empty backpack behind, Franz began walking west in his heavy boots.

Franz looked for road signs to Berchtesgaden, but someone had torn them down. He chain-smoked. Whenever the pines creaked, he stopped, looked, then resumed his trek. The Party's propaganda had told him the Americans would be vengeful, and after they had worked a prisoner over they would hand him to the French or Soviets for further punishment. Franz hoped this was not true. After his experience in the desert he would have preferred to be a prisoner of the British. Franz passed through a tiny hamlet of a half dozen homes on either side of the swift-flowing stream. There, along the side of the road, he stopped and looked up. Hanging from a telephone pole was a dead German soldier in a gray Army uniform. Franz looked back the way he had come and thought, *Maybe this was not so smart*. He shook the idea from his mind. The Americans had not done this. They wanted the Germans to surrender, not to run away and keep fighting.

Franz continued. A half a mile later, he came to a split in the road. To his right, the concrete road continued through the mountain pass. To his left, a small wooden bridge led across the stream to a dirt logging road. The logging road hugged the mountainside and was dark with shadows. Franz decided to take the logging road because it was more likely to be deserted.

Franz set out again, his boots now crunching the dirt. Through gaps in the pine trees, he kept his eyes on the bright, flowing stream and the main road beyond the stream, where he expected to see American tanks. Turning a bend, Franz stopped in his tracks. In the path ahead of him stood twenty or more SS soldiers. He instantly recognized them by their camouflage smocks with light green and brown spots. Some were digging in. Others were setting up machine guns over fallen trees and aiming their rifles across the stream toward the main road. A few sat on rocks along the mountainside, smoking and cradling machine pistols. Franz realized they had hung the soldier he had found earlier. It was a message to other Germans to stay away. They had most likely mined the main road and were waiting for the same American tanks Franz had expected to see.

Now you've done it, Franz thought to himself, cursing his decision to take the logging road. Franz resumed his stride toward the SS soldiers. He knew he could not turn back, having discovered their ambush. He hoped he could give the impression of complete disinterest and walk through them like a passerby. He reached his hand into his right pocket and grabbed his rosary. His fingers had long stripped the black paint from the beads, completing their transformation to a pale purple color. As he passed the first soldiers, Franz tried not to look at the silver runes that resembled small lightning bolts on the soldiers' gray collars. This was the mark of the SS. Some wore soft caps with the death's head patch above the brim. Others wore helmets with fabric covers that matched their smocks. Some of the SS soldiers snickered and joked at the pilot without a plane.

Clad in his crumpled gray officer's cap, cracked leather flight suit, and heavy, muddy boots, Franz looked haggard but tough. Some of the SS soldiers glared as Franz walked between them. Franz stared ahead and trudged along.

Franz knew the soldiers on either side of him were the toughest and most ruthless in Germany. No pilot of the German Air Force, except for Goering, would ever be convicted of a war crime. The same could not be said of the SS men whom Franz walked past.

With every step away from them, Franz expected to hear the crack of a rifle and to feel the punch of a bullet in his back. But none came. By some miracle, as if he were invisible, they let him live.

Several miles later, the logging road merged with the main road. Stepping into the light and onto the concrete, Franz saw a green armored vehicle facing him, its gun leveled on the road. He knew he had reached the outskirts of Berchtesgaden. The vehicle wore a white American star on its hood. Franz raised his arms in surrender.

━━━━━━━━

THE AMERICAN INFANTRYMEN initially assumed Franz was an SS man posing as a pilot (for more lenient treatment) because of the direction he had come from. They had known that the SS were there the whole time. At first, the GI interrogators were rough, operating under the assumption that Franz was an SS officer. Then they realized otherwise and passed Franz along to interrogators of the Army Air Forces.*

The Air Forces interrogators recognized Franz immediately, having received JV-44's surrender at Salzburg Airport and that of Galland

---

* Franz would remember, "When they interrogated me, within the first minutes they knew I couldn't be SS because I showed them my logbook."

at Tegernsee. Over the next fourteen days, Franz submitted to a number of interrogations. The new interrogators immediately took his logbook, and overestimating its technological value, they never returned it. When Franz sat down for his first interrogation, he agreed to tell the American officers about the 262 but with a stipulation: "I still am a soldier, so I can only tell you so much."

24

WHERE BOMBS HAD FALLEN

THE FOLLOWING YEAR, MARCH 1946, STRAUBING, BAVARIA

THE TOES OF Franz's flying boots dragged along the rough, upturned stones as the three German police officers hauled him through the streets. Two men carried him, their arms under his. The third man, the officer in charge, walked ahead of the others leading them. Franz's senses returned. He caught his footing and limped on his own power. But the policemen would not let go. Behind Franz, the men at the brick works poured out into the street, silently watching the drama. The townspeople on both sides of the street looked on Franz with hollow eyes and frowns. They remained silent. The war had made them apathetic to uniformed brutes dragging a man away.

Franz knew he was in trouble when the officer in charge turned and entered the first dark alley they came to. The policemen pulled Franz into the alley and dropped him in the darkness between two buildings. Franz looked toward the street he had come from, warm with light, and knew he had been safe in the sight of the crowds.

The police officers were bigger than him. Franz clenched his fists, anticipating a beating. The officers adjusted their collars the way a man might when rolling up his sleeves before a fight. Franz glanced toward the street, contemplating a run. He knew he wouldn't get far in his heavy boots.

But then the policemen took a step back nonchalantly. The officer in charge reached in his pocket and pulled forth a pack of cigarettes. He offered Franz a cigarette. Franz hesitated. The man shook the packet. "It's all right," he told him. Franz drew a cigarette. One of the other officers extended his lighter. Franz puffed the cigarette to life; it was an American brand. The other men lit up, too. Everyone shook out his shoulders and seemed to relax. Franz apologized for punching the brick yard manager, explaining that the man was refusing him work because he had been a fighter pilot.

"Don't worry," the officer in charge told Franz. "We're not going to do anything about it." The officers went on to explain what the three of them had done in the war.* The officer in charge had led a flak battery. One of his men had been a guard on airfields. The other officer had been in the infantry.

The officer in charge asked Franz about his unit and where he had fought. Franz told him. The men had all heard of JV-44, "Galland's unit." The officer in charge explained that he was from Straubing and had finagled his way to end the war at a battery there. He told Franz with a laugh, "I watched you fly!" He explained that he had once seen 262s, high overhead.

Franz laughed and said it was possible. The officer in charge glanced at his watch and stamped out his cigarette butt in the gutter. His men did the same.

With the click of his boots, the officer in charge saluted Franz, holding his salute with his hand pressed to the brim of his cap. His men did the same. The three policemen held their salutes, their eyes locked on Franz. In his threadbare coat and fingerless gloves Franz

---

* Franz would remember, "They were all old sergeants, mostly from the Air Force."

raised his hand to his brow, clicked together the heavy heels of his fly-ing boots with a thud, and saluted them back.

The policemen wheeled and walked out of the alley. Stepping into the sun, they turned toward the brickyard to continue their patrol. Franz followed them but turned the other direction, away from the scene of the incident. He walked back the way he had come, toward the sun and along the road where bombs had fallen.

FOR MONTHS FRANZ scraped by in Straubing, delivering what money he made to his mother and Eva. Finally in 1947, he found work fixing sewing machines at an unlikely place: the Messerchmitt company in Augsburg, near the former jet school at Lechfeld. No longer did the builder of 109s and 262s make fighters. After the war they had transi-tioned to building knitting looms and personal sewing machines at the same factories.

In 1948, Franz married Eva. They settled into their new postwar life together. As the years passed, Franz stayed in touch with some of his old comrades, including Roedel. In winter 1953, they met at a pub halfway between their homes and went drinking for the last time. Franz told Roedel that he was leaving soon for Canada, where he had secured the job of a lifetime—to work as an engineer on a new Cana-dian fighter plane. Roedel tried to talk Franz into staying. He had heard rumors that the German Air Force was soon to be rebuilt. Offi-cers who had served with honor in World War II would be invited back for a chance to lead.*

Roedel told Franz that if he stayed, they both could join together

---

* In 1949, the Allies had given West Germany her sovereignty back. They needed an ally and knew that if the Cold War turned hot, Germany would be its battlefield. To block the "Red Tide" from invading Europe, the Americans were preparing to train German pilots to fly American jets to shoot down Soviet bombers before they dropped their nukes on Europe. With the Allies' blessing, a group of German generals had quietly gathered in 1950 to plan the revival of the military that would be called the Federal Defense Force or Bundeswehr.

and continue their careers in the new Air Force. They could fly along-side American and British pilots instead of against them. Roedel had talked to Trautloft and the Count, who were contemplating the op-portunity. Roedel said that even Steinhoff, who had survived his burns, was hoping the Allies would let him wear his uniform again. But Franz told Roedel he was done with the notion of following or-ders. He had seen what "following orders" had done to Germany. Ger-many had become a land dotted with strange new hills. The hills had sprung up outside of new towns where villagers had piled the debris that had once been their old towns before they were destroyed in the war. The last order Franz had followed was from Lieutenant Pirchan who asked him to visit his mother and sister in Graz to convey his good-byes. Franz had traveled to Graz immediately after the Ameri-cans released him and would never talk about that experience.

Franz told Roedel that he wanted to build and fly airplanes. It was all he had ever wanted. Through friends at the Messerschmitt com-pany, Franz had secured an offer to work on the proposed Canadian fighter called "the Arrow." The job was in "payload weight and balanc-ing"—if the jet was approved for production by the Canadian govern-ment. Seeing Franz's enthusiasm, Roedel encouraged him to take the leap and go to Canada. He warned Franz, "You'll have to learn En-glish, you know." Franz told Roedel he was already practicing. Franz wished Roedel luck in trying to rejoin the Air Force, "if there ever is a German Air Force again." The two parted with a silent handshake. After what they had seen together, words were inadequate.

Franz found the experience of leaving his homeland easier than he had thought it would be. In Germany, the ghosts of the war were close to home. Whenever a plane flew overhead, Franz thought of his young pilots. He saw the suffering in the eyes of his countrymen. He also re-membered how some of them had turned on him. In the forests and camps of Germany, Franz saw the ghosts of the Holocaust, the crimes of the minority that had spoiled every German fighting man's honor. One German fighter pilot spoke for the fighter forces when he wrote,

"The atrocities committed under the sign of the Swastika deserve the most severe punishment. The Allies ought to leave the criminals to the German fighting soldiers to bring to justice."[1]

SEVERAL MONTHS LATER, SPRING 1953, CANADA

When Franz and Eva relocated to Canada they settled with Eva's brother, who had moved to Vancouver, on the west coast, to work in the lumber industry. There, Franz waited to be called to work on the Arrow. When the Canadian government approved the Arrow for production that July, the military classified the jet as top secret. Franz lost his job before it began. When he applied for a security clearance, he was refused because he had been a German officer. Franz took the setback in stride. His brother-in-law helped him find a job at a logging camp in the Queen Charlotte Islands. There, Franz worked as a diesel mechanic, fixing logging trucks. He lived in the company of twenty-seven lumberjacks and their families. He quickly learned English and liked working with his hands and amid nature. He and Eva had a daughter named Jovita, but the couple's relationship was not to last. Some would say that a good relationship requires "a sun and a moon," and Franz and Eva were both suns—strong and stubborn. Their divorce, when it came in 1954, was amicable.

Because the job paid well, Franz stayed on at the lumber camp after Eva had departed. The distant sight of the Canadian Rockies and their snowy peaks reminded him of the Bavarian Alps and the life he had once loved. He began to write home, at night, to his mother, the men he had served with, and the people he had known.

On a whim, he wrote to Mr. Greisse, the kindly bureaucrat who had supervised pensions, whose address he had saved. But Mr. Greisse did not write back. Instead, his daughter, Hiya, did. She told Franz that her father was ill. Because he had been a member of The Party, the Soviets had locked him up in a camp at the war's end. An average-sized man before the war, he came back to his daughter five years later weighing just ninety pounds. Hiya had been a short thirteen-year-old kid with strawberry-blond hair when she and Franz first met. Now she was twenty-three and eager to explore the world. She asked Franz questions about Canada. Franz wrote back. Despite the fifteen-year age gap between them, the two began to correspond.

Hiya told Franz about her experiences after the war's end, how she traded her mother's china for food from local farmers. She wrote about the Soviet soldiers who had moved into her house, washing their potatoes in the toilets, shattering her mother's crystal glasses, and getting drunk every night while singing "Lili Marlene." "They were mostly nice, but boy if they got drunk you didn't want to be around them as a girl," she told Franz. Hiya confided that the Soviets had raped most of the women in and around Berlin in the year after the war. She would not talk about what happened to her sister.

For the better part of two years, Franz and Hiya corresponded weekly. Every so often Franz called her from the only phone on the island, one located in the office of the lumberyard.

In 1956, Hiya boarded a plane and traveled to Vancouver, where she and Franz met for the first time in twelve years. Her blond hair curled above her ears and her posture was impeccable. She wore a sky-blue skirt and blouse with white buttons that led up to a high collar and tiny black gloves. Franz had come to know Hiya's beautiful personality, but he never guessed that the short little girl would one day grow up to be so gorgeous. Their plan had been an unspoken one. Within a year of meeting they headed to the city hall in Vancouver and were married.

Hiya enjoyed moving with Franz to his island in the Queen Charlottes, where they shared a small cabin. On their first night together on the island Franz led Hiya outside, to look at the sky just as they had during the war. He held her hand as he showed her the Aurora Borealis, the colorful Northern Lights. But when Hiya saw the lights flickering on the horizon, she cried hysterically. The Northern Lights had triggered flashbacks in her mind, memories of Potsdam and Berlin burning. With time, she came to appreciate the lights, but she never saw the same beauty in them that Franz did.

Franz's mother came to visit him and Hiya even though she was not thrilled about the idea of them having married in city hall instead of a church. She stayed for four months. When Franz would tell old fighter pilot jokes during their dinners together, his mother would always chide him. "Franz, you're lucky Dad is not around!" Franz's mother asked him to go to church with her and to attend confession. He did and confessed to a priest that he had not attended church for twenty years because he had been caught dueling. The priest laughed, welcomed Franz back, and said, "In that case, you're overdue for communion." Franz and Hiya tried to convince Franz's mother to stay with them longer, but she refused. She missed her friends—but more than anything she missed her beer.

Hiya and Franz seldom discussed the war. Hiya discovered a story from Franz's past one night, by accident. In the logging camp, the families often threw parties. After one party, Franz had too many drinks. As Hiya steered him on the path to their cabin, they came across a mother bear in the moonlight. She was leaning over a fence, grunting, calling her cub that was stuck on the other side. But in his drunken state, Franz forgot where he was. "It's my bear!" he told Hiya. But she did not understand. "I have to say hi to him," Franz pleaded. Hiya whispered that it was a bad idea. She held Franz back. But Franz insisted that it was his bear and struggled. Hiya knew he was going to get himself mauled. When Hiya could no longer hold Franz back she kneed him in the rear. As he was distracted by his hurting backside, Hiya pulled him home and put him to bed. The next morning, as Hiya served breakfast, Franz ate standing. He told her, "I must have hurt myself last night—I don't know how, but I can't sit." From her seat at the table, Hiya explained why he was so sore. Franz slowly took a seat across from her, wincing. Then he told her the war story of a lovable bear.

25

WAS IT WORTH IT?

TWENTY-FOUR YEARS LATER, 1980, VANCOUVER

THE ARRIVAL OF the eighties found Franz and Hiya happily enjoying their retirement years, exploring the mountains of Vancouver and fishing from its lakes. Time had shrunken Franz's stature. Now sixty-five, he had grown shorter and thicker. His neck seemed to shrink into his shoulders, but his face remained strong. As his cheeks sagged, they gave a sterner impression when he was not smiling. He still dressed like every day was a day in the office, wearing dress slacks, a long-sleeved shirt, and a fleece vest over top, the look of a Silicon Valley entrepreneur well before its time. Hiya cut her hair short but retained her youthful charm, her sassy German spirit only growing.

Together they had bought a ranch and raised a Shetland pony in a barn behind their home. Franz smoked like a chimney until one morning he felt winded after walking to feed the pony. That afternoon, he told Hiya, "I don't smoke anymore." "Since when?" she asked. "Since this morning," he told her. In a moment, Franz kicked a nearly forty-year habit. For fun, Franz took to flying sport planes and even purchased a Messerschmitt 108, a four-seat personal transport plane with elegant lines just like his old 109's. He even painted the 108 like his wartime 109 and flew it at air shows as "the bad guy" that P-51s would chase around the sky to the crowd's delight.

One day, Franz's old commander, Galland, came to visit him. When Galland arrived at Franz's doorstep, he was a smaller, gentler version of his larger-than life self in World War II. His trademark mustache was gray, and he still wore his hair slicked back, only now it was gray at the temples. Galland's black eyes pierced from heavier eyelids. His smirk was unchanged. After the war, he had found work as a forestry agent, maintaining game lands, hunting, and reflecting on the war. Then German aircraft designer Kurt Tank invited Galland to join him in Argentina, where he was building a fighter jet for Juan Peron, the country's dictator. Peron needed someone to train his pilots and build his Air Force, so Tank recruited Galland. After that stint, Galland had returned to Germany and flown an air race with Edu Neumann and in air shows. He had consulted on the movie *Battle of Britain* and ran the Association of German Fighter Pilots. He had married three times, raised a family, and often vacationed with his former British enemies, fighter pilots Robert Standford Tuck and Douglas Bader.

Galland wanted to go hunting with Franz, so Franz borrowed a Beaver floatplane from a doctor friend. He flew Galland to a lodge on a river in northern Canada. When Franz taxied the floatplane to shore, he approached too fast and beached the craft on the sand. Galland gave him heck for the bad landing. Franz laughed him off, telling Galland, "You always have to be the general, eh?" Franz was not one for hunting but accompanied Galland, who shot a moose. They gave its meat to a local Native American tribe then hauled the moose's head back to Vancouver, where Franz shipped the horns to Germany for Galland. In the days that followed, Franz and Galland talked once a week by phone.

FIVE YEARS LATER, 1985

Franz looked at the party invitation in his hands with disbelief. The Boeing Company had learned of Franz through his air show flying and invited him to attend their 50th Anniversary party for the Boeing B-17 Flying Fortress. Franz pondered the invitation, unsure if he should attend. He began thinking about the war again. A memory resurfaced, one long locked away. In his mind, he saw the battered bomber he had let escape. He told the story to Hiya for the first time. The question began troubling him again, like an unhealed wound: "Did the B-17 make it home to England?" He knew the only people he could ask would be the plane's crew. But the odds were slim that they had made it across the sea, let alone survived the war. Of the twelve thousand B-17s built, five thousand had been destroyed in combat. Even slimmer was the prospect that if the crew had survived, they would still be alive forty-one years later, or even possible to locate. Franz had no names to reference. No tail number, just a memory. But Franz knew he had taken a great risk in helping the bomber escape, and he longed to know: *Was it worth it?*

"You should go to the party and ask around," Hiya advised Franz. "It may be your last chance."

Despite his hesitation, Franz traveled to the Museum of Flight at Paine Field to attend Boeing's party. Once again, Franz found himself a lone German traveling through a swarm of Americans. Some five thousand former B-17 pilots and crewmen had attended. Franz nervously wandered around the three B-17s that had been flown in for the veterans to tour. He expected his old enemies to hate him. Instead, the old B-17 veterans—who now wore thick glasses with big frames—crowded around him and bombarded him with questions. "How did you have time to aim when attacking us?" one asked. "You only had a fraction of time then you had to go right through," Franz explained. "Yes, you used to go right through us!" another B-17 vet chimed in, to which Franz laughed, "*Ja,* more or less." Franz asked every veteran he met if the man knew of a bomber that had been escorted to safety by a German fighter. None had heard of such a thing. Colonel Robert Morgan, the former captain of the famed B-17 *Memphis Belle*, was there and Franz asked him. Morgan had heard of no such thing, but the notion gave him a chuckle.

A camera crew from the local King 5 TV station was filming the party and interviewing veterans for a TV special. They filmed Franz, who described the B-17 he was looking for, the most badly damaged B-17 he had witnessed. "I've seen a B-17 flying without the rudder," Franz said in their TV program. "I saw him flying with half the tail shot off and still flying." Franz did not know the name *Ye Olde Pub*, or the name of its pilot, Charlie Brown. And he had long forgotten the date, December 20, 1943—but he knew what he had seen. "We knew we had a job to do—defend our country," Franz said in the program, "and we knew the boys in those airplanes had a job to do, too, because they had orders to get the war finished and it was just such fierce combat." Franz left Boeing's party with new friends among former adversaries and an invitation from the American Fighter Aces veteran's association to attend future reunions as their guest. Franz returned to Vancouver certain that he would never know the B-17 crew's fate.

———

AT THE OPPOSITE corner of the continent, in Miami, Florida, Charlie Brown was pondering his half of the December 20 encounter. Charlie's life after WWII had been idyllic. During college in West Virginia he had met a girl named Jackie, a petite brunette who always wore her hair in a neat bun. She was from a small West Virginia town like Charlie's and captivated him with her colorful dresses and classiness. Jackie understood what Charlie had endured during the war. She was a young war widow whose first husband had been a fighter pilot killed over Europe. Charlie and Jackie hit it off and married in 1949. That same year Charlie returned to the Air Force and made a career in military intelligence and even served in London as an attaché to the RAF.

During this time, he and Jackie had two children, daughters Carol and Kimberly. In 1965, Charlie retired early, as a lieutenant colonel, to work for the State Department in Southeast Asia during the Vietnam War. There, for six years, he supervised the flow of food and aid to America's regional allies.

When Charlie retired for good in the early seventies, he moved to Florida, bought a house, and drove a big Cadillac with Air Force wings on its license plate. Charlie seemed to grow taller and lankier with age, and lost only a few inches of his hairline. He wore yellow-tinted glasses, high-waisted pants, and long shirts with their sleeves always rolled up. He was never without a bolo tie. He drank a martini each night and always carried a "first aid kit" of gin, vermouth, two glasses, and a shaker in the trunk of his car. As a hobby, Charlie pursued his passion for science and invention and worked with other inventors to develop environmentally friendly diesel engines long before such research was popular. He spent hours on the golf course, volunteered at his church, and doted on Jackie, who still wore her colorful dresses and makeup every day. She was calm, dignified, and a great cook. Charlie's daughters lived nearby and often came for dinner. He knew he had a wonderful life.

In these, his golden years, Charlie's war memories resurfaced. He had attended a bomb group reunion in 1957 but nothing more. Back then, the memories were too fresh and painful. Now he began having nightmares again. He would dream about December 20, and the dream always ended with *The Pub* spinning to earth in a death dive from which he could not recover. Charlie always awoke just before he crashed in the dream. Standing in his bathroom looking in the mirror, Charlie tried to tell himself that December 20 was long over. But something deep within him was eating at his subconscious, and he knew it was not just the spin. He needed closure.

Charlie joined the 379th Bomb Group Association, as well as the association for his pilot class, to reconnect with his old buddies. At the 1985 Las Vegas reunion of his pilot class, Charlie and his classmates sat in a circle in the hotel's hospitality suite, swapping war stories. One of the men in the circle was Charlie's former classmate, Colonel Joe Jackson. Jackson had a round, friendly face and still wore his hair in a military crew cut. He told his war stories with an upbeat Georgian accent. Jackson had been a bomber pilot in WWII and a fighter pilot in Korea. In Vietnam, he had flown transport planes, and his actions had earned him the Medal of Honor. Jackson did not tell that story, but Charlie and the others had heard what he had done. Jackson had landed a transport on an airfield that was being overrun by the enemy. Miraculously, he had rescued three Air Force combat controllers, picking them up and whisking them away. His plane came back with countless holes and even an unexploded rocket-propelled grenade in the nose.

Charlie stunned his Scotch-sipping buddies when he casually remarked, "You'll never believe this, but one time I was saluted by a German pilot." Jackson and the others were so intrigued that they prompted Charlie to reveal the full story. Charlie told them of the German pilot who had spared him and his crew.

"You should look for him," Jackson urged Charlie. "He might still be out there." Charlie knew the odds were slim. The German fighter pilots had been all but wiped out. How could he find an unknown enemy pilot he had flown with for ten minutes, neither having exchanged a single word? It was forty-two years later, but still he wondered, *Who was he and why did he let us go?*

Charlie began his search for the German pilot. In his free time during the next four years, Charlie used his Air Force connections to cull the archives in America and England and discovered his crew's after-action report from December 20. It had been stamped CLASSIFIED but contained nothing sensitive. Charlie recalled the man who had written the report—Seething's lanky intelligence officer, Lieutenant Robert Harper. So Charlie contacted the 448th Bomb Group Association and discovered that Harper resided in New England. Charlie called Harper, who remembered him instantly. Harper told Charlie that he had stayed on for another tour in England then become an architect after the war. Having retired, Harper told Charlie his new hobby was painting. That gave Charlie an idea.

"Do you think you could paint a portrait of our plane?" Charlie asked him. Harper remembered *The Pub* and agreed. "This time is it safe to include the German?" Charlie joked. Harper laughed and agreed to paint the 109 flying alongside *The Pub*, his way of making amends for having quashed the story during the war. Harper painted the scene in watercolors then hit a roadblock. He called Charlie. He did not know what markings to paint on the German plane. Charlie had no idea either. "Let's leave that part blank," Charlie told Harper. "Just in case I find him."

Charlie had read in an aviation magazine that Germany's most famous pilot, General Adolf Galland, had recently made an amazing reunion of his own. Galland had reunited with his wartime crew chief, Gerhard Meyer, by placing an ad in a newsletter called *Jaegerblatt*. *Jaegerblatt* ("*Fighter Journal*") was the official publication of the Association of German Fighter Pilots, the reunion group for past and current pilots. So Charlie wrote to the editor of *Jaegerblatt* and asked if the editor would publish his short letter describing the December 20 incident and the German pilot he was trying to find. But the editor was not eager to help a former bomber pilot. He declined Charlie's request. So Charlie tried another route and wrote to Galland to ask for his help. Galland replied by letter that he had never heard of a 109 sparing a B-17, but he would order *Jaegerblatt*'s editor to publish Charlie's note. Galland could do this because he had once served as the organization's president. He told Charlie to resubmit his letter, and Charlie eagerly complied.

In his letter, Charlie outlined the time, place, and general details of the encounter, in which "a single Bf-109 made a non-firing gun camera run on the B-17 and ended up flying formation on the right wing." Charlie listed his address in Florida where he could be reached. But Charlie did not mention that his bomber's left horizontal stabilizer had been blown away or that his rudder was nearly gone or that his tail gunner had been killed. His years in military intelligence had bred a sense of skepticism. He saved those details and one last fact as a secret test in the event that a German pilot actually came forward.

SEVERAL MONTHS LATER, JANUARY 1990, VANCOUVER

At his mailbox, Franz saw that his *Jaegerblatt* had finally come from Germany. He plodded slowly along his driveway. Inside his house with its walls filled with woodcarvings, cuckoo clocks, and paintings of mountains, Franz dropped into his easy chair. He perused his *Jaegerblatt* expecting to discover who had died since the previous issue. Then he saw it.

"Hiya!" Franz shouted.

Hiya came running. She assumed something bad had happened—maybe Galland had died.

"Here, look, this was him!" Franz shouted. Hiya looked confused. "The one I didn't shoot down!" Franz clarified.

Over Franz's shoulder, Hiya read the newsletter, amazed. As Galland had promised, *Jaegerblatt* had published Charlie's "looking for" letter. Like a small ad it occupied a quarter of a black-and-white page. Franz stood up and shuffled to his den, with its wallpaper that resembled old newspaper print. He opened the cover on his typewriter, slipped a piece of paper within the rollers, and quickly pounded out a letter that read:

Jan. 18, 1990

Dear Charles,

All these years I wondered what happened to the B-17, did she make it or not? As I am a guest of the American Fighter Aces, I inquired time und again, but without any results. I have been a guest at the 50th Anniversary of the B-17, and I could still [not] find any answers, whether it was worth to risk a court marshal. I am happy now that you made it, and that it was worth it.

I will be in Florida sometime in June, as guest of the American Fighter Aces and it sure would be nice to talk about our encounter. By the way, after I landed at Bremen Airport, I borrowed the Fieseler Storch from the airport commander to fly out to a B-17 which I shot down. The field I landed in just was not cooperating, and I stood on my head or prop. I just wanted to be sure that the crew was treated correctly. My landing was not appreciated, I told in the officer's mess, as I was forced to stay overnight to have one of my radiators changed, which had a 50 caliber bullet stuck in it.

For now, Horrido

Yours,
[Signed] Franz
Franz Stigler

Five days later in Miami, Jackie brought Charlie his mail as he sat at his desk, listening to the radio. He sliced the letter with an opener. "My God," Charlie muttered as he read the letter in disbelief. He called his wife. "Could it be him?" Jackie asked. Thinking like an intelligence officer, Charlie pointed out that Franz had asked for nothing. He had not listed his phone number or said they needed to write a book together and tell the world of their encounter. He simply had suggested that maybe they could meet someday and that he was happy Charlie had made it. "I've got a good feeling this is the guy," Charlie told his wife. "But I'm not getting my hopes up, yet." Charlie sat down to type a letter back to Franz. Midway through the process he became impatient and stopped. "The heck with it," he said. Picking up the phone, Charlie dialed information. He asked for the Vancouver phone directory and if there was a Franz Stigler listed. The operator told him there was and gave him Franz's number. Charlie called and Franz picked up.

"Is this Mr. Franz Stigler?" Charlie asked.

"Ja," Franz replied. "This is he."

"The Franz Stigler who flew in World War Two?" Charlie asked.

"Ja," Franz replied, sounding confused.

"Franz, I think we go way back. This is Charlie Brown."

The conversation was strange and awkward at first. Charlie asked Franz a series of questions to figure out if he was really the one. Franz described the bomber's battle damage. He mentioned the missing stabilizer. He said the rudder was nearly gone. He told Charlie the tail gunner's position was shattered. Charlie's heart skipped a beat. He had never mentioned the stabilizer, rudder, or tail gun position in his *Jaegerblatt* letter—but Franz knew everything. Then Franz told Charlie, "When I let you go over the sea, I thought you'd never make it across."

"My God, it is you!" Charlie said. Tears ran down his cheeks and onto the phone's handset. Charlie had purposely never mentioned anything in the letter about flying over the water. That was his secret test. All Charlie had mentioned was that the encounter had happened over land. Yet Franz knew they had flown together out and over the sea. His emotions flowing, Charlie asked Franz the first thing that came to mind. "What were you pointing for? You kept pointing and trying to tell us something?"

"To get you to land in Sweden!" Franz told Charlie, choking up himself.

"I had no idea!" Charlie replied, "Otherwise I would have flown there and would still be speaking Swedish today!"

———

THE DAY AFTER their conversation, Charlie wrote:

Receiving your letter was one of the greatest thrills of my life. I had to know for sure and obtained your telephone number from the Vancouver operator. My conversation with you totally dispelled any doubt, when you mentioned going over the water with us. That has never been advertised in any of the letters seeking the 109 pilot.

In his letter, Charlie asked Franz about the markings on his fighter, so his friend Robert Harper could complete his painting. He also asked Franz to keep him informed if he was indeed coming to Florida to the American Fighter Aces convention, where he hoped they could meet. Charlie closed the letter by writing:

I have the distinct feeling that some power greater than that of our respective governments was looking out for most of us on Dec. 20, 1943. To say THANK YOU, THANK YOU, THANK YOU on behalf of my surviving crewmembers and their families appears totally inadequate.

Even though we still had one functional gun left in the top turret we were effectively out of the war. I am not only thankful that you did not bring about our demise . . . but also grateful you did not pull out a Walther P-38 [pistol] or slingshot and finish us off, while you were flying close formation with our right wing.

I am sure that your skill and daring made you an extremely successful fighter pilot; however, if you repeatedly exhibited that type of camaraderie/chivalry, and daring, your chance of surviving combat would not have been too great. I join you in being most grateful that you were not court marshaled for your chivalry on Dec. 20, 1943.

With warmest
regards,
[Signed] Charlie
Charles L. Brown

Charlie wrote to Franz unaware that Franz was an ace or where he had served. He just knew that Franz was a good man. But Charlie still needed to know why Franz had spared him. That spring, Franz suffered lung ailments and had to cancel his trip to Florida. Charlie offered to travel to Seattle, instead, if Franz would meet him there. Franz agreed and the men set a date.

SEVERAL WEEKS LATER, JUNE 21, 1990, SEATTLE

On the day of their planned reunion, Charlie paced within the Embassy Suites hotel wearing one of his baggy gray suits and bolo ties. He knew Franz and Hiya were due to arrive at 11:30 A.M. and that emotions would run high, so he planned a good-spirited joke. Charlie had recently received prints from Harper of his finished painting that showed Franz's 109 flying with Charlie's B-17. Harper entitled the work, *The Ultimate Honor.* Harper's talents had come a long way. Charlie gave one of the prints to the lady at the front desk and asked her, "When Mr. and Mrs. Stigler check in, can you please give this to Mr. Stigler and ask him if he is the famous German fighter ace?" The girl agreed to play along.

Charlie watched and waited from a raised balcony overlooking the hotel's atrium. At noon, Franz and Hiya appeared in the lobby and approached the desk. Charlie recognized Franz from photos they had exchanged. The lady at the front desk handed Franz the print and played along. Franz looked around frantically, knowing Charlie had to be behind such a joke. "That's enough," Charlie chuckled to himself. He took the elevator down to the lobby and stepped out. Franz saw Charlie and ran to him. The two former enemies hugged and cried.

Charlie's wife had been unable to travel with him to meet Franz, so he had brought a friend—Joe Jackson, the Medal of Honor recipient who had first suggested he look for Franz. The following morning, Jackson joined Franz and Charlie as they sat in Charlie's hotel room and talked. Jackson had brought his video camera and filmed their discussion. He knew he was watching history in the making.* "The odds against this happening are millions to one," Charlie told the camera. "First, of either of us surviving for forty-six-plus years, and then being able to get in contact." Jackson interjected and asked Franz what he was feeling, having finally met Charlie. Franz struggled with his words. "It wasn't easy," Franz said as he fought tears and began to sniffle. "I hugged him." Wiping his eyes with one hand, he slapped Charlie on the shoulder to keep from crying and said, "I love you, Charlie."

OVER THE NEXT two days, Charlie and Franz revived old memories as they toured Seattle. Franz told Charlie about his brother, the reason he became a fighter pilot. Charlie told Franz about growing up on a farm and losing his mother. Charlie learned that Franz had not been out of ammo when he flew alongside *The Pub*, as Charlie had assumed. Franz revealed quite the opposite. His guns had been full. Charlie also discovered that the man who spared him was not just any pilot. He was one of Germany's great aces, a man who had served in the "Squadron of Experts." Charlie wanted to learn more about JV-44. Franz said many of the stories were too painful—but he promised to give Charlie a book about the unit. In parting, Charlie told both Franz and Hiya, "You'll be pleased to know that our B-17, *Ye Olde Pub*, never dropped bombs on Germany again." Back at his home in Miami, Charlie told Jackie, "It was like meeting a family member, a brother you haven't seen in forty years."

"Did you find out why he spared you?" she had asked.

Charlie nodded.

"I was too stupid to surrender," Charlie said. "And Franz Stigler was too much of a gentleman to destroy us."

---

* "It was such an incredible, once-in-a-lifetime thing," Charlie would remember. "I believed that I had a better chance of winning the lottery than finding him alive, some forty years later." Jackson's film of Charlie and Franz's reunion is now available for viewing on the author's website.

Charlie never had his nightmares of "the spin" again after meeting Franz.

———————————

AFTER HAVING MET Charlie, Franz talked with Galland by phone. Franz admitted to Galland that he had let the B-17 escape. All Galland had to say was "It would be you." Galland revealed that he had ordered *Jaegerblatt* to publish Charlie's letter. Franz could sense that Galland was neither thrilled nor angry that he had let the bomber escape. Instead, Galland had mixed feelings, having lost his younger brothers in the war. Even forty-six years later, he considered Franz's act to be dereliction of duty—and yet the right thing to do. Franz and Galland would continue to talk week after week until Galland's death in 1996.

As news of Charlie and Franz's reunion circulated, it made the headlines. *Jaegerblatt* ran a story about Franz's reunion with Charlie under the title "An Act of Chivalry in the Skies over Europe." Franz began receiving phone calls from Germany that delivered the same message.

"Is this Franz Stigler?"

"*Ja.*"

"You pigheaded asshole." *Click.*

Others began, "Are you Franz Stigler, who didn't shoot the B-17 down?"

"*Ja.*"

"Traitor!" *Click.*

The calls disturbed Hiya until Franz told her, "You have to understand that people were being killed by the B-17s, and this person who called may have lost his family to a bombing raid." As the story of Franz and Charlie's reunion circulated in North America, Canadian and American TV stations ran the story with teasers like "Why did this Luftwaffe ace spare an American bomber crew and risk a date with Hitler's firing squad?" and "A change of heart, a mystery that would remain unsolved for decades . . . a Remembrance Day story you won't soon forget." Despite being widely well received, the stories were not appreciated by everybody. Franz received a few calls from his Canadian neighbors who were surprised to discover that "the enemy" lived among them.

"Is this Franz Stigler?"

"*Ja.*"

"Go home, you Nazi bastard." *Click.*

"They'll never understand," Franz would say to calm Hiya.

TWO MONTHS LATER, SEPTEMBER 13, 1990, MASSACHUSETTS

The cameraman, producer, and sound technician with his boom microphone backpedaled as they led Charlie and Franz in a walk-around inspection of the olive-colored B-17 that sat on the sunlit tarmac. Charlie walked slowly to keep pace with Franz, who hobbled with his cane. The two talked as the camera recorded every nuance.

Charlie wore a blue vinyl jacket covered with Air Force patches. A smattering of pewter pins of B-17s covered his matching blue ball cap, with an 8th Air Force patch in its center. At Charlie's side, Franz wore a navy blazer over khaki pants, free of pins or patches. But on his head he wore a blue ball cap with a square patch that surrounded a yellow embroidered B-17 and the title THE 379TH BOMB GROUP.

Old veterans and their families milled around and through the bomber, posing for photos in the waist windows and under the open bomb bay. A reunion of the 379th Bomb Group was under way. Charlie and the veterans of the 379th Bomb Group had invited Franz to attend as their guest. They had given him the hat he wore. They would one day make him an honorary member of the 379th Bomb Group.

The cameramen were filming for the CBS News *This Morning* show. At a time when the world was focused on a pending war in the Persian Gulf, anchor/reporter Wayne Freedman had gotten wind of another big story—a human interest tale of redemption that he would later bill as "The story of a war reunion that only took place because of the compassion of an enemy."

Around the bomber, the 379th veterans and their families grew respectfully silent as Charlie, Franz, and the camera crew circled the plane. "This one looks nice compared to yours," Franz said offhandedly to Charlie, who chuckled in agreement. Under the bomber's wing, Hiya and Charlie's wife, Jackie, watched from the shade, having just met.

After the CBS crew lowered their cameras and departed, Charlie and Franz remained with their wives, chatting. Charlie looked over his shoulder periodically, toward a shadowy hangar, as if expecting someone. Finally, two old veterans emerged from the hangar and hobbled toward the small gathering under the wing. The sight was not unusual for a reunion, two veterans with their wives, sons, and daughters behind them. But these men who approached Charlie and Franz were special. Charlie knew them but Franz did not.

"Franz, there's two gentlemen who would like to meet you," Charlie said, fighting a grin. He steered Franz out from under the wing and into the light. The first veteran to reach Franz was Charlie's old ball turret gunner, Sam "Blackie" Blackford, whose wide mustache was gray and whose head was bald but for wispy gray hair above his ears. Blackie started crying as he shook Franz's hand vigorously, refusing to stop. The other veteran was Charlie's radio operator, Dick Pechout, whose hair had turned white and whose eyes remained meek behind tortoiseshell glasses. Charlie looped his arms over Franz and Blackie, hugging them. Blackie broke down. Through sobs, he thanked Franz for sparing his life and said that because Franz had not pulled the trigger on him, his children and grandchildren were able to experience life. Pechout draped his arms silently around Franz and the others as the four huddled.

Blackie's tears made Franz sob, and Franz's crying made Charlie well over. The veterans' families and the other old men of the 379th kept their distance at first. Then, when they could stand it no more, they converged around the sobbing veterans who were their husbands or fathers or grandfathers or buddies.

From above it must have looked funny, the circle of people crowding around one small man in the center, hugging him and one another amid sounds of tears and laughter. But everyone that day owed something to Franz Stigler, the man in the middle. Because of him, twenty-five men, women, and children—the descendants of Charlie, Blackie, and Pechout—had the chance to live, not to mention the children and grandchildren of Charlie's other crewmen.

But Franz thought he had been the one given a gift. When he presented Charlie a book about the Squadron of Experts, inside the cover he penned an inscription, quiet words that the world was never meant to hear. When Charlie read it, he could hear Franz's voice.

In 1940, I lost my only brother as a night fighter.

On the 20th of December, 4 days before Christmas, I had the chance to save a B-17 from her destruction, a plane so badly damaged it was a wonder that she was still flying.

The pilot, Charlie Brown, is for me, as precious as my brother was.

Thanks Charlie.
Your Brother,
Franz

From above, the circle of people blended as they hugged near the bomber's wing, becoming just one mass, bigger and greater as the gaps between them vanished.

AFTERWORD

IN 1955, THE United States and her allies formally welcomed West Germany into NATO and revived the German Air Force. In recognition of their honorable service to their country during World War II and absence of affiliation with The Party, the following officers were reinstated at their old ranks and led successful careers in the new German Air Force.

Gerhard "Gerd" Barkhorn retired as a three-star general.

Gustav Roedel retired as a one-star general.

Hannes Trautloft served as the inspector general and retired as a three-star general.

Erich Hohagen retired as a one-star general.

Walter "the Count" Krupinski retired as a three-star general.

Erich "Bubi" Hartmann joined the new Air Force after ten years in Soviet P.O.W. camps and later retired as a colonel.

Johannes "Macky" Steinhoff joined the new Air Force and climbed the ranks in spite of his severe disfigurement from his burns. He eventually served as the Air Force's commander and retired in 1974 as a four-star general. In 1997, the German Fighter Wing 73 was given the honorary name "Steinhoff," one of the few wings named after a man. Today, the Steinhoff Wing flies regularly alongside the Richthofen Wing, named for the Red Baron.

———

IN 1957, AT a 379th Bomb Group reunion, Charlie revealed his true age to his crew. The Quiet Ones were surprised but not offended. They figured Charlie had done a fine job of getting them home, the only measure that mattered.

———

CHARLIE NEVER HAD contact with Marjorie after the war, but last heard she had gotten married and never stopped flying.

———

IN THE YEARS following their reunion, Franz and Charlie traveled across North America telling their story to any civic clubs, air museums, or military units that requested them. This was their last act of service to build a better world. Their message was simple: enemies are better off as friends.

Franz Stigler succumbed to illness in March 2008. Shortly before he died, Franz asked Hiya to cremate his body but to keep his ashes close. "I promise I won't be a bother," he said. After fifty-two years of marriage he died in Hiya's arms.

Charlie Brown died in November 2008, eight months after Franz.

Prior to Charlie's death, the U.S. Air Force completed a lengthy investigation into the events of December 20, 1943, and the actions of Charlie and his crew. The Air Force ruled that military officials had made a mistake in how they had handled the case sixty-four years earlier. In April 2008, the Air Force summoned Charlie to the Florida State Capitol and awarded him the nation's second highest medal for valor—the Air Force Cross. The Air Force also presented Charlie's last living crewman, Albert "Doc" Sadok, with the Silver Star and posthumously awarded a Silver Star to each of the eight deceased members of the crew.

Today, with a combined nine Silver Stars and one Air Force Cross, the crew of *Ye Olde Pub* remains one of the most decorated bomber crews in history.

Franz Stigler never got the Knight's Cross, but as he always said, he got something better.

Franz Stigler   Surrey, Jan.18/90
Surrey,B.C.
V3W 4P8
C a n a d a

                    Dear Charles,

        Allthis years I wondert what happend to the B17,
dit she make it or not.As I am aguest of the American
Fighter Aces,I inquired time und again,but without any
results.Ihave been a guest at the 50thuniversary of the
B17,und Ikould still find any answers,wheter it was
worth to risk a Court Marshal.I am happy now that you
made it,and that it was worth it.

                    I will be in Florida sometimes in June
as guest of the Am.Fighter Aces and it sure would be
nice to talk about ouer encounter.By the way after I
landet at Bremen Airport,Iborrowed the Fieseler Storch
from the airport Commander to fly out to a B17 wich I
shot down.The field I landet in just was not cooperating
and I stood on My head or prop.I just wonted to be sure,
tha the crew was treated correctly.My landing was not
appreciated,Ihave been told in the Off.Mess,as I was forced
to stay overnight to have one of my radiators changed,
Wich had a 5o cal.bullet stuck in it.

                            For now

                            horrido

                                yours

Pilot Class 43-D Association, Inc.
A Non-Profit Organization

January 24, 1990

Mr. Franz Stigler
Surrey, B. C.
V3W 4P8
Canada

Dear Franz,

Receiving your letter was one of the greatest thrills of my
life. Although I normally try to anticipate events and prepare
myself for a variety of circumstances, I was ecstatic at
receiving your letter and totally unprepared to write this
response; so if you will bear with me here goes.

First, do not be discouraged by the mass of data you find
enclosed with this letter. Once you have read THE 13 MINUTE GAP
and then THE 13 MINUTE GAP-REVISITED you will be able to better
understand my interests. I will also enclose the first two
stories of an Anthology I am compiling which will also provide
additional background. And finally, I will enclose just a bit on
my combustion research efforts, especially as they relate to
diesel engines.

When I read your letter and saw your photo's I was so elated
that all I could think of was that perhaps your actions related
to another aircraft. I had to know for sure and obtained your
telephone number from the Vancouver operator. My conversation
with you totally dispelled any doubt, when you mentioned going
over the water (North Sea) with us. That has never been
advertised in any of the letters seeking the 109 pilot. Do you
remember the exact area where we exited the coast?

I know that you realize that the probability of each of us
surviving for these forty six plus years since Dec. 20, 1943 is
in and of itself incredible. Further, our being able to identify
and communicate with each other at this time is nothing short of
a miracle. My most sincere congratulations to your fighter pilot
association and especially to your wonderful newsletter which
provided the vehicle for our correspondence.

Now for a few specific comments, observations, questions, etc.:

1) I would appreciate your further comments as to the reason
that you did not fire at us during the encounter. I felt that
perhaps you were one of the pilots who had previously engaged
us, were out of ammunition, and finally saluted/waved as an act
of respect/camaraderie. If you had ammunition the alternative

was that you felt that due to the excessive damage to our aircraft we would not make it back to England. In the latter case the wave/salute would just be to wish us well. During our conversation you mentioned that you had thought that we would try to make it to Sweden. If you and I had been able to communicate and you had suggested that to me I would be speaking Swedish today. As the narrative points out, I was a very, very inexperienced aircraft commander, and had just turned 21 years of age. Fortunately the thought of going to Sweden rather than facing the North Sea never crossed my mind. You will be pleased to know that "167" never flew combat again.

2) After we barely made it back to England and landed at Seething, the casualties were removed and the uninjured survivors were debriefed. Later, as I revisited the aircraft one of the senior officers and I were inspecting the almost destroyed tail section. He asked, "Lieutenant, why in the world would you try to fly such a badly damaged aircraft back to England?" I replied, "Well Sir, I had one dead and three more seriously injured crew members who had little or no chance of surviving a bailout; and <u>fortunately</u> I could not see the rear of the aircraft and did not truly know how badly it was damaged." With that he replied "Young man I am going to recommend you for out nation's highest award." The rest of the story is covered in the GAP narratives.

3) As you can ascertain from the story and the painting "THE ULTIMATE HONOR" the assumption was made that you were one of the pilots who had previously attacked us, although your aircraft color seemed different. At this time I see no reason to change the title; however the caption will be altered. One of the points I stress in the narratives is to have as near totally accurate data as it is possible to obtain. The lack of accurate markings on the Bf-109 is all that has kept me from having the painting lithographed. In addition to the symbolic markings you actually were parked on my right wing. Bob Harper, the artist took artistic license in moving you further out in order to obtain a better perspective and increase the size of the 109. Per our discussion please, please get me YOUR ACTUAL AIRCRAFT MARKINGS AS SOON AS POSSIBLE. Since you had the best air view of our aircraft, obtained during your audacious inspection, I would be most interested in your observations as to the visible damage to the aircraft. Also, <u>**what was your rank?**</u> Thanks.

4) After you read the basic GAP how would you feel about writing about that day (Dec. 20, 1943) in your life, along the lines that I covered? I think that with what has now transpired it would make a fantastic conclusion to the GAP segments.

5) Please keep me posted on the details of your June visit to Fort Lauderdale with the American Fighter Aces.

6) Hopefully one or more of the fifteen attacking Bf-109 and FW-190 pilots survived the war. The 190's had wing tips and nose

painted yellow and blue and looked like a circus. The Bf-109's were gray with blue trim. Perhaps you could assist in locating one of the survivors. It would really add to the story in terms of interest if we could obtain one of the fighter pilot's perspective of the engagement, and perhaps their frustration in not having finished us off. I have the distinct feeling that some power greater than that of our respective governments was looking out for most of us on Dec. 20, 1943.

To say THANK YOU, THANK YOU, THANK YOU on behalf of my surviving crew members and their families appears totally inadequate. Even though we still had one functional gun left in the top turret we were effectively out of the war. I am not only thankful that you did not bring about our demise with your machine guns and cannon, but also grateful that you did not pull out a Walther P-38 or slingshot and finish us off, while you were flying close formation on our right wing. I am sure that your skill and daring made you an extremely successful fighter pilot; however, if you repeatedly exhibited that type of camaraderie/chivalry, and daring, your chance of surviving combat would not have been too great. By the way I assume that you did not fly formation with enemy aircraft as a regular procedure. Did you in fact ever do such a thing either before or after our chance airborne meeting? I join you in being most grateful that you were not court martialed for your chivalry on Dec. 20, 1943.

We should both be grateful to Mrs. Shirley Haskell of Dallas, Texas who gave me a gift of a great book titled SIGNED WITH THEIR HONOR, by Piet Hein Meijering, a Dutch author. I then wrote Piet Hein and he in turn contacted Gen. Galland and the author of your association newsletter. Nothing has ever worked out so well , or so quickly, as that series of events. It truly is still A SMALL WORLD CHARLIE BROWN. If you have not read Piet's book please let me know and I will send you a copy. It is a shame that you were not featured in his book as, unfortunately, he was not aware of your most unusual actions.

I hope that you enjoy these results of very extensive research efforts on behalf of dozens of dedicated individuals. My rather biased and amateur reporting efforts leave much to be desired, but hopefully the unusual results will more than make up for any lack of professionalism in presentation. I hope you and yours enjoy.

As my RAF compatriots would say "WELL DONE, GOD BLESS, AND KEEP."

With warmest regards,

Charlie

Charles L. Brown

Enclosures: Page 4

THE UNITED STATES OF AMERICA

TO ALL WHO SHALL SEE THESE PRESENTS, GREETING:

THIS IS TO CERTIFY THAT
THE PRESIDENT OF THE UNITED STATES OF AMERICA
AUTHORIZED BY TITLE 10, SECTION 8742, UNITED STATES CODE
HAS AWARDED

THE AIR FORCE CROSS

TO

SECOND LIEUTENANT CHARLES L. BROWN

FOR

EXTRAORDINARY HEROISM IN MILITARY OPERATIONS
AGAINST AN OPPOSING ARMED ENEMY

20 DECEMBER 1943

GIVEN UNDER MY HAND IN THE CITY OF WASHINGTON

4 FEBRUARY 2008

_____
CHIEF OF STAFF

_____
SECRETARY OF THE AIR FORCE

AF FORM 2260, 20060101

SPECIAL ORDER #: G-094 CONDITION: 5

PAS CODE: N/A RDP: N/A

CITATION TO ACCOMPANY THE AWARD OF

THE AIR FORCE CROSS

TO

CHARLES L. BROWN

The President of the United States of America, authorized by Title 10, Section 8742, U.S.C, awards the Air Force Cross to Second Lieutenant Charles L. Brown for extraordinary heroism in military operations against an armed enemy of the United States as a B-17 Pilot over Germany, 20 December 1943. On this date while attacking a heavily defended target over occupied Germany, Lieutenant Brown's aircraft sustained severe flak damage, including destruction of the Plexiglas nose, wing damage, and major damage to the number two and four engines. Lieutenant Brown provided invaluable instructions to the co-pilot and crew requiring the number two engine to be shut down. He then expertly managed to keep the number four engine producing partial power. This action enabled his crew to complete the improbable bombing run and bomb delivery on this important strategic target. Immediately upon leaving the target, severe multiple engine damage prevented maintaining his position in the formation. During this extreme duress, the demonstrated airmanship displayed by Lieutenant Brown could only be described as crucially pivotal to the aircraft's survival and displayed by only more seasoned and experienced aviators during the War. His violent, evasive tactics to counter the multiple enemy efforts to destroy their airplane directly contributed to his crew and his aircraft's survival. Alone and outnumbered, the aircraft was mercilessly attacked by the enemy in which crew difficulties were compounded when discovered only three defensive guns were operational, the others frozen in the -75 degree Fahrenheit temperatures. The results of this brief, but devastating aerial battle was one crew member dead; another critically wounded that would require amputation of his leg; serious damage of the third engine; the complete destruction of the aircraft's left elevator and stabilizer; the inoperability of bomber's oxygen and communications systems; and the complete shredding of the rudder by enemy fire that produced a death roll of the plane as it spiraled helplessly out of control causing the entire crew to temporarily lose consciousness. Miraculously, prior to ground impact, Lieutenant Brown and the co-pilot regained consciousness and managed to regain full flight control by pulling the heavily damaged aircraft out of its' nose-dive. Although managing to recover this aircraft from certain doom, the crew's plight was further complicated when a lone German fighter witnessed the maneuver, now attempted to force the crippled aircraft to land. Displaying the coolness, courage and airmanship of more senior pilots, he boldly rejected the enemy fighter's attempts at a forced landing and directed the struggling aircraft to the North Sea. While attempting this improbable, treacherous return to home station, Lieutenant Brown's command and control was instrumental to the remaining crew's survival. While in the cockpit, he provided the essential engine control, fuel management, and piloting skills necessary to the cockpit team during their hazardous, yet miraculous return of the aircraft's perilous crossing of the North Sea back to home station in England. Through this extraordinary heroism, superb airmanship, and aggressiveness in the face of the enemy, Lieutenant Brown reflected the highest credit upon himself and the United States Army Air Corps.

ACKNOWLEDGMENTS

My thanks go out to the following people for their help with *A Higher Call*.

To Charlie Brown, for opening the door to this epic story when I came knocking. Your lifelong devotion to your crew made this book possible. To Franz Stigler and Helga Stigler, for welcoming this outsider into your lives and sharing stories that were fascinating for me—and painful for you. May the world grant you the peace you deserve.

To my editor at Berkley Publishing Group, Natalee Rosenstein, who had faith in the transcendental power of this story. Thanks for rolling the dice with this first-time author. To my publisher at Penguin Group, Leslie Gelbman, and her team, thanks for giving the green light to share this book with the world.

To Charlie's daughters, Carol Dawn Warner and Kimberly Arnspiger. To the sons of Sam Blackford—Paul Blackford and Chris Blackford—and to Richard Sadok (the son of Al Sadok) and Franz Stigler's godson Jim Berladyn. The memories, photos, and diaries you shared enriched this book immensely.

To Larry Alexander, a seasoned author and newspaperman who

helped me shoulder the mountain of research and writing to complete this book. From digging up B-17 flight manuals to finding P-40 pilots to interview, your guidance was a gift.

To David Harper of Eagle's Nest Historical Tours, my guide and liaison to all things German. From driving me to WWII sites in Germany to placing ads in German newspapers seeking the descendants of Willi Kientsch, your help was instrumental. You are one of Europe's top tour guides for good reason.

To Byron Schlag, the jolly old B-17 tail gunner veteran who took me to England to tour 8th Air Force bomber bases with him during a reunion of his bomb group. Thanks for being my 8th Air Force mentor for so many years.

To Professor Colin Heaton, America's expert on WWII German pilots. The author of *The German Aces Speak*, Colin was stationed in Germany during the 1980s as a soldier in the U.S. Army. During that time he interviewed countless German pilots, treasured interviews he shared with me so I could know his friends—the aces.

To Robert Forsyth, a British historian and the world's preeminent JV-44 expert. When Franz Stigler gifted a book about JV-44 to Charlie Brown, he chose Robert's book, *JV-44*. In addition to freely answering my questions, Robert opened his photo library and shared many of the rare JV-44 pictures that appear in this book.

To Dr. Kurt Braatz, who wrote Gunther Luetzow's biography *Gott oder ein Flugzeug* (*God or an Airplane*) and translated key components of his book to help me understand Luetzow, a largely forgotten man whose legacy Braatz works to keep alive.

To Master Sergeant Craig Mackey and the staff at the Air Force Historical Research Agency, thanks for providing the most professional research and archives service I've ever encountered.

To my focus group of critical readers, Eric Carlson, Joe Gohrs, Matt Hoover, Pete Semanoff, and Justin Taylan, your feedback made this a better book.

To the lovely Austrian and German girls who helped me from afar,

Julia Loisl (for her translations), Jaqueline Schiele (who helped me search for Willi Kientsch's family), and Carolin Huber (who helped me locate August Stigler's grave site). Special thanks to Carolin for lending her critical eye and critiquing the manuscript from a German perspective. The word "brilliant" does not adequately describe the job you did.

To America's preeminent aviation artist, John D. Shaw, whose painting adorns this book, thanks for using your masterful brush-strokes to spread this story.

To the composers whose scores were the rousing soundtrack to my typing, to Michael Giacchino for your *Medal of Honor: Allied Assault*, to Hans Zimmer for your song, "Woad to Ruin," and to my talented friends in the band the Airborne Toxic Event.

To the historians, experts, and friends who shared their insight: Robin Barletta, Bianca Del Bello, Christer Bergström, Steve Blake, Andy Boyd, Cheryl Cerbone, Dr. Thomas Childers, Mark Copeland, Ferdinando D'Amico, Patricia Everson, Wayne Freedman, Uwe Gelfert, Wilhelm Göbel, Jon Guttman, Greg Johnson, Matt Hall, Mike Hart, Roger Hesse, Kelly Kalcheim, Julee MacDonald, Carl Molesworth, Carina Notzke, Gordon Page, William S. Phillips, Andrew Rammon, Christopher Shores, Vince Tassone, Odette Trellinger, John Weal, Rick Willett, Bob Windholz, and Paul Woodadge.

To my high school English teacher, Mr. G. David Friant, who edited our magazine for a decade without pay or reward, just to help a bunch of kids develop their talents—anything I've learned about writing I owe to you.

To the World War II veterans whose advice and corrections made for a better book—W.A.S.P. pilot Betty Blake, B-24 pilot Joe Jackson, P-40 pilot Jack Pinkham, B-24 bombardier William Reichle, B-17 radio operator George Roberts, Bf-109 pilot Kurt Schulze, and flak gunner Otto Wittenburg. Special thanks to this book's chief historical advisors, B-17 pilot John Noack and Me-262 pilot Jorg Czypionka, who worked with me from start to finish. John flew a B-17 in the bloody Second Schweinfurt raid and was later shot down into the North Sea and taken prisoner, whereas Jorg's career paralleled that of Franz Stigler. Jorg was a flight instructor-turned-109 pilot who later flew 262s in combat—only with a catch—he flew jets at night, as a night fighter. Not only did Jorg know Franz Stigler after the war, but he, too, had a close encounter of his own with a British Spitfire pilot (a story too amazing for this short space, so I've posted it, along with other bonus content on my website: www.ValorStudios.com).

To my parents, Robert and Karen Makos, and my sisters, Erica Makos and Elizabeth Makos. I've always looked to you first, for a critical read or an opinion, for encouragement or a reality check. I can work harder and sleep better knowing that you're in my life and always pushing me forward.

To my brother, Bryan Makos, my right-hand man and toughest critic, you've worked with nearly everyone credited above, freeing me up to write. Yours was no easy task—to gather historical facts, stories, and human resources spanning three continents, eight countries, and both sides of a world war. Your name is not on the cover. Your work may go unnoticed. But few people, if anyone, could have done the job you did.

Lastly, to my grandfathers, WWII veterans Mike Makos and Francis Panfili, when anyone asks how I became interested in history, it's due to you—the air shows you took Bryan and me to as kids, the plastic models of WWII planes that you built for us, your old photo albums, your patches and pins and reminders of a time gone by—who would have thought it would lead to this?

TO LEARN MORE

To view rare WWII aircraft such as those described in this book, the author encourages you to explore these fine aviation museums and organizations. An asterisk* indicates where a B-17 or Bf-109 is available for public viewing.

The Collings Foundation (Stow, Massachusetts)*
USS Intrepid Museum (New York, New York)
Air Mobility Command Museum (Dover, Delaware)*
National Air and Space Museum (Washington, DC)*
The Military Aviation Museum (Virginia Beach, Virginia)*
The Mighty Eighth Air Force Museum (Pooler, Georgia)*
Museum of Aviation (Warner Robins, Georgia)
Fantasy of Flight (Polk City, Florida)*
Stallion 51 (Kissimmee, Florida)
Air Force Armament Museum (Eglin AFB, Florida)*
National Museum of the United States Air Force (Dayton, Ohio)*
Grissom Air Museum (Peru, Indiana)*
Yankee Air Museum (Belleville, Michigan)*
The Air Zoo (Portage, Michigan)
Museum of Science and Industry (Chicago, Illinois)

EAA Experimental Aircraft Association (Oshkosh, Wisconsin)*
National Naval Aviation Museum (Pensacola, Florida)
USS Alabama Museum (Mobile, Alabama)
National WWII Museum (New Orleans, Louisiana)
Eighth Air Force Museum, (Barksdale AFB, Louisiana)*
Lone Star Flight Museum (Galveston, Texas)*
Commemorative Air Force Gulf Coast Wing (Houston, Texas)*
Cavanaugh Flight Museum (Addison, Texas)
Airman Heritage Museum (Lackland AFB, Texas)*
Commemorative Air Force Museum (Midland, Texas)
The Liberty Foundation (Tulsa, Oklahoma)*
Strategic Air and Space Museum (Ashland, Nebraska)*
Wings Over the Rockies Air and Space Museum (Denver, Colorado)
Spirit of Flight Museum (Erie, Colorado)*
Hill Aerospace Museum (Hill AFB, Utah)*
Pima Air and Space Museum (Tucson, Arizona)*
Commemorative Air Force Arizona Wing (Mesa, Arizona)*
Flying Heritage Collection (Everett, Washington)*
Museum of Flight (Seattle, Washington)*
Evergreen Aviation and Space Museum (McMinnville, Oregon)*
Tillamook Air Museum (Tillamook, Oregon)
Wings of Freedom (Milwaukie, Oregon)*
Planes of Fame (Chino, California, and Valle, Arizona)*
Palm Springs Air Museum (Palm Springs, California)*
Lyon Air Museum (Santa Ana, California)*
March Field Museum (Riverside, California)*
Castle Air Museum (Atwater, California)*
San Diego Air and Space Museum (San Diego, California)
Imperial War Museum (London and Duxford, England)*
The American Air Museum (Duxford, England)*
Royal Air Force Museum, Hendon (London, England)*
Vintage Wings of Canada (Quebec, Canada)
Canada Aviation and Space Museum (Ontario, Canada)*
Messerschmitt Foundation (Munich, Germany)*

NOTES

CHAPTER 3
1. Paul Berben, *Dachau: 1933-45,* 81–82.
2. Colin D. Heaton and Jeffrey Ethell interview with Franz Stigler.

CHAPTER 4
1. Christopher Shores and Hans Ring, *Luftkampf zwischen Sand und Sonne,* 194.

CHAPTER 5
1. Franz Kurowski, *German Fighter Ace Hans-Joachim Marseille,* 142.
2. Robert Tate, *Hans-Joachim Marseille: An Illustrated Tribute to the Luftwaffe's "Star of Africa,"* 83.

CHAPTER 6
1. Colin D. Heaton and Anne-Marie Lewis, *The German Aces Speak,* 155.

CHAPTER 8
1. Colin D. Heaton Interview with Gustav Roedel.
2. Jeffrey Ethel, *P-38 Lightning,* 21–23.

CHAPTER 9
1. Colin D. Heaton and Anne-Marie Lewis, *The German Aces Speak,* 127.
2. Heinz Knocke, *I Flew for the Fuhrer,* 97.
3. Author interview with Dr. Kurt Braatz.
4. Ibid.

5. Johannes Steinhoff, *Messerschmitts Over Sicily*, 11.

6. Colin D. Heaton and Anne-Marie Lewis, *The German Aces Speak*, 29–31.

7. Elliott Arnold and Richard Thruelsen, *Mediterranean Sweep: Air Stories from El Alamein to Rome*, 103.

8. 79th Fighter Group press release, June 1943.

9. Franz Stigler, "Palm Sunday Massacre," *Luftwaffe: Deadly Aces, Deadly Warplanes* 1, no. 1 (1989): 16–21, 96. In the absence of his logbook, Franz's water landing was wrongly attributed in this article to April 18 when it actually occurred on June 10. Franz refers to a corporal who was shot down with him and later returned to Sicily by raft. This was correct. The man was Corporal Karl Burger who was shot down on June 10.

10. The dialogue between Steinhoff and the Gestapo that follows is according to Johannes Steinhoff, as told to Colin D. Heaton.

11. Beth Griech-Polelle, *Bishop von Galen: German Catholicism and National Socialism*, 80.

12. Colin D. Heaton and Jeffrey Ethell interview with Franz Stigler.

13. Johannes Steinhoff, *Messerschmitts Over Sicily*, 181.

14. Albert Speer, *Inside the Third Reich.*

CHAPTER 10

1. Colin D. Heaton and Jeffrey Ethell interview with Franz Stigler.

CHAPTER 13

1. Harry Crosby, *A Wing and a Prayer*, 39.

2. Elmer Bendiner, *Fall of the Fortresses*, 91.

3. Air Force Historical Research Agency interview with General Maurice Preston.

4. Philip Kaplan and Rex Alan Smith, *One Last Look*, 197.

5. Elmer Bendiner, *Fall of the Fortresses*, 13.

6. Ibid., 73.

CHAPTER 15

1. Frank Geary, "Courage, Faith, Culminate in Brotherhood of Friendship Among Former Enemies in Skies Over WWII Europe," *Jax Air News* (1998): 14–15.

2. Ibid., 14–15.

CHAPTER 16

1. Rudolph Herzog, *Dead Funny: Humor in Hitler's Germany*, 167–168.

CHAPTER 17

1. Elmer Bendiner, *Fall of the Fortresses*, 206.

2. Ibid., 114–115.

CHAPTER 18

1. Joseph Mizrahi, *Knights of the Black Cross*, 63.

2. Ibid., 55.

CHAPTER 19

1. Joseph Mizrahi, *Knights of the Black Cross*, 64.
2. Joseph Deichl interview, "The Last Mission," King 5 TV, Seattle, October 9, 1985.
3. Johannes Steinhoff, *The Final Hours*, 21.
4. Willi Heilmann, *I Fought You from the Skies*, 150.
5. Joseph Mizrahi, *Knights of the Black Cross*, 63–64.
6. The dialogue that follows is compiled from Johannes Steinhoff's memoir, *The Final Hours*, and Colin D. Heaton's interview with Gustav Roedel.
7. Johannes Steinhoff, *The Final Hours*, 95.
8. The dialogue between Luetzow and Goering that follows is according to Johannes Steinhoff's memoir, *The Final Hours*.
9. Colin D. Heaton and Anne-Marie Lewis, *The German Aces Speak*, 168.
10. Ibid., 168.

CHAPTER 20

1. Robert Forsyth, *JV 44: The Galland Circus*, 102.
2. Johannes Steinhoff, *The Final Hours*, 127.
3. Colin D. Heaton and Anne-Marie Lewis, *The German Aces Speak*, 58.

CHAPTER 21

1. Robert Forsyth, *JV 44: The Galland Circus*, 147.
2. Philip Kaplan, *Fighter Aces of the Luftwaffe in World War 2*.
3. Colin D. Heaton, *The Me 262 Stormbird: From the Pilots Who Flew, Fought, and Survived It*.
4. Ibid.
5. Robert Forsyth, *JV 44: The Galland Circus*, 164.
6. Ibid., 165.

CHAPTER 22

1. Johannes Steinhoff, *The Final Hours*, 139.
2. Trevor Constable and Raymond Toliver, *Horrido! Fighter Aces of the Luftwaffe*, 139.
3. Colin D. Heaton interview with Johannes Trautloft.
4. Joseph Moser, *A Fighter Pilot in Buchenwald*, 123–124.
5. United States Holocaust Memorial Museum, "The Holocaust," *Holocaust Encyclopedia*, http://www.ushmm.org/wlc/en/article.php?ModuleId=10005144.
6. Colin D. Heaton and Anne-Marie Lewis, *The German Aces Speak*, 135. Some authors have placed Franz in air on the day of Steinhoff's crash when really he was preparing to fly. The reason for this confusion is easy—no official JV-44 flight rosters survived the war so the record of who flew on which day could only be determined by the veterans' memories. When fans and historians asked Franz, "Were you flying on the day when Steinhoff crashed?" Franz would answer "Yes, of course." This is because he did fly that day, after Steinhoff's crash.
7. Colin D. Heaton, *The Me 262 Stormbird: From the Pilots Who Flew, Fought, and Survived It*.

8. Ibid.

9. Ibid.

10. Robert Forsyth, *JV 44: The Galland Circus*, 229.

11. Ibid., 188.

CHAPTER 23

1. Adolf Galland, *The First and the Last*, 299.

2. Joseph Goebbels, "25 April 1945: Last Broadcast," YouTube.

3. Levi Bookin, "April 26, 1945," *What Happened Today?*, http://dailytrh.tripod.com/0426.html.

4. Adolf Galland, *The First and the Last*, 301.

CHAPTER 24

1. Heinz Knocke, *I Flew for the Fuhrer*, 187.

BIBLIOGRAPHY

A few words about sources and authenticity. It's important to note that Franz Stigler flew 487 combat missions during WWII, and Charlie Brown flew 29. Both men had documented the time, date, and place of every mission in their logbooks, but only Charlie's logbook survived the war. In May 1945, American interrogators seized Franz's logbook and it was never seen again. When I began my interviews with Franz and Charlie, it had been nearly fifty-nine years since the war's end. Both men shared their memories with me in the best detail they could remember. They also shared outstanding stories they had written in years prior, much of which had never been published. Combining these accounts with wartime records and using the sources below, I've reconstructed the timeline, events, and anecdotes of each veteran's service as accurately as possible. I've also taken the liberty to translate German words and names into their English equivalents as well as converting metric measurements to imperial measurements.

Primary sources include interviews, letters, diaries, and written accounts from WWII veterans Franz Stigler, Charlie Brown, Al Sadok, Sam Blackford, Dick Pechout, Hiya Stigler, Bill Reichle, Joe Jackson,

Viktor Widmaier, John Noack, George Roberts, Betty Blake, John Whitley, Kurt Schulze, Jorg Czypionka, Otto Wittenburg, and others too numerous to list.

379th Bomb Group (H) WWII Association, Inc. *Anthology Volume One: November 1942–July 1945.* Paducah, KY: Turner Publishing, 2000.

379th Bomb Group (H) WWII Association, Inc. *Anthology Volume Two: November 1942–July 1945.* Paducah, KY: Turner Publishing, 2000.

Arnold, Elliott, and Richard Thruelsen. *Mediterranean Sweep: Air Stories from El Alamein to Rome.* New York: Duell, Sloan and Pearce, 1944.

Baker, David. *Adolf Galland: The Authorised Biography.* London: Windrow & Greene, 1996.

Bekker, Cajus. *The Luftwaffe War Diaries.* New York: Ballantine Books, 1966.

Bendiner, Elmer. *Fall of the Fortresses.* New York: G.P. Putnam's Sons, 1980.

Berben, Paul. *Dachau: 1933–1945.* London: Comite International De Dachau, 1980.

Bookin, Levi. "What Happened Today? April 26, 1945." September 10, 2011. http://dailytrh .tripod.com/0426.html.

Boyne, Walter. *Messerschmitt Me 262: Arrow to the Future.* Atglen, PA: Schiffer Publishing, 1994.

Braatz, Kurt. *Gott oder ein Flugzeug.* Germany: Neunundzwanzig Sechs Verlag, 2005.

Caidin, Martin. *Me 109.* New York: Ballantine Books, 1968.

Caldwell, Donald. *JG26: Top Guns of the Luftwaffe.* New York: Ivy Books, 1991.

Childers, Thomas. *In the Shadows of War: An American Pilot's Odyssey Through Occupied France and the Camps of Nazi Germany.* New York: Owl Books, 2004.

Constable, Trevor, and Raymond Toliver. *Horrido! Fighter Aces of the Luftwaffe.* New York: Ballantine Books, 1970.

Coppa, Frank. *The Papacy, the Jews, and the Holocaust.* Washington, DC: The Catholic University of America Press, 2006.

Crosby, Harry. *A Wing and a Prayer.* New York: HarperCollins, 1993.

Cull, Brian, et al. *Spitfires Over Sicily.* London: Grub Street, 2000.

Ethel, Jeffrey. *P-38 Lightning.* New York: Crown Publishers, 1983.

Forsyth, Robert. *Jagdverband 44: Squadron of Experts.* New York: Osprey Publishing, 2008.

Forsyth, Robert. *JV-44: The Galland Circus.* UK: Classic Publications, 1996.

Freedman, Wayne. *This Morning.* CBS, New York, September 26, 1990.

Freeman, Roger. *The Fight for the Skies.* New York: Cassell & Co., 1998.

Freeman, Roger. *The Mighty Eighth: A History of the Units, Men and Machines of the US 8th Air Force.* London: Cassell & Co., 2000.

Freeman, Roger, and David Osborne. *The B-17 Flying Fortress Story.* London: Arms & Armour, 1998.

Galland, Adolf. *The First and the Last: The German Fighter Force in World War II.* London: Methuen, 1955.

Geary, Frank. "Courage, Faith, Culminate in Brotherhood of Friendship Among Former Enemies in Skies Over WWII Europe." *Jax Air News,* October 8, 1998, 14–15.

Geary, Frank. "German Air Ace 'Knighted' for Sparing Ye Olde Pub." *Jax Air News*, August 20, 1998, 12–14.

Goebbels, Joseph. "25 April 1945: Last Broadcast." Speech, April 21, 1945. YouTube, July 20, 2011.

Griech-Polelle, Beth. *Bishop von Galen: German Catholicism and National Socialism.* New Haven, CT: Yale University Press, 2002.

Hammel, Eric. *Air War Europa.* Pacifica, CA: Pacifica Press, 1994.

Heaton, Colin D., and Anne-Marie Lewis. *The German Aces Speak.* Minneapolis, MN: Zenith Press, 2011.

Heilmann, Willi. *I Fought You from the Skies.* New York: Award Books, 1966.

Herzog, Rudolph. *Dead Funny: Humor in Hitler's Germany.* New York: Melville House, 2011.

Hoffmann, Peter. *The History of the German Resistance: 1933–1945.* Quebec: McGill-Queen's University Press, 2001.

Kaplan, Philip. *Fighters Aces of the Luftwaffe in World War 2.* UK: Pen & Sword Books Limited, 2007.

Kaplan, Philip, and Rex Alan Smith. *One Last Look.* New York: Abbeville Press, 1983.

Kaplan, Philip, and Jack Currie. *Round the Clock.* New York: Random House, 1993.

Knoke, Heinz. *I Flew for the Fuhrer.* London: Greenhill Books, 1991.

Kurowski, Franz. *Hans-Joachim Marseille.* Atglen, PA: Schiffer Publishing, 1994.

"The Last Mission," King 5 TV, Seattle, October 9, 1985.

MacDonogh, Giles. *After the Reich: The Brutal History of the Allied Occupation.* New York: Basic Books, 2009.

Mizrahi, Joseph. *Knights of the Black Cross.* Granada Hills, CA: Sentry Books, 1972.

Moser, Joseph, and Gerald Baron. *A Fighter Pilot in Buchenwald.* Bellingham, WA: Edens Veil Media, 2009.

Murawski, Marek. *Luftwaffe Over the Desert from January till August 1942.* Poland: Kagero Publishing, 2010.

Price, Alfred. *The Last Year of the Luftwaffe: May 1944 to May 1945.* London: Arms and Armour Press, 1991.

Ring, Hans, and Christopher Shores. *Fighters Over the Desert.* New York: Arco Publishing, 1969.

Ring, Hans, and Christopher Shores. *Luftkampf zwischen Sand und Sonne.* Germany: Motorbuch Verlag, 1978.

Rudel, Hans Ulrich. *Stuka Pilot.* New York: Ballantine Books, 1958.

Scutts, Jerry. *Bf 109 Aces of North Africa and the Mediterranean.* London: Osprey Publishing, 1994.

Shuck, Walter. *Luftwaffe Eagle: From the Me 109 to the Me 262.* UK: Crecy Publishing, 2009.

Steinhoff, Johannes. *The Final Hours: The Luftwaffe Plot Against Goering.* Dulles, VA: Potomac Books, 2005.

Steinhoff, Johannes. *Messerschmitts Over Sicily.* Mechanicsburg, PA: Stackpole Books, 2004.

Stigler, Franz. "Palm Sunday Massacre," *Luftwaffe: Deadly Aces, Deadly Warplanes* 1, no. 1 (1989): 16–21, 96.

Toliver, Raymond, and Trevor Constable. *Fighter General: The Life of Adolf Galland*. Atglen, PA: Schiffer Publishing, 1999.

United States Holocaust Memorial Museum. "The Holocaust." *Holocaust Encyclopedia*. http://www.ushmm.org/wlc/en/article.php?ModuleId=10005144, accessed on June 4, 2011.

Verfasser, D. "Rationing in Germany." Online posting, November 9, 2009. AxisHistory .com Forum Index—Life in the Third Reich & the Occupied Territories, November 16, 2011. http://forum.axishistory.com/viewtopic.php?f=46&t=159844.

Weal, John. *Jagdgeschwader 27 'Afrika'*. UK: Osprey Publishing, 2003.